Praise for *Moral Leadership*

"This collection of essays takes a fresh look at one of today's most urgent concerns: moral leadership in the public domain. The book is important reading for anyone who believes that moral leadership may still be possible, even during a time of ethical degradation in many key social institutions."

—William Damon, professor of education, Stanford University

"A stellar group of well-known thinkers. A topic of commanding importance. Articles that make hard ideas fascinating and readable. What's not to like in this striking new collection of essays? It is hands-down the best anthology on practical ethics to appear in many years."

—Thomas Donaldson, Mark O. Winkelman Professor, the Wharton School of the University of Pennsylvania

"The heavy hitters in business ethics are well represented in this timely volume. Their message is of compelling interest to scholars and business leaders alike."

—Robert H. Frank, Henrietta Johnson Louis Professor of Management and professor of economics, Cornell University

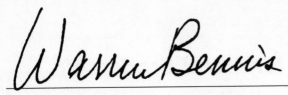

A WARREN BENNIS BOOK

This collection of books is devoted exclusively to new and exemplary contributions to management thought and practice. The books in this series are addressed to thoughtful leaders, executives, and managers of all organizations who are struggling with and committed to responsible change. My hope and goal is to spark new intellectual capital by sharing ideas positioned at an angle to conventional thought—in short, to publish books that disturb the present in the service of a better future.

Books in the Warren Bennis Signature Series

Branden	*Self-Esteem at Work*
Mitroff, Denton	*A Spiritual Audit of Corporate America*
Schein	*The Corporate Culture Survival Guide*
Sample	*The Contrarian's Guide to Leadership*
Lawrence, Nohria	*Driven*
Cloke, Goldsmith	*The End of Management and the Rise of Organizational Democracy*
Glen	*Leading Geeks*
Cloke, Goldsmith	*The Art of Waking People Up*
George	*Authentic Leadership*
Kohlrieser	*Hostage at the Table*
Rhode	*Moral Leadership*

Moral Leadership

The Theory and Practice of Power, Judgment, and Policy

Deborah L. Rhode
Editor

Foreword by Warren Bennis

JOSSEY-BASS
A Wiley Imprint
www.josseybass.com

Published by Jossey-Bass
A Wiley Imprint
989 Market Street, San Francisco, CA 94103-1741   www.josseybass.com

Readers should be aware that Internet Web sites offered as citations and/or sources for further information may have changed or disappeared between the time this was written and when it is read.

Jossey-Bass books and products are available through most bookstores. To contact Jossey-Bass directly call our Customer Care Department within the U.S. at 800-956-7739, outside the U.S. at 317-572-3986, or fax 317-572-4002.

Jossey-Bass also publishes its books in a variety of electronic formats. Some content that appears in print may not be available in electronic books.

Library of Congress Cataloging-in-Publication Data

Moral leadership : the theory and practice of power, judgment, and policy / by Deborah L. Rhode, editor ; foreword by Warren Bennis.
    p. cm.
  Includes bibliographical references and index.
  ISBN-13: 978-0-7879-8282-9 (cloth : alk. paper)
  ISBN-10: 0-7879-8282-2 (cloth : alk. paper)
  1. Business ethics. 2. Management—Moral and ethical aspects. 3. Leadership—Moral and ethical aspects. 4. Social responsibility of business. I. Rhode, Deborah L.
  HF5387.M649 2006
  174'.4—dc22

                                                                    2006008774

Printed in the United States of America
FIRST EDITION
HB Printing   10 9 8 7 6 5 4 3 2 1

For Lawrence Quill

Contents

Introduction: Where Is the Leadership in Moral Leadership?   1
Deborah L. Rhode

Part One:
Ethical Judgment   55

1. Making Sense of Moral Meltdowns   57
David Luban

2. Three Practical Challenges of Moral Leadership   77
Joshua Margolis, Andrew Molinsky

3. Ethical Judgment and Moral Leadership:
Three Barriers   95
David Messick

4. Morals for Public Officials   111
Russell Hardin

Part Two:
The Psychology of Power   127

5. The Psychology of Power: To the Person?
To the Situation? To the System?   129
Philip G. Zimbardo

6. Taming Power   159
David G. Winter

7. Power and Moral Leadership   177
Dacher Keltner, Carrie A. Langner, Maria Logli Allison

Part Three:
Self-Sacrifice and Self-Interest   195

8. Orchestrating Prosocial Motives   197
    C. Daniel Batson

9. Self-Sacrifice and Self-Interest: Do Ethical Values
    Shape Behavior in Organizational Settings?   213
    Tom R. Tyler

Part Four:
Serving the Public Through the
Public Sector: Accountability
of Nonprofit Organizations   227

10. Strategic Philanthropy and Its Malcontents   229
    Paul Brest

11. Ethics and Philanthropy   249
    Bruce Sievers

Part Five:
Moral Leadership:
Perspectives and Implications   265

12. Exercising Moral Courage: A Developmental Agenda   267
    Linda A. Hill

13. Perspectives on Global Moral Leadership   291
    Kirk O. Hanson

Notes   301

Acknowledgments   359

About the Authors   361

Index   369

Foreword

"The trouble with the world is that everyone has
his reasons."

—*Jean Renoir*

Books of readings—compendia, collections, and anthologies, that
sort of undertaking—are notoriously difficult to pull off. Especially
those with *original* essays. To begin with, publishers don't like them
because they, er, don't sell. And mostly for good reasons: the typical
anthology includes a dizzying assortment of unrelated papers fas-
tened uneasily together by typographic artifices. We're all too familiar with the usual pitfalls: papers of uneven quality; first drafts that
were never quite in shape and were gathering dust in some desk
drawer; and assemblages of articles that fit uneasily, like unmatched
socks. Most important, many such "readers" lack a clear and coherent conceptual armature.

Deborah Rhode's choices of authors and their seminal contributions is a relief, a startlingly fresh exception to all of the usual
mishaps that beleaguer those intrepid souls who agree to undertake
such a thankless task. Rhode's challenge is unusually daunting: to
create a framework that is useful, balanced, objective, *and* with a
carapace generous enough to address the key aspects of a topic as
forebodingly complex as "moral leadership." This book—it's not
bold or hyperbolic to say—will soon become required reading for
anyone who wants to understand the vexing issues that inhere in
this complicated topic.

As a veteran "foreword writer" who's come in from the cold, I long ago vowed that I would never write another one. The importance of this book made it an obligation. First of all, Rhode's introductory essay is a masterpiece. With super lucidity she confronts the issues and conundrums facing this nascent field of inquiry. If some of the other essays didn't measure up to her standard, I would stop here and simply say as they do on menus, "that one alone is worth the price of admission." Well, Rhode's is, but there are many others and to mention one would imply that others weren't of the same quality; that's not the case.

There are two reasons for my enthusiasm. First, all of the authors know what they're talking about. They do not avoid complexity or try to avoid the dangerous shoals of this regularly contested terrain. Whether they dwell on the dispositional factors, as some do, or situational factors, which others do, or the systemic factors, as still others do, their eyes are wide open and make legitimate their own dubiety. Second, the values they express, indirectly or directly, comport with what our democratic institutions should be about: transparency, freedom, parity, and moral awareness of its leaders. Not only did I feel uplifted reading this book, I felt that it helped to disperse the shadows where moral leadership restlessly resides. This book should make it more difficult for leaders to hold on to the "reasons" that trouble the world.

March 2006

Warren Bennis
WB Series Editor
Santa Monica, California

Moral Leadership

INTRODUCTION: WHERE IS THE LEADERSHIP IN MORAL LEADERSHIP?

Deborah L. Rhode

Moral leadership has always been with us, but only recently has the concept attracted systematic attention. Political philosophers dating from the early Greeks and theologians dating from the Middle Ages occasionally discussed virtue in the context of leadership.[1] However, not until the later half of the twentieth century did leadership or business ethics emerge as distinct fields of study, and attention to their overlap has been intermittent and incomplete. In the United States, it took a succession of scandals to launch moral leadership as an area of research in its own right. Price fixing in the 1950s, defense contracting in the 1960s, Watergate and securities fraud in the 1970s, savings and loans and political abuses in the 1980s, and massive moral meltdowns in the corporate sector in the late 1990s and early 2000s underscored the need for greater attention to ethics.

Moral leadership is now in a boom cycle. At last count, a Web search revealed some forty-seven thousand sites. National leaders have clamoured that "Something Must Be Done."[2] Dutiful platitudes have been uttered, and a thriving cottage industry has been churning out courses, commissions, conferences, and consultants.

Parodies of all of the above also have been in ample supply. In the post-Watergate era, cartoonist Gary Trudeau satirized hastily assembled professional ethics courses as "trendy lip service to our better selves." The 1980s and 1990s debacles prompted publications like *Wall Street Ethics*, which opened to nothing but blank pages.

1

And Enron and its disciples have generated comparable comic relief. The *New York Times Magazine* ran a mock job application for a corporate ethics officer that included multiple-choice questions such as the following:

Experience (check all that apply)

☐ MFA in fiction writing

☐ Accounting Department, Enron

☐ Congressman

Analogies

Please choose the best word or phrase to complete the analogy. *Shoplifting* is to *accident* as *accounting fraud* is to

a. misunderstanding

b. rounding error

c. friendly disagreement

d. subject to interpretation

e. impossible

I believe that the truth is

☐ objective

☐ subjective

☐ for sale[3]

The *New Yorker* featured a similar spoof under the caption, "Bush, Cheney Blister Shady Business Ethics." In this account, the president displayed his customary "can-do attitude" in solving the "real problems facing American business," such as theft of hotel shampoo, soap, and sewing kits by corporate executives traveling at company expense. To combat such abuses, the president reportedly announced plans to form a "cabinet level department of Homeland Personal Toiletries."[4]

Serious scholars have also expressed reservations about whether there is any "there" in the moral leadership literature. In evaluating the field of leadership studies during its early years, one of its most prominent experts, Warren Bennis, observed that "more has been written and less is known" than on any other topic in the social sciences.[5] While that may no longer be true about the discipline generally, the subdiscipline of moral leadership remains an academic backwater. One recent survey of some eighteen hundred articles in psychology, business, religion, philosophy, anthropology, sociology, and political science found only a handful that addressed leadership ethics in any depth.[6] Few of those articles, or the books recently released on this topic, are informed by relevant research outside their field. Publications written by and for managers have typically been at best superficial and at worst misleading, littered with vacuous platitudes and self-serving anecdotes. Many of the all-purpose prescriptions marketed in the popular press are at odds with the limited scholarship that is available.

Given the centrality of ethics to the practice of leadership, it is striking how little systematic research has focused on key questions.[7] How do leaders form, sustain, and transmit moral commitments? Under what conditions are those processes most effective? What is the impact of ethics officers, codes, training programs, and similar initiatives? How do norms and practices vary across context and culture? What can we do at the individual, organizational, and societal levels to foster moral leadership?

To assist inquiry along these lines, this Introduction surveys the state of moral leadership literature. It aims to identify what we know, and what we only think we know, about the role of ethics in key decision-making positions. The focus is primarily on leadership in business contexts, because that is where most work has been done and where the need in practice appears greatest. However, the overview that follows also draws on research from related fields and offers insights applicable to other organizational contexts. Part One explores definitions of moral leadership, and Part Two chronicles the increasing recognition of its importance. Part Three analyzes the circumstances under which "ethics pays," and Part Four examines the individual and contextual factors that influence ethical conduct. Part Five identifies strategies of moral leadership, and Part

Six concludes with proposals to promote it. This overview offers a sense of what is missing in both the theory and practice of moral leadership and what is necessary to fill the gaps.

Moral Leadership Defined

A central difficulty plaguing analysis of leadership in general, and moral leadership in particular, is the lack of consensus on what exactly it means. A related problem is the failure even to recognize that such definitional incoherence is a problem. One comprehensive review of twentieth-century publications on leadership found that two-thirds did not even bother to define the term.[8] The difficulties are compounded when, as is usually the case, qualifications like "moral," "ethical," or "value-driven" are also left undefined.[9]

One reason that much of the literature simply bypasses definitional issues may be that authors assume some long-established common core of meaning. "To lead" comes from the Old English word *leden* or *loedan*, which meant "to make go," "to guide," or "to show the way," and the Latin word *ducere*, which meant "to draw, drag, pull, guide, or conduct."[10] Although popular usage sometimes conflates leadership with status, power, or position, scholars generally draw distinctions among them. Leadership requires a relationship, not simply a title; leaders must be able to inspire, not simply compel or direct their followers.

Most leadership literature also assumes a commonsense understanding of key value-laden terms. *Ethics* is generally traced to the Greek words *ethikos*, which means pertaining to custom, and *ethos*, which refers to character. *Morality* comes from the Latin word *mores*, which refers to character, or custom and habit. Philosophers often use *ethics* when discussing the study of morality and *morality* when discussing general principles of right and wrong. However, in both popular usage and work on leadership, the terms are largely interchangeable, and that convention will be followed here. To be "moral" or "ethical," as commonly understood, is to display a commitment to right action. That generally includes not only compliance with law but also with generally accepted principles involving honesty, fair dealing, social responsibility, and so forth.

Yet while there may be substantial consensus about the core meanings of moral leadership at the abstract level, there is far less agreement about what they mean in practice. Dispute centers around several key issues. What constitutes effective leadership? Does all leadership, or all effective leadership, have an ethical content? How should the moral dimensions of leadership be defined and assessed? To what extent are there shared understandings of ethically responsible behavior in contexts where values are in conflict?

Ethics and Effectiveness

Innumerable models have come and gone, and each generation rediscovers and recasts many of the same concepts.[11] Some frameworks stress the traits of leaders, others the relationship with followers. The past quarter-century has witnessed the rise, fall, and occasional resurrection of transactional leadership, transformational leadership, charismatic leadership, authentic leadership, autocratic leadership, steward leadership, servant leadership, collaborative leadership, laissez-faire leadership, and value leadership. What is striking about this literature is how little has traditionally focused on ethics. The gaps are apparent in the field's most encyclopedic overview, Bass and Stogdill's *Handbook on Leadership*; this 1990 handbook on leadership runs over nine hundred pages, but only five have indexed references to ethics. None of the book's thirty-seven chapters centers on moral issues.[12]

Although more recent overviews find somewhat greater attention to ethics, there is surprisingly little systematic analysis of a key issue: whether all leadership has a moral dimension. To borrow Machiavelli's classic formulation, can one be a "good" leader in terms of effectiveness without being a "good" leader in terms of morality? The limited leadership commentary that focuses on this question stakes out a range of views.

The first is that leadership is inescapably "value-laden": "all leadership, whether good or bad, is moral leadership at the descriptive if not the normative level."[13] In the most relevant empirical study to date, about half of surveyed business executives agreed that ethically neutral leadership was impossible.[14] Yet while virtually no commentators dispute the fact that ethical views shape the means and ends of leaders, this is not the sense in which "moral" leadership is commonly understood. In conventional usage, *moral* conveys "morally justified." And a purely descriptive account leaves the interesting definitional question unanswered: can leadership be successful without being moral in a more demanding, prescriptive sense?

On this issue, commentators divide. An increasingly common position, encountered in both scholarly and popular literature, is that the essence of effective leadership is ethical leadership. The first prominent theorist to take this view was historian James McGregor Burns. In his 1978 account, *Leadership*, Burns distinguished between transactional and transformational leadership. The first involves an exchange relationship between leaders and followers, who cooperate on the basis of self-interest in pursuit of mutual gains. By contrast, in transformational leadership, leaders and followers "raise one another to higher levels of motivation and morality," beyond "everyday wants and needs." They aspire to reach more "principled levels of judgment" in pursuit of end values such as liberty, justice, and self-fulfillment.[15] Similarly, John Gardner, in *The Moral Aspect of Leadership*, argued that leaders should "serve the basic needs of their constituents," defend "fundamental moral principles," seek the "fulfillment of human possibilities," and improve the communities of which they are a part.[16] To Gardner, like other contemporary commentators, men such as Hitler and Stalin can be considered rulers but not leaders.[17]

Many scholars see this definition as too limiting. Some argue that effective leadership requires morality in means, although not necessarily in ends. Underlying this distinction is the assumption that widely shared principles are available for judging process but no comparable consensus exists for judging objectives.

According to this view, leadership cannot be coercive or authoritarian, but it can seek ends that most people would regard as morally unjustified.[18]

Yet this distinction is inconsistent with conventional understandings and not particularly helpful for most purposes. As Bennis notes, "People in top positions [can often be] doing the wrong thing well."[19] "Like it or not," others point out, Hitler, Stalin, and Saddam Hussein were animated by a moral vision and were extremely effective in inspiring others in its pursuit.[20] In her recent account, *Bad Leadership*, Barbara Kellerman similarly suggests that it is unproductive to exclude from definitions of leadership those whose means or ends are abhorrent but nonetheless effective, and therefore instructive. As she puts it, "How can we stop what we don't study?"[21]

Values-Based Leadership

A similar point could be made about controversies over the ethical dimensions of "values-based" leadership. Although the label is relatively recent, the concept is longstanding.[22] In essence, as Philip Selznick's classic 1957 study put it, leaders must be "experts in the 'protection of values.'"[23] Contemporary commentators on management generally agree and emphasize the need to build a shared mission that extends beyond financial achievement.[24] For example, Thomas Peters and Robert Waterman's study of high-performing businesses concludes that the primary role of top executives is to "manage the values of the organization."[25] Successful leadership requires infusing employees' "day to day behavior with long-run meaning" and inspiring commitment to a "grand vision" about quality, service, and excellence.[26] Yet most of the values literature skirts the central questions. How are values determined and transmitted? Under what circumstances are those processes effective? To what extent do the values have an explicitly ethical content?

In its early original formulation, the concept of values-based leadership had crucial moral dimensions. However, as it has been popularized and adapted to the management context, those dimensions have often been eclipsed by more pragmatic concerns. One representative survey of corporate value statements found that about three-quarters mentioned ethics or integrity, but generally accompanied by other missions such as customer satisfaction, accountability, profitability, innovation, and teamwork.[27] And much of the discussion of "excellence" in values commentary carries little moral content. What is left is leadership ethics without the ethics. In a sense, the trend resembles what has sometimes happened with the concept of leadership more generally as it has acquired increasing corporate cachet. The result is epitomized by the billboard for a southern California restaurant: "Seafood Leadership: Anthony's Fish Grotto."[28]

Moreover, even commentators who see an ethical dimension to values leadership often discuss it in only the most perfunctory and platitudinous terms. Publications aimed at managerial audiences frequently just list a few key qualities that have "stood the test of time," such as integrity, honesty, fairness, compassion, and respect, without acknowledging any complexity or potential conflict in their exercise.[29] Other commentators simply add "moral" as an all-purpose adjective in the mix of desirable characteristics: leaders should have "moral imagination," "moral courage," "moral excellence," and, of course, a "moral compass."[30] Homespun homilies abound:

- "Lead with your heart."
- "Be true to core values."
- Recognize that "moral judgment is not a luxury."
- "Value integrity."
- Create a "climate of goodness."
- "Be an evangelist selling the mission of honorable ethical conduct."
- "Trust yourself and others will trust you too."
- Show "commitment to integrity, which beyond doing everything right, means doing the right thing well."[31]

Trade press publications sometimes attempt to spruce up the sermonizing with catchy historical allusions: *If Aristotle Ran General Motors* and *Leadership Secrets from Attila the Hun*.[32] Or they include words to live by from great philosophers, Chinese proverbs, and favorite fortune cookies.[33] It is hard to imagine that anyone finds much of actual use in these truisms. Part of the problem is that few of the publications marketed to leaders make any concessions to complexity. Only rarely does a note of realism creep in, typically by way of acknowledgment that reconciling priorities may be difficult or that most people, including leaders, act from mixed motives, not all of them disinterested.[34] But rarer still are any real insights about how to strike the appropriate balance among competing concerns. When examples are given, they generally appear as stylized, often self-serving morality plays in which virtue is its own reward and dishonesty does not pay.[35] The party line is that violating "timeless values" is always wrong, "pure and simple."[36] In this uncomplicated leadership landscape, the "right thing for business and the right thing ethically have become one in the same."[37]

Would that it were true. But the leadership literature by and for leaders is generally not much interested in evidence, only anecdotes. In the conventional narrative, when abuses occur, the problem is one of "flawed integrity and flawed character"; top managers are sending the wrong moral messages and failing to align practice with principle.[38] Although the underlying assumption is that leaders' personal values are critical in shaping subordinates' conduct, this literature offers no systematic evidence about how values are conveyed and interpreted or what makes the process effective.[39] The research we do have paints a much more complicated portrait than the mainstream commentary conveys.

The discussion that follows focuses on this process of moral leadership, using the term in its colloquial sense of exercising influence in ways that are ethical in means and ends. In essence, the point is that however definitional issues are resolved, effective leadership requires a moral dimension too often missing or marginal in American business and professional organizations.

The Historical Backdrop and Current Need for Moral Leadership

Although the need for moral leadership is longstanding, only in the past half-century has that need given rise to formal ethics initiatives.[40] And despite a recent flurry of efforts, fundamental challenges remain.

The Emergence of Ethics Initiatives

A few corporations began adopting internal codes of conduct early in the twentieth century, but it was not until a sequence of scandals, starting in the 1960s, that interest in business ethics and corporate social responsibility gained significant attention. By the mid-1980s, repeated exposés of fraud and corruption among American defense contractors led to the creation of the Defense Industry Initiative; its participants established ethical compliance programs that eventually became models for other corporate sectors.[41] During the 1970s and 1980s, the need for such programs became increasingly apparent, given recurrent waves of securities fraud, insider trading, international bribery, antitrust violations, environmental hazards, unsafe products, and related abuses. One representative survey of America's largest corporations in the early 1990s found that two-thirds had been involved in illegal activities over the preceding decade.[42]

In 1991, the U.S. Sentencing Commission responded to such patterns by substantially increasing fines for organizational crimes, but permitting reduced penalties if the defendant had adopted "effective programs for preventing and detecting" wrongful behavior.[43] This initiative, together with the enormous legal expenses and reputational damage that often accompanied criminal and civil liability proceedings, intensified pressure for reforms. By the turn of the twenty-first century, about 75 to 80 percent of surveyed companies and 90 percent of large corporations had ethical codes, up from 15 percent in the late 1960s. About half of all businesses provided formal ethics training.[44] A third also had ethics officers, and the percentage increased to over half among Fortune 500 companies after another spate of Wall Street scandals in the early twenty-first century.[45]

Corporate Social Responsibility

A parallel and partly overlapping development has involved corporate social responsibility. The term had its origins in a 1953 book by Bowen, *Social Responsibilities of the Businessman*, and over the next several decades, it came to encompass a broad range of initiatives.[46] According to the global organization Business for Social Responsibility, the concept involves "operating a business enterprise in a manner that consistently meets or exceeds the ethical, legal, commercial and public expectations society has of business."[47] By this definition, corporate social responsibility encompasses multiple strategies concerning governance, philanthropy, product safety, health and labor standards, the environment, and related issues. A wide variety of nongovernmental organizations has emerged to monitor organizational performance along these dimensions and to provide standards for socially concerned investors. A recent Web search revealed over thirty thousand sites for corporate social responsibility.[48]

By the end of the twentieth century, in the United States alone, close to 150 mutual funds, with almost $100 billion in assets, invested only in "socially responsible" companies. Several times that number of funds used some "social screens" and either avoided companies that marketed certain products (such as tobacco or firearms) or favored businesses that met specified standards on matters of ethical concern. Altogether an estimated $1.1 trillion of the $13 trillion in funds under professional management in the United States reflect some consideration of corporate social responsibility.[49]

Business Ethics: Competing Perspectives on the Problem

Although compliance with legal and ethical obligations can be viewed as one aspect of corporate social responsibility, business leaders generally distinguish between them and place more emphasis on compliance. In one poll, senior executives at American-based multi-national companies were asked to evaluate their organization on a variety of dimensions. Over 90 percent rated their corporations' "business ethics" as excellent or good. About half gave similar ratings to social or environmental impact.[50]

Whether disinterested observers would give the same high rankings to business ethics is open to doubt. Empirical evidence is mixed. In a Gallup poll on public confidence in some twenty major institutions taken around the same time as the executive survey, Americans rated "big business" second to last. Only about a fifth expressed high levels of confidence, which placed large corporations lower than Congress and organized labor.[51] In other recent polls, close to half of Americans said they had "not much trust" or "no trust" in large U.S. companies, and almost three-quarters believed that wrongdoing was widespread.[52] Only 10 percent thought that current rules designed to promote responsible and ethical corporate behavior were working "pretty well"; almost half thought they needed "major changes" or a "complete overhaul."[53]

Public perceptions of business leaders are similar, although many employees seem to view their own company's CEO as an exception. In one national 2002 survey, only a quarter of Americans viewed top executives as honest.[54] In another 2004 poll, when asked, "How much of the time do you think you can trust the executives in charge of major companies in this country to do what is right?" only 1 percent said "always," and only a fifth said "most of the time"; about a quarter said "almost never."[55] When it comes to their own organization's leaders, assessments are more favorable, but not uniformly positive. About 90 percent of those responding to a large 2003 Ethics Resource Center survey felt that their organization's leader set a good example of ethical behavior; 85 percent said that honesty was practiced frequently and that employees were held accountable for ethics in their workplace.[56] By contrast, in another 2004 survey of some fifteen hundred workers, almost half said that their company's leaders did not lead by example.[57]

These assessments are, of course, highly subjective and may often be skewed by highly salient but atypical events, as well as other well-documented response biases. Many workers have little reliable information about top executives' day-to-day conduct, and those who feel loyal to their organization are likely to view its leadership in the most favorable light.[58] Efforts to provide more objective evidence of corporate ethics have been plagued by multiple methodological difficulties. Corporations have been understandably wary of granting access to information that would reveal wrongdoing, and employee reports of others' misconduct yield widely varying results. In one survey at the turn of the twenty-first century, three-quarters of workers had observed violations of the law or company standards during the previous year.[59] By contrast, an Ethics Resource Center study from around the same time found that only a third of employees had observed misconduct. When that study was repeated in 2003, the percentage had dropped to 22 percent. Only 10 percent reported pressure to engage in unethical activity.[60] Yet even that survey, which offered the most positive findings of recent studies, found some grounds for concern. Almost half (44 percent) of employees who observed misconduct did not report it, largely out of concerns that a report would do no good or not remain confidential, or that they would suffer retaliation and be viewed unfavorably by coworkers.[61]

Other empirical research also suggests too wide a gap between professed commitments to ethical integrity and actual workplace practices. For example, one recent survey of executive members of the American Management Association found that about a third believed that their company's public statements on ethics sometimes conflicted with internal messages and realities. Over a third indicated that although their company would follow the law, it would not always do what would be perceived as ethical.[62] In another study involving responses to hypothetical fact situations based on Securities and Exchange Commission cases, almost half of top executives expressed a willingness to make fraudulent financial statements under at least some circumstances.[63] The consequences of such attitudes are not just hypothetical. Business and professional leaders' involvement in recent corporate misconduct contributed to losses in shareholder value estimated as high as $7 trillion.[64]

Societal Interests and the Limits of Regulation

Shareholders' economic interests are only part of society's enormous stake in the moral leadership of business and professional organizations. These organizations shape the quality of our lives across multiple dimensions, including health, safety, jobs, savings, consumer products, and the environment. As leading economic and legal theorists have long noted, neither market forces nor regulatory strategies are a full substitute for ethical commitments that leaders can help institutionalize in organizational cultures. Amartya Sen and Kenneth Arrow have both underscored the dependence of markets on shared moral expectations and behaviors.[65] Economic institutions depend on mutual confidence in the honesty and fair dealing of multiple parties. Yet market forces provide inadequate protection against free riders: those who seek to benefit from general norms of integrity without observing them personally. Market processes also provide insufficient correctives for information barriers and social externalities. If, for example, consumers lack cost-effective ways to assess the quality of goods, services, and investment opportunities, sellers may lack adequate incentives to meet socially desirable standards. So too, the public often bears unwanted external costs from transactions that parties find advantageous. Environmental hazards are the most obvious example: the past quarter-century provides ample accounts of the enormous health, safety, and aesthetic costs of socially irresponsible organizational behavior.

Legal regulation is a necessary but not sufficient response. Legislatures and government agencies often have inadequate information or political leverage to impose socially optimal standards. Industry organizations frequently exercise more influence over regulatory processes than unorganized or uninformed stakeholders do.

Oversight agencies may also be uninformed or understaffed, or captured by special interests.[66] Enforcement may be too costly or penalty levels that are politically acceptable may be too low to achieve deterrence.[67] Where regulation falls short, the health and financial consequences can be irreversible. The problem is particularly acute in countries that lack the economic or governmental strength to constrain powerful global corporations. And the inability of these nations to impose appropriate health, safety, labor, and environmental standards affects many outside their borders. In an increasingly global market, it is difficult for countries that have socially desirable safeguards to compete with countries that do not. It is also impossible for nations that accept the costs of such requirements to escape the environmental degradation caused by others that are unwilling or unable to do the same.

In this world of imperfectly functioning markets and regulatory processes, the public interest in self-restraint by socially responsible corporate leaders is obvious. What is less obvious is the extent to which corporations' own interests point in similar directions and what can be done to insure a closer alignment.

Doing Good and Doing Well: When Does Ethics Pay?

"Ethics pays" is the mantra of most moral leadership literature, particularly the publications written by and for managers. *If Aristotle Ran General Motors* offers a representative sample of reassuring homilies: a "climate of goodness will always pay," "you can't put a simple price on trust," and "unethical conduct is self-defeating or even self-destructive over the long run."[68] A dispassionate review of global business practices might suggest that Aristotle would need to be running more than GM for this all to be true. But no matter; in most of this commentary, a few spectacularly expensive examples of moral myopia will do: companies that make "billion-dollar errors in judgment" by marketing unsafe products, fiddling with the numbers in securities filings, or failing to report or discipline rogue employees.[69] The moral of the story is always that if "values are lost, everything is lost."[70]

Even more hard-headed leadership advice is often tempered with lip-service to the cost-effectiveness of integrity and reminders that profits are not an end in themselves. "The top companies make meaning, not just money," Peters and Waterman assure us.[71] Jack Welch, a CEO best known for his pursuit of profits, not ethics, similarly insists that "numbers aren't the vision, numbers are the product." Although they cannot be disregarded, they should not achieve "such priority that [leaders] fail to deliver on the things that matter to the company in the long run—its culture . . . its values."[72] In fact, that is useful advice, and had he followed it, his record might have been less mixed.[73] But when and whether ethics pays is much more complicated than moral leadership commentary generally suggests.

Corporate Social Responsibility, Ethical Conduct, and Financial Performance

A wide range of studies have attempted to address the "value" of values. The most systematic research seeks to assess the correlation between corporate social responsibility and financial performance. Such efforts have been complicated by the absence of any consistent, standardized measures of social responsibility. The concept encompasses a wide range of conduct, and there are no widely shared methodologies for comparing businesses' records on many dimensions such as diversity, community relations, philanthropy, and environmental stewardship.[74] Moreover, correlations do not establish causation, and any documented relationships between financial and social performance may run in either or both directions. In some cases, profitability may drive benevolence: companies that are doing well have more resources to invest in doing good. Alternatively, attention to moral values may improve financial performance by improving relations with various stakeholders: employees, customers, suppliers, and community members. These factors also may be interrelated and mediated by other variables. Social performance could be both a cause and consequence of financial performance, but the strength of either relationship could be significantly affected by additional industry-specific factors.[75]

Despite these methodological complications, the overall direction of research findings is instructive. Some studies have compared the social performance of companies with high and low financial returns.[76] Other surveys have looked for relationships between social and financial performance among all Standard and Poor 500 companies.[77] Although results vary, few studies find a purely negative correlation. In one overview of ninety-five surveys, only four found a negative relationship, fifty-five found a positive relationship, twenty-two found no relationship, and eighteen found a mixed relationship.[78]

A similar pattern emerges from qualitative and quantitative research that addresses the impact of specific ethical behaviors on financial results or on measures likely to affect such results, such as employee relations and public reputation. The vast majority of these studies find significant positive relationships. For example, companies with stated commitments to ethical behavior have a higher mean financial performance than companies lacking such commitments.[79] Employees who view their organization as supporting fair and ethical conduct and its leadership as caring about ethical issues observe less unethical behavior and perform better along a range of dimensions; they are more willing to share information and knowledge and "go the extra mile" in meeting job requirements.[80] Employees also show more concern for the customer when employers show more concern for them, and workers who feel justly treated respond in kind; they are less likely to engage in petty dishonesty such as pilfering, fudging on hours and expenses, or misusing business opportunities.[81] The financial payoffs are obvious: employee satisfaction improves customer satisfaction and retention; enhances workplace trust, cooperation, and innovation; and saves substantial costs resulting from misconduct and surveillance designed to prevent it.[82]

Such findings are consistent with well-documented principles of individual behavior and group dynamics. People care deeply about "organizational justice" and perform better when they believe that their workplace is treating them with dignity and respect and ensuring basic rights and equitable reward structures.[83] Workers also respond to cues from peers and leaders. Virtue begets virtue, and observing moral behavior by others promotes similar conduct.[84] Employers reap the rewards in higher morale, recruitment, and retention.[85] A number of studies have also found that employee loyalty and morale are significantly higher in businesses that are involved in their communities and that corporate giving levels correlate positively with public image and financial performance.[86]

Ethical Reputation and Financial Value

A reputation for ethical conduct by leaders and organizations also has financial value. Most obvious, it can attract customers, employees, and investors and can build good relationships with government regulators.[87] Survey data from the United States and abroad also reveal that most individuals believe that companies should do more than simply make a profit, create jobs, and obey the law. In one international poll, two-thirds agreed that businesses should set high ethical standards and contribute to broader social goals; a quarter reported rewarding or punishing a company for its social performance.[88] Representative surveys of American consumers find that between one-third and two-thirds say that they seriously consider corporate citizenship when making purchases, and a quarter recall boycotting a product because of disapproval of the company's actions.[89]

The reputational penalty from engaging in criminal or unethical conduct can be substantial and can dramatically affect market share and stock value.[90] According to some research, most of the decline in shareholder value following allegations or proof of illegal behavior reflects damage to reputation, not prospective fines or liability damages.[91] A substantial body of research also suggests that the goodwill accumulated by doing good can buffer a company during periods of difficulty resulting from scandals, product or environmental hazards, or downsizing.[92]

A celebrated case in point is Johnson & Johnson's decision to recall Tylenol after an incident of product tampering. It was a socially responsible decision that was highly risky in financial terms; pulling the capsules cost more than $100 million, and many experts at the time believed that it would doom one of the company's most profitable products. But Johnson & Johnson's reputation for integrity, reinforced by the recall decision, maintained public confidence, and the product bounced back with new safety features and no long-term damage.[93] Examples of unhappy endings also abound. A notorious example of a public relations disaster that could have been averted was Royal Dutch Shell's decision to sink an obsolete oil rig with potentially radioactive residues in the North Sea despite strong environmental protests. The adverse publicity and consumer boycotts took a huge financial toll.[94]

When Ethics Doesn't Pay: The Case for Values

Such examples are not uncommon. Business ethics textbooks offer countless variations on the same theme. But the reasons that the examples are so abundant also point out the problems with "ethics pays" as an all-purpose prescription for leadership dilemmas. As Harvard professor Lynn Sharp Paine puts it, a more accurate guide would be "ethics counts."[95] Whether doing good results in doing well depends on the institutional and social context. The "financial case for values," Paine notes, is strongest when certain conditions are met:

- Legal and regulatory systems are effective in enforcing ethical norms.

- Individuals have choices in employment, investment, and consumption and are well informed concerning those choices.

- The public expects organizations to operate within an ethical framework.[96]

Berkeley professor David Vogel adds that virtue generally makes economic sense on corporate social responsibility issues only when the costs are relatively modest.[97] In short, when "ethics pays," it is generally because the public wants it to and because leaders in business, government, and the professions have designed effective incentive and compliance systems.

It is, however, naive and misleading to suggest that these systems are always in place.[98] It is also self-defeating. To make the case for "values" turn solely on instrumental considerations is to reinforce patterns of reasoning that undermine ethical commitments. We respect moral conduct most when it occurs despite, not because of, self-interest. Moreover, to view corporate charitable contributions as requiring a financial payoff can distort philanthropic priorities. This attitude is what leads some business leaders to use corporate giving as a form of social currency that buys them status or perks like seats on prestigious nonprofit boards and preferential treatment at splashy charitable events.[99] The demand for "value added" from corporate donations has also led certain companies with poor reputations to spend more on advertising their good deeds than on the donations themselves.[100]

Ultimately what defines moral behavior is a commitment to do right whether or not it is personally beneficial. What defines moral leadership is adherence to fundamental principles even when they carry a cost. Our challenge as a society is to find ways of minimizing these costs and reinforcing such leadership. That, in turn, will require a clearer understanding of the dynamics of moral conduct.

Individual and Contextual Dimensions of Moral Conduct

By definition, moral leadership involves ethical conduct on the part of leaders, as well as the capacity to inspire such conduct in followers. Any adequate account of the foundations of moral leadership accordingly requires an account of the influences on moral behavior. This is a subject of considerable complexity, and one on which the leadership literature is especially unsatisfying. Recent work in psychology generally suggests that moral conduct is a function of the interplay of individual personality and social influences. However, moral leadership commentators seldom draw from research on these reciprocal influences in any integrated and systematic way. Some scholars simply borrow from one body of work, such as cognitive development, cognitive bias, or organizational psychology. Others ignore these disciplines altogether or eclectically invoke a few selected theorists.

The following discussion offers a more comprehensive overview. Although a full exploration of the topic is beyond the scope of this survey, it is possible to identify the major individual and contextual dimensions of ethical leadership.

Moral Character and Moral Decision Making

Moral and religious philosophers since Aristotle have generally assumed the existence of fixed character traits that are largely responsible for ethical and unethical behavior.[101] Much of the widely read work on moral leadership shares that assumption. A recurrent theme is that "character is the defining feature of authentic leadership" and that most recent problems are a "function of flawed integrity and flawed character."[102] The perception that personality traits are consistent, deeply rooted, and responsible for ethical conduct reinforces our sense of predictability and control. It is also consistent with a widely documented cognitive bias that psychologists label the "fundamental attribution error": our tendency to overvalue the importance of individual character and undervalue the role of situational factors in shaping behavior.[103] Yet social science research makes clear that many such assumptions about personality traits are a "figment of our aspirations."[104] As discussion below indicates, moral conduct is highly situational and heavily influenced by peer pressures and reward structures.[105]

Although the importance of personal qualities should not be overstated, neither should their role be overlooked. Individuals vary in their approach toward ethical issues in ways that matter for understanding leadership. In his influential analysis of moral development, psychologist James Rest identified four "components of ethical decision making":

- Moral awareness: recognition that a situation raises ethical issues
- Moral reasoning: determining what course of action is ethically sound
- Moral intent: identifying which values should take priority in the decision
- Moral behaviors: acting on ethical decisions[106]

Moral Awareness and Ethical Culture

Moral awareness, the first element, reflects both personal and situational factors. One involves the moral intensity of the issue at stake. Intensity is, in turn, affected by both social consensus about the ethical status of the acts in question and the social proximity of their consequences.[107] When issues arise in workplace contexts, it is the degree of consensus in these settings that has the greatest influence on moral awareness.[108] Organizations that place overwhelming priority on bottom-line concerns encourage individuals to "put their moral values on hold."[109] Such workplace cultures may help account for the large numbers of surveyed managers and professionals who claim never to have faced a moral conflict.[110]

A second influence on moral awareness involves the "feeling of nearness (social, cultural, psychological, or physical)" that the decision maker has for victims or beneficiaries of the act in question.[111] Individuals' capacity for empathy and their sense of human or group solidarity positively affect ethical sensitivity, which encourages altruistic action and receptiveness to principles of justice, equality, and fairness.[112] Conversely, peoples' capacity to distance, devalue, or dehumanize victims leads to moral disengagement and denial of moral responsibility.[113] These capabilities are themselves influenced by childhood socialization, religious and political commitments, direct exposure to injustice, and educational approaches that build awareness of others' needs.[114]

A wide array of quantitative and qualitative research also demonstrates the effect of workplace cultures on ethical sensitivity. Two widely reported case studies are Sunbeam under the leadership of "Chainsaw" Al Dunlop and Enron under the direction of Kenneth Lay, Andrew Fastow, and Jeffrey Skilling. Dunlop was notorious for moral myopia in defining the company's vision and moral callousness in carrying it out. In his view, the notion of ethical responsibility to stakeholders such as employees, customers, suppliers, or local community residents was "total rubbish. It's the shareholders who own the company."[115] Consistent with that view, Dunlop subjected subordinates to abusive working conditions, punishing schedules, and unrealistically demanding performance expectations; "either they hit the numbers or another person would be found to do it for them."[116] This bottom-line mentality did not ultimately serve the bottom line. Sunbeam ended up in bankruptcy, and Dunlop ended up settling a civil lawsuit by paying a $500,000 fine and agreeing never to serve again as an officer or director of a major corporation.[117] So too, Enron's plummet from the nation's seventh largest corporation to a bankrupt shell has been partly attributed to its relentless focus on "profits at all costs."[118] The message conveyed by corporate leaders was that accounting and ethics rules were niceties made to be stretched, circumvented, and suspended when necessary.[119] Those who advanced were those able to "stay focused" on corporate objectives "unburdened by moral anxiety."[120]

Moral Reasoning, Situational Incentives, and Cognitive Biases

Rest's second key element in moral leadership is moral reasoning. Individuals vary in their analysis of moral issues, although here again, context plays an important role. The most widely accepted theory of moral reasoning, developed by Harvard psychologist Lawrence Kohlberg and adapted by many others, posits three primary stages. At the preconventional stage, people analyze right and wrong in terms of rewards and punishment, and attempt to further their own self-interests. At the conventional stage, people focus on what is socially acceptable and seek to avoid disapproval, dishonor, and guilt. At the postconventional stage, people base judgments on abstract principles that reflect universal concerns and focus on maintaining their self-respect.[121]

Most evidence suggests that individuals have a relatively poor grasp of their own reasoning processes and use different, typically lower, levels of reasoning in business contexts than in other aspects of their lives.[122] As one manager put it in Robert Jackell's famous case study, *Moral Mazes*, "What's right in the corporation is not what is right in a man's home or his church."[123] Abundant evidence indicates that this view is pervasive, that organizational reward structures affect the judgments of leaders, and that their decisions have a corresponding impact on subordinates.

One powerful influence involves compensation. In a culture where money buys not just goods and services but also power and status, economic rewards can skew decision-making processes in predictable ways. For top managers, stock options are an increasingly important factor. They account for about 60 percent of the pay of chief executives at the largest corporations and can give rise to large fortunes.[124] This incentive structure may encourage leaders to seek short-term increases in stock prices even when that involves cutting ethical corners and damaging the corporation's performance over the long term.[125]

So too, the moral judgments of both leaders and followers can be adversely affected by growing inequalities in compensation. The salary ratio between CEOs and the average worker is now about five hundred to one, and nonsalary perks for top executives have also mushroomed.[126] A textbook case of the corrosive impact of this reward system involves L. Dennis Kozlowski, Tyco's former CEO, who has been convicted for fraud and misappropriation. Under his leadership, corporate funds financed expensive art, a six thousand dollar shower curtain, and a fifteen thousand dollar umbrella stand for the company apartment in which he resided, as well as half the cost of his wife's $2 million birthday party. In defending his conduct, Kozlowski maintained ignorance about the cost of at least some of the items; he apparently gave a blank check to consultants. He also stated, "People think that I'm a greedy guy; that I was overcompensated. . . . But while I did earn enormous sums of money . . . I worked my butt off and it was all based on my performance in Tyco's long established pay-for-performance culture."[127] Professionals who pad expenses or inflate their hours to meet unrealistic quotas offer similar rationalizations: their work is really worth more than the time they actually spent, or everyone else does it, and expects it, under long-established hourly billing structures.[128]

The adverse effects of these incentive structures are readily apparent. The rationalizations that support petty dishonesty in billing or profligate use of corporate resources can readily spill over to other issues.[129] Such abuses also encourage subordinates to respond in kind. A wide range of research indicates that employees' perceptions of unfairness in reward systems, as well as leaders' apparent lack of commitment to ethical standards, increase the likelihood of unethical behavior by subordinates.[130] People often reason in terms of retributive justice and rationalize their own misconduct as a justifiable response to organizational norms.

Other forms of self-interest can similarly skew ethical decision making. Psychologists have documented a variety of cognitive biases that contribute to moral myopia. Those who obtain leadership positions often have a high confidence in their own capacities and judgment.[131] That can readily lead to arrogance, overoptimism, and an escalation of commitment to choices that turn out to be wrong either factually or morally.[132] As a result, individuals may ignore or suppress dissent, overestimate their ability to rectify adverse consequences, and cover up mistakes by denying, withholding, or sometimes destroying information.[133] A related bias involves cognitive dissonance; individuals tend to suppress or reconstrue information that casts doubt on a prior belief or action.[134] Such biases may lead individuals to discount or devalue evidence of the harms of their conduct or the extent of their own responsibility.

In-group biases similarly can result in unconscious discrimination or in ostracism of inconvenient and unwelcome views. Those dynamics in turn generate perceptions of unfairness and encourage team loyalty at the expense of moral candor and socially responsible decision making.[135]

Moral Intent, Moral Conduct, and Situational Pressures

Yet individuals' moral reasoning processes, however affected by these cognitive biases, are only part of what explains moral conduct. Indeed, most research finds only a modest correlation between ethical reasoning and behavior.[136] It is not enough for people to make a sound moral judgment. They must also have "moral intent"—the motivation to give priority to moral values—as well as the ability to follow through and act on that intent.[137] Moral motivations are in part a reflection of the centrality of moral concerns to individuals' identity and self-esteem.[138] Much depends on how they weigh these concerns in relation to other needs for power, status, money, peer approval, and so forth. So too, what psychologists label "ego strength" will help determine whether individuals are able to put their moral values into action. Factors include the person's ability to work around impediments, cope with frustration, and remain focused on moral objectives.[139]

A variety of situational pressures can affect that ability. Some of the best documented involve time and authority. A famous example of the influence of time constraints grows out an experiment by Princeton psychologist John Darley. It found that seminary students en route from a lecture on the Good Samaritan were unlikely to behave like one if they were late for another obligation; most passed by a moaning man in seeming need of medical care rather than stop and provide assistance.[140] Stanley Milgram's classic obedience-to-authority experiment offers an even more chilling example of how readily the good go bad if pressures are substantial. When asked to administer electric shocks to another participant in the experiment, about two-thirds of subjects fully complied, up to levels marked "dangerous," despite the victim's screams of pain.[141] Yet when the experiment was described to subjects, none believed that they would comply, and estimates of compliance by others were no more than one in a hundred.[142] Variations of the study also documented the importance of peer influence. When the subject was paired with someone who refused to comply, 90 percent followed suit; when that person uncomplainingly complied, 90 percent of the subjects did so as well.[143]

Moral Behavior: Diffusion of Responsibility, Socialization, and Peer Pressure!

Studies on behavior in group settings similarly underscore the malleability of moral conduct. This research typically finds that individuals are more likely to engage in unethical conduct when acting with others. Three dynamics often work to "protect people from their own conscience": diffusion of responsibility, socialization to expedient norms, and peer pressure.[144]

The dilution and displacement of responsibility in group settings emerge clearly in studies involving bystander intervention; people are less likely to aid someone in distress when others fail to do so.[145] This same diffusion of responsibility is apparent in corporate settings. A well-known example involves the failure of top Salomon Brothers officials to report or take prompt corrective action against a trader who submitted false auction bids to evade Treasury Department purchase limits. Four top executives knew of the misconduct and failed to act for several months: the CEO, the president, the general counsel, and the vice chairman, who was the trader's supervisor. According to findings by the Securities and

Exchange Commission, each of these officials "placed responsibility for investigating [and curbing the trader's] conduct . . . on someone else."[146] The result was a major financial crisis when the threat of a public investigation ultimately forced disclosure. The firm's share price plummeted, many clients withdrew their business, and a government lawsuit imposed almost $300 million in fines and penalties. No one who had evaded responsibility lived happily ever after. Both the president and the CEO were forced to resign.[147]

A similar displacement of responsibility may help account for the passivity of many corporate boards during periods of massive misconduct. In the cases noted earlier involving Al Dunlop, Dennis Kozlowski, and Andrew Fastow, directors approved grossly excessive compensation and failed to heed warning signals of financial and ethical difficulties. Indeed, Enron's board even twice suspended conflict-of-interest rules to allow Fastow to profit at the corporation's expense.[148] Part of the problem, as a former Enron prosecutor notes, is that directors generally lack individual accountability for collective decision making; their reputations rarely suffer and insurance typically insulates them from personal liability.[149]

A famous simulation by Wharton professor Scott Armstrong illustrates the pathologies that too often play out in real life. The experiment asked fifty-seven groups of executives and business students to assume the role of an imaginary pharmaceutical company's board of directors. Each group received a fact pattern indicating that one of their company's most profitable drugs was causing an estimated fourteen to twenty-two "unnecessary" deaths a year and would likely be banned by regulators in the company's home country. The drug accounted for some 12 percent of the company's sales and a larger percentage of its profits. A competitor offered an alternative medication with the same benefits at the same price but without the serious side effects. More than 80 percent of the boards decided to continue marketing the product both domestically and overseas and to take legal and political action to prevent a ban. Some of the remaining 20 percent that would not fight the prohibition would continue marketing until it went into effect. None of the boards decided to recall the drug. By contrast, when a different group of individuals with similar business backgrounds was asked for their personal views on the same hypothetical situation, 97 percent believed that continuing to market the product was socially irresponsible.[150]

Other group dynamics apart from diffusion of responsibility also help explain the gaps between personal principles and practices. Socialization and peer pressure play important roles in signaling what ethical norms are appropriate and in penalizing those who fail to comply. Under circumstances where bending the rules has payoffs for the group, at least in the short term, members may feel substantial pressure to put their moral convictions on hold. That is especially likely when organizations place heavy emphasis on loyalty and offer substantial rewards to "team players."[151] Strategies of disengagement such as euphemistic labeling, reattribution of blame, and denigration of victims then enable individuals to deny problematic aspects of their collective conduct.[152]

The cognitive biases described previously also conspire in this process. For example, once individuals yield to group pressure when the moral cost seems small, the commitment bias and the desire to reduce cognitive dissonance may kick in and entrap them in more serious misconduct. The result is what is known as "the boiled frog" problem: a frog thrown into boiling water will jump out of the pot; a frog placed in tepid water that gradually becomes hotter and hotter will calmly boil to death.[153]

In "The Inner Ring," C. S. Lewis describes the process by which peoples' need to belong to a favored circle undermines moral commitments:

> Just at the moment when you are most anxious not to appear crude, or naif, or a prig—the hint will come. It will be the hint of something which is not quite in accordance with the rules of fair play: something which the public, the ignorant, romantic public would never understand . . . but something, says your new friend, which "we"—and at the word "we" you try not to blush for mere pleasure—something "we always do." And you will be drawn in, if you are

drawn in, not by desire for gain or ease, but simply because at that moment you cannot bear to be thrust back again into the cold outer world. . . . And then, if you are drawn in, next week it will be something a little further from the rules, and next year something further still. . . . It may end in a crash, a scandal, and penal servitude; it may end in millions [and] a peerage. . . . But you will be a scoundrel.[154]

Organizational Structure, Climate, and Reward Systems

Other characteristics of organizations can be similarly corrosive and add a further dimension to the personal frameworks that theorists like Rest propose. One such characteristic involves the fragmentation of information. The size and structure of bureaucratic institutions and the complexity of the issues involved may work against informed ethical judgments. In many of the recent scandals, as well as earlier financial, health, safety, and environmental disasters, a large number of the upper-level participants were not well informed.[155] Lawyers, accountants, financial analysts, board members, and even officers often lacked knowledge about matters raising both moral and legal concerns. In some instances, the reason may have been willful blindness: keeping one's eyes demurely averted is a handy skill, particularly when the alternative might be civil or criminal liability. In other cases, the problem has had more to do with organizational structures and practices. Work has been allocated in ways that prevented key players from seeing the full picture, and channels for expressing concerns have been inadequate. Shooting the messenger was the standard response to unwelcome tidings in cases like Enron, and ultimately, it was not just the messenger who paid the price.[156]

Additional aspects of the organizational culture play a critical role. As earlier discussion indicated, a key factor is ethical climate: the moral meanings that employees place on workplace policies and practices.[157] Organizations signal their priorities in multiple ways: the content and enforcement of ethical standards; the criteria for hiring, promotion, and compensation; the fairness and respect with which they treat employees; and the social responsibility they demonstrate toward other stakeholders. Some of the messages are blatant and the consequences readily foreseeable. For example, in the 1990s, Sears Roebuck leadership changed the company's compensation structure for auto service personnel. In effect, these employees received a lower straight salary supplemented by a commission on services sold or amount of labor performed. Under the new structure, mechanics had to do 60 percent more work to earn an amount equal to their previous hourly wage. Reports of massive fraud and unnecessary repairs quickly began to surface. Yet despite mounting evidence, Sears Roebuck's leadership adopted a public posture reminiscent of the scene in *Casablanca* where the gambling casino owner professes to be "shocked, shocked" that illegal conduct was occurring at his establishment. The company did not implement the necessary reforms until after officials filed misconduct charges in over forty states, defrauded consumers brought eighteen class action lawsuits, and jokes appeared on national television. David Letterman's "Top Ten" repair jobs recommended by the Sears automotive department included "grease the ashtrays" and "add a redwood deck."[158]

In other cases, the reward structure has been less blatantly distorted, but the relative importance attached to money and morals has been nonetheless clear. One surveyed company that invested significant resources in its "world-class" ethics/compliance program had leaders who failed to take it seriously. As a disillusioned senior manager noted, at their monthly two-hour meetings with the chief operating officer, "we spend 5 minutes on compliance and 115 minutes on profitability. So, you tell me—what matters here?"[159]

In the moral meltdowns recently on display, a range of factors contributed to the unethical climates. However, the scandals generally shared one fundamental characteristic: the elevation of decision makers' short-term interests over moral values. In this respect, Enron was a "perfect storm."[160] The corporation's hypercompetitive, profits-at-any-cost culture and reward structure had a predictably pathological impact on ethical commitments. Under the company's "rank and yank" evaluation system, employees who rated the lowest in financial performance were publicly demoted, passed over, or let go.[161] Board directors who signed off on huge compensation packages for top managers were rewarded in kind. They all received highly generous option-based payments for service. Some who headed allied businesses got lucrative contracts with Enron; others who worked for nonprofit institutions got six-figure charitable donations.[162] Many of the "independent" professionals—lawyers, auditors, and financial analysts—who blessed ethically problematic transactions were part of organizations with similarly skewed incentives. The leadership of Enron's outside law and accounting firms generally placed such a high priority on maintaining lucrative client business that they could not avoid complicity in client misconduct.[163] Precisely how much complicity is unclear and likely to remain so, given the massive destruction of potential evidence and the protections of confidentiality for many key decisions. But what is abundantly clear about Enron and other major scandals is that many participants in leadership roles failed to exercise appropriate moral oversight and create a climate that would encourage it.

Yet these were not, for the most part, individuals who appeared demonstrably immoral. Rather, they were caught in corrosive cultures and seemed indifferent or insensitive to the ethical consequences of their activities. The problem was a less acute variation of the "banality of evil" that Hannah Arendt described among the Third Reich. In observing Adolph Eichmann at his trial in Jerusalem, she was "struck by a manifest shallowness . . . that made it impossible to trace the incontestable evil of his deeds to any deeper level of roots or motives. . . . There was no sign in him of firm ideological convictions or of specific evil motives and the only notable characteristic one could detect in his past behavior was . . . thoughtlessness." Indeed, "except for an extraordinary diligence in looking out for his personal advancement, he had no motives at all."[164] Designing correctives for such ethical indifference is one of the central leadership challenges of our era. Addressing that challenge will require strategies on two levels. We need to enable those in positions of power to exercise moral leadership more effectively. And we need to increase the willingness of leaders to make moral leadership a priority.

Strategies of Moral Leadership

What is ultimately most disturbing about the literature marketed directly to leaders is the superficiality of ethical guidance. The connection between theory and practice is weakest at the very point where the need for integration is greatest. A broad range of research on organizational culture and regulatory compliance is available, but it seldom informs the most widely circulated work on leadership. Rather, the dominant approach in the popular press is to combine platitudes with profiles. It couples vague exhortations to righteousness with snapshots of exemplary workplace cultures, often, coincidentally, featuring, the authors' own companies.[165] The difficulty with these anecdotal case histories, apart from their selective and patently self-serving descriptions, is that the analysis seldom proceeds in any depth. Never does it offer any systematic empirical evidence of the company's ethical climate. And many of the lauded corporate citizens fall from grace within embarrassingly short intervals.[166] It is particularly grating to read of the exceptional corporate citizenship of companies like Enron, which was lauded for its philanthropy and progressive environmental policies, or Wal-Mart, which ranked third in "social responsibility" in a widely cited 2000 survey.[167] Sam Walton's much touted commitment to make every Wal-Mart store a "pillar of the local community" seems especially ironic in the light of recent evidence of the company's widespread violations of labor and antidiscrimination laws.[168]

What we need instead are more solidly grounded strategic analyses, packaged in forms accessible to those in leadership positions. At a minimum, such analyses should address the role of ethical codes and compliance programs, the importance of integrating ethical concerns and stakeholder responsibilities into all organizational functions, and the necessity for visible moral commitment at the top. That commitment must include adherence not only to legal requirements, but also to widely accepted principles of social responsibility. In contexts where there is no consensus about ethically appropriate conduct, leaders should strive for a decision-making process that is transparent and responsive to competing stakeholder interests.

Ethical Codes and Compliance Programs

The vast majority of large organizations have ethical codes and compliance programs. In principle, their rationale is clear. Codes of conduct can clarify rules and expectations, establish consistent standards, and project a responsible public image. If widely accepted and enforced, codified rules can also reinforce ethical commitments, deter ethical misconduct, promote trust, reduce the organization's risks of liability, and prevent free riders (those who benefit from others' adherence to moral norms without observing them personally).[169]

In practice, however, the value of codes is subject to debate. Skeptics often fault current documents as either too vague or too specific. Some seem never to "get past the stage of endorsing motherhood"; they are framed too broadly to be useful in resolving day-to-day dilemmas.[170] Others seem too detailed and "legalistic"; they are overly long and insufficiently flexible to cope with variations across cultures and contexts.[171] According to Robert Haas, Levi Strauss's experience was that "rules beget rules. . . . We became buried in paperwork, and any time we faced a unique ethical issue another rule or regulation was born." And because eliminating all gaps and ambiguities was impossible, the approach proved counterproductive. As Haas explained, "Our compliance-based program sent a disturbing message to our people—'We don't respect your intelligence or trust you!' . . . [This] approach didn't keep managers or employees from exercising poor judgment and making questionable decisions."[172] Other research on compliance programs bears this out. Programs that focus only on punishing deviations from explicit rules are less effective in promoting ethical behavior than approaches that stress values by encouraging self-governance and commitment to ethical aspirations.[173] Poor outcomes are particularly likely where employees feel that the programs' primary concern is protecting top management from blame or liability and where they have had little involvement in shaping the content of conduct standards.[174]

A related issue involves enforcement. In many organizations, ethical codes and compliance structures are viewed primarily as window dressing—public relations gestures or formalities needed to satisfy the federal sentencing guidelines.[175] As noted earlier, these guidelines reduce organizations' criminal liability for misconduct if they have ethics programs meeting prescribed standards. However, empirical studies find no correlation between these programs and a reduction in illegal conduct.[176] Many scandal-ridden companies have had programs that appeared on paper to comply with these standards. "Good optics" was how one manager discussed Enron's ethical code, and shortly after the company's collapse, copies of the document were selling on eBay, advertised as "never been read."[177]

Some organizations attempt to address the problem by requiring employees to certify their compliance with codified rules. However, the effectiveness of such requirements is open to question. In one study, none of the middle managers surveyed were aware of their company's code, even though all of them had signed it as a condition of employment.[178] In another large-scale survey, whether employees were familiar with the corporation's code or had referred to it frequently was not significantly related to the incidence of unethical conduct.[179] So, too, studies that have looked at the correlation between ethical codes and ethical behavior have reached mixed results and are frequently plagued with methodological difficulties. Many surveys rely only on self-reports, and the most systematic research often finds no significant relationship between codes and conduct.[180] In interpreting such findings, experts generally agree that much depends on the organization's overall ethical climate and the extent to which ethical standards are enforced and integrated into its daily functions.[181]

Recognition of this fact has prompted recent amendments to federal sentencing guidelines. In order to reduce culpability for criminal conduct, organizations must have ethical compliance structures that satisfy more rigorous requirements. These requirements track many of the recommendations commonly offered by experts in the field. For example, under the amended guidelines, organizations must not only exercise due diligence to detect criminal conduct, they must also "promote an organizational culture that encourages ethical conduct and a commitment to compliance with the law." To that end, they must provide "appropriate incentives" as well as disciplinary sanctions. The organization's governing authority, typically the board of directors, must be "knowledgeable" and must "exercise reasonable oversight" concerning the ethics program. "High-level personnel" must have "overall responsibility" for the program's effectiveness. Opportunities must be available for employees to seek ethics guidance and provide confidential or anonymous reports of misconduct. Upper-level personnel must have ethics training and make periodic evaluations of the compliance program.[182]

How many organizations will attempt to comply with these requirements, how they will be interpreted in practice, and how much effect they will have on ethical conduct remains to be seen. But at the very least, the guidelines identify minimum characteristics of an appropriate ethics program. An increasing array of research is also available that can guide program design and suggest best practice standards. One key finding is that employees should have opportunities for involvement in the development of codes, training, and evaluation structures. This approach is inconsistent with many companies' strategy of having outside consultants supply a standardized ethics program. Such prepackaged approaches do not adequately respond to organizations' distinctive cultures and needs, and frequently are interpreted as efforts by management simply to protect itself from liability.[183] In contexts like investment banking, where existing company rules have proven inadequate, development of an industrywide code and related enforcement and educational initiatives could be a useful catalyst for reform.[184]

Most organizations also need to do a far better job of providing adequate power, status, and resources for compliance officers and of evaluating the performance of their ethics programs. How often are ethical issues raised? How well does the organization follow up on reports of misconduct? How effectively does it protect whistle-blowers from retaliation? How do employees perceive the program? Do they feel able to deliver bad news or make confidential reports without reprisals? These are all key factors in predicting ethical conduct, and too few organizations have made serious attempts to assess them.[185] More systematic strategies of program evaluation are necessary, such as surveys of employees and stakeholders, exit interviews, focus groups, and independent audits.[186]

Establishing an effective ethics and compliance structure is a demanding task. The common practice of offloading responsibility to an outside consultant or underfunded midlevel manager is a setup for failure. Efforts to institutionalize ethics can succeed only if they are integral to the workplace culture and taken seriously by those at leadership levels.

Integrating Ethics

A true commitment to moral leadership requires the integration of ethical concerns into all organizational activities. In business and professional contexts, that means factoring moral considerations into day-to-day functions, including planning, resource allocation, hiring, promotion, compensation, performance evaluations, auditing, communications, public relations, and philanthropy.[187] Responsibilities to stakeholders need to figure in strategic decision making at more than a rhetorical level. To that end, assessments of organizational performance need to reflect values in addition to profits.

In designing such assessments, it is often helpful to benchmark, or to evaluate the organization's performance in the light of industrywide best practice standards. In essence, benchmarking requires identifying other organizations that have achieved the desired ethical objectives, analyzing the processes that led to such success, and adapting those processes to the organization's own culture.[188] The Ethics Resource Center has also devised questionnaires and related materials that can help employers assess their ethical cultures and compare their results.[189] Large international companies can measure their corporate social responsibility against standards such as the Caux Roundtable Principles for Business or the Principles of the United Nations Global Compact.[190]

Assessments of organizational culture should focus not just on compliance with legal and ethical rules but also on organizational justice. As noted earlier, employees' ethical conduct, job performance, and loyalty to the organization partly depend on their perceptions of the fairness of its treatment of workers and other stakeholders.[191] Those perceptions are, in turn, influenced by whether reward structures seem equitable, whether performance standards seem reasonable and impartially applied, and whether employees feel respected and valued.

A wide array of social science research confirms what common sense suggests: that rewards and punishments for unethical conduct affect its frequency.[192] Yet obvious though this seems, many leaders appear oblivious to how it plays out in practice; neither the formal nor informal reward structures of many organizations pay serious attention to the ethics of upper-level personnel or of the units that they supervise. Performance evaluations that focus only on short-term, bottom-line outcomes are particularly likely to skew moral decision making.[193] Most of the scandals discussed earlier were partly attributable to reward structures that encouraged pushing the ethical edge and failed to sanction conduct on the fringes of fraud.

Compensation structures are the most visible measure of an organization's values, and executive pay would be a good place for reform efforts to start. A substantial body of empirical research indicates that current compensation systems are frequently not well tailored to reward merit, even if merit is narrowly defined in terms of an organization's short-term financial performance.[194] Nor are these systems generally perceived as fair. Almost 90 percent of Americans believe that CEOs are paid more than they deserve and that they are becoming rich at the expense of ordinary workers.[195] Excessive disparities between the salaries of top company officers and the average worker adversely affect the organization's ethical climate and employees' conduct.[196]

The Ethical Commitment of Leaders

One consistent finding of research on organizational culture is the significance of leaders' own ethical commitments.[197] That commitment is critical in several respects. First, leaders set a moral tone and a moral example by their own behavior.[198] Employees take cues about appropriate behavior from those in supervisory positions. Whether workers believe that leaders care about principles as much as profits significantly affects the frequency of ethical conduct.[199] Consistency between words and actions is particularly important in conveying a moral message.[200] Day-to-day decisions that mesh poorly with professed values send a powerful signal. No corporate mission statement or ceremonial platitudes can counter the impact of seeing leaders withhold crucial information, play favorites with promotion, stifle dissent, implement corrosive reward structures, or pursue their own self-interest at the organization's expense. Hypocrisy may be the bow that vice pays to virtue, but it is a singularly unsuccessful leadership strategy.

One obvious but often overlooked opportunity for moral leadership is for those in top positions to keep their own compensation within reasonable bounds. Particularly when the organization is downsizing or undergoing financial difficulties, leaders need to share at least some of the hardships of the troops. Given the pay levels commonly prevailing in executive suites, those hardships are unlikely to be substantial. It is ludicrous to hear messages about ethical responsibility from a CEO whose pay is a thousand times that of the average worker, who wants her personal yacht shipped across the country at company expense, or who sends a corporate jet to pick up a pair of shoes for his wife.[201]

At a less obvious level, leaders face a host of issues where the moral course of action is by no means self-evident. Values may be in conflict, facts may be contested or incomplete, and realistic options may be limited. Yet while there may be no unarguably right answers, some will be more right than others: that is, more informed by available evidence, more consistent with widely accepted principles, and more responsive to all the interests at issue. A defining feature of moral leadership is a willingness to ask uncomfortable questions: Not just, "Is it legal?" but, "Is it fair?" "Is it honest?" "Does it advance societal interests or pose unreasonable risks?" "How would it feel to defend the decision on the evening news?"[202]

Not only do leaders need to ask those questions of themselves, they also need to invite unwelcome answers from others. To counter the self-serving biases and organizational pressures noted earlier, individuals in positions of power should actively solicit diverse perspectives and dissenting views. That will require more protection for whistle-blowers and more channels for disagreement over ethical issues. Studies of whistle-blowing consistently find that those who seek to expose legal or ethical violations typically encounter harassment, ostracism, and retaliation; some become permanent pariahs in their fields.[203] The costs do not appear significantly lower for those who report the misconduct to supervisors rather than to external agencies or the media.[204] And all too often, disclosures go largely unheeded or produce no lasting change. In commenting on the odds of vindication, one whistle-blower wryly predicted, "If you have God, the law, the press, and the facts on your side, you have a 50-50 chance of [victory]."[205] Fear of reprisals, along with lack of confidence that reports would be productive, are the major reasons that employees give for not disclosing abuses or airing ethical concerns.[206] Many doubt that anonymous or confidential disclosures would remain so or that paper protections against job retaliation would prove effective.[207]

Those who are seriously committed to moral leadership need to create more safe spaces for both reports of misconduct and moral disagreements generally. The problem in too many organizations, as one expert puts it, is "not only does no one want to listen but no one wants to talk about not listening."[208] It is of course true that some dissenters are unbalanced or vindictive employees who air unmerited claims or self-serving grievances. But creating adequate internal channels even for these reports is the best way to prevent the far greater costs of external whistle-blowing. And even those whose motives are tainted may have valid concerns. A widely publicized case in point is the disgruntled Texaco employee who leaked tapes of racist slurs and plans for document destruction in order to protect his own job during restructuring.[209] Whatever the costs of coping with unjustified internal dissent, the price of suppression is likely to be greater. Candid dialogue on ethical issues is essential for informed decision making. Every leader's internal moral compass needs to be checked against external reference points. Recognizing ways in which they might be wrong is crucial in determining what is likely to be right.

Promoting Moral Leadership

A final set of strategies should focus on promoting moral leadership. As a society, we need to do more to reward and reinforce exemplary leaders. And as educators, we need to make moral leadership a more central curricular and research priority.

Societal Strategies

A wide range of public policy initiatives is necessary to build commitment to and capacity for moral leadership. Among the most promising directions of reform are those that involve increasing information about performance, strengthening rewards and sanctions, and enhancing capacities for monitoring those incentive structures.

One set of strategies should seek to increase the information available both to leaders of organizations and to the government regulators and stakeholder constituencies that can hold those leaders accountable. Recent federal legislation, such as the Sarbanes-Oxley Act, exemplifies that approach.[210] It includes new requirements for publicly traded companies that will make evidence of illegal conduct more likely to reach top management and boards of directors. For example, the act provides additional procedures and protections for internal whistle-blowing. It also obligates lawyers to report evidence of material legal violations to either a qualified legal compliance committee or the organization's chief legal officer or executive. If no appropriate and timely response is forthcoming from the counsel or CEO, the report must go to the organization's governing board.[211]

Systematic research will be necessary to assess how effective these requirements prove in practice and whether all of the provisions justify the costs of compliance. However, it is already clear that further initiatives will be necessary for organizations and conduct that are not covered by the legislation. One approach is for government agencies, industry associations, and public interest organizations to establish more voluntary codes or best practice standards, along with more ways of encouraging and monitoring compliance. Many recent social responsibility issues have substantially improved corporate performance, particularly on matters involving health, safety, labor, diversity, and the environment.[212] Additional progress along these lines is possible by expanding incentives for participation. For example, more government regulators could follow the practice of some agencies and offer participating companies reductions in inspections and penalties for minor violations, as well as certification for meeting quality standards.[213] More rankings and ratings on various measures of corporate social responsibility by nongovernmental organizations could also be effective, especially if accompanied by greater publicity on the best and worst performers.[214]

Governments and industry organizations could also do more to increase information by expanding reporting requirements. One central obstacle to monitoring corporate legal compliance and social responsibility is the lack of standardized public data. Mandatory reporting on these measures could assist stakeholders and public interest organizations in assessing organizational performance and in enabling leaders to benchmark their own progress.[215] Governments and stock exchanges could also improve the quality of information provided by requiring more independent auditing.[216]

Expanded safeguards for whistle-blowing, both internally and externally, could be equally useful. The current patchwork of federal and state law leaves far too many workers unprotected from retaliation.[217] At a minimum, we need comprehensive legislation that makes it an unfair labor practice to discharge an employee who reports to management or governmental agencies conduct reasonably believed to be illegal, against specific public policy, or inconsistent with employer ethical rules.[218] In the absence of statutory protections, more courts could interpret contract and employment law to prevent retaliation against justifiable whistle-blowing. States that have such safeguards have not experienced undue difficulty with frivolous claims, in part because powerful informal as well as formal sanctions are available for abuse. In addition to legal protections, whistle-blowers need greater public support; more resources should be available to organizations that provide publicity, advice, and legal assistance.[219]

A second cluster of strategies should focus on increasing the rewards and punishments for leadership behavior and organizational performance. Greater recognition for exemplary conduct is essential, such as awards, rankings, and media coverage. Harnessing the purchasing power of socially concerned consumers should be a key priority. Public opinion surveys find that about two-thirds of consumers report considering social responsibility when making purchase decisions, three-fourths say that they would be likely to switch to a brand associated with a good cause, and about half say that they would be likely to pay more for a product or service associated with such a cause. However, only a fifth indicate that they actually bought a product or service in the past year because of such an association, and only a quarter could identify the "most socially responsible" companies.[220] Other studies on purchasing behavior reveal an even greater gap between what consumers say and what they actually do based on business' ethical reputation.[221] Individuals need more readily accessible information about which companies deserve support and more reminders about the need to align their purchases with their principles.

The same is true of investors. Although large majorities of Americans claim to consider social responsibility in determining what stocks to buy, the record of investment behavior suggests otherwise.[222] The market share of socially screened funds remains small, and many decision makers who claim to consider ethical records do so on only one or two issues.[223] David Vogel, in *The Market for Virtue*, underscores an obvious point. More companies would make social responsibility a higher priority if more investors as well as consumers were willing to pay the price.[224] So, too, pressure by large shareholders on particular moral issues is an often effective but underused strategy.[225]

Not only do we need more rewards for leadership that is ethically and socially responsible, but we also need fewer rewards for leadership that is not. One possibility is to find ways of altering compensation structures that unduly favor short-term profit maximization. Organizations that are now caught in an arms race for executive salaries and stock options would benefit from some collective solutions. Examples include tying compensation to performance measures other than short-term profits; ensuring more transparency concerning the total package of pay, perqs, and deferred income; and encouraging more stakeholder organizations to exert pressure for reform.[226] Passage of proposed federal legislation requiring shareholder approval for executive compensation would also be a step in the right direction.[227]

An equally obvious strategy is to increase the sanctions for illegal and unethical conduct. Recent increases in white-collar criminal prosecutions and civil liability proceedings against those who abuse their leadership positions are a promising development.[228] However, most state and federal regulatory agencies are still woefully understaffed and underfunded, and much socially irresponsible but not clearly illegal behavior falls through the cracks. More enforcement resources and more creative use of penalties would help to reinforce desirable conduct and the leadership necessary to achieve it. Many experts believe that strategies focused on shaming offenders and improving internal compliance structures are prefer-able to the modest fines that courts and regulators often impose.[229]

Finally, the government could require corporate leaders to engage in more systematic self-evaluation of their companies' ethical performance. Such evaluations could include surveys of employees and stakeholders, as well as reviews of legal compliance and internal complaint records. Requirements for self-assessment could be incorporated in licensing and regulatory standards or imposed in response to legal violations.[230] The results of these evaluations could then be made available to stakeholders, courts, and government agencies and could become the basis for designing more effective internal and external regulatory structures. Corporate leaders are now drowning in data about their organizations' financial performance. They need comparable information about their ethical records and more prodding to collect it.

Educational Strategies: The Limits of Character Screening

A final approach to promoting moral leadership is to enlist business and professional schools in both screening applicants and educating students along ethical dimensions. As a public relations gesture, an increased focus on candidates' moral character during the admission process makes perfect sense. Who could dispute the importance of integrity among future leaders in business and the professions, and the desirability of identifying that quality in applicants? To that end, many business schools have intensified their scrutiny of the information that applicants provide by verifying the accuracy of grades, prior experience, and recommendations.[231] Other institutions have put additional questions concerning ethics to applicants and references and are paying more attention to the responses.[232] For example, Harvard Business School requests authors of letters of recommendation to rank a candidate's integrity on a five-point scale and asks applicants to discuss an ethical dilemma that they have faced.[233] In evaluating answers to such questions, schools like the University of Chicago are committed to rejecting "evil nerds."[234] Insead, an international business school, uses alumni interviews to screen candidates and send a message: "No ethics, no entry."[235]

Whether the means chosen are adequate to the task is another matter, and one that too few institutions are considering, at least publicly. The assumption that applicants' descriptions of an ethical dilemma or responses to interview questions will generally reveal much about their moral character seems dubious at best. Given the competitive nature of the admission process, it is unlikely that most candidates will view this as an occasion to bare their souls. Indeed, if experience with personal essays in college applications is any guide, we can expect the rise of a new market in moral dilemmas. The ethically challenged will be able to purchase advice manuals, coaching, and probably even prepackaged narratives, suitable for adaptation to personal circumstances. Moreover, the references selected by applicants are unlikely to be good sources of compromising information, and whatever knowledge they do have will have limited predictive value. As the research summarized earlier makes clear, moral behavior is highly situational. While individuals differ in their responses to temptation, contextual pressures have a substantial impact on ethical conduct. How applicants will cope with moral dilemmas in their later careers depends heavily on factors that cannot be anticipated at the time of admission, such as financial circumstances, peer pressures, and organizational reward structures.[236] Prior behavior is relevant, but it is necessary to know a great deal about how and why individuals responded to earlier situations in order to gauge how they will react in different future circumstances.[237] Admissions officers seldom, if ever, have that kind of knowledge.

The current popularity of character inquiries may be another example of the fundamental attribution error described earlier: our tendency to overvalue the importance of character and undervalue the role of situational influences in shaping moral conduct. Those whose ethical indifference and willful ignorance contributed to the recent spate of scandals were not all "evil nerds." Nor is it likely that their role would have been predicted by a more intensive screening process at their admission to business and professional schools.

That is not to suggest that all character screening efforts should be abandoned. However limited their effectiveness in revealing an applicant's true values and capacity to live up to them, such inquiries may send a useful message about the school's own values and willingness to institutionalize them. At the very least, giving moral character a more prominent role in the admission process is a relatively low-cost way of deterring fraudulent applications and reinforcing the message that morality matters. But that message needs to be conveyed by schools' entire curricula and by those who hire their graduates.

In that effort, we still fall far short. Indeed, when résumé fraud is exposed, too many businesses treat it as business as usual. A case in point involves Bausch & Lomb, which acknowledged that its chief executive officer had falsely claimed to have earned an M.B.A. from New York University. The company's board of directors initially called the lie an "unfortunate mistake" and reaffirmed its support for the CEO. In the wake of adverse publicity, the board elevated the mistake to a "serious matter" and announced it would withhold his $1.1 million bonus. But the board also declined to accept the CEO's resignation because he remained the "right person to carry on the resurgence of the company."[238] The national leaders who demand more character screening by business schools should direct comparable concern to the business community.

Ethics Curricula

A second strategy that business and professional schools have been urged to pursue involves increased curricular attention to ethical issues. President Bush, joined by a host of others, has called on these schools to be "principled teachers of right and wrong and not surrender to moral confusion and relativism."[239] Even students have joined the chorus. In one representative survey, over 80 percent of prospective business graduate students felt that M.B.A. programs should include greater emphasis on ethics.[240]

On the surface, ethics instruction as a response to ethics scandals has much to recommend it. As William Hazlett once wryly observed, we can conveniently "applaud what is right and condemn what is wrong, when it costs us nothing but the sentiment."[241] Compared with other structural responses to corporate misconduct, curricular refurbishment is a cheap fix, particularly if it involves only what most schools have done, which is to add a few courses or programs here and there.

Even this minimalist response is not entirely unwelcome, given the current state of applied and postgraduate ethics instruction. In law schools, what often passes for professional responsibility courses is legal ethics without the ethics: the focus is primarily (and uncritically) on bar disciplinary rules, which fails to include many key issues of social justice or to provide future practitioners with the foundations for reflective judgment.[242] Although ethical issues arise in every subject, that would not be apparent from core curricula or leading casebooks, which devote less than 2 percent of their total coverage to professional responsibility concerns.[243] With a few notable exceptions, business schools do no better.[244] Almost two-thirds do not even require ethics instruction.[245] In one representative poll by the Aspen Institute of some seventeen hundred M.B.A.s, only about a fifth thought that their schools were doing "a lot" to prepare them to manage value conflicts. Another fifth said they were not being prepared at all.[246] The dominant focus in business education is on maximizing organizational wealth, and surveyed students' priorities shift accordingly.[247] The marginalized treatment of other values undercuts the point of including them in the first instance. Specialized courses on ethics in management, professional, and leadership curricula need to be supplemented by coverage everywhere else.[248] Students learn from subtexts as well as texts, and silence is a powerful socializing force.

What stands in the way is largely a combination of faculty iner-
tia, self-interest, and skepticism. Some professors simply cannot be
bothered to invest even a modest effort in retooling their courses to
include ethics coverage. Others doubt that the effort would be productive. If, as President Bush suggested, the goal is teaching "right
and wrong," courses on professional and business ethics offer too little too late. A few hours of classroom discussion are unlikely to alter
the values that individuals have acquired over a lifetime from families, relatives, schools, peers, and the culture generally. As Irving
Kristol put it in a widely circulated *Wall Street Journal* editorial,
"Corporate leaders know the fundamentals of what is right and
wrong."[249] If that knowledge has somehow eluded them by the time
they get to business school, it will take more than the curricular
equivalent of "compulsory chapel" to set them straight.[250]

A related objection is that teaching skills of moral reflection is
"useless" in preventing immoral practices.[251] The problems most
often arise not because individuals lack knowledge of ethical distinctions but because they lack the strength to act on what they know
under situational pressure. And as one expert notes, "Teaching crooks
a little Aristotle won't make them better human beings."[252]

These objections, while not without force, misconceive the
mission of well-designed ethics curricula. The objectives that
experts in the field identify do not involve pontificating about right
and wrong. Rather, the goal is to help students develop their own
capacities for moral reasoning in applied contexts and heighten
their understanding of legal and ethical boundaries as well as the
organizational pressure to cross them. While the contributions of
ethics curricula in that effort should not be overstated, neither
should they be undervalued. Most research indicates that strategies
for dealing with ethical issues change significantly during early
adulthood and that well-designed curricular coverage can improve
capacities for moral reasoning.[253] Such coverage can increase students' understanding of concrete professional dilemmas, the structural pressures and cognitive biases that contribute to unethical

conduct, and the strategies, both personal and organizational, that can assist in solutions. "People are fond of saying that you learn ethics at your mom's knees," Wharton professor Tom Donaldson observes. But "my mother didn't tell me about highly leveraged derivative transactions."[254] Nor will most professional students have thought about competing obligations of client loyalty, confidentiality, and prevention of fraud in circumstances like those arising in Enron and other corporate scandals. The issues most worth discussing in postgraduate courses are not ones on which students already have well-informed intuitions. And there is value in having them confront ethical dilemmas before they have vested economic interests in the resolution.

Well-designed curricula can also explore the structural conditions underlying these dilemmas and the most promising regulatory responses. Many experts view ethics courses as opportunities to identify "good institutional design."[255] Similar approaches can be part of leadership curricula and continuing executive education programs for senior managers. Such a focus would be more productive than many of the jazzed-up, dumbed-down motivational courses now peddled to upper-level employees. It is, as Jean Lipman-Blumen notes, easier to "get leaders to do different things than change who they are."[256] Any effective response to the misconduct recently on display will require policy responses like those detailed earlier, which demand more attention from business and professional schools.

Finally, ethics courses can offer an opportunity to consider some larger questions that are too often eclipsed by daily demands. Through innovative teaching strategies, including literature, case studies, and dialogues with former white-collar criminal offenders, such courses can invite participants to think more deeply about the lives they want to lead and the world they want to leave behind.[257]

In short, the objectives for business, professional, and leadership programs should be less about attempting to screen out the morally myopic or constructing some single ethics class that will convert them. Rather, ethical issues need to be integrated throughout the curricula. The focus should be on equipping the great majority of students to deal responsibly with the ethical challenges that they will encounter and to design organizational structures that will be part of the solution, not the problem.

Responsibilities in Research

Any effective strategies for promoting moral leadership will require more leadership from the academic community. Despite the importance of ethical responsibility among those in key positions, we know far too little about how best to secure it. As noted earlier, most of the mainstream leadership literature is long on platitudes and short on data, and little serious scholarship from allied fields has focused on the issue. Particularly in the works written by and for leaders, discussion of ethics tends to be superficial and simplistic. Much ink is spilled on the "vision thing" and the importance of values. Little informed guidance is provided about how to realize them in practice.

We urgently need more empirical research about what works in the world. Systematic assessment is essential for formal structures such as ethics courses, training programs, hot lines, codes, and compliance systems. For example, we know that many corporations and universities are spending substantial sums on ethics education, which varies considerably in goals, methods, and instructors. What we do not know is whether these initiatives have measurable effects on ethical conduct. To the extent that evaluation occurs, it generally involves asking participants to rate their satisfaction with the educational experience.[258] It would be far more useful to know whether they do anything differently as a result. Research on behavior is necessary to determine whether particular approaches are more likely than others to be effective in promoting specific goals, such as legal compliance or other socially responsible decision making.

More attention should also focus on organizational structure. Are there better and worse ways of aligning responsibilities for ethical compliance, philanthropy, auditing, and community relations?

How are moral values best transmitted in particular organizational contexts? What are the effects of recent legislative reforms? Are further regulatory initiatives necessary? What concrete leadership strategies are most likely to promote ethical climates?[259]

Finally, we need not only to expand our research agenda but also to rethink its substantive focus. Not only should we be collecting new data, we should also be questioning how best to present them. In particular, we need to challenge prevailing definitions of successful leadership that do not encompass moral responsibility. As obvious as this point seems, it is often missing or marginalized in management publications, executive education, and the business community generally. Two recent, widely circulated books are cases in point.

Jim Collins's *Good to Great* analyzes what has enabled "good" organizations to become "great" performers over a sustained period. "Great," as Collins's research team defines it, involves exceptional stock returns independent of industry performance for fifteen years. Although the team considered including measures such as "social impact" and "employee welfare," they settled on a definition of success that reflected only more objective financial measures.[260] Among their "great" companies was Philip Morris, which had the "longest record of exceptional performance" of any of the businesses profiled.[261] Researchers did make an oblique acknowledgment that not everyone would consider maximizing sales of a deadly carcinogen by suppressing information about its addictive qualities a mark of "greatness." However, they concluded that it is not the "content of a company's values that correlate with performance but the strength of conviction with which it holds those values."[262]

Similarly, *Lasting Leadership* profiles twenty-five executives whom a panel of viewers of the Nightly Business Report and Wharton School considered the most influential business leaders of the past quarter-century. The criteria for selection focused on the ability to create new business ideas or opportunities and cause dramatic political, social, or industry changes. Like *Good to Great*, the index to *Lasting Leadership* provides no listings under ethics, corporate social responsibility, or related topics. Although a few individuals are singled out for leadership with a moral dimension, the vast majority are not.[263] Several have personal histories or business records that are anything but distinguished in ethical terms.[264]

We urgently need more balanced definitions of success, which include ethical and social responsibility as well as financial profitability. Those who occupy leadership positions in the research community have unique opportunities and corresponding obligations to underscore the importance of moral values in leadership roles. As a profession and a society, we cannot afford to treat issues of ethical responsibility as someone else's responsibility. If we are seriously committed to promoting moral leadership, we need to make good on that commitment in our own research priorities.

Part One

ETHICAL JUDGMENT

1

MAKING SENSE OF
MORAL MELTDOWNS

David Luban

The wave of corporate scandals that began in 2001 produced a remarkable parade of business executives partaking in what has become an American ritual: the Perp Walk. In the ensuing four years, we have witnessed trials and mistrials and retrials of John and Timothy Rigas (Adelphia), Dennis Kozlowski and Mark Swartz (Tyco), Bernard Ebbers (WorldCom), Richard Scrushy (Health South), and Andrew and Lea Fastow (Enron), and we are approaching trials of Enron's Kenneth Lay and Jeffrey Skilling. Scrushy was acquitted, and Kozlowski dodged the conviction bullet once, only to be retried and convicted.

The successful defense of Richard Scrushy was that he did not know what his underlings were doing. Kozlowski worked the same defense in his first trial, while Ebbers and the Rigas (father and son) attempted it but failed. Legal observers expect Lay to venture the same defense of ignorance. The defense is in its own way as damning of these executives' leadership as the charges against them. If the defense fails, they stand convicted of orchestrating crimes and frauds. If it succeeds, they stand acquitted because they did not know what

I originally delivered a version of this chapter as the keynote address at the 2003 Ninth Circuit conference and a second, substantially modified, version at Rhodes College. A version of this will appear in Susan Carle (ed.), *Lawyers' Ethics and the Pursuit of Social Justice: A Critical Reader* (New York University Press, 2005). My principal acknowledgment goes to Deborah L. Rhode, who has served as an interlocutor and midwife on all the versions.

was going on in the companies they led. Acquittal signifies that their leadership was at best utterly inept. At worst, acquittal indicates that they not only fostered an amoral, win-at-all-costs moral climate, they also succeeded in engineering their own deniability. Either they were ostriches, hiding their heads in the sand as their managers committed crimes, or they were foxes who understood the importance of not knowing too much and then managed to persuade juries that their carefully contrived ignorance was exculpatory.[1] In all cases, these were disastrous examples of moral leadership. The remarkable fact is that before their businesses crashed, all these people were among the most successful and innovative business leaders in America. Those one tier down—the lawyers, accountants, consultants, and other professionals involved in different aspects of the crooked deals and cooked books—have also gotten into trouble. Arthur Andersen accounting partner David Duncan pleaded guilty to obstruction of justice charges based on Enron document shredding; and, based on the conduct of Andersen's lawyer, Nancy Temple, the accounting giant was itself convicted. (The U.S. Supreme Court overturned the conviction because it deemed the jury instructions inadequate, but Andersen had already been ruined, and it could still face retrial.)

My aim in this chapter is to explore why executive and professional leadership goes sour. The examination proceeds along four principal dimensions: ethical, cultural, economic, and psychological.

The Ethical Dimension: Adversarial Ethics

At its simplest, what we seem to have witnessed in Enron, WorldCom, Global Crossing, Arthur Andersen, Merrill Lynch, and the other high-profile cases of the past few years is an epidemic of dishonesty, self-dealing, cheating, and even outright theft—an incredible failure to honor the most basic rules of Sunday school morality by executives and professionals who people trusted to know better than that and to do better than that. Obviously it was not the first such epidemic: the 1980s were marked by spectacular insider-trading scandals (at least two financial titans, Ivan Boesky and Michael Milken, went to jail), followed by the savings-and-loan catastrophe. It will not be the last either.

What conclusions we should draw from pandemic business scandals is likely to depend on one's overall outlook on business regulation. Those who think that our economy works best when executives have lots of power and discretion to make innovative, high-risk decisions are likely to favor tough enforcement over new regulation. According to their view, the fraudulent executives are bad apples in a basically sweet barrel. Whatever we do, let us make sure we do not kill the apple tree with a regulatory chainsaw. Others argue that the problem is not a few bad apples but a system that allows gross conflicts of interest and cries out for regulation. Their view is that the rottenness goes a lot deeper into the barrel than the notorious bad apples on top. With a system that makes self-dealing so easy and so profitable, it is no wonder that basic honesty goes out the window.[2]

I take a different outlook from both of these. My proposition is that most of the people who brought us these scandals have ethical belief systems that are not much different from yours and mine. I suspect that if you asked them whether they think lying and cheating are okay, they would answer with an indignant no, and if you gave them a lie detector test when they said it, the needle would not budge. I do not pretend to see into people's brains, but I would be willing to bet that virtually none of the architects of these scandals— not the executives, not the accountants, not the lawyers—really thinks he or she did anything wrong. In that case, you might be asking what planet these people come from, but the answer, of course, is that we are standing on it. In their basic moral outlook, most will not turn out to be that much different from anyone else.

The fact is that everyday morality does not have settled principles for hypercompetitive, highly adversarial settings.[3] For example, when the other side fights dirty, can you fight dirty too? On this issue, most people's moral intuitions are conflicted. Even Sunday school sends a double message. On the one hand, we say that two wrongs do not make a right and tell ourselves to turn the other cheek. On the other hand, we say that turnabout is fair play, we say an eye for an eye, we say you have to fight fire with fire.

Consider a legal example that has become all too familiar to litigators: discovery abuse. Both plaintiffs and defendants in high-stakes civil litigation are notorious for abusing the system of civil discovery. Plaintiffs' counsel attempt to bury the other side in interrogatories, aiming self-consciously to make the process so expensive and time-consuming for defendants that they will settle the case favorably. Defendants retaliate in kind by withholding documents on specious legal theories or sometimes by burying the smoking-gun documents in a truckload of paper. While legal scholars disagree about the extent of discovery abuse, everyone agrees that it goes on.[4] A question I have often asked lawyers is this: If the other side does it, can you retaliate? The legal answer is no. The federal rule against discovery abuse (Rule 26) does not have a "they started it!" exception. But many lawyers think that if the other side starts playing discovery games, they would be hurting their clients to turn the other cheek. The legal rules may be clear, but the moral rules are anything but. In a classic case, a law firm was sanctioned $325,000 for egregious discovery abuse, but fourteen prominent experts testified that the firm's behavior was ethical, and in more than a decade, only one other court has followed the precedent that this case set.[5]

Our society's moral ambivalence about hardball behavior in highly competitive settings obviously carries over to the business world, because business is as competitive as it gets outside war. Take an example: the 1970 fraud case *United States* v. *Regent Office Supply*.[6] This case presented the question whether it is fraud for salesmen to lie their way past secretaries so they can make their pitch to a purchasing agent if their goods are high quality and their prices are honest. In *Regent Office Supply*, the government and the defendant companies stipulated the facts in the mail fraud indictment and in effect asked the court for an advisory opinion on lies told by salesmen to get their foot in the door. The Second Circuit Court of Appeals made no secret that it was annoyed to be asked, as the opinion puts it, "to give approval or disapproval to the myriad of sales pitches used for various purposes in the diversified world of commerce." It was an awkward, embarrassing question. The court did not want to condone lying, but it also did not want to put the discount stationery industry out of business. It found the Solomonic solution: it held that deceit by itself does not necessarily amount to fraud, but then proceeded to denounce deceit as "repugnant to 'standards of business morality.'" I suspect the judges on the panel understood very well that the evidence before them showed the opposite: that these lies are an accepted part of business morality.

I am not suggesting that "everyone does it" is a legitimate moral excuse. Rather, I am suggesting that there are very few consensus moral rules for highly adversarial, competitive settings. That implies a lot of moral uncertainty and ambiguity in a culture as addicted to competition as ours is.

The Cultural Dimension: America's Love Affair with Winners

This takes me to the second point: the cultural obstacles to dealing with Enron-type ethical meltdowns. The fact is that our culture loves the Fastows and Skillings of the world as long as they succeed. The explanation of success worship goes all the way back to Max Weber's classic study of the Protestant ethic and the spirit of capitalism. According to Weber, capitalism flourished in religious climates that emphasized the idea that business is a secular calling, just as much a part of the divine plan as religious callings. And in these religious traditions, worldly success was a sign of divine approval. It would be a mistake to place too much weight on the Protestant origins of American capitalism: four hundred years and millions of non-Protestant immigrants have largely effaced the theological specifics of the Protestant ethic. But the cultural residue remains, and it is hard to deny that Americans still worship success and love winners. The employees, managers, accountants, and attorneys who work for the winners are no exception.

More than that, I think it is undeniable that American culture has always had a soft spot in its heart for bad boys who break rules to get results, as long as they do it in style. A favorite Hollywood genre is movies whose heroes are a gang of thieves pulling off an intricate heist: *The Sting, Ocean's 11*, all the way down to forgettable summer fluff like *The Italian Job*. True, the thieves usually steal from other bad guys or target the idle rich who have more jewelry than is good for them. But they are still crooks—and we kind of like them. Almost as popular is the Hollywood good guy who breaks rules to get results, from John Wayne in *The Man Who Shot Liberty Valance*, to Stallone in *Rambo*, to *My Cousin Vinnie*. The main thing is that they have to be winners, and they have to do it in style. We are willing to forgive a lot when it comes to flamboyant rascals who also happen to be winners. Jesse Ventura parlayed a bad boy image into a governor's mansion. And there is no denying that Enron reveled in a kind of high-octane flamboyant aggressiveness, where top performers got million-dollar bonuses and then joined Skilling for Land Cruiser racing in Australia.[7]

Having a soft spot for bad boy winners seems harmless enough, but the flip side is a little uglier. As a culture, we have little patience with losers. If they did something wrong, we do not cut them the same slack we do for winners. Even if they were blameless, we are unlikely to find them all that appealing. In a fascinating series of experiments, the social psychologist Melvin Lerner discovered that the worse someone is treated, the more likely observers are to rate the victim as an unattractive, flawed person.[8] Lerner explains this phenomenon as an unconscious attempt to ward off the scary thought that if unfair stuff can happen to her, it can happen to me. We unconsciously disparage the victim in order to find a distinction, some distinction, between her and us in order to reassure ourselves that *we* will not get victimized next.[9] I find this explanation entirely plausible. Whatever the explanation, though, the experiment provides powerful evidence that we do not tend to find losers beautiful.

I think everyone instinctively understands this, and the implications for business ethics are disturbing. Given the choice between breaking rules and winning or being a law-abiding loser, you are far more likely to win friends and influence people if you break the rules—especially if you can portray the rules as red tape crying out to be cut. No wonder that Enron executives took the most aggressive accounting positions they possibly could. Pushing rules as hard as you can in order to be a winner is exactly what our culture prizes.

Admittedly, this phenomenon explains the top executives better than the accountants and lawyers who papered the dubious deals. Except for a few celebrated personal injury lawyers, the bar is not known as a haven for flamboyant bad boys, and neither is the accounting profession. Of course, business law has its share of tough guys who would rather be feared than loved, like the famous New York City bankruptcy lawyer who sometimes grabs other lawyers by the necktie to pull their faces into convenient screaming range. But he is not really a flamboyant bad boy. He is merely a jerk.

The accountants' and lawyers' job is to keep the flamboyant bad boys out of trouble. The problem is that when a successful client is flying high, as high as Enron flew, no one wants to be the doomsayer who puts on the brakes. A hundred years ago, Elihu Root, one of the founders of Cravath, Swaine & Moore, said, "The client never wants to be told he can't do what he wants to do; he wants to be told how to do it, and it is the lawyer's business to tell him how."[10] The same ethos permeates large accounting firms. The culture's love affair with bad boy businessmen creates a behavioral echo among the employees whose job is to hold them in check but who may see their real job as guarding the CEO's back.

The Economic Dimension: The Feudal and Socialist Character of American Capitalism

The argument so far has called attention to two important facts: the ethical fact that the basic rules of everyday morality do not have a lot of traction in adversarial or highly competitive settings, and that our culture is more willing to tolerate stylish scoundrels who come out on top than honorable, rule-following losers. We will see the significance of these conclusions once we turn to the third major challenge to reform.

This is the economic fact that a capitalist economy always produces losers. In one way, this is obvious: competition means that some people win and others lose. But I mean to be pointing to something a bit less obvious. One of the fundamental puzzles of economic theory is why corporations exist in the first place. For a century, economists have pointed out a paradox: corporations are little islands of central planning at the very heart of the market system. Corporations are miniature command economies. Managers gather and process information, set targets, and give their employees instructions. That is perfectly obvious. What makes it puzzling is that we know command economies do not work very well compared with market economies. Why do big corporations exist, then, instead of dissolving into a federation of small independent contractors?

Nobel Prize winner Ronald Coase, the granddaddy of law and economics, answered the question in 1937.[11] Coase's explanation was simple and elegant. Even if free-market theory holds that it would be more efficient to structure corporations as internal markets, setting up markets costs money. Sometimes they are worth it, but sometimes it is cheaper and more efficient to settle for a command structure inside the firm. That is why corporations exist.

So far, so good. But the fact remains that centrally planned economies have built-in infirmities. The reason that market economies beat planned economies is that they are better at processing information and responding to change. As Ludwig von Mises and Friedrich Hayek argued almost a century ago, the world changes faster than the planners can gather and process information. Planners are perpetually behind the curve. A central planning system simply cannot respond the way that a decentralized pricing system does.

We must keep this lesson in mind because it constitutes an iron law of economics that applies to corporate executives just as much as it applied to commissars in the dinosaur socialist economies of yesteryear. It does not matter how smart executives are or how fast on their feet. The world around them is faster. Inevitably they set their quarterly targets based on inadequate or obsolete information. And sometimes reality catches up with them. The economy goes south just when they have placed their bets on a few more golden quarters of going north.

The problem is that a manager who has set an impossible target has usually put his boss and employees on the line as well. Robert Jackall, who authored one of the best studies ever on the moral world of corporate managers, points out that corporate hierarchies are almost feudal in structure.[12] Ask a contemporary corporate manager what his job is, and he is likely to answer, "I work for Joe Smith."[13] He answers the question by naming his boss, not by offering an impersonal description of his job, a startling echo of Marc Bloch, the great historian of feudal society, who wrote, "To be the 'man' of another man: in the vocabulary of feudalism, no combination of words was more widely used or more comprehensive in meaning."[14]

Like the vassalages of medieval Europe, American corporate hierarchies are networks of personal patron-client relations. Managers offer perks and protection in return for loyalty and performance. A manager extracts targets and promises from subordinates and on the basis of those numbers makes promises to his own boss, who does the same with her own boss. When one of those promises fails, it runs the risk of taking down not just yourself but the people above and below you as well. In an odd way, executives fighting desperately to hide their losses and stay in business act in part out of a warped sense of fiduciary obligation to other people in the company. The moral pressure to meet your numbers, combined with self-interest, is overwhelming.

Jackall studied old-economy companies: textile manufacturers and chemical giants. How different are the new-economy companies like Enron? The details are different, but the pressure to set extravagant targets and meet them by hook or by crook (mostly by crook, it appears) was, if anything, even more intense. Enron was structured as a perpetual tournament. New employees picked ten other employees to rate their performance, with all the gamesmanship possibilities that that implies. In addition, management kept a database where any employee could comment on any other. At the end of the year, all the ratings were put on a bell curve, and those at the bottom were ruthlessly fired. Winners went hiking in Patagonia with Skilling.[15] The heat was on full blast.

What do you do when you cannot keep your promises and meet your targets? You have four choices. One is to pin the blame on someone else. Claiming you did not know what others were doing is the simplest way, but more subtle methods exist as well. For example, Jackall discovered a system of "milking" factories in the chemical giant he studied. A manager struggling to meet his numbers shortchanges essential maintenance on the equipment. Eventually the equipment breaks down in a very expensive way, but by that time the manager has been promoted, and the meltdown happens on someone else's watch. Top management had little interest in tracking accountability, because in Jackall's company, everyone knew that the boss got to the top the same way.[16]

If you cannot pin the blame on someone else, a second option is to arrange things so the losses fall on your customers, your shareholders, your employees—anywhere but yourself. Michael Lewis's classic memoir of his years as a 1980s Wall Street bond trader recalls that whenever it came down to the choice between absorbing a loss yourself or passing that loss onto a customer—"blowing up your customer," as Lewis puts it—traders blew up their customers without thinking twice about it.[17] Enron's management dumped their own stock while locking their employees' stock in soon-to-be-worthless 401(k) plans.

Option three, Enron's main strategy, is to smear on the cosmetics, cover up the losses as long as possible, and hope for a miracle turnaround to pull you from the fire. Rational managers should know better than to rely on miracles. But look at the character traits that make for successful entrepreneurs: boundless optimism, big egos, a taste for risk, unwillingness to take no for an answer. Exactly these traits predispose high-flying CEOs to bet the farm on one last roll of the dice and assume that Lady Luck will smile on them. Surely the economy will rebound and get you out of your troubles. Only sometimes it does not.[18]

These are the three dishonest strategies: blame someone else, shaft someone else, or cover up and hope against hope. The fourth strategy is to accept that you have lost, take your lumps, and move on.

The fourth strategy is not always fatal. During the heyday of the dot-coms, a failed e-business was a badge of honor on your résumé, like a Purple Heart. If you were twenty-five years old and had not burned through your investors' money at least once in some failed e-business, it just showed you were not ambitious enough.[19]

But e-business never-never land was obviously the exception. In real business, big business, new economy or old, failure is failure. In that case, given the choice between cheating, covering up, or watching your career evaporate, it is fanciful to expect that executives will seriously entertain the last option; and unfortunately, the others are dishonest. Remember my previous arguments: a powerful strain in our culture admires rogue winners more than honest losers, and in hypercompetitive settings, everyday morality does not give firm guidance. What we now see is that the failures that drive executives to cheat and cover up are built into the very nature of a corporation, which is a planned economy that cannot avoid placing high-risk bets. Put these three factors together, and you have a recipe for scandals. The conclusion seems unavoidable: the crooks, like the poor, will always be with us.

The Psychological Dimension: Cognitive Dissonance and Moral Compass

But none of this explains our original puzzle of why the crooks continue to think they are not crooks. Here social psychology offers an answer. The basic reason is cognitive dissonance. Whenever our conduct and principles clash with each other in a way that threatens our self-image as an upstanding person, the result is a kind of inner tension—dissonance. And dissonance theory tells us that wired into us is a fundamental drive to reduce dissonance. How do you accomplish that? Obviously, you cannot change your past conduct. Instead, you change your beliefs. That is what fifty years of research have taught. In situation after situation, literally hundreds of experiments reveal that when our conduct clashes with our prior beliefs, our beliefs swing into conformity with our conduct, without our noticing that this is going on.

In one classic dissonance experiment, subjects were asked to perform a boring, repetitive task: rotating screws in holes of a pegboard. Afterward they were paid to tell the next student waiting to perform the same task that it was really very interesting. This is "counterattitudinal advocacy," known more colloquially as "lying." Behaviorists or economists might predict that the higher the pay, the more likely the subjects were to start believing what they told the other students. But dissonance theory makes the opposite prediction. Deceiving your fellows for little or no benefit to yourself creates dissonance, and so it was the low-paid advocates who internalized the belief they were advocating. That is what the experiments confirmed.[20] Apparently when my own behavior makes me, in Saint Augustine's words, "a great riddle to myself," I solve the riddle in the simplest way: *if I said it, I must believe it; if I did it, I must think it is right.* All this, I want to emphasize, goes on unconsciously.

How can this happen? The answer, as any psychiatrist will tell you, is that we do not automatically know our own beliefs. Instead, we figure them out by examining our own behavior. If I ate that piece of chocolate cake, I guess that means I like chocolate cake. If I covered up losses with smoke-and-mirrors accounting, I must think that smoke-and-mirrors does not really count as a cover-up. And what if this contradicts what I have always been taught and always thought I believed in the past? I tell myself that only a fanatic refuses to learn from experience—and I am no fanatic.

One surprising result follows. Most of us are inclined to think that the big problem in the ethics scandals is lack of integrity on the part of the principals. But if integrity means doing what you think is right, these men and women had integrity to burn. They got it the cheap way: once they did things, they believed those things were right. Integrity does not help very much when you are in the grips of self-deception.[21]

The problem is not simply that we unconsciously adjust our moral beliefs so they inevitably make us look good. Psychologists have also shown that our judgment is deeply affected by the people around us. Show a group of people two lines, and if eleven of them say that the shorter line is longer, the twelfth is likely to see it that way as well.[22]

The same thing is true with moral judgment, and that is the special problem that organizational settings create: you are always in the room with eleven other people. In the 1960s, a young woman named Kitty Genovese was assaulted and murdered in Queens, New York, as dozens of people in their apartments witnessed the assault. Not a single person called the police. The media were filled with dismay at this sign of social indifference. But two social psychologists had a different explanation: they conjectured that groups of people are usually less likely to help out in emergencies than single individuals are. To test their hypothesis, they had subjects fill out questionnaires in a room. While a subject worked on the questionnaire, a staged emergency happened—either the sound of crashing equipment and screams from the next room or smoke billowing into the room where the subject was sitting. The results were remarkable: when subjects were by themselves, most responded quickly to the emergency. But when another person sat next to them and failed to respond, they mimicked the other person and did nothing themselves. Evidently we respond to unusual situations by first checking to see how other people respond. And just as we take cues from the other person, he or she takes cues from us. We reinforce each other, sometimes in disastrously wrong beliefs. Pedestrians stepping around the body of a homeless man collapsed in the street may not be heartless or callous. They may simply be taking their cues from each other. The evidence suggests that if they were alone when they encountered the unconscious man, they would stop to help.[23]

The conclusion is disturbing. Our moral compass may point true north when we are by ourselves; but place us next to a few dozen other compasses pointing east, and our needle falls into line with theirs—and contributes to the magnetic field influencing the needles of other people's compasses.

The Kitty Genovese effect goes a long way toward explaining why no one blew the whistle on the corporate scandals: insiders simply took their cues from each other. They saw everyone else acting as though everything was perfectly all right, and they acted that way themselves, each reinforcing the others' passivity. But it is also important to realize that cognitive dissonance and the social nature of perception fit together. Both ideas are variations on a single theme: that the human conscience has a tendency to take its cues from the situation we are in, a situation defined partly by our own past actions and partly by the actions of the people around us. No doubt being wired this way served some important purpose for our evolutionary ancestors at the dawn of time. But it can lead to tragic results when we stumble into a social situation that seems to demand morally compromising behavior.

The desire to fit in with those around us helps explain how lower-level employees, such as lawyers and accountants, become fatally implicated in corporate wrongdoing. In large organizations, decisions get parceled out among many people, and every piece of work is the product of many hands. Information filters in piecemeal, a little at a time. As a result, decisive moral moments are not obvious. They are not really moments at all. They do not scream out, "You've reached the crossroads!" Changes come gradually, like walking in a very large circle. Not only that, the consequences of decisions are often nearly unfathomable. And working in teams, it is seldom obvious whose responsibility any choice ultimately is. It may be everyone's or nobody's at all. The ground is fertile for the Kitty Genovese effect.

No one had a keener eye for the moral pitfalls of bureaucratic organizations like big businesses than C. S. Lewis, who once warned an undergraduate audience, "To nine out of ten of you the choice which could lead to scoundrelism will come, when it does come, in no very dramatic colours. Obviously bad men, obviously threatening and bribing, will almost certainly not appear."[24] Instead, the problem starts the first time that your supervisor asks you to bend a rule for the company's good. "Next week," Lewis tells us, "it will be something a little further from the rules, and next year something further still, but all in the jolliest, friendliest spirit. It may end in a crash, a scandal, and penal servitude; it may end in millions, a peerage and giving the prizes at your old school. But you will be a scoundrel."[25] And dissonance theory suggests that you will never even notice.

Suppose, for example, that a chief financial officer calls in an in-house lawyer, and a consultant, and an accountant, and says that he would like to structure some deals that will help push accounting losses off the books. (Think Andrew Fastow.) The lawyer may not know off the top of her head whether there is a legal way to do it, but that is what she gets paid to figure out. The last thing the lawyer thinks about is that an ethical rule forbids her from counseling or assisting in a client fraud. The conversation is about business goals, not about fraud (such an ugly word!). The lawyer, accountant, and consultant accept the business goal of making business losses vanish from the balance sheets, and reason backward to whatever compli-cated structure it will take to achieve it. So what if the law requires a proper business purpose other than sanitizing an annual statement? The whole lawyering problem is figuring out some way to package the client's goal as a proper business purpose, although that might require drifting into the gray zone at the margin of the law. Trans-parency avoidance feels to the lawyer, accountant, and consultant like little more than a formalistic game, not much different from tax avoidance.

The trouble is that transparency is what the law requires, and transparency avoidance bears an uncanny resemblance to fraud. By the time the smoke clears, the CFO may be looking at ten years in jail and the *Wall Street Journal* will be doing exposés of the deals. Or maybe not, as Lewis says. Maybe you will all get rich. You will still be a scoundrel. But rich or poor, while the deals are under construction, from the professionals' point of view, it all looks like an interesting challenge, nothing more. Charles Davidow, a Washington lawyer involved in the Powers Committee's investigation of Enron, reports that when he talked with the lawyers about all the special-purpose entities that Fastow created, they were proud of their handiwork, not ashamed. Yet Neal Batson, the Enron bankruptcy examiner, has found legal malpractice and violations of fiduciary duty on the part of Enron's general counsel and two Houston law firms. All of it is documented in his final report, two hundred pages spent unraveling transactions of such incredible complexity that even the lawyers who papered them admitted that they did not understand what they were doing. Or maybe they were simply saying they did not understand because it is better to admit that you were engaged in malpractice than that you did know what you were doing and were committing fraud.

Nothing demonstrates the power of organizational roles to distort conscience more strikingly than the famous Stanford Prison Experiment (see Chapter Five in this volume). Male college students were divided randomly into "guards" and "inmates" in a mock prison for a two-week role-play experiment. In less than a day, the guards began bullying and brutalizing the inmates, and the inmates started developing the depression, uncontrollable weeping, rage, and anxiety of real-life prisoners. By Day Two, the prisoners revolted, and the guards put down the rebellion by blasting them with fire extinguishers. By Day Seven, the experimenters decided they had to terminate the experiment early before anyone was permanently damaged.[26]

The attitude changes in the subjects almost defy belief. One guard wrote in his diary before the experiment, "As I am a pacifist and non-aggressive individual, I cannot see a time when I might maltreat other living things."[27] By Day Five, the same student wrote: "This new prisoner, 416, refuses to eat. That is a violation of Rule Two: 'Prisoners must eat at mealtimes,' and we are not going to have any of that kind of shit. . . . Obviously we have a trouble-maker on our hands. If that's the way he wants it, that's the way he gets it. We throw him into the Hole ordering him to hold greasy sausages in each hand. After an hour, he still refuses. . . . I decide to force feed him, but he won't eat. I let the food slide down his face. I don't believe it is me doing it. I just hate him more for not eating."[28]

The power of situations to wreak havoc on conscience is hard to believe, but in experiment after experiment, the evidence is irrefutable. Consider the famous Milgram shock experiments.[29] Two people out of three will administer what they think are near-fatal electric shocks to an innocent volunteer if an experimenter orders them to do so in the name of scientific research. But not a single person who heard the experiment described believed that they would do it. Apparently the situation takes over when we are actually in it. Give the shocker a teammate, and the result is even more dramatic: if the teammate will not administer the next shock, only 10 percent of people obey the experimenter. But if the teammate goes along with the next shock, compliance shoots up to 90 percent. Social pressure affects conscience to an extent few of us would believe possible.

In a corporate culture, the incredible plasticity of conscience that social psychology reveals creates perhaps the biggest challenge to reformers. If you cannot trust your own conscience to tell you the difference between right and wrong, how are you supposed to do what is right? Remember what we have learned so far: the stakes in business are high, the corporate culture puts out powerful cues, the wider culture reinforces them, and no settled guidelines about morality in competitive settings push hard in the opposite direction. It should hardly astonish us that the result is ethical self-deception on a grand scale.

It may sound as though I am saying dishonesty is a social disease that is nobody's fault. That is not my intention at all. The goal is to understand, not to make excuses. In fact, I am not a great believer in the idea that to understand all is to forgive all. People make their choices under constraints, including psychological ones, but in the end, all sane adults are still accountable for the choices they make. We should never forget that not everyone gives in to social pressures.

If my conscience lets me down, the fact remains that it is *my* conscience, not the company's conscience and not society's conscience.

Lessons for Leaders?

It is customary to end on an optimistic note. My basic message has been that ethics, culture, economics, and psychology all pose tremendous challenges to efforts at corporate reform. Changing the rules of conduct will not necessarily change the conduct, because rules alone will not change the ethos, the culture, the economics, or the psychology that make up the moral world of corporate America. People who think there are magic vaccines or magic bullets are fooling themselves.

But challenging is not the same as impossible. Even if Wall Street does have new scandals to deal with, the insider trader scandals of the 1980s have not recurred. The savings and loan crisis is history. Messes can be cleaned up, even if we know that the crooks will always be with us, and sometimes they will not even realize that they are crooks.

What advice can I offer to managers, accountants, and lawyers in corporate settings? Is it really true that forces you are barely aware of can disconnect your conscience as thoroughly as the Stanford prison guards or the administrators of electric shocks? If the answer is yes, then how can anyone deal with forces they are barely aware of?

I have three suggestions.[30] First, all the experimental studies suggest that cognitive dissonance disconnects the wires of conscience slowly and one step at a time. That is what C. S. Lewis suggests, and I am certain that Lewis got it right. We get cooked like the legendary frog who does not notice that he is being boiled as long as the water is heating up slowly. For that reason, it becomes critically important to give ourselves some kind of warning. Set yourself some telltale sign—something that you know is wrong. Write down on a piece of paper, "I will never backdate a document." Or "I will never let a coworker get blamed for something that was my fault." Or "I will never paper a deal that I don't understand." Or "I will never do anything that I couldn't describe to my dad while looking him in the eye." Pick your telltale sign carefully, and the moment the alarm rings, evacuate the building.

Second, we may take a cue from Stanley Milgram's electric shock experiments. When Milgram debriefed his compliantly murderous subjects afterward, he asked them whose fault the shocks were: the scientist who ordered the shocks, the victim who provoked them by getting wrong answers on a test, or the subject who administered them. Not too surprisingly, the compliant subjects usually blamed the other two (while the defiant subjects, who refused to follow murderous orders, took on themselves primary responsibility for their conduct).[31] My advice, then, is to notice when you are blaming someone else. Right or wrong, the very fact that you are blaming it on the CFO or the accountant is a telltale sign that your own conscience is on the road to perdition.

Finally, I suggest that a certain amount of self-doubt and self-skepticism is not such a bad thing. Moral meltdowns happen when the reactor overheats. There is a kind of euphoria that comes from working on big cases, big deals, for high-energy businesses and high-powered clients. Intoxicating though it may be, it is a bad idea to trust euphoria. My version of Socrates' "know yourself!" is "doubt yourself!" This is hard advice in a nation that admires self-confident, don't-look-back leaders. "Doubt yourself!" sounds like a recipe for neurosis. But without some healthy skepticism, the temptation to take your cues from the client-executive with the most hubris may be unavoidable. Icarus makes a terrible role model.

2

THREE PRACTICAL CHALLENGES
OF MORAL LEADERSHIP

Joshua Margolis, Andrew Molinsky

The business scandals that unraveled in the early years of the twenty-first century provoked renewed interest in the roots of misconduct. Journalists and academic researchers alike have documented a range of misdeeds, traced their origins to everything from public policy to personality disorders, and proposed theories designed to help prevent future recurrences. What about the other side of the picture? What enables people to be effective moral leaders: to engage in exemplary conduct that reflects conscientious judgment and principled deliberation, conduct that attends to the rights, needs, and claims of others, conduct that meets these standards especially when it may be inconvenient or exact a personal cost? The answer depends on the academic discipline you subscribe to.

There seem to be four dominant portraits of human beings that emerge from the study of moral conduct across academic disciplines: human beings as functions of layered forces, human beings as deliberate actors, human beings as obligated agents, and human beings as heroic characters. Each of these portraits carries different implications for moral leadership. Cognitive and social psychology, sociology, and organizational behavior document the ways in which a range of forces within us and external to us operate beyond conscious control to lead us to do wrong. Human cognitive faculties, social pressures, institutional norms, and structural features all conspire to lead well-intentioned people to do harm. We human beings are products of forces that often elude our control—and even our notice. Moral leadership thus requires tuning in to these cognitive and social forces and, once attuned, taking care in how they are managed.[1]

On the other side of the spectrum, philosophy implies a fully deliberative portrait of human beings. Philosophical approaches to ethics help people identify, sort through, and weigh underlying issues and claims, providing lenses for discernment and standards necessary for judgment. Moral leadership is then possible when people engage in careful analysis, thoughtful reflection, principled judgment, and action consistent with this deliberative process. A third portrait emerges from economic approaches to individual behavior. Economic accounts often cast managers as agents whose responsibility lies in their duties to principles. What enables moral leadership is a well-designed context: a set of incentives, controls, and contracts that facilitate the fulfillment of an agent's duty to his or her principles. Structural features foster moral leadership by influencing individuals' rational, self-interested calculation so it coincides with the interests of those whom they represent. Studies of leadership present a fourth portrait: human beings who triumph over limitations, adversity, and flaws. What emerges are individuals who exercise wisdom in weighing options; they negotiate the narrow pass between expedience and principle, between ambition and social welfare, and they recognize human and material costs in a humane way, but they do not waver from what must get done and do what must get done with expert proficiency. Just as the philosophical portrait contrasts with the social-psychological one, so too this portrait contrasts with the economic one. What enables moral leadership is not the context that surrounds people but what resides within them: their character.

These portraits provide vital guidance for fostering moral leadership, especially when taken together. But they constitute an incomplete gallery, and in one particularly acute way. They do not capture the actor's firsthand experience of encountering ethical challenges in practice. While the other portraits can provide practical insight, they can be significantly augmented with a systematic grasp of the look and feel of lived moral experience. An individual's firsthand raw experience of pressure-filled and ambiguous organizational settings, as well as of the vying expectations of professional roles, poses significant demands that must be met to exercise moral leadership. A person situated in a well-structured context, intent on being a moral leader, equipped with robust character and vigilant awareness of psychological tendencies, may know how he or she would ideally want to act in a particular situation. What cannot be anticipated is the person's actual experience of that situation. That real experience of pressure, ambiguity, and vying demands creates obstacles to moral leadership. Grasping that firsthand experience can attune people to those obstacles and develop their capacity to convert the practical guidance that emerges from other ethical portraits into moral action.

In this chapter, we describe three practical challenges that shape how people experience the ethical demands of their work. These challenges emerge from our research on professionals' performing "necessary evils," tasks that entail doing harm in order to advance a valued objective. These tasks, such as laying a person off or evicting a family from its home, entail great responsibility and embody ethical tensions. Necessary evils shed light on the realistic texture of what people experience when they encounter ethical tensions in their work. Recognizing these tensions can prepare people to meet the ethical demands of professional roles and organizational settings. That alone, though, neither amounts to moral leadership nor guarantees it. However, it is an essential ingredient if those from whom society expects moral leadership are to manage the ethically complex environments they face.

Many features of organizations and professional roles shape a person's ethical experience and capacity to enact moral leadership. We focus on three that tend to get overlooked: time pressure, ambivalence, and how people see themselves, or what we call self-construal. These three features share two characteristics in common.

First, they constitute the current of ethical experience that must be navigated. That current rarely gains the attention that a salient obstacle or impediment, such as a distorting incentive system, receives. These three features receive little notice in discussion of ethics because they lurk beneath the surface of events. They rush invisibly through the ethical challenges that arise routinely in professional roles and organizational settings, perhaps treated as bothersome distractions at best. Second, these three features are all double-edged swords. If ignored, they can capsize efforts to exercise moral leadership. If managed, they can propel moral leadership. Exercising moral leadership is never guaranteed, but recognizing these three features and preparing to manage them exposes people to the realities of ethical challenges that must be mastered for moral leadership to be possible. We introduce the three features in the sections that follow, drawing from our own and others' research to illustrate why they can be such crucial points of leverage in preventing or enabling moral leadership.

Time

Time in professional and organizational settings is often scarce. We have studied how professionals in four different occupations handle tasks that entail harming another human being in order to advance a professional or organizational objective. We spoke to managers about firing people, police officers about evicting people, doctors about performing painful procedures, and addiction counselors about disciplining clients. The time available for performing these tasks is short of the ideal. Not only because police officers must complete twenty evictions in a day, or doctors have to see a certain number of patients to satisfy a contract, or a company wants all laid-off employees out by noon. It is also because another pressing situation calls, with another aggrieved party seeking restitution, another patient in need, or another employee needing patience and understanding. A doctor of emergency medicine, one of the 111 professionals we studied, described this reality for us:

You could walk out of a situation, where you just told somebody their kid is dead, and have to walk into somebody pissed off that they've waited for two hours because their kid has an ear infection. And you can't say to that parent, "Look someone else's kid just died. Shut the f— up and just let me do this." . . . You can't just call in your crisis management team, or your debriefing team, or let the whole place go slide while you take care of how you feel emotionally. . . . And no one else in the situation is going to either. The charge nurse is trying to deal with all the backup in the department from the fact that you've been—I've been—tied up with this sick kid, and she's not going to come out and say, "Boy, do you need a break. Why don't you take a half hour, go eat." She's going to come up to me with a list of people who are waiting and mad.

It is at this very moment that the emergency department and the patients most need moral leadership. It is also at this chaotic, time-pressured moment when it is most difficult for the doctor, or any other professional in a comparable situation, to exercise moral leadership: to model conduct by putting others' needs and her own responsibility above the din of the situation and the pressures of the moment.

Grave mischief can be done when people have too little time. The Enron board of directors exemplifies the dangers of limited time. The U.S. Senate investigation of Enron found that at a single special meeting held by teleconference on June 28, 1999, the board of directors covered a number of significant matters. Among them, CEO Kenneth Lay discussed a reorganization occurring at Enron, and the board reviewed resolutions to authorize a stock split, alter the company's stock compensation plan, purchase a corporate jet, and invest in a power plant in the Middle East. At this same meeting, a vote was also taken to establish one of the notorious special-purpose entities, LJM1; the company's code of conduct was waived, thereby permitting the chief financial officer, Andrew Fastow, to head the special-purpose entity despite a conflict of interest; and the entity's first transaction, with Rhythms NetConnections, was reviewed. All of these issues, mundane and questionable alike, were covered in no more than one hour.[2]

Time was not the cause of misdeeds at Enron, but this example illustrates how moral leadership can easily be compromised when time is scarce. Not only can limited time aid and abet mischief, inhibiting a board full of business leaders from deliberating thoroughly and questioning troubling practices, it can also frustrate natural human tendencies to aid others. In their famous study of helping behavior, John Darley and Dan Batson discovered that the most influential factor determining whether a bystander would respond to a person in distress was whether the bystander had sufficient time. A bystander late to an appointment was less likely to heed a plea for help.[3] Moral leadership in aiding others, much like moral leadership in stopping misconduct, gets squeezed in the hands of the clock.

Is more time the antidote? Not necessarily. Too much time, it turns out, can also contribute to grave mischief. Philip Zimbardo has related his classic Stanford prison experiment to the inhumane treatment of prisoners at Abu Ghraib.[4] One contributing factor at Abu Ghraib, Zimbardo has noted, was the endless, vacant, and unsupervised time that guards had on the night shift. Again, time alone did not cause guards to mistreat prisoners. However, with so much time on their hands, immoral conduct sprouted. Copious time, it would seem, is no guarantee of moral leadership.

Too little time and too much time both inhibit moral leadership. But too little time defines the reality of professional and organizational settings, especially in an era striving for greater efficiency. Quite simply, moral leadership entails managing time. Therefore, for those who wish to exercise moral leadership, one imperative is to be cognizant of time and manage it actively rather than just lament its swift passage. Little is known about how time as a dimension of ethical conduct can be managed. As a crucial variable, time has garnered growing attention in research on organizations,[5] and ethicists have considered intriguing questions about time,[6] but the intersection of the two fields is where we need greater practical insight. What does seem clear is that ethical conduct can be advanced or impeded based on how time is handled.

Our research suggests that organizational and individual mechanisms can help effectively manage the impact of time on ethical conduct. For example, some organizations have structures and systems that build in pauses and second looks. They provide a safety valve against the impact that limited time can have on decisions with ethical implications. What these structures and systems share is that they are designed as much to educate as they are to monitor. In one hospital where we spoke with doctors about necessary evils, clinical teams comprise medical students, interns, residents, fellows, and attending physicians. Although not unusual for a teaching hospital, this structure reassured the medical students and interns and gave them the opportunity to handle cases that otherwise would have been beyond their level of experience. The direction and oversight provided by more senior doctors exists primarily for educational purposes, but it ensures that multiple eyes, from a novice's to a veteran's will consider a difficult case. No one individual may have the ideal amount of time, but the overlapping attention of multiple people equipped with different sensibilities increases the likelihood that all dimensions of the situation, including ethical implications and the humanity of the patient, will get noticed.[7]

So too with an addiction facility we studied. Although individual counselors make the decision about expelling clients who violate rules, the entire team of counselors must discuss the decision and then treat it as a collective decision. For the addiction facility, the team system is designed to foster collective responsibility for life inside the facility. What it also does is build in time between making a momentous decision and sealing it. Teams at the addiction facility and hospital thus share two characteristics, which help manage the dangers of time. First, the addiction counseling team and medical teams turn deliberation from a private activity inside one person's head into a public event that occurs through discussion. Second, multiple sets of eyes review a single situation. These structures thus build in natural pauses that decelerate action without impeding it, and they offset the constrained time of any one individual by building in time devoted from multiple people.

Limited time is still a reality of organizational life and professional roles. So individuals also must find ways to manage time and manage their reactions to time pressures. Construing time as a resource rather than as a constraint can help people be more conscious of it and more conscientious in their use of the amount of that available resource, whether it is plentiful or scarce.[8] In addition, we found that seasoned managers, doctors, police officers, and addiction counselors all took time for short breaks, no matter how hectic the day, to collect themselves, step away from the pressure, and simply take stock of the rapid pace, as did the doctor whose comment opened this section. More than providing a solution to the rush of time, these breaks alert professionals to the impact of time and the care needed to manage it as one manages all other factors that may bear on one's conduct.

Ambivalence

Moral leadership often requires people to act in a manner they sense is right even as it unleashes uneasiness and misgivings. Here a manager and a doctor describe this experience as they laid off an employee and cleaned a wound, respectively:

Manager: "I think there is compassion, there is a, you know, sense of angst about these people. However, I have a practical side and I know this is what we need to do for the business."

Doctor: "When the man was writhing in pain, shaking, sweating and calling out in pain, I felt awful. I started to get very hot and sweaty and nervous. I knew that I had to finish, but felt like I was doing an inadequate job of both breaking loculations and of packing the wound."

Ambivalence describes the manger's clash between "compassion" and "what we need to do for the business" and the doctor's clash between feeling "awful," "nervous," and "inadequate," but knowing "I had to finish." A sense of professional responsibility motivates an action, but that action provokes a conflicting visceral reaction to do no harm. Ambivalence is about the disquieting internal tension that comes from competing duties, colliding considerations, and dissonant emotions. Although natural in situations with conflicting demands, ambivalence unchecked and unmanaged can lead to dysfunctional consequences for the leader attempting to take action.

However, the practical challenge may have less to do with ambivalence run amok than with failure to acknowledge the reality of ambivalence. The implicit ideal of moral leadership conjures up a conscientious individual who deliberates over various options, all imperfect; weighs principles, rights, responsibilities, and consequences, both good and bad; and ultimately commits with resolve to a course of action, whatever its drawbacks and costs, exuding confidence that propels others to commit and thereby increases the likelihood of successful action. All the while, the individual is open to learning and adjustment, but not squeamishness, indecision, or paralyzing analysis. Contrary to this judicious and poised image, professionals in each of the occupations we studied revealed a different portrait of actual experience. Here are two managers and a police officer relating that experience:

> *Manager conducting a layoff:* "Internally there is a nervous stomach, you feel on edge. Sometimes you get physically nauseous or a headache. Very often the night before or after you have very bad dreams that are not necessarily related to the downsizing itself, but from that stress."
>
> *Manager firing someone:* "It is very difficult from an emotional standpoint knowing you are dealing with somebody's livelihood. Dealing with somebody's ego. Dealing with somebody's ability to provide for their family."

Officer evicting a family: "You feel bad for the family sometimes, especially like the mothers or the wives with their
   little babies in their arms."

Ambivalence is a hard fact of professional practice, especially in
situations such as necessary evils, in which individuals are pulled in
vying directions, trying to honor intuitive sensibilities to avoid harming others while also fulfilling their responsibility to achieve a greater
good or purpose. However, as third-party observers, people often have
difficulty accepting ambivalence. As observers, people seem uncomfortable when they hear that a doctor feels torn about performing a
lumbar puncture on a child who absolutely needs it in order to diag-
nose the source of that child's ailment. As observers, we do not want
to hear that our doctors have second thoughts and uneasy feelings
about procedures that seem essential for health.

So too people feel uneasy when they learn that Scott Sullivan,
the CFO at WorldCom, or his loyal assistant, Betty Vinson, had
reservations about committing accounting fraud. Reservations
about what? Where, we as observers wonder, is the good they were
weighing? How could they not see the patent wrongness of their
deeds? Observers search for the virtuous side of these managers'
actions, the side that induced ambivalence, and have difficulty
grasping it. People would prefer to hear that Sullivan and Vinson
had moral clarity and indulged gluttonously in violating accounting standards at WorldCom,[9] just as we would prefer to hear that a
doctor's moral clarity leads to his or her unquestioned performance
of a procedure. In real-life ethical dramas, we want our heroes and
our villains. Our empathy breaks down for some reason when we
learn of people's qualms.

There is a gulf between experiencing ambivalence and witnessing it.[10] How an action looks differs from how that action feels if
you are the actor. There is no more compelling evidence than Stanley Milgram's famous experiments on obedience to authority. Psychiatrists were asked to predict the maximum shock they believed
people would administer. The psychiatrists predicted that most sub-

jects would not administer more than 150 volts and that only one in one thousand subjects would administer the maximum 450 volts. Psychiatrists were also asked to predict how they would likely behave, as were college students and middle-class adults. Only 4 of the 110 (3.6 percent) people asked thought they would go as high as 300 volts, and only 25 of the 110 (22.7 percent) thought they would administer more than 150 volts. The data from Milgram's experiment revealed that people's actual conduct defied these expectations. In the main version of Milgram's experiment, 25 subjects (62.5 percent) administered the maximum shock, and 36 of 40 subjects (90 percent) went beyond 150 volts.[11] Analysis from the eyes of an observer differs markedly from experience in the shoes of an actor.

An experiment we conducted also revealed the discontinuity between detached observation and involved action. We found that people judge the fairness of a hardship imposed on employees similarly whether they are observers of the hardship or managers about to inflict the hardship. Reducing pay or laying off employees are both seen as more unfair when done to augment corporate profits than when done to offset a corporate loss. This holds true for third-person observers reading about a company cutting pay, and it holds true for first-person actors who must lay someone off. Although observers' ethical judgments may parallel actors' ethical judgments, actors' real experience overwhelms that arm's-length judgment. We put people through a simulation where they took on the role of a project manager. They were introduced (on paper) to the project manager's team, given the project manager's schedule for the coming week, and asked to respond to a series of e-mails inquiring about scheduling and strategic decisions. When pressed to lay off a member of the team, the emotional experience reported by those in the manager's role was just as intense whether the layoff was intended to augment corporate profits or offset a dire loss, and the amount of severance subjects granted was comparable across those conditions. When people must do the deed, the subjective experience of causing harm to someone else produces a comparable experience across fairness conditions despite differing objective judgments of those conditions. And that subjective experience revolves around ambivalence.

When people experience ambivalence, it provokes efforts to resolve the ambivalence, to rationalize away one side of the equation and thereby calm the emotions and discomfort. Often people favor the side that protects them from their deepest fear: the loss of livelihood, the admission of failure, or the implication of guilt. But that may not foster leadership, whereas sustaining ambivalence may.

In situations that involve an ethical trade-off, even though one side of the trade-off must ultimately be selected—for example, harming a person to help an organization perform better—the other side of the trade-off does not disappear. A person still loses his or her job, and a tenant still loses a place to live. Philosopher Ruth Barcan Marcus refers to this as the "residue" of moral dilemmas.[12] Action requires that we select a path, but the path selected does not eradicate the legitimate claims and concerns of the losing side. Here is where ambivalence can foster moral leadership. First, ambivalence helps those who encounter ethical challenges keep track of the moral residue and attend to that residue, even as they select the other side of the dilemma. As one manager commented, "If there's a person across the table, even though from a business perspective I've rationalized that it makes sense to do this, there's still an individual across the table whose life I'm impacting." Second, ambivalence sustains moral sensibility and guards against callousness. A senior human resource manager and a veteran addiction counselor explained their ongoing struggle with the cross-cutting emotions unleashed by necessary evils, despite the myth that the task simply becomes routine:

> *Human resource manager*: "I just know that I have to fight internally with myself not to say something that I want to say like, 'I really feel sorry for you and I wish I could remove the pain for you.' . . . It's painful to think you may be putting somebody on welfare. Or you may be causing somebody's

family to break up or somebody's kids not to be able to have food. . . . Somebody else might tell you that it's a piece of cake, it's nothing, it doesn't bother me, it's a job, I have to do my job. But it's always fighting it off for me."

Addiction counselor: "We're human. You're not supposed to get close. You're supposed to leave the work at the door. You're supposed to go home completely devoid of what happened in the eight hours that you're there. Anybody that can do that, please write the book and give them the million dollars and then send me a copy of the book. It doesn't work. It works for those people who are not doing this for the right reasons."

Ambivalence reminds managers and doctors, police officers and addiction counselors, that whatever their conduct in this instance, multiple considerations and ethical claims were in play, and the resolution was neither clean nor clear. We suggest that people prepare for ambivalence so that they can use ambivalence constructively. Ambivalence signals an unresolved collision of considerations, emotional reactions, and concerns. Ambivalence can therefore serve as a cue to take quite seriously all sides of the situation, to heed one's instincts and intuitions, which are not completely resolved. Preparing people for the experience of ambivalence is essential, in part because this experience seems unfathomable to us as observers not in the actor's shoes.

To prepare people to exercise moral leadership, especially young professionals and students, a different portrait of practical professional action must be conveyed, one that illuminates the reality of ambivalence. To be clear, we are not advocating indecision, excessive rumination, or paralyzing guilt. What we suggest, though, is that if individuals in professions and organizations are to exercise moral leadership—to judge wisely, plan action in the light of principle, act with proficiency and resolve, and engage in exemplary conduct—we may need to prepare them for what moral action feels like in practice. That includes the feeling of ambivalence.

Sense of Self

Morality focuses on what we owe others: on the rights they can claim, on our duties toward them, and on the consequences of our actions for them.[13] Moral leadership thus entails exemplary conduct in attending to the rights, needs, and claims of others, even when it is inconvenient and exacts a personal cost. In what might therefore be seen as a paradox, how a person treats others often hinges more on how a person understands himself or herself than on any thought that person gives to others. A manager, a doctor, and an addiction counselor interviewed for our research illustrate how self-construal guided what they did in ethically challenging situations:

> *Manager conducting a layoff*: "I am not there as myself. I am there as the company. The company is an entity and the company is ice and in many cases, people did not have full responsibility for the decision, and in this one I had some if not most of the responsibility."

> *Doctor performing a painful procedure*: "When the white coat is on and when you're being a doctor, it makes perfect sense that you have to do this because it's part of the job and you know that you're expected to rise above the situation that most people might have emotional difficulty doing. You're the one everyone is counting on, so you fulfill your role."

> *Addiction counselor expelling a client from a tough love program*: "I really liked this kid, and I really saw potential in him, but he just couldn't do it, and part of what I do is create a safe environment for other clients. And I really had to step back and allow myself to take on the responsibility of my title and who I am, and it was extremely hard for me."

How people make decisions, James March has proposed in his "logic of appropriateness," is a function of how people implicitly understand three things: the situation they face, their role in that situation, and the way that someone occupying their role in such a situation typically acts.[14] People intuitively enact behavior assumed to be appropriate to the role they occupy in a given situation. How they see themselves guides what they do.

An example comes from the forty-four managers in our study of necessary evils—tasks that entail doing harm to advance an organizational objective. The managers manifested two dominant ways of approaching necessary evils.[15] Some emphasized fairness, quarantined their own emotion, and focused on conveying information to the harmed party. Others emphasized compassion, sought ways to integrate their emotion into their conduct, and focused on assisting the harmed party. The orientation of each group emerged from the different ways they construed their roles. The first group saw their role as protecting the company from threat, whereas the second group saw their role as protecting the target of harm from further injury. Neither group neglected ethical considerations, but how they saw themselves in their roles shaped the type of moral conduct they adopted.

An experiment we conducted also revealed the effect of self-construal on moral conduct.[16] Students had to inform peers that those peers had been denied a scholarship. When subjects' empathy was primed subconsciously through a scrambled-sentence task and a brief questionnaire, they came to see themselves not merely as messengers but as helpers for the students. The emotion students experienced toward unjust procedures and the compassion and compensation they offered differed from the emotional experience and compensatory actions of students not primed for empathy. Even when the consequences of a situation remain the same for affected parties—in this case, losing scholarship money—salient aspects of an individual actor's identity influence that person's moral conduct.

If moral conduct depends as much on how an actor sees himself or herself as it does on how that actor views others, then there is a curious implication for educating those whom we expect to exercise moral leadership. The content of what students and future professionals learn about morality and ethics may be matched in importance by the implicit message sent by that content about who they are. What do we mean by this? Beyond what philosophers teach about different theoretical approaches to ethics, beyond what psychologists teach about the causal antecedents of moral conduct and misconduct, and beyond what other disciplines teach about the content of moral responsibilities and action, each discipline conveys to its students an implicit sense of who they are. Social science tells us we are much more products of our surroundings and cognitive equipment than we may otherwise care to admit. Social science has illuminated just how vulnerable we human beings are to act in unethical ways. Breathtaking findings sober us to just how much human behavior can be influenced by organizational features,[17] social pressures,[18] and cognitive tendencies.[19]

In contrast, philosophy and even economic models ride on assumptions about human beings' capacity to act deliberately, on the basis of reasoned assessments and conscious intentions. For budding professionals, philosophical approaches to ethics model careful analysis, precise logic, and reflective equilibrium that moves between tutored intuitions and rational principles.[20] Who we are, philosophy implies, are beings capable of exercising careful thought and control over our conduct.

Moral leadership requires that people see themselves through both lenses. It requires an appreciation for the tremendous impact that forces beyond our awareness may be exerting on our behavior. Moral leadership also requires a sense of one's capacity to exercise deliberate control over choices and behavior. That is what sustains our sense of ourselves as rational and reasonable actors. Internalizing both portraits of who we are can help people guard against invisible, corrupting influences, on the one hand, and rise to the level of our potential rational capacity, on the other.

It is not just the juxtaposed portraits of human beings as agent and actor that are important. Rather, moral leadership may require people to see themselves as a combination of actor and agent. Consider time and ambivalence. When people experience time pressures and the uneasiness of ambivalence, they are in the grips of powerful forces that can unobtrusively shape conduct. They are agents of causal influences. People cannot step outside those forces. While being buffeted about, however, they can exert their creative capabilities to operate constructively. They can function as actors resourceful in their handling of the forces they face. A sense of self that tells us we are responsible—literally, able to respond to the forces that bombard and grip us—may be crucial for those moments when moral leadership is most needed and least likely because the forces seem so overwhelming and insurmountable.

Conclusion

Budding moral leaders must be ready to manage time, use ambivalence, and draw on dueling, and integrated, senses of self. These provide no guarantee of moral leadership, but they do reflect the demanding experience of encountering real ethical challenges in practice. Expecting them and being ready to encounter them may make the challenging waters that call for moral leadership more navigable. Moral leadership is often identified with clear conviction, a capacity to check impulsive temptations against principles, steadfast commitment to a course of action, and courage in the face of personal costs. We do not deny the need for clarity, resolve, and courage. But if they are to survive the rapids of real ethical challenges, those from whom we expect moral leadership must be equipped to handle those rapids. The relentless pace of organizations and professional roles, the destabilizing experience of ambivalence, and the implicit sense one has of one's identity and role churn those rapids. Learning that these challenges are coming and then actively navigating them can only help increase the odds that moral leadership will indeed emerge.

3

ETHICAL JUDGMENT AND MORAL LEADERSHIP

Three Barriers

David Messick

There are three barriers to sound ethical judgments in situations requiring moral leadership. The first of these is the invisibility of bias. People are usually unaware of the factors that bias or skew our ethical judgments, and we suffer from what we might call the illusion of objectivity. How this happens is rather well known. I think there are at least two components of this illusion. The first is the tendency to see issues as lacking an ethical dimension. Tenbrunsel and Messick have outlined several factors that lead to what we have called *ethical fading*.[1] We use the verb *to fade* in the sense that colors fade and lose their saturation and vibrancy. Ethical fading refers to the gradual loss of ethical coloration in many situations. Language euphemisms, the gradual slippery slope of many practices, and our ability to find causal links in complex situations can lead to the inference that a situation is devoid of ethical content.

However, even if we are aware of the ethical aspects of a situation, we easily form self-serving interpretations of the nature of the ethical content. Research that Keith Sentis and I conducted many years ago showed the self-serving quality of judgments of fairness, for instance, and many subsequent studies have elaborated these findings.[2] It is in some ways impossible for us to avoid the constraints of our histories and our experiences. I can try to see the world from the perspective of a Cambodian sugar palm farmer, but

I can never escape the fact that it is I who is imagining what this other person is seeing. We rarely can know how our judgments are being formed or influenced by irrelevant events.

The second barrier is the fact that often ethical principles do not exist alone for us to admire and respect in isolation. It is often the case that conflicting ethical principles arise in the same situation. For instance, a case that was related to me recently happened in the Philippines when the manager of an agricultural products company was informed that one of his salesmen had had his laptop computer stolen. The theft rate was suspiciously high, and the laptops were quite valuable. The manager found out that the report of theft was false and that the salesman had merely kept the laptop for his personal use. The decision had to be made as to whether the salesman should be prosecuted by the law. The salesman was an educated man with a potentially fine future, and the manager knew that the minimum penalty under the criminal law of the Philippines would result in a six-year sentence in prison, with the possibility of as many as twenty years. Considerations of justice dictated that the man should be prosecuted, but considerations of mercy led to the belief that the man should be given a second chance and that the penalty would be too harsh. The manager had been grappling with this dilemma for weeks and had been unable to make a judgment, not because there were no ethical standards to apply but because there were at least two and they led to diametrically opposite judgments. Ethical judgments become difficult when more than one principle is evoked and when the principles lead to opposing judgments. Kidder has written extensively about such right-versus-right conflicts.[3]

The third and final problem is that of having the courage to make an ethical judgment in situations in which one may be wrong or unpopular or ineffective for having done so. In the extensive literature on whistle-blowing, Micelli and Near claim that the primary reason potential whistle-blowers do not come forward is that they believe that nothing will be done about their allegations.[4] Moreover, some psychologists who study conformity, the tendency for people to make erroneous judgments when they witness others having done the same, claim that there are two fundamental desires in conflict in these situations: the desire to be right and the desire to be liked. In situations with real moral ambiguity, like the right-versus-right situations, a person might be both wrong and unpopular by taking a stand. Declining to take a stand, and thereby failing to exercise moral leadership, reduces these risks. We know a good bit about the dynamics of these situations, thanks to the pioneering research of people like Latane and Darley and like Stanley Milgram, but more emphasis needs to be placed on the design of cultures and environments that promote moral leadership and sound ethical judgments.

Ethical Fading

The first barrier that needs to be addressed is the process that allows situations to become devoid of ethical content or coloration. As Tenbrunsel and Messick use the phrase "ethical fading," it refers to the observation that situations that once may have evoked a strong ethical response fail to do so. A number of processes can cause this phenomenon.[5] One such process is the slippery-slope phenomenon that is well known in organizational contexts. An executive needs to make the numbers expected by the "street" to maintain the price of his stock. As the close of the financial period approaches, the executive sees that she is likely to be slightly short. To avoid this, she brings forward the revenue from a deal that technically will not close until after the books are closed. This is a violation of generally accepted accounting standards, but it is not a huge one. The revenue from the deal is recognized this term instead of next. It is wrong, but no big deal. However, this causes the executive to begin the next period in the hole by the amount of the deal. She hopes for a really big quarter, so the loss of the revenue from the one deal will not be obvious. The miracle does not happen, however, so she needs to bring the revenue from two deals forward this quarter: one to get back to where she should have started and the other to make the targets expected. The gradual accumulation of ethical infractions begins to make the early ones seem innocuous and innocent. If the practice is commonplace, it must not be wrong. Related to this is the comment attributed to Stalin that "a single death is a tragedy but a thousand deaths is a statistic."

I often experience a version of this phenomenon in my classes when discussing bribery. In some firms, bribes are paid as a matter of routine. The people who report that this is an ordinary way of doing business, especially in some parts of the world, are shocked to learn that others are outraged at the practice and that these people earnestly believe that people who pay bribes should be fired and firms that condone such actions should be shut down. In some industries, in some parts of the world, the ethical prohibition and shame of bribery has simply faded, and "considerations" are a mundane business practice.

Calling bribes "considerations" illustrates nicely the second process Tenbrunsel and Messick identified as maintaining the illusion of objectivity: the use of euphemisms reduces or eliminates ethical opprobrium. Bribes are surely bad, but considerations, or facilitation fees, or priority access contributions, or any of a dozen other euphemisms, are less so, often because a euphemistic phrase is so abstract that its meaning is obscure.

Even without seeking to intentionally bowdlerize descriptions of one's conduct, the choice of words can make us look good, especially in comparison to others. I quoted a student in one study who said that her roommate "stole" her food from their joint refrigerator, while she "borrowed" her roommate's food.[6] The clever but probably mindless choice of words made her actions seem ethically acceptable while her roommate's were not. In a follow-up study to the one cited above, we explicitly examined the tendency of people to select words that would fade any ethical connotations of their acts relative to those of others. Previous research had shown that people tend to differentiate themselves from others in terms of the frequency or likelihood that they would do ethically positive or negative acts. We tend to believe that we do good things more often and bad things less often than others. Cates and Messick actually allowed people to select, from a predesigned list, the frequentative adverb that best described their behavior and that of others. The choices ranged from Never to Always.[7] The results were very clear. With all of the morally laden actions described, people chose adverbs that made them appear better than others. For instance, with the phrase, "keep (my) (their) word," the subjects who selected the adverb for "keep my word" selected Always or Usually on average. The modal category was Usually. When the action was describing others, "keep their word," the modal categories were Often and Sometimes. The differences were statistically significant for "I usually keep my word" and "They sometimes keep their word." These choices of adverbs seem to describe reality to the respondents, hence the illusion of objectivity and superiority that allows each of us, like the children of the fictional Lake Wobegone, to be above average.

We should be reminded that while the use of language can have subtle and unconscious effects on our ethical judgments, others may see the intentional manipulation of language as unacceptable and even fraudulent. A good case arose in the context of the Enron debacle. Enron's accounting firm, Arthur Andersen (AA), had approved many of the devious accounting ploys that Enron had invented to mislead its investors. Shortly before the Securities and Exchange Commission (SEC) and the Department of Justice (DOJ) announced their investigations, the AA accountants had begun to destroy the documents that pertained to many of these activities. The criminal charge of obstruction of justice was brought by the DOJ against AA. One document that was to play a pivotal role in the eventual conviction of AA was written by Nancy Temple, an attorney working for AA, to David Duncan, who headed AA's Enron team. This document, an e-mail, concerned Enron's proposal to describe a cost as nonrecurring, meaning that it would not have to be entered as an ordinary cost on Enron's books. David Duncan had said that such a representation would be "misleading." Temple's e-mail suggested that Duncan change the word *misleading*. She also requested that her name be removed from the e-mail making this suggestion. The jury hearing the obstruction-of-justice case against AA found this memo and the suggested change to be evidence of the presence of a "corrupt persuader," a finding they needed to bring in a verdict of guilty. So AA was convicted of attempted bowdlerization, of trying to "fade" the unethicality of Enron's deceptions.[8]

The third way people lose or transform the ethical quality of an act is to find a causal interpretation that avoids the ethical connotations. While the use of euphemisms involves the choice of the right words or phrases, causal "cleansing" involves the selection of the right causes. Social psychologists (and others) have long referred to the role of self-serving bias, that is, the tendency for people to take credit (causal responsibility) for successes and shun credit for failures.[9] In situations of even moderate complexity, the causal structures are ambiguous. In retaliatory spirals, for instance, like family fights or violence escalation in the Middle East, all parties may claim that they are "reacting" to a provocation initiated by others. No one thinks he or she "started it."

If the causes of undesirable outcomes are many and intertwined, one becomes more or less able to find a causal story that eliminates ethical culpability for the story teller. One famous exercise of this sort is the "Message to the Public" left by Robert F. Scott after his failure to reach a safe haven for himself and his men following his trek to the South Pole in 1911–1912. Scott and the four men with him died on the return, perishing a mere eleven miles from a supply depot that could have saved their lives. This failure and the consequent fatalities have been attributed to a series of poor decisions and blunders by Scott, the leader of the expedition.[10] However, Scott's own account highlights the environmental causes: "The causes of the disaster are not due to faulty organization, but to misfortune in all risks which had to be undertaken." He then describes the planning and preparation as "perfection."[11] What was conspicuous to Scott as he was dying and writing his defense was the poor weather and paralyzing cold. He did not focus on the fact that the depot that they failed to reach ought to have been about thirty miles closer to the

South Pole. Had the depot been laid in its intended position, they would have secured the food and fuel. Scott himself had failed to reach the intended position for the depot the previous summer, so the fact that they were starving was his fault, but it was less obvious than the cold and the blizzard.

A final illustration of the use of causal selection to fade ethical responsibility may be seen in Eichenwald's account of the Enron debacle.[12] Again, the failure of this huge American corporation was the result of a multitude of factors ranging from the criminal conduct of some of its officers to the inattention of others who should have observed, reported, and halted the criminal conduct. As the company was beginning to evoke hard questions about its financial health from business reporters, it found itself in more and more trouble concealing its secrets. The stock price was falling, and this decline was creating trouble with its ability to service its debts. Kenneth Lay, the CEO, expressed his view that the company's trouble was caused by a hostile business press. The *Wall Street Journal*, he said, has "a hate-on" for Enron.[13] Mark Palmer, the head of corporate communications, corrected him: "We've got forty billion dollars in obligations and no cash flow. *That's* the problem."[14] Lay was looking for a cause that would shield him from blame. But Palmer was right on target.

Perhaps the most profound and least tractable reason that our biases are invisible is that we cannot be aware of how "we" might have seen the world and the events in it had we been someone else. We can only see the world as we see it. This seems banal on the one hand, but it is profound on the other. Let me illustrate with a recent example.

I recently wanted to buy a pair of binoculars. I could shop around and look through the different alternatives and see how the world looked through those lenses. I bought the pair that I thought most suited my purposes. I can think of my own consciousness as a pair of binoculars through which I see the world. But I cannot shop around to see how it looks from your consciousness or someone else's. The best I can do is to pretend to be able to see through yours while still looking through mine. So I can never see how the world might look were I someone else. Nor can anyone else.

So consider the case of an engineer who is making a staffing decision to decide who from among several candidates is going to be promoted to a staff-level technical position. He has made a provisional choice of a woman with excellent qualifications. Before making the choice public, he takes it to his boss for approval. His boss says, "I don't think this is a good choice." The engineer asks why, and the boss replies, "You come from India, and many of the people on your staff are of Indian background. There is a rumor that you give preferential treatment to people of Indian ethnicity, and the woman you have chosen fits this category. Her parents were immigrants from India." The engineer is offended and furious. He is being accused of an ethnocentric bias in favor of Indian engineers. He claims the people he promoted were better qualified than any of the other candidates. It had nothing to do with ethnicity. But how can he know that? Would he have made the same promotion decisions if he had been born and educated in the United States? Who can say? We can be sure that he was not consciously trying to advance the careers of ethnic Indians and that he was doing his absolute best to get the best people. But that is irrelevant to this point.

Contextualizing Ethics

The second generic barrier to sound ethical judgment arises from the fact that most of the ethical decisions and judgments that people make in their lives are made in situations that are rich in contextual detail and built-in conflicts. It is rare that a situation evokes one and only one ethical norm. When multiple principles become engaged, considering only one and ignoring the others would usually be seen as an oversimplification. Let me illustrate. Consider a physician who works for an health maintenance organization (HMO) that treats several million customers or patients. Each of the patients has purchased a policy that describes the treatments permitted under the policy and the cost of the policy. The more one pays, the more services one gets. Our physician's job is to deal with atypical requests that arise when a patient seeks a treatment that is not covered under the policy that the person has purchased. As the physician described it, the treatment being sought is often for a child with a newly diagnosed illness that could be fatal if untreated. Sympathy and the desire to help the parents and the child dictate that the treatment should be approved. However, justice, adhering to the terms of the contract, denies the treatment. Which ethical standard should rule? If one makes all calls in favor of the parents in these cases, there is no incentive for people to purchase more expensive options because they can receive treatments whether or not they have paid for them. Furthermore, the profitability and, in extreme cases, the very existence of the HMO could be jeopardized. However, to decide always in favor of the HMO would be inhumane, allowing people to go untreated when treatment is possible. No matter which choice one makes in a situation such as this, it will seem immoral and wrong to one of the parties. If the decision is to approve the treatment, the physician's boss can accuse the physician of behaving irresponsibly, of "giving away the company's money." But a decision to deny treatment could lead to the patient's death, and family members could claim that the physician was responsible. There is no single or simple "correct" decision here.

This is one illustration of what Kidder calls right-versus-right ethical conflicts.[15] He differentiates these conflicts from temptation conflicts, conflicts between right and wrong, where one knows that one of the options is ethically wrong but is still tempted to choose it. Sometimes people act as if the heart of ethical judgment and decision making involves making the right type of choices in temptation conflicts, but my own experience is the opposite. The most common types of ethical problems plaguing the people I encounter are right-versus-right conflicts.

Kidder discusses four types of right-versus-right conflicts and suggests that these categories may be exhaustive. One type he calls individual-versus-community conflicts. These are conflicts in which the interests of one party are in opposition to those of a larger, more inclusive party. For instance, an executive in charge of marketing for a gaming company whose profits derive from gambling would face this type of conflict if the executive also believed that gambling was injurious to the health of the communities that supported it. It has been claimed that negative political ads, ones that attack an opponent's character, are effective in damaging the opponent, but they also do damage to the credibility of all candidates and the political system more broadly. Deciding whether to attack one's opponent would also be a conflict of this type.

A second type of right-versus-right conflict involves short-term versus long-term trade-offs. A standard illustration of this type of conflict occurs when individuals or organizations stand to gain in a negotiation or a sale by concealing unfavorable facts. In the short term, concealment produces an advantage. In the long term, trust is lost and reputation suffers if the deceived person discovers the deception. A second illustration involves a customer who inadvertently pays too much for a service or product. The question is whether to bring the error to the attention of the customer and refund the overpayment, or to allow the overpayment to stand. Refunds involve a short-term cost, but they may buy long-term loyalty.

A third type of conflict Kidder labels truth versus loyalty. One generic example occurs during economic downturns, when some employees must be laid off. An executive involved in the downsizing knows that a good friend is going to be among the victims. If the friend is given advance warning, she can begin to look for a job, delay major purchases, and deal intelligently with the bad news. But the executive is bound by a commitment not to reveal who the victims will be, and in some cases, even that there will be layoffs. Many executives have found these conflicts to be highly difficult and stressful. Loyalty to the friend requires disclosure of the bad news, while loyalty to the firm prohibits it. Where does ethical judgment lead one in a case like this?

The final type of conflict that Kidder discusses involves justice versus mercy. The case of the physician working for an HMO is an illustration of this type of conflict. Justice requires that all parties abide by their contractual commitment, whereas mercy dictates that a family member receive treatment. Another classic example of this type of conflict arises when an employee is found to have violated company rules. An executive in one of my classes told of discovering that an employee in her company (a large pharmaceutical firm in Beijing) had been pilfering inexpensive office supplies. She had been taking paper, ballpoint pens, staplers, and the like home. When the employee, a promising college graduate with a degree in biochemistry, was interviewed about the theft, she confessed and said she was taking the material to give to her brother who was a student. Her family, she claimed, was poor and could not afford to buy these supplies that her brother needed for his studies. The theft of even such inconsequential things was a clear violation of the company's policies, and the required response was termination of the employee. However, this happened in China, where a dossier is kept on every Chinese citizen, according to the executive. Dismissal for theft would have been entered on this young employee's dossier, and that stain would have marked the employee for the rest of her life. She would not have been able to get a job with a multinational company ever again, she would have been denied a passport to permit her to travel abroad, and she would probably have been required to take a job teaching science in a rural school. The consequences would have been harsh and permanent if she were fired. Mercy dictated that the employee be given a second chance, while justice required that she be dismissed. It is hard to see which of these actions represents moral leadership. The compromise that the executive reached was to advise the employee to resign and look for another job. No black mark was entered in her dossier, but the spirit of the corporate policy was upheld. Ethical judgments often require such compromises among competing ethical principles, making leadership a matter of compromise, balance, and half-steps.

The Need for Moral Courage

The final barrier that I mention is one of the most difficult and most studied: the need for moral courage. When I speak of moral courage, I am referring to the conviction to do what one believes is the right thing despite the risk of unpleasant consequences. Three prototypical situations can be identified in which moral courage is necessary for moral leadership: resisting immoral authority, risking unpopularity, and blowing the whistle.

Resisting Immoral Authority

One common dilemma for executives concerns a boss who wants to involve them in immoral conduct. Examples include refusing to tell a customer about a quality problem in a product that the customer has bought, promising a customer a timetable that is known to be impossible, terminating or promoting an employee for inappropriate reasons, misrepresenting the testing that has been done on a product prior to sale, or falsifying a report to save money or time. One recent illustration of this type of problem arose for a physician whose hospital was scheduled to be closed by a new patient health care corporation in order to save money. One consequence of the closure was the virtually certain reduction in the assistance available for a dependent subpopulation that had long been served by the hospital. The physician, who was chief of staff of one of the hospital's sections, worked with community and activist groups to create political support that would prevent its closure. When the CEO of the corporation heard about those efforts, he called the physician into his office and warned him that if he continued working with the opposition, he would lose his position as chief of staff. The physician chose not to stop working with the community groups, the hospital stayed open, and the physician was replaced as chief of staff.

There has been a good deal written about situations of this sort, and this is not the occasion for a full review. Experimental research goes back at least to Milgram's seminal studies on obedience to authority, followed by Kelman and Hamilton's work on "crimes of obedience," and extended recently by Badaracco's inquiries about how people manage to do the right thing through "quiet leadership."[16] While the literature offers many suggestions for coping with immoral demands, the options generally boil down to four qualitatively different choices. First, one can display moral courage (or recklessness), doing what one thinks is right and accepting the consequences. This was the option that the physician chose. Second, one can solve the problem by leaving the organization. Although quitting is often the best option, the costs may sometimes be extremely high; leaving the armed services is an example. Third, one can follow orders and do something that seems wrong and immoral. The short-term solution may create long-term costs to one's conscience and self-regard. Finally, one can try to negotiate one's way around the orders and find a way to do the right thing without being downright disobedient or disrespectful. The physician, for instance, might have tried to convince the CEO that keeping the hospital open was in the long-term best interest of the corporation, as well as the patients to whom he was committed. Badaracco offers wise ideas about how to conduct this type of negotiation. While the last option may seem like one that compromises moral courage, it may in fact be the most effective in the long run in creating morally desirable consequences. In the long run, however, people are well advised to exit organizations in which they feel that their moral integrity is regularly assaulted.

Risking Unpopularity

Taking positions that can be predicted to be socially unpopular also requires moral courage. Among the leaders who have shaped the modern social and political landscape are many people who have braved fierce opposition not only from powerful opponents but also from extremists within their own group. The most visible examples of this type of moral courage are individuals like Dr. Martin Luther King Jr., Nelson Mandela, and Mahatma Gandhi. The ferocity and pervasiveness of the forces opposing such leaders are sufficient to deter most of us from taking such risks. One need only remember the brutal assaults on civil rights demonstrators in the American South in the 1960s, or the quarter of a century that Nelson Mandela spent in a South African prison, or the beatings and imprisonment of Mahatma Gandhi, to understand the stakes. And the dangers such leaders face are not just from the "other side." Gandhi, a Hindu, was assassinated by a Hindu. Itzak Rabin, the Israeli peacemaker, was assassinated by an Israeli. His Egyptian counterpart, Anwar Sadat, was assassinated by Egyptians. Indeed one reason that moral leaders of this sort are so widely admired is precisely that they are so rare.

Whistle-Blowing

The final situation in which moral courage is called for (and is often missing) entails whistle-blowing. Typically these are situations in which an observer witnesses wrongdoing and must decide whether to expose it. The dynamics of the conflict depend on the details of the situation. A student who witnesses his roommate cheating on a take-home exam may have to decide whether to report the infraction. A police officer, like the fabled Frank Serpico of the New York Police Department, may daily witness other officers accepting money to protect gambling, prostitution, or drug operations, and may experience powerful pressure to join in the graft. Here the conflict is, first, whether to participate, and, second, whether to report. In some cases, the activity is clearly illegal, as was the case with Serpico, but in others, the legality may be ambiguous, as was the case with the accounting deceptions that were created by officers of Enron and reported in a memo by Sherron Watkins. Watkins's memo sent on August 15, 2001, asked questions about the viability and legitimacy of some of the special-purpose enterprises that were being created within Enron to hide debt and create the illusion of income. It is also relevant that Watkins's memo was originally anonymous. She did not sign it, presumably to avoid possible retaliation. Anonymous whistle-blowing or leaking has the protection that the leak may be shielded from the consequences of its actions.

Moral courage is required to blow the whistle on another person or institution for many reasons. There may be personal recriminations or threats, and injury or even death may result. In some organizational cultures, like the New York Police Department, a whistle-blower is considered a traitor. In others, like Enron, someone who questioned the financial gimmicks was considered hopelessly stupid, someone who just "did not get it." Few self-respecting executives wanted to risk getting this reputation. In religious organizations, one risked excommunication by taking reports of wrongdoing outside the organization. In such cases, the threats concern the most important aspects of one's identity and livelihood. No wonder it is so rare.

Two additional factors tend to suppress whistle-blowing. One is the ambiguity about whether something is truly wrong. For instance, in Enron, the accounting machinations were of such complexity that casual observers could not judge if they were proper. Employees were often assured that the arrangements had the blessing of the lawyers and the accountants. So even if they suspected fraud or criminal activity, they could not be sure. Yet their failure to report could (and often was) taken as assent and approval.

The second factor is the perception that even if the infraction were reported, nothing would be done about it. Why go to the trouble and risk social ostracism if no remedies would be forthcoming? Micelli and Near, in their study of whistle-blowing, cite research that suggests that the fear of futility is more a deterrent to whistle-blowing than the fear of retaliation.[17] Even worse, if the person or agency to which the problem is reported is actually part of the problem, then blowing the whistle gives a warning signal to those responsible. This was part of the problem that Serpico came to perceive: that the higher-ups to whom he was reporting were part of the criminal conspiracy. The sense that disclosure may be futile or counterproductive often becomes a major barrier to publicly denouncing wrongdoing.

An obvious strategy to reduce such barriers is to reduce the ambiguity about what is and is not permitted in an organization and to have policies to clarify reporting channels when gray activity is observed. Anonymous hot lines are a possibility, as is outsourcing the reporting system to independent agencies that are empowered to investigate the allegations. To combat the perception of futility, organizations need to have some effective responses to allegations of wrongdoing. At a minimum that will require launching investigations of any reported misconduct, all charges, reporting the findings to the whistle-blower, and providing some positive recognition to the person making the allegations regardless of the outcome. Such policies can reinforce the moral courage that is often required to stand up and make a clear and public ethical judgment.

Conclusion

The three barriers to ethical judgment that I have discussed—one's conviction of moral rectitude and objectivity, the moral complexity of many situations faced by leaders, and the need for moral courage—may be thought of as three forces that tend to render our judgments self-serving, defensible, and safe. While I have made suggestions for coping with each of these barriers, I also acknowledge that these three C's constitute a formidable coalition to sound ethical judgment.

4

MORALS FOR PUBLIC OFFICIALS

Russell Hardin

In political leadership, the brunt of the problem of moral judgment that leads to action is how well the judgment is institutionalized and how effectively the action can be regulated. In particular, public officials must be subjected to some degree of institutional oversight. This follows from two central facts. First, these officials are in positions to take massive advantage of their roles, whose purpose is public service. Second, in a complex modern society, individually generated moral principles are not likely to constitute a coherent and consistent body. Oversight must be guided by principles for action that are clear to all. These principles constitute much of what we might call the ethics of public officials.

Principles is perhaps a misleading term here. What is necessary is something more nearly like laws or a code of behavior. Ethics in public office is first and foremost a political problem in this sense: the rules for behavior should generally be what the political process has established them to be. No lawyer, no moral philosopher, no religious leader can tell us what those rules have to be or what they a priori should be. Such experts might help us understand the problems and help resolve our minds on what to expect and what to do. They cannot tell us what the "right" rules ought to be. There are very few, if any, right rules that should specifically govern the actions of public officials. Our code will not be an ideal code devised according to abstract principles; it will be contextual in the sense that it will be socially constructed by us for particular purposes.

At the same time, the enforcement of morals should not be purely political. We should not let the mood of the public decide every case as it arises. There should be general rules and standard procedures. As much as possible, I think we want to take actual cases out of politics, although of course in some circumstances—such as the impeachment of Bill Clinton, Richard Nixon, and Andrew Johnson—the issues may be inherently political. But depoliticizing standard, everyday cases can yield a substantial political benefit to us in our politics. It should lead politicians and public officials to give more attention to public policies, less to ideology and personality. It also deflates the public tendency to deal emotionally with current cases in the heat of the moment. Forcing the consideration of cases through dull, even partly bureaucratic institutional procedures helps to defuse emotional charges.

Now turn to the basic nature of the ethics of public officials. Public officials—elected and appointed—are trustees, and we want them to act as trustees. They are our agents. This is the problem that public ethics must address. Unfortunately, it is often virtually impossible to determine what actions fulfill the office of a political trustee, especially an elected official as opposed to an official appointed to do a fairly specific range of things in a well-defined job. Officials are elected by only a fraction of their constituents, and even those constituents who vote for them may not have all their views represented. Hence, holding such officials accountable is extremely difficult and complicated.[1]

Such accountability is being aggravated in this new era of de facto party realignment in many nations. In the United States, the previously quasi-libertarian Republican party is now the great advocate of government monitoring and control of private lives. Republican politics now heavily revolves around social issues and their regulation by central government. These issues are quite diverse and not ideologically related in systematic ways. In the United States, for example, a traditional libertarian might oppose gun control, oppose giving religion a greater role in government and also oppose giving government greater power to monitor citizens. Many

Republican elected officials currently oppose gun control while supporting the other two issues. A social libertarian is out of luck on this package of views. The multiplicity of noneconomic issues and their partial lack of coherence severely undercuts accountability.

Perhaps the biggest complaint against what some people call the current ethics binge in the United States is that it distracts us, or our public officials, from policies. Give us ethical policies, and we will care less about the ethics of the policymakers. And we may be using ethical concern with personal foibles to escape from the harder issues of policy. These are the claims of various editorials, and there is some truth to such complaints. Against even the little bit of truth in them, note that it is also true that we can depoliticize the treatment of ethical misfeasance by formalizing rules and setting up relatively autonomous agencies to handle it. Then we could also expect officeholders to pay keener attention to the content of policies rather than to the behavior of their fellow officials.

I will focus on a priori versus conventional ethics, on ordinary individual-level morality versus institutional arrangements, and on political versus legal and regulatory agency control of public ethics. In general, I will argue that morality for public officials should be functional in the sense that what it is right for some official to do is what makes the official's role work as intended. Indeed, professional ethics should also be functional in this sense, as Deborah Rhode argues for lawyers' ethics.[2] Far more generally, we might agree with David Hume that most of ethics is artificial in the sense that it depends on social arrangements to make our ethics functional.[3] Those arrangements entail the creation of particular kinds of role with expectations of particular kinds of behavior in each role. These claims are perhaps most conspicuously clear for the ethics codes of various professional groups, such as doctors and lawyers.[4] Those codes change to reflect changing circumstances, including changing institutional circumstances such as the rise of big hospitals and large law firms.

To characterize acting according to the requirements of an institutional role as moral requires that the purpose of the institution and its roles is at least benign. That is, we first have to justify the institution and its purpose, and then we can justify the behavior of role holders in the institution. I assume here that the governmental institutions at issue are at least benign. My focus here is on individual behavior in institutions that exist to fulfill justifiable purposes.

A Priori Versus Conventional Ethics

In principle, the ethics of public officials must be what the law has determined. There is no other and, especially, no higher authority available to determine the content of such ethics. Legislators or their advisers might refer to philosophical ethics, social psychology, or organization theory for ideas, but the final force of whatever principles are adopted will likely be their backing by legislation and enforcement by other officials. These ethical standards cannot depart from positive law, which is conventional in this same way. Individuals might commonly suppose that their ethics is a priori: there is a right or a wrong action, a good or a bad outcome. Ethics of public officials, by contrast, must turn on many contingent facts about the natures of public institutions.

Popular personal ethics has in fact often been a priori or intuitionist.[5] Intuitionism in moral debate is used in two quite different but intellectually related ways. First, there is the idea that we all simply know what is the truly moral choice in various contexts—or at least the former students of upper-class English public schools such as Eton can do so, as H. A. Prichard believes. Prichard says when we face a difficult moral problem, we merely have to let "our moral capacities of thinking do their work."[6] Immanuel Kant had nothing but scorn on this move. "To appeal to common sense," he writes, "is one of the subtle discoveries of modern times, by means of which the most superficial ranter can safely enter the lists with the most thorough thinker, and hold his own."[7] Twentieth-century intuitionist ethics has largely been a disgrace to philosophy more generally.

Second, there is the supposition that serious moral philosophers can test various moral deductions from theory against their direct substantive moral intuitions. This supposition is slightly perverse because it implies that we could skip our theories and go directly with our intuitions. If the supposition is valid, why waste time with theory?

These are both absurd propositions absent any explanation of just how it is that we come to have true substantive moral ideas lodged in our minds. Earlier philosophers supposed that God was responsible.[8] That peculiar move is not available to most of us today. Any claim that we all know what is morally right or good falters in the face of the variety of moral ideas that people, including philosophers, view as self-evident. There are compelling social psychological explanations of how we might come to believe in particular moral claims, and those explanations do not entail or require that the beliefs are true.[9]

For public officials, the process of ethical decision making is quite different and entails the functional relation of role holders' actions to their institutional purposes. Morality for these individuals is at least partially conventional. It is like law in that it is legislated or devised by some governing or advisory body. It is also likely to be written into a code, such as the Code of Conduct of the City of Chicago Board of Ethics. Unlike a body of rules in ordinary morality, the code can be overseen, enforced, and revised by an authoritative body. By comparison, the ordinary ethics of a modern society is a morass of often conflicting, seldom enforceable rules grounded in quite different background principles. Any spontaneous ruling on what should be the ethics of the roles in an agency would therefore likely be incoherent and inconsistent.

The law and a code of enforced ethics can regularize behavior more readily and pervasively than any ordinary ethics can. If we want moral guidance for public officials and leaders, this is the form we should want it to take: consistent, relatively thorough, codified, transparent, institutionalized, enforceable, and subject to revision with experience. Enforcement must be consistent but not partisan. This is admittedly hard to guarantee because public office enforcement is likely to be subject to political constraints. As in the example of the three U.S. presidential impeachment proceedings, having one's own party in control of Congress is likely to be a protection against removal from office.

Individual-Level Morality Versus Institutional Arrangements

It is generally true that we want to have particular political institutions because of what they will do for us. We should therefore want their design to be functional. Morality within a role in an institution is therefore at least partially conventional and contingent. Moreover, institutional morality is at least partially consequentialist because we create institutions in order to accomplish various objectives; we want them for their consequences. As Thomas Nagel notes, consequentialist considerations and impartiality play special roles in the moral assessment and justification of institutions.[10] To judge a political institution or role or act without attention to its consequences would typically make no sense. The chief reason for creating any institution is to affect the world in some way, to have consequences. One might hold that personal ethics should not be consequentialist, but it is incoherent to suppose that politics is not consequentialist.

In sum, we require institutional help if we are to accomplish many of our purposes, such as maintaining an orderly society in which individuals can prosper, maintaining fair standards in bringing people to account for misbehavior of various kinds, and carrying out collective purposes, such as building infrastructures for our activities. To accomplish these ends, an institution must address moral behavior. For example, it constrains its role holders to keep them from doing some things, and it enables them to do other things. When an institution fails to achieve its purpose, we may charge the failure to one of two causes. The first is misdesign of the institution for its purpose; the second is failure of role holders within the institution.[11] Of course, a well-designed institution includes devices for correcting failures of role holders.

Political Versus Legal and Regulatory Agency Control

The view of the functional morality of officials and role holders more generally is especially congruent with one of the traditional conceptions of law, as associated roughly with Thomas Hobbes, Lon Fuller, and many others. This conception is that law is facilitative, that it serves a coordination function.[12] Through helping us coordinate our activities, law serves our mutual advantage. It is concerned, for example, not with whether we make an exchange but whether, if we wish to do so or we stand to gain from doing so, it will facilitate our doing so. Contract law, tort law, and much else are, in this sense, parts of the facilitative branch of the law. Fuller even argues that laws that are not facilitative but that attempt to block voluntary mutual choices, such as laws against crimes without victims, fail because their moral status as law is unjustifiable.

We can accept Fuller's more or less causal account without accepting his vocabulary of the morality of law. The reason for the seeming failure of laws against crimes without victims is that those laws do not serve mutual advantage. By contrast, regulation of the ethics of public officials, if it is directed at their fit with their functionally defined roles, is mutually advantageous to the larger society. It establishes guidelines for behavior and sets expectations. It is prospective and facilitative and therefore has the character of law, but law that is directed at the institutions of government and its legal system rather than at the larger society.

Indeed, one may sensibly claim that in the adjudication of any litigation, the judicial focus should be "not the resolution of the immediate dispute but its impact on the future conduct of others."[13] This view might even be read as the focus of the common law, as argued by Justice Learned Hand in what is now called the Hand rule. When a judge resolves a case, the most important part of the resolution is its effect on future behavior. This should therefore be a central part of the judge's concern in reaching a verdict.

There is an important side benefit of making ethics a matter of regulation and law and not merely of political discretion. Clarifying rules and expectations induce people to be less careless about their actions. This was the experience of the early days of the Board of Ethics of the City of Chicago (established under the Ethics Ordinance of 1987).[14] Many, perhaps most, of the cases that arose in the first years were inquiries about whether certain actions would be prohibited under the ethics ordinance. Officeholders seemed at first to be mildly irritated when the board initiated inquiries. In the longer run, they become more attentive to the appearance of conflict of interest and developed patterns for insuring ethical compliance.

Division of Labor in Official Ethics

One of the great advantages of making ethics a matter of institutional rather than strictly personal determination is the reliance on a division of labor in developing, codifying, and appropriate standards of conduct overseeing ethics. Reliance on individual moral beliefs would not generate a coherent set of norms. By contrast, a code that has experts contributing to its design and content enables others to focus on their institutional roles. For everyone to attempt to assess the ethics of their actions would not contribute significantly to getting their jobs done or even done well.

If it is implausible that individuals' spontaneous choices would lead to a coherent code, it is also inconceivable that a single individual or even committee could craft a complete code that would stand the test of time. The many failed efforts to construct utopian societies suggested the problem. To read, for example, James Harrington's *Commonwealth of Oceana* is to be teased with the extraordinarily dreamlike character of the argument. How could anyone have thought to lay out, in essentially fictional form, how a society should be constructed by a single clever designer? Harrington has various participants in his idealized society give long speeches on how things are to work. None of these speeches appears plausible, and none of the complicated structures he proposes (down to specific salaries for certain officials) would survive long even if they could be gotten under way to begin with. Harrington's utopia is presented in a dazzling display of silliness not unlike science fiction at its most bizarre.

In the division of labor in modern society, no one person could have a comprehensive overview of the organization of leadership. If we are to create a workable code that would affect behavior in morally positive ways, we will need multiple participants in the design. This is true of legal standards more generally, both in codified law such as the Napoleonic Code or the Anglo-Saxon common law. Both have been refined continually; no one could have formulated them in anything like their present forms without the experience of centuries. A code of ethics for political leaders is not complicated, but it too requires the distillation of experiences from multiple perspectives.

Consider one historical example of the development of such a body of ethical principles. George Washington Plunkett of the Tammany political machine in New York City spoke proudly of his practices, which today would count as corrupt but that he thought honorable and astute. He distinguished honest and dishonest graft and claims that "I seen my opportunities and I took 'em." Plunkett died as a highly honored millionaire. Today, those in positions such as Plunkett's who take similar opportunities risk ending their careers in jail. Today we understand official misfeasance better for having read of Plunkett's practices and his rationalizations of those practices. As noted later, the very idea of conflict of interest was not clearly articulated in Plunkett's time (he died in 1924), and its specific significance for a governmental ethics was not yet a crucial concern. Since his time, the standards on conflicts have seen a sea change.

The functional fit of a code of ethics with the purposes of institutions it governs recalls a distinction between Ronald Dworkin's and Richard Posner's views of the law more generally.[15] Dworkin looks to constitutional and moral theory to resolve contested issues; Posner looks to economic efficiency. Posner's stance would often require empirical rather than normative data. Posner believes that when judges engage in legal reasoning, the process is not much different from ordinary reasoning about nonmoral issues. Rarely do they engage in distinctly "moral reasoning." And when they do, academic moral philosophy is unnecessary. For example, "such political innovations as republicanism, the separation of powers, the system of checks and balances, and the secularization of politics can be . . . detached from their philosophical aegis and evaluated without regard to philosophical principles."[16]

In fact, this process is rarely easy for a typical judge, who, when the law runs out, will likely flounder. Few if any judges are expert in academic moral theory or in the social sciences that would be necessary for determining the functionality of a rule in a case at hand. Fortunately, we have a division of labor in law to deal with such concerns. We can refer them to a legislative body or to higher courts that specialize in cases where competing values are at issue. Most judges will be well served if the law is clear enough to resolve ordinary disputes. Similarly, the overseers of ethical code will be at their best when rules are clear and speak directly to conduct at issue. When they fall short as decision makers they should follow Posner's vision rather than Dworkin's. The basic rationale for a code of conduct is to fit behavior with the purposes of the institution. Its reputation should be procedural rather than moral and should draw more from empirical data than abstract theory.

We might also take advantage of the power of an institution to enforce morality of other kinds, as in policies on affirmative action or on sexual harassment, imposing these norms on influential institutions such as major corporations, universities, hospitals, and public accommodations. In general, it seems likely that the best agency for enforcing these broader social values would be a public oversight agency, not a body within the institution at issue. The public policy objective is to make it effective, consistent, and fair enforcement of these values. That task is best undertaken through officials accountable to society generally, not to particular institutions.

Conflicts of Interest

Conflicts of interest are a pervasive feature of human life, and there is nothing inherently immoral about them. You and I may have a conflict of interest over which of us gets a particular job or public benefit, and it is typically not wrong for one of us to end up the winner. But there are many conflicts of interest that compromise the role of public officials. The rewards of public office—mostly salary and related benefits—are established by law. Government employees should not use the power of their office to extract additional rewards in the form of bribes, gifts, jobs for relatives, and so forth. To take an obvious example, public officials should not help to award a government contract to their spouse's construction firm, law firm, travel agency, or consulting firm. Self-interest should not distort the prices your agency pays for the relevant services.

Some well-known case histories bring the point home. Former U.S. Attorney General Ed Meese arranged government jobs for people who loaned him money when his credit rating was very bad. Spiro Agnew, while governor of Maryland, took bribes for giving out contracts for public works. Dozens of other examples over the past quarter-century come readily to mind. Many involve illegal actions, as in Agnew's case. They would not even qualify as Plunkett's honest graft.

To ensure public trust, government officials would do well to avoid even the appearance of a conflict of interest. This may raise the most difficult issues for codes of public ethics. Should we prohibit conduct that raises the appearance of conflicts? The answer largely should turn on how much difference we think it makes to the functioning of public officials and of public agencies overall. This will be a matter of political sociology, not of a priori morality. If prohibition on apparent conflicts of interest means that public bodies such as legislative committees or ethics boards must invest great effort in investigating actual conflicts of interest, that may be all to the good. Perhaps more important, if appearances of conflicts of interest cast public doubt on an official's reliability, that is also a strong reason for the public to ban them.

The term *conflict of interest* first appeared in a court decision in the United States in 1949.[17] Now it is in hundreds of codes and statutes governing behavior of public officials. It also applies to certain activities of private citizens such as insider trading. Unless we are total hermits with no ties to anyone (and therefore not reading this discussion), we all face conflicts of interest. Until about a hundred years ago, almost no one thought this fact to be a problem except in extreme cases, such as bribery or treason. Today it is one of the central crises of eroding trust in government. Why? In part, because large government institutions affect ever more of our lives. We want the officials within these organizations to act disinterestedly to serve public, not private, objectives. Their motivations should be transparent and untainted by their own priorities.

Given their pervasiveness in all our lives, conflicts of interest are not intrinsically immoral. To suffer a conflict of interest does not require evil intention or character weaknesses. Whether a particular action constitutes unjustifiable conflict of interest is a contingent fact. Often it is the role of the actor that is definitive. For example, investment firms sell stocks on behalf of companies; they also advise individual investors on which stocks to buy. They clearly face an inherent conflict of interest, although their agents may claim to be entirely honest in their recommendations.[18] But private citizens can advise someone to buy their stocks on which they expect to incur losses. Because they are not acting in an agency relationship, they may profit from the transaction as long as they make no fraudulent representation.

Three Potential Distortions

If we establish enforcement mechanisms for ensuring the ethics of public officials, several complications can arise. For example, the enforcers might punish an action that is functional, fail to punish one that violates the institution's purpose, or even abuse their power to sanction officials who have not violated their role requirements. All three of the presidential impeachment proceedings happened when the president's party was in the minority in both houses of Congress. In all three cases, much of the motivation was self-evidently political rather than moral or constitutional, although Nixon was sufficiently involved in covering up criminal activity to constitute grounds for removal from office. A completely independent, apolitical Justice Department might have pursued the case against Nixon but likely not the other two. In addition to the possibilities of such enforcement problems, which are characteristic of legal systems in general, there are at least three distinctive difficulties connected with ethics and public officials.

First, institutional roles can encourage actions that violate ordinary principles of personal morality. Nagel notes that an agent might be expected to do for the principles what the principles ought not do for themselves.[19] Reinhold Niebuhr similarly notes that individuals with the best of intentions may serve vicious policy.[20] Ironically, public immorality seems to be less tarnishing than private immorality despite the extent of the consequences. In Nagel's example, Vice President Spiro Agnew is far more reviled for his personal corruption than Henry Kissinger is for his policies that resulted in civilian casualties on a massive scale. Hume remarks that "there is a system of morals calculated for princes, much more free than that which ought to govern private persons."[21] His point was to describe, not to justify, that system. His explanation of the disparity between official and personal morality intended to distinguish between states that have less frequent and more distant human interactions than do individuals. The highest costs of Kissinger's policies were borne by Vietnamese and Cambodian citizens far removed from the concerns of most Americans.

The Agnew and Kissinger examples are not strictly comparable in an important sense. Agnew's actions of taking bribes from construction companies that wanted to do business with the state of Maryland were a violation of his role morality. Kissinger's behavior in bombing Cambodia was not such a violation. To judge immoral requires some general moral theory. From that vantage, although Kissinger's actions were not in violation of his role morality, it was his role that enabled him to act immorally. We might want our standards of ethics for public officials to encompass acts that are immoral by conventional definitions, but finding a consensus on what those actions are may be impossible except in extreme cases.

A second problem is what theorists label *professional deformation*. Officials may tend to see it in their personal interest (or even their duty) to work for what seems to be the good of their agency, even where it conflicts with broader social interests. We must want a code for officeholders. One function of a specific ethical code is to restrain such organizational loyalty.

A third difficulty arises when violations of ethical codes raise issues of criminal liability. When public officials are accused of crimes, they are entitled to the same constitutional protections as any other citizen. Those protections are designed to ensure a just system free of constitutional abuse, and public servants should not be required to waive their rights and testify against themselves as a condition of retaining their office. For example, mere refusal on their part to testify about their activities cannot be used as prima facie evidence of their guilt.

By contrast, when public officials are questioned about their ethics outside the criminal justice system, they deserve no such protections; we need not suppose they are protected by such rights. When an ethics committee oversight body investigates a conflict of interest, it *can* take an employees' refusal to answer questions as prima facie evidence of an actual conflict. This is simply a cost of serving as a public trustee.

Conclusion

We might see society as a collection of individuals or as an organized endeavor for mutual purposes. Philosophical ethics often is tacitly founded on the first view. The second view is necessary to understand the ethics of role.[22] Few of today's moral theorists actively address politics in the rich ways that Hume, William Paley, John Stuart Mill, and almost all other major philosophers before the twentieth century. Paley entitled his book *The Principles of Moral and Political Philosophy*. Almost no one writing today could label their books in a way to imply that they see the enterprise of moral and political philosophy as one, as Paley, Hume, and Mill obviously believed. It is a peculiarity of twentieth-century moral philosophy that it became almost exclusively personal or individual in its focus. The shift in thinking began with a flood of intuitionist moral philosophy (for example, Prichard's writings) early in the twentieth century and G. E. Moore's (1903) idealistic and practically irrelevant variant of utilitarianism.[23] These works rightly lie almost entirely unread today, although intuitionism is still a significant, if intellectually destitute, enterprise. When contemporary philosophers discuss leadership in the context of an organization, they commonly focus on personal responsibilities of its occupants. All too often these theorists neglect the issues of institutional function and design.

Those are the issues that must be acted on ethical codes and standards of public officials. For these agents of the state, moral behavior in role must align individual behavior with the institutional purposes. Often our standards of a judgment will be essentially utilitarianism. Depending on the institution, the question may be what ethical requirements for officeholders will best serve the public welfare, enhance fairness, and uphold individual rights.

If we wish to promote conduct by public officials that will serve such institutional purposes, we should focus on two organizational strategies. First, at the stage of designing public institutions, we should build in natural incentives for behavior consistent with institutional goals.[24] Second, we must create oversight to monitor officials' behaviors. The morality we seek is morality that functionally serves the purposes of our political institutions.

Part Two

THE PSYCHOLOGY
OF POWER

5

THE PSYCHOLOGY OF POWER

To the Person? To the Situation?
To the System?

Philip G. Zimbardo

Evil is intentionally behaving—or causing others to act—in ways that demean, dehumanize, harm, destroy, or kill innocent people. This behaviorally focused definition makes a leader responsible for purposeful, motivated actions that have negative consequences to other people. It excludes accidental or unintended harmful outcomes, as well as the broader, generic forms of institutional evil, such as poverty, prejudice, or destruction of the environment by agents of corporate greed. But it does include responsibility for marketing and selling products with known disease-causing, death-dealing properties, such as cigarette manufacturers, or other drug dealers. It also extends beyond the agent directly accountable for aggression to encompass those in positions of authority whose orders or plans are carried out by subordinates. This is true of political and military leaders, such as Hitler, Stalin, Mao, Pol Pot, Idi Amin, Saddam Hussein, and other tyrants.

The same human mind that creates the most beautiful works of art and extraordinary marvels of technology is equally responsible

This chapter is a modified version of my presentation for the Stanford Center on Ethics Symposium on Moral Leadership February 25, 2005. It relies on my recent chapter, "The Social Psychology of Good and Evil: Understanding Our Capacity for Kindness and Cruelty," published in *The Social Psychology of Good and Evil*, ed. Arthur Miller (New York: Guilford Press, 2004), 21–50.

for the perversion of its own perfection. This most dynamic organ in the universe has been a seemingly endless source for creating ever more vile torture chambers and instruments of horror: the concentration camps of the Third Reich, the "bestial machinery" of Japanese soldiers in their rape of Nanking, and the recent demonstration of "creative evil" of 9/11 by turning commercial airlines into weapons of mass destruction.[1] How can the unimaginable become so readily imagined?

My concern centers around how normal individuals can be recruited, induced, and seduced into behaving in ways that could be classified as evil and the role of leaders in that process. In contrast to the traditional approach of trying to identify "evil people" to account for the evil in our midst, I will focus on the central conditions that underpin the transformation of good, or average, people into perpetrators of evil.

Locating Evil Within Particular People: The Rush to Judgment

"Who is responsible for evil in the world, given that there is an all-powerful, omniscient God who is also all-Good?" That conundrum began the intellectual scaffolding of the Inquisition in the sixteenth and seventeenth centuries in Europe. As revealed in *Malleus Maleficarum*, the handbook of the German Inquisitors from the Roman Catholic church, the inquiry concluded that the devil was the source of all evil. However, these theologians argued that the devil works his evil through intermediaries, lesser demons, and, of course, human witches. Therefore, the hunt for evil focused on those marginalized people who looked or acted differently from ordinary people, who might, under rigorous examination or torture, be exposed as witches and then put to death. As historian Ann Barstow notes, the victims were mostly women who could readily be exploited without sources of defense, especially when they had resources that could be confiscated.[2]

Paradoxically, this early effort of the Inquisition to understand the origins of evil and develop responses to evil instead created new forms of evil. It exemplifies the risk of simplifying complex problems by blaming individual perpetrators.

The same risk emerged following World War II, when a team of psychologists sought to make sense of the Holocaust and the broad appeal of national fascism and Hitler.[3] Their focus was on the authoritarian personality: a set of traits underlying the fascist mentality. However, what they overlooked was the host of processes operating at political, economic, societal, and historical levels of analysis that influenced so many millions of individuals to revere their dictator and hate Jews.

This tendency to explain observed behavior by reference to dispositions, while ignoring or minimizing the impact of situational variables, is what Stanford psychologist Lee Ross has called the fundamental attribution error.[4] We are all subject to this dual bias of overemphasizing dispositional analyses and underemphasizing situational explanations. We succumb to this effect because so much of our education, training, and law enforcement are geared toward a focus on individual orientations. Dispositional analyses are a central operating feature of cultures that are based on individualistic rather than collectivist values.[5] Thus, it is individuals who receive praise, fame, and wealth for achievement and are honored for their uniqueness, but it is also individuals who are blamed for the ills of society. Our legal, medical, educational, and religious systems are all founded on principles of individualism.

Dispositional analyses always include strategies for behavior modification to assist deviant individuals, by education or therapy, or to exclude them from society by imprisonment, exile, or execution. Locating evil within selected individuals or groups has the virtue of rendering society blameless. The focus on people as causes for evil then exonerates social structures and political decision making for contributing to underlying conditions that foster evil: poverty, racism, sexism, and elitism.

Most of us take comfort in the illusion that there is an impermeable boundary separating the evil (them) from the good (us). That view leaves us with less interest in understanding the motivations and circumstances that contributed to evil behavior. But in fact, as is clear from the Russian novelist Alexander Solzhenitsyn, a victim of persecution by the Soviet KGB, that the line between good and evil lies in the center of every human heart.

It has been my mission as a psychologist to understand better how virtually anyone could be recruited to engage in evil deeds that deprive other human beings of their lives, dignity, and humanity. So I have always begun my analyses of all sorts of antisocial behavior, even the most horrendous instances of evil, with the question, "What could make me do the same thing?" And furthermore, I wonder what set of situational and structural circumstances empowered others—maybe similar to me—to engage in deeds that they too once thought were alien to their nature.

The answers underscore the extraordinary capacity of the human mind to adapt to virtually any environmental circumstances in order to survive, create, and destroy as necessary. We are not born with tendencies toward good or evil but with mental templates to do either, more gloriously than ever before, or more devastatingly than ever experienced before—as the terrorist attacks of September 11, 2001, revealed. It is only through the recognition of our shared human condition that we can acknowledge vulnerability to situational forces. Although the research summarized in this chapter focuses on identifying processes by which ordinary people can be seduced or initiated into engaging in evil deeds, the time has also come to better understand how ordinary people can resist such forces and promote prosocial behavior. If we want to develop mechanisms for combating transformations of good people into evil perpetrators, it is essential to learn first the causal mechanisms underlying those behavior changes.

Blind Obedience to Authority: The Milgram Investigations

Stanley Milgram developed an ingenious research procedure to demonstrate the extent to which situational forces could overwhelm individual will to resist.[6] He shocked the world with his unexpected finding of extremely high rates of compliance to the demands of an authority figure to deliver apparently dangerous electric shocks to an innocent victim.[7] He found that about 67 percent of research participants went all the way up to the top shock level of 450 volts in attempting to "help" another person learn appropriate behaviors. Milgram's study revealed that ordinary American citizens could so easily be led to engage in "electrocuting a nice stranger" as the Nazis had been led to murder Jews.

After this initial demonstration with Yale College students, Milgram went on to conduct eighteen experimental variations on more than a thousand subjects from a variety of backgrounds, ages, and educational levels. In each of these studies, he varied one social psychological variable and observed its impact on the extent of obedience by a subject to shock the "learner-victim," who pretended to be suffering. The data told the story of the extreme pliability of human nature. Almost everyone could be totally obedient, or almost everyone could resist authority pressures; it depended on situational differences. Milgram was able to demonstrate that compliance rates could soar to 90 percent of people who delivered the maximum 450 volts to the learner-victim, or could be reduced to less than 10 percent of total obedience by introducing one variable into the compliance recipe.

Want maximum obedience? Provide social models of compliance by having participants observe peers behaving obediently. Want people to resist authority pressures? Provide social models of peers who rebelled. Interestingly, almost no one shocked the learner-victim when he actually asked to be shocked. They refused authority pressure when the target seemed to be a masochist. In each of the other variations on this diverse range of ordinary Connecticut citizens, low, medium, or high levels of compliant obedience could be readily elicited as if one were simply turning a human nature dial.

What is the expected rate of such obedience in the Milgram setting according to experts on human nature? When forty psychiatrists were given the basic description of this experiment, their average estimate of the number of United States citizens who would give the full 450 volts was only 1 percent. Only sadists would engage in such behavior, they believed. These experts on human behavior were totally wrong because they ignored situational determinants. Their training in psychiatry had led them to overly rely on dispositional explanations. This is a strong instance of the operation of the fundamental attribution error in action.

Ten Steps to Creating Evil Traps for Good People

What were the procedures in this research paradigm that seduces many ordinary citizens to engage in such apparently abusive behavior? These procedures parallel compliance strategies used in many real-world settings by "influence professionals" such as salespeople, cult recruiters, and national leaders.[8]

These are the influences that will lead ordinary people to do things they originally believe they would not:

1. Offering an ideology that justifies any means to achieve a seemingly desirable goal. In clinical experiments like Milgram's, the rationale is helping people improve their memories. For nations, it is often a "threat to national security" that justifies going to war or suppressing dissident political opposition. This is the excuse that fascist governments and military juntas have frequently used to destroy socialist or communist opposition. When citizens fear that their national security is being threatened, they are all too willing to surrender their basic freedoms. In the United States, the fear of terrorism has led many citizens to accept torture of prisoners as a necessary tactic for securing information that could prevent further attacks. As research by Susan Fiske and her colleagues indicates, that reasoning contributes to ordinary people's willingness to torture enemy prisoners in contexts like Abu Ghraib prison.[9]

2. Arranging some form of contractual obligation, verbal or written.

3. Giving participants meaningful roles to play (teacher, student) that carry with them previously learned positive values and response scripts.

4. Presenting basic rules to be followed that seem to make sense prior to their actual use, but then can be arbitrarily used to justify mindless compliance. Make the rules vague, and change them as necessary.

5. Altering the semantics of the act, the actor, and the action (from hurting victims to helping learners); replace reality with desirable rhetoric.

6. Creating opportunities for diffusion of responsibility or suggesting that others will be responsible or that the actor will not be held liable.

7. Starting the path toward the ultimate evil act with a small, insignificant first step (only 15 volts in the Milgram experiment).

8. Gradually increasing steps on the pathway to abuse, so that they appear no different from prior actions. Increases of only 30 volts presented no noticeable difference in harm to the Milgram participants.

9. Changing the nature of the influence authority from initially "just" and reasonable to "unjust" and demanding, which elicits confusion but continued obedience.

10. Making the exit costs high by allowing the usual forms of verbal dissent (that make people feel good about themselves), while insisting on behavioral compliance ("I know you are not that kind of person; just keep doing as I tell you").

Such procedures can prepare people psychologically to do the unthinkable.

On Being Anonymous: Deindividuation and Destructiveness

The idea for my doing research that used anonymity as an independent variable in the study of aggressive behavior came not from a psychological theory but rather from William Golding's Nobel prize–winning novel, *Lord of the Flies*. It chronicles the transformation of good British, Christian choir boys into murderous little beasts by centering on changes in external physical appearance that lead to changes in mental states and behaviors.[10] Painting their faces, changing their outward appearance, made it possible for some boys to kill a pig for food. Once that alien deed of killing another creature was accomplished, they could continue to kill with pleasure, both animals and people alike. In a real-world setting, could similar changes in external appearance affect internal and behavioral processes? That is the question I answered with a set of experiments and field studies on the psychology of deindividuation.[11]

The basic procedure involved having young women deliver a series of painful electric shocks to each of two other young women whom they could see and hear in a one-way mirror before them. Half the subjects were randomly assigned to a condition of anonymity, or deindividuation, and half to one of uniqueness, or individuation. The four college student subjects in each deindividuation cluster were treated as members of a group, not as individuals; their appearances were concealed by hoods, and their names were replaced by numbers. The comparison group consisted of individuals who wore name tags and were made to feel unique. Both sets of subjects were asked to make the same responses of shocking each of two woman "victims" over the course of twenty trials. The cover story was that these "victims" were trying to be creative under stress, so the job of our subjects was to provide stress through painful electric shocks while I, as the experimenter, gave them the creativity test. Unlike the Milgram paradigm, there was no authority insisting on their aggressive behavior because I was in the adjacent room, seen in the two-way observation mirror by the subjects along with each of the two alleged women in the creativity study. The dependent variable was the duration of shock administered, not shock level intensity. Again, no shocks were actually administered, although all participants believed they were doing so and that the two victims were suffering.

The results were clear: women in the deindividuation condition delivered twice as much shock to both victims as did the women in the individuated comparison condition. Moreover, they shocked both victims, the one previously rated as pleasant and the other unpleasant victim, more over the course of the twenty trials, while the individuated subjects shocked the pleasant woman less over time than they did the unpleasant one. One important conclusion flows from this research and its various replications and extensions, some using military personnel from the Belgian army: anything that makes people feel anonymous reduces a sense of accountability and increases their propensity to evil under situations inviting violence.

Cultural Wisdom: How to Make Warriors Kill in Battle But Not at Home

Some societies go to war without having young male warriors change their appearance, while others always include ritual transformations of appearance by painting or masking the warriors (as in *Lord of the Flies*). Does that change in external appearance make a difference in how warring enemies are treated? Harvard anthropologist John Watson posed that question.[12] The Human Area Files were his data source to compare societies with different practices in preparing warriors for war and the extent to which they killed, tortured, or mutilated their victims.

The results are striking confirmation of the prediction that anonymity promotes destructive behavior when permission is also given to behave in aggressive ways that are ordinarily prohibited. Of the twenty-three societies for which these two data sets were present, 80 percent (twelve of fifteen) of societies in which warriors changed their appearance were among those noted as most destructive, while that was true of only one of the eight where the warriors did not change appearance before going to battle. Ninety percent of the time when victims were killed, tortured, or mutilated, it was by warriors who had first changed their appearance.

A key ingredient in transforming ordinarily nonaggressive young men into warriors who can kill on command is to change how they look. War is about old men persuading young men to harm and kill other young men. It becomes easier to do so if they first alter their usual external facade by putting on uniforms or masks or painting their faces. As they acquire anonymity, they lose their usual internal focus of compassion and concern for others. When the war is over, the warriors can return to their peaceful status, encouraged by removing their uniform, taking off the mask, and resuming their former facade.

Moral Disengagement and Dehumanization

Psychologist Al Bandura has developed a model of moral disengagement that specifies the conditions under which anyone can be led to act immorally, even those who usually ascribe to high levels of morality.[13] The model outlines a set of cognitive mechanisms that alter a person's (1) perception of the reprehensible conduct (engaging in moral justifications, making palliative comparisons, using euphemistic labeling); (2) sense of the detrimental effects of that conduct (minimizing, ignoring, or misconstruing the consequences); (3) sense of responsibility for the link between reprehensible conduct and its detrimental effects (displacing or diffusing responsibility); and (4) view of victims (dehumanizing or blaming them).

Bandura and his colleagues designed a powerful experiment that is an elegantly simple demonstration of the power of dehumanizing labels.[14] It reveals how easy it is to induce normal, intelligent individuals to accept a dehumanizing label of other people and then to act aggressively based on that classification. A group of four participants were led to believe they were overhearing a research assistant tell the experimenter that the students from another college were present to start the study in which they were to deliver electric shocks of varying intensity (allegedly as part of a group problem-solving study). In one of the three randomly assigned conditions, the subjects overheard the assistant say to the experimenter that the other students seemed "nice." In a second condition, they heard that the other students seemed like "animals," In a third variation, the assistant did not label the students.

This situational manipulation clearly affected behavior. Experimental subjects gave the most shock to those labeled "animals," and their shock level increased over the ten trials. Those labeled "nice" were given the least shock, and the unlabeled group fell between these extremes. Thus, a single word, *animals*, was sufficient to induce intelligent college students to treat others as if they deserved to be harmed.

What is also of interest is the progressive nature of abuse. On the first trial, there is no difference across the three experimental situations in the level of shock administered, but with each successive opportunity, the shock levels diverge. Those shocking the so-called animals shocked them more and more over time, a result comparable to the escalating shock level of the deindividuated female students in my earlier study. That increase in aggression over time, with practice or with experience, illustrates a self-reinforcing effect of abuse. Perhaps its appeal is not so much in inflicting pain to others as in the sense of power and control in such a situation of dominance.

A more positive finding was that individuals receive more respectful treatment if someone in authority labels them positively. Those perceived as "nice" were least harmed. There is an important message here about the power of words, to be used for good or evil.

Suspension of the Usual Cognitive Controls Guiding Moral Action

Part of what is necessary to get good people to engage in evil is to minimize or reorient normal cognitive control processes. That process suspends conscience, self-awareness, sense of personal responsibility, obligation, commitment, liability, morality, and analyses in terms of costs and benefits of given actions. The two general strategies for accomplishing this objective are reducing cues of social accountability of the actor (no one knows who I am or cares to) and reducing concerns for self-evaluation. The first strategy minimizes concerns for social evaluation and social approval by making the actor feel anonymous. It works in an environment that masks identity and diffuses personal responsibility across others in the situation. The second strategy stops self-monitoring by relying on tactics that alter one's state of consciousness (such as by drugs, strong emotions, or hyperintense activity) and projecting responsibility outward onto others.

The Hostile Imagination
Created by Faces of the Enemy

The importance of situational influences is also apparent in the ways that nations prepare soldiers to engage in wars and prepare citizens to support the risks of going to war, especially a war of aggression. This difficult transformation is accomplished by a special form of cognitive conditioning. Images of the "enemy" are created to prepare the minds of soldiers and citizens to hate those who fit the category. This mental conditioning is the military's most potent weapon.

Archetypes of the enemy are created by propaganda. These visual images often create a societal paranoia that focuses on the threats these enemies pose for women, children, homes, and the religion of the soldier's nation, way of life, and so forth. Psychologist Sam Keen's analysis of this propaganda on a worldwide scale reveals that there are a select number of categories used by "homo hostilis" to invent an evil enemy in the minds of good members of righteous tribes.[15] The enemy is aggressor; faceless; rapist; godless; barbarian; greedy; criminal; torturer; death; a dehumanized animal, or just an abstraction. Alternatively, there is a vision of the enemy as worthy, combatant, a powerful opponent to be crushed in "mortal combat"—as in the video game of the same name.

Can Ordinary Old Men
Become Murderers Overnight?

One of the clearest illustrations of the transformation of ordinary people into agents of mass atrocities comes from the chronicle of Nazi genocides by British historian Christopher Browning.[16] In March 1942 about 80 percent of all victims of the Holocaust were still alive; eleven months later, about 80 percent were dead. In this short period of time, the Endlösung (Hitler's Final Solution) was energized by mass murder squads in Poland. This genocide required mobilization of a large-scale killing machine at the same time as able-bodied German soldiers were needed on the collapsing Russian front. Since most Polish Jews lived in small towns and not the large cities, the question that Browning raised about the German High Command was, "Where had they found the manpower during this pivotal year of the war for such an astounding logistical achievement in mass murder?"[17]

His answer came from archives of Nazi war crimes, in the form of the activities of Reserve Battalion 101, a unit of about five hundred men from Hamburg, Germany. They were family men from working-class and lower middle-class backgrounds and were too old to be drafted into the army. They had no military or police experience. They were just raw recruits sent to Poland without warning of, or any training in, their secret mission: the total extermination of all Jews living in the remote villages of Poland. In just four months they had shot to death at point-blank range at least thirty-eight thousand Jews and deported another forty-five thousand to the concentration camp at Treblinka.

Initially their commander acknowledged that this was a difficult mission and any individual could refuse to execute these men, women, and children. Records indicate that at first, about half the German police reservists refused and let others engage in the mass murder. But over time, social modeling processes took their toll, as did guilt-induced persuasion by those who had been doing the shooting. By the end of their journey, up to 90 percent of the men in Battalion 101 were involved in the shootings, even proudly taking close-up photographs of their killings. Like the guards at Abu Ghraib Prison, these policemen put themselves in their "trophy photos" as proud exterminators of the Jewish menace.

Browning makes clear that there was no special selection of these men. They were as ordinary as can be imagined—until they were put into a situation in which they had official permission and encouragement to act sadistically against those labeled as the "enemy." He also compares the underlying mechanism operating in that far-off land at that distant time to both the psychological processes at work in the Milgram research and the Stanford Prison Experiment discussed below.

Educating Hatred and Destructive Imaginations

The second broad class of operational principles by which otherwise good people can be recruited into evil is through educational and socialization processes that are sanctioned by the government in power, enacted within school programs, and supported by parents and teachers. A prime example is the way in which German children in the 1930s and 1940s were systematically indoctrinated to hate Jews, to view them as the all-purpose enemy of the new German nation.

As the Nazi party rose to power in 1933, no objective took higher priority than the reeducation of Germany's youth. Hitler wrote, "I will have no intellectual training. Knowledge is ruin to my young men. A violently active, dominating, brutal youth—that is what I am after."[18] To teach the youth about geography and race, special primers were created for elementary schools. These "hate primers" were brightly colored comic books that contrasted the beautiful blond Aryans with the despicably ugly caricatured Jew. They sold in the hundreds of thousands. One was titled: *Trust No Fox in the Green Meadows and No Jew on His Oath*. What is most insidious about this kind of hate conditioning is that it included "facts" to be learned and to be tested on, or from which to practice new penmanship. In the *Trust No Fox*, a series of cartoons illustrates all the ways in which Jews deceive Aryans, get rich and fat from dominating them, and are lascivious, mean, and without compassion for the plight of poor and elderly Aryans. The final scenarios depict the retribution that Aryan children achieve first by expelling Jewish teachers and children from their school, so that "proper discipline and order" can be taught, and then prohibiting them from community areas like public parks, and finally expelling them from Germany. The sign in the cartoon reads ominously, "one-way street." Indeed, it was a unidirectional street that led eventually to the concentration camps and crematoria that were the center pieces of Hitler's Final Solution. Thus, this institutionalized evil was spread, diverting education from its central mission of encouraging critical thinking and opening student minds to new ideas.

The institutionalized evil that George Orwell vividly portrays in *1984*, his fictional account of state dominance, now strikes us as prophetic. For example, there are direct parallels between the mind control strategies and tactics Orwell attributes to "The Party" and those that Reverend Jim Jones used in dominating the members of his religious/political cult, Peoples Temple.[19] Jones orchestrated the suicide/murders of more than nine hundred American citizens in the jungles of Guyana twenty-five years ago, the finale of his grand experiment in institutionalized mind control. Not only did Jones read *1984*, he talked about it often and had a song commissioned by the church's singer entitled "1984 Is Coming," which everyone had to sing at some services.

The Stanford Prison Experiment: Institutional and Systemic Power to Corrupt

My own 1971 prison experiment synthesized many of the processes and variables outlined earlier: anonymity of place and person, dehumanization of victims, and a setting with differentials in control and power. This experiment was designed to extend over a two-week period to provide our research participants with sufficient time to become fully engaged in their assigned roles of either guards or prisoners. Having participants live in that setting day and night as prisoners, or work there for long eight-hour shifts as guards, would also allow sufficient time for situational norms to develop and patterns of social interaction to emerge, change, and become crystallized. A second feature of this study involved screening all research participants to find individuals as normal as possible: healthy physically and mentally, and without any history in drugs, crime, or violence. These preconditions were essential if we were to untangle the situational versus dispositional knot. A third feature of the study was the absence of any prior training in how to play the randomly assigned roles of prisoner and guard, to leave that up to each subject's prior societal learning. A fourth feature was to make the experimental setting as close to a functional simulation of the psychology of imprisonment as possible.[20]

Central to this mind-set were issues of power and powerlessness, dominance and submission, freedom and servitude, control and rebellion, identity and anonymity, coercive rules and restrictive roles. We gave these social-psychological constructs a practical reality by putting all subjects in appropriate uniforms, using assorted props (handcuffs, police clubs, whistles, signs on doors and halls), replacing corridor hall doors with bars to create prison cells, having no windows or clocks to tell time of day, replacing individual names with numbers (prisoners) or titles for staff (Mr. Correctional Officer, Warden, Superintendent), and giving guards control power over prisoners.

Subjects were recruited from among nearly one hundred who answered our advertisements in the local city newspaper. They were given a background evaluation that consisted of a battery of five psychological tests, personal history, and in-depth interviews. The twenty-four who were evaluated as most normal and healthy in every respect were randomly assigned to the role of prisoner or guard. The student-prisoners underwent a realistic surprise arrest by officers from the Palo Alto Police Department, who cooperated with our plan. The arresting officer took "felons" to the police station for booking, after which they came to the prison in the reconstructed basement of Stanford's Psychology Department. The prisoner's uniform was a smock/dress with a prison ID number. The guards wore military-style uniforms and silver-reflecting sunglasses to enhance anonymity. Data were collected through systematic video recordings, secret audio recordings of conversations of prisoners in their cells, interviews and tests at various times during the study, postexperiment reports, and direct, concealed observations.[21]

In essence, the situational forces overwhelmed individuals' dispositional tendencies. The Evil situation triumphed over the Good people. Our projected two-week experiment had to be terminated after only six days because of the pathology we were witnessing. Normal students were behaving sadistically in their role of guards, inflicting humiliation, pain, and suffering. Some guards even reported they were enjoying doing so. Others had "emotional breakdowns" and stress disorders so extreme that five of them had to be excused within that first week. Those who adapted better to the situation were prisoners who mindlessly followed orders, became blindly obedient to authority, and allowed the guards to dehumanize and degrade them.

I terminated the experiment not only because of the escalating level of violence and degradation by the guards against the prisoners, but also because I became aware of my own personal transformation. I had become a Prison Superintendent, the second role I played in addition to that of principal investigator. I began to talk, walk, and act like a rigid institutional authority figure more concerned about the security of "my prison" than the needs of the young men entrusted to my care as a psychological researcher. In a sense, I consider that the most profound measure of the power of this situation was the extent to which it transformed my own personality. Fortunately, there appeared to be no lasting negative consequences of this powerful experience. At the end of the study, we had extended debriefing sessions of guards and prisoners and periodic checkups over many years to promote a healthy response to the unhealthy environment we had simulated.

The Evil of Inaction

British statesman Edmund Burke aptly observed, "The only thing necessary for evil to triumph is for good men to do nothing." Our usual take on evil focuses on violent, destructive actions, but non-action can also become a form of evil, when assistance, dissent, or disobedience are called for. Social psychologists heeded the alarm when the infamous Kitty Genovese case made national headlines. As a young woman was being stalked, stabbed, and eventually murdered, thirty-nine people in a housing complex heard her screams and did nothing to help. It seemed obvious that this was a prime example of the callousness of New Yorkers, as many media accounts reported. A counter to this dispositional analysis came in the form of a series of classic studies by Bibb Latane and John Darley on bystander intervention.[22] One key finding was that people are less likely to help when they are in a group, when they perceive others are available who could help, than when those people are alone. The presence of others diffuses the sense of personal responsibility of any individual.

A powerful demonstration of the failure to help strangers in distress was staged by John Darley and Dan Batson.[23] Imagine you are a theology student on your way to deliver the sermon of the Good Samaritan in order to have it videotaped for a psychology study on effective communication. Further imagine that as you are heading from the Psychology Department to the videotaping center, you pass a stranger huddled in an alley in dire distress. Are there any conditions that you could conceive that would not make you stop to be that Good Samaritan? What about the press of time? Would it make a difference if you were late to give that sermon? Most of us would like to believe it would not make a difference, that we would stop and help no matter what the circumstances. That may be particularly the case for theology students, thinking about helping a stranger in distress, which is amply rewarded in the biblical account.

The researchers randomly assigned students of the Princeton Theological Seminary to three conditions that varied how much time they had to get to the Communication Department to tape their Good Samaritan speeches. The conclusion: don't be a victim in distress when people are late and in a hurry, because 90 percent of them are likely to pass you by. The more time the seminarians believed they had, the more likely they were to stop and help. So the situational variable of time press accounted for the major variance in helping, without any need to resort to dispositional explanations about theology students being callous, cynical, or indifferent, as Kitty Genovese's nonhelpers were assumed to be.

In situations of evil, there are almost always those who know what is going on and do not intervene to help. There were "good" guards in the Stanford Prison Experiment who did no harm to the prisoners, but they never once opposed the demeaning deeds of the bad guards. In the recent Abu Ghraib Prison abuse case, it is clear that many people knew of the abuse, even doctors and nurses, but never intervened to prevent it.[24]

Torturers and Executioners: Pathological Types or Situational Imperatives?

There is little debate but that the systematic torture by men of their fellow men and women represents one of the darkest sides of human nature. Surely, people assume, here is a place where dispositional evil would be manifest. To test that assumption, my colleagues and I focused on Brazil policemen who long tortured "enemies of the state." We began by focusing on torturers, trying to understand both their characters and circumstances, but we had to expand our analytical net to capture their comrades-in-arms, who chose or were assigned to another branch of violence: death squad executioners. They shared a "common enemy"—men, women, and children who, though citizens of their state, even neighbors, were declared by "the authorities" to be threats to the country's national security. Some had to be eliminated efficiently, while others who might hold secret information had to be made to yield it up and confess to their treason.

In carrying out this mission, these torturers could rely in part on the "creative evil" embodied in torture devices and techniques that had been refined over centuries since the Inquisition by religious and later government agents. But the Brazilians added a measure of improvisation to accommodate the particular resistances and resiliencies of the enemies standing before them, claiming innocence, refusing to be intimidated or acknowledge culpability. It took time and emerging insights into human weaknesses for these torturers to become adept at their craft, in contrast to the task of the death squads, who with hoods for anonymity, good guns, and group support, could dispatch their duty swiftly and impersonally. For the torturer, it could never be just business. Torture always involves a personal relationship, essential for understanding what kind of torture to employ, what intensity of torture to use on this person at this time. With the wrong kind or too little, there will be no confession. With too much, the victim dies before confessing. In either case, the torturer fails to deliver the goods. Learning to select the right kind and degree of torture makes rewards abound and praise flow from the superiors.

What kind of men could do such deeds? Did they need to rely on sadistic impulses and a history of sociopathic life experiences to rip and tear the flesh of fellow beings day in and day out for years on end? Were these violence workers a breed apart from the rest of humanity? Or is it conceivable that they could be schooled in sadism by some identifiable and replicable training program? Could a set of external conditions, situational variables that contributed to the making of these torturers and killers, be identified? If their evil deeds were not traceable to inner defects but rather to external forces, such as the political, economic, social, historical, and experiential components of their police training, then we might be able to generalize principles responsible for this remarkable transformation.

Martha Huggins, Mika Haritos-Fatouros, and I interviewed several dozen of these violence workers in depth and have published a summary of our methods and findings.[25] Our results were largely congruent with an earlier study of torturers trained by the Greek military junta.[26] Contrary to conventional wisdom, these torturers were not motivated by sadistic impulses. Individuals with those tendencies were screened out of the training process because they would not be reliable; they would get off on the pleasure of inflicting pain and not sustain the necessary focus on the goal of confession. From all the evidence we could muster, Brazil's violence workers were not unusual or deviant in any way prior to practicing this new role. Nor did they show any persisting deviant tendencies or pathologies in the years following their work as torturers and executioners. Their transformation was a consequence of the training they were given, group camaraderie, national security ideology, and a belief that socialist-communists were enemies of their state. Torturers were also influenced by their sense of being special, above and better than peers in public service; by the secrecy of their duties; and by the constant pressure to produce desired results regardless of fatigue or personal problems. Such conditions are all too replicable when a nation becomes obsessed with national security and allows fears of terrorism to suspend basic individual rights.

Suicide Bombers: Mindless Fanatics or Mindful Martyrs?

The transformation of Brazilian violence workers is similar to the evolution of Palestinian students to suicide bombers. There have been close to one hundred suicide bombings by Palestinians against Israelis since September 2000. Initially the bombers were all young men, but recently women have joined the ranks. What appears senseless, mindless murder by those under attack is anything but that to those intimately involved. A common assumption is that those bombers are poor, desperate, socially isolated, illiterate young people with no career prospects. That stereotype does not match the actual portraits of these young men and women. Many are students with hopes for a better future, intelligent, attractive, connected with their family and community.

Ariel Merari, an Israeli psychologist, outlines the common steps on the path to these explosive deaths. Leaders of an extremist group first identify particular young people who appear to have an intense patriotic fervor; declarations at a public rally against Israel or support at some Islamic cause or Palestinian action might set them apart. These individuals are then invited to discuss how serious they are in their love of their country and hatred of Israel; they are asked to translate their commitments into action. Those who are willing join a small group of three to five similar youths who are at varying stages of progress toward becoming agents of death. They learn the tricks of the trade from elders: bomb-making, disguise, and selection of targets. Then they make public their private commitment by preparing a videotape on which they declare themselves to be "living martyrs" for Islam and for the love of Allah. In one hand, they hold the Koran, in the other, a rifle. This video binds them to the final deed, since it is sent home to their family before they execute their final plans. The recruits believe that they will earn a place beside Allah and that their relatives will be similarly blessed because of their martyrdom. A sizable financial payment goes to their family as a gift for their sacrifice.

Their photo is emblazoned on posters that will be put on walls everywhere in the community the moment they succeed in their mission, to become inspirational models. To stifle concerns about the pain from wounds inflicted by exploding nails and other bomb parts, leaders assure them that before the first drop of their blood touches the ground, they will already be seated at the side of Allah, feeling no pain. A further incentive for young males is the promise of heavenly bliss with scores of virgins in the next life. They become heroes and heroines, modeling self-sacrifice to the next cadre of young suicide bombers.

This program relies on various social, psychological, and motivational principles to assist in turning collective hatred into a dedicated, seriously calculated program of indoctrination and martyrdom. It is neither mindless nor senseless, but involves a very different mindset with sensibilities that Americans are not used to witnessing among young adults. A recent television program on female suicide bombers went so far as to describe them as more akin to the girl next door than to alien fanatics. What is so frightening about the emergence of this new social phenomenon that is spreading, in both the Middle East and recently in Europe, is that so many intelligent young people can be directed toward ending normal, joyous lives in murderous explosive blasts.

To counteract the powerful tactics of these extremist leaders will require providing meaningful life-affirming alternatives to this next generation. It requires new national leadership that explores every negotiating strategy that could lead to peace and not to death. It requires persuading these young people to share their values, their education, and their resources in projects that focus on human commonalities, not differences. Suicide/murder is a gash in the fabric of the human connection that leaders from every nation must unite to prevent. To encourage the sacrifice of youth for the sake of advancing ideologies of the old might itself be considered a form of evil that transcends local politics.

Summing Up Before Moving On

It is a truism in psychology that personality and situation interact to generate behavior, as do cultural and societal influences. Acknowledging the power of situational forces does not excuse the behaviors channeled by their operation. However, a situational perspective provides a knowledge base to shift our attention away from simplistic and ineffective individualistic efforts to change the evildoer and moves our focus toward causal networks that should be modified. Sensitivity to situational determinants of behavior also suggests ways to alter situations of vulnerability. To that end, several related dimensions bear emphasis. First, a range of apparently simple situational factors can function to have an impact on our behavior more compellingly than seems possible. The research outlined here and in other chapters in this book points up the force of influences such as group pressure, social modeling, authoritarian directives, semantic framing, and stereotypical labels.

Second, the situationist approach redefines heroism. When the majority of ordinary people can be overcome by such pressures toward compliance and conformity, the minority who resist should be considered heroic. Acknowledging the special nature of this resistance points up the need to understand how they are able to withstand compelling pressures.

Third, the situationist approach encourages personal humility. When trying to understand "unthinkable," "unimaginable," "senseless" acts of evil, we should, on this view, avoid embracing the high moral ground that distances us "good folks" from those "bad ones." A situational approach gives others the benefit of attributional charity. It reminds us that any deed, for good or evil, that any human being has ever done, you and I might also do given the same situational forces. If so, it becomes imperative to keep our immediate moral outrage in check and look for the causal factors that could have led individuals in morally reprehensible directions.

An obvious current application of these principles involves the rush to denounce terrorists and suicide bombers instead of also working to understand the psychological, economic, and political conditions that foster such generalized hatred of an enemy nation, including our own. The "war on terrorism" can never be won solely by plans to find and destroy terrorists, since millions of individuals, anywhere, at any time, could become potential terrorist recruits. It is only by understanding the situational determinants of terrorism that programs can be developed to win the hearts and minds of potential terrorists away from destruction and toward creation. This is not a simple task, but it is an essential one that requires implementation of social-psychological perspectives in a comprehensive, long-term plan of attitude, value, and behavior change.

Understanding What Went Wrong in Abu Ghraib Prison

The situational influences of evil came to the fore in recent trials of American prison guards at Abu Ghraib. In October 2004, I testified via closed circuit television to the military trial judge in Baghdad in defense of one of the guards, Sergeant Ivan Frederick. The abuse of

Iraqi prisoners horrified the sensibility of people around the world, in part because it was the first time in history that such conduct was publicized in graphic photographic images. The guards directly responsible were widely condemned as "morally corrupt" and presented by American leaders as exceptions to the norm of American soldiers. The initial focus of the government "to get to the bottom" of this mess clearly reflected a dispositional orientation; blame was attributed to sadistic personalities and related pathologies.

My expert testimony involved an army reserve sergeant in charge of the night shift where all the mayhem occurred. Everything I could learn about the Abu Ghraib Prison, Tier 1-A, the "soft torture" interrogation center of that prison, revealed virtually all of the social psychological processes operating in the Stanford Prison Experiment. In fact, one of the independent investigations, headed by James Shiesinger, specifically details the parallels between the two prisons.

The Abu Ghraib guards were army reservists forced into this role with no mission-specific training. They lacked supervision and personal accountability. Prison norms encouraged the abuse and humiliation of detainees as a way to soften them up for interrogation. These norms were reinforced by civilian contract interrogators, the military police, the Central Intelligence Agency, and the entire chain of military and political command.

I offered evidence in three areas:

Dispositional: Evidence for any personal pathologies or sadistic tendencies, as well as positive traits and values

Situational: Evidence of the working conditions on that prison's night shift

Systemic: Evidence of the broader conditions that spawned and sustained that situation, particularly the leadership and the objectives of that interrogation center

With regard to disposition, this soldier was totally and unequivocally normal on all measures assessed by an army clinical psychologist (and independently validated by a civilian expert in assessment). There was no evidence of any psychopathology or sadistic tendencies. Rather, Frederick matches our stereotypes of the All-American man. He is a patriotic son of a West Virginia coal miner. He hunts, fishes, plays softball, attends Baptist church services regularly, and has a strong marriage to an African American woman. As a reserve soldier, he had a blameless record as a guard in a low-security, small-town civilian prison with one hundred inmates. He was proud to serve in Iraq and initially worked with children in a small village where he was starting to learn Arabic.

The situational conditions, the behavioral context, involved working conditions that bordered on the inhumane for both guards and prisoners. The processes operating in that prison were directly comparable to those in the Stanford Prison Experiment: deindividuation, dehumanization, moral disengagement, social modeling, pressures for conformity, passive bystanders, power differentials, use of enforced nakedness, and sexually humiliating tactics. The worst abuses in both settings took place on the night shift. The working conditions for Frederick included twelve-hour night shifts (4:00 P.M. to 4:00 A.M.), seven days a week, for forty days with not a day off, then fourteen days after one day off. Exhaustion and stress were exacerbated by chaotic conditions: unsanitary and filthy surroundings that smelled like a putrid sewer, with limited water for showering. Frequent electrical blackouts created dangerous opportunities for prisoner attacks. This young man with no mission-specific training was put in charge of more than three hundred prisoners initially; that number soon swelled to more than a thousand. He was also in charge of twelve army reserve guards and sixty Iraqi police, who often smuggled contraband to the inmates. He rarely left the prison. When off duty, he slept in a cell in a different part of prison. He missed breakfasts and stopped exercising or socializing. Tier 1-A became his total reference setting.

This of itself would qualify anyone for total job burnout.[27] But guards were also under the stress of frequent insurgency attacks. Five U.S. soldiers and twenty prisoners were killed, and many others were wounded by almost daily shelling during Frederick's service. Finally, there were abusive acts by the prisoners themselves. Seven had rioted in another part of the prison and were sent to Tier 1-A for "safe keeping." Four others had raped a fellow boy prisoner. Five separate military investigations concerning Abu Ghraib acknowledge its horrendous conditions. They also acknowledge "failures of leadership, lack of leadership, indifferent leadership, and conflicting leadership demands." What is clear from these independent investigations is a total absence of accountability and oversight and an encouragement of stress interrogation.

The military judge took none of these conditions into account when he issued his sentence. Frederick received the maximum penalty: imprisonment for eight years, a dishonorable discharge, and loss of twenty-two years of army reserve retirement funds. This verdict represents yet another failure of leadership. It ignores the systemic conditions encouraging abuse and absolves the military and political officials responsible.

Promoting Civic Virtue, Moral Engagement, and Human Goodness

There are no simple solutions for the evils addressed here; if there were, they would already have been enacted by those far wiser than I. But the past half-century of psychological research provides some insight about what might be done at the individual and situational levels.

At the individual level, let us first imagine the reverse of the Milgram experiment. Suppose our objective is to create a setting in which people would comply with ever increasing demands to do good, behave in more altruistic ways, undertake ever more positive, prosocial actions. Instead of a paradigm to facilitate the slow descent into evil, we need a paradigm for the slow ascent into goodness.

Consider an altruism scale, which begins by pressuring subjects to provide thirty minutes or an hour of time for a good deed. The demands would then escalate to longer periods and regular commitments to worthy causes. One could imagine, for example, a progression on behalf of a sustainable environment. Individuals would be encouraged to engage in activities that required increasing commitment of time and money to "green" causes.

Some of the same social-psychological forces that fostered the abuses described could also be harnessed for positive ends. We could, for example, construct an eleven-step plan for promoting civic virtue that parallels the ten steps toward evil outlined earlier:

1. Openly acknowledge errors in judgments. This reduces the need to justify mistakes and continue immoral action. It undercuts the motivation to reduce dissonance by reaffirming a bad decision.

2. Encourage mindfulness. People need reminders not to live their lives on automatic pilot, but to reflect on the situation and consider its ethical implications before acting.[28]

3. Promote a sense of personal responsibility and accountability for all of one's actions. People need a better understanding of how conditions of diffused responsibility disguise their own individual role in the outcomes of their actions.

4. Discourage minor transgressions. Small acts—cheating, gossiping, lying, teasing, and bullying—provide the first steps toward escalating abuses.

5. Distinguish between just and unjust authority. The fact that individuals occupy a position of authority, as in the Milgram experiment, does not entitle them to obedience in unethical actions.

6. Support critical thinking. People need to be encouraged to demand evidence and moral justifications and to evaluate their credibility.

7. Reward moral behavior. More recognition needs to be available for those who do the right thing under difficult situations, such as whistle-blowers in public and private sector positions.

8. Respect human diversity. Appreciating difference is key to reducing in-group biases and prejudices.

9. Change social conditions that promote anonymity. Making people feel special and accountable can promote socially desirable actions and reinforce individuals' sense of self-worth.

10. Challenge pressures for conformity. Individuals need strategies for resisting group influences and maintaining their own moral compass.

11. Refuse to sacrifice crucial freedoms for elusive promises of security. These sacrifices are often the first step toward fascism, and the price is often prohibitive.[29]

6

TAMING POWER

David G. Winter

My title, taken from a chapter in Bertrand Russell's book, *Power*, reflects my strong conviction that power is something to be tamed.[1] Let me stipulate at the outset, therefore, that power is a necessary dimension of all human enterprises and that it brings many important benefits. For one thing, power seems to be a necessary dimension of all organized human social life (at least for activities larger than face-to-face groups); therefore, it is a necessary feature of all human institutions.[2] Furthermore, charismatic leaders are people who love power, or at least can take pleasure in wielding it.[3] Thus power can inspire and illuminate us; as two disciples said of Jesus after the dinner at Emmaus, "Did not our heart burn within us, while he talked with us?" (Luke 24:32).

But power also has a negative face. Lord Acton argued that "power tends to corrupt, and absolute power corrupts absolutely."[4] David Kipnis, and Annette Lee-Chai and John Bargh, have documented these corruptions and abuses through the "metamorphic" effects of power on attributions, attitudes, judgments, and moral thinking.[5] Even charismatic power is not immune from evil effects; it was charisma, after all, that brought the Holocaust, the Twin Towers of September 11, 2001, and the corrupt brutality of Baghdad's Abu Ghraib Prison (whether the guards were loyal to Saddam Hussein or George W. Bush). In our everyday world, untamed power emerges in family violence and playground bullies. Michael Adams even describes a future dystopia of a human and natural environment destroyed by untamed power: "One can almost hear those SUVs rolling into their gated communities, where millions of

cable- or satellite-equipped TVs in millions of well-appointed living rooms unobtrusively mutter news about melting polar ice-caps,
faraway wars, terrorist threats, and the raging violence of American
inner cities."[6]

Taming power therefore is one of the central moral and ethical
problems of human social existence, not only in our own time but
through history and culture. It is the great theme of Western literature and social science, ranging from Richard Wagner's epic "Ring"
opera cycle, which portrays the epic struggle of power and love, to
Lee-Chai and Bargh's survey of social science mechanisms that
might preserve the use of power while guarding against its misuse.[7]

Candidate Variables for Taming Power

It is well to recognize at the outset that taming power is certainly
not easy and may not even be possible. Taoism, for example, holds
that power cannot be tamed but rather must be allowed to run its
course; individuals are advised to yield, to embrace "nonaction"
(*wuwei*) rather than laws, controls, or arguments: "The student of
Tao loses day by day. Less and less, until nothing is done. Do nothing, and everything is done. The world is ruled by letting things
take their course. It cannot be ruled by interfering."[8] Such a response, which can be termed "instrumental inaction,"[9] is often the
wisest alternative—indeed, the only one—for people who are powerless; as the Roman lawyer and political leader Cicero asked,
"What can be done against force, without force?"[10] From this perspective, the American habit of dividing into "good" and "bad,"
and then setting the good free to expel and destroy the bad, when
applied to power, is a recipe for disaster—leading to such outcomes
as the extermination of Native Americans, Woodrow Wilson's "war
to end wars" that only set the stage for an even more terrible war,
and the massacre of Vietnamese villagers in My Lai.

I would like to approach the problem of taming power from the
perspective of a psychologist, though my argument will range
widely beyond psychology into literature and history. What follows

is a critical exploration and analysis of some ways people have sought to tame people's power drives. It is certainly not an exhaustive catalogue. I will focus particularly on research involving power motivation or the desire to have impact on other people and the world at large.[11] To anticipate my conclusion: many methods have been proposed for taming power; each can be effective sometimes, but none is foolproof. All are vulnerable to being hijacked by power itself. Such a conclusion should not be a counsel of despair but rather a call to vigilance and critical thinking.

Love and Affiliation

Perhaps the most obvious psychological mechanism for taming power is love or affiliation. Affection, mutuality, and concern for others would seem to be natural brakes on the excesses of power; as Hans Morgenthau put it, "Power is redeemed by an irreducible residue of love."[12] In his correspondence with Albert Einstein, Sigmund Freud explained this braking effect on the basis of his dualistic theory of human motivation: "If willingness to engage in war is an effect of the destructive instinct, the most obvious plan will be to bring Eros, its antagonist, into play against it. Anything that encourages the growth of emotional ties between men must operate against war."[13]

In fact, there is considerable evidence that affiliative concerns can temper power. At the individual level, David McClelland has found that high levels of affiliation motivation block the aggressive impulses of the power motive. At the collective or national level, high levels of power motive imagery are associated with war[14] and crisis escalation,[15] but only if levels of affiliation imagery are low. In international relations, affiliation motivation promotes peaceful outcomes because it is associated with concessions and compromise.[16]

There is also evidence that affiliation motivation, either by itself or in combination with power motivation, does not promote "good" power in the sense of effective, charismatic leadership.[17] And under some circumstances, love and affiliation reinforce trends toward violent power. As Morgenthau warned in the same passage quoted above: "Love is corrupted by an irreducible residue of power." Thus, Samuel Stouffer and his colleagues concluded that in wars, most soldiers fight not out of ideological fervor but rather because of affiliative bonds with their primary group of fellow soldiers.[18] In 2005, an American soldier being redeployed to Iraq expressed these sentiments in his blog: "If I get shot at or placed in danger, I'm going to kill everything that moves on the other site. I won't enjoy doing it, but it's my job, and my battle buddies are more important to me than life itself, and THEY are the reason I'm going. Screw Iraq, screw Bush, screw the army—just remember that it's me and my battle buddies out there."[19] Such ties can easily transform the death of a close friend or buddy into a desire for revenge, to continue the fight so that (in Lincoln's words at Gettysburg) "these dead shall not have died in vain." Similar effects can be seen among individuals, perhaps especially when love is threatened, scorned, or betrayed.[20] Avonne Mason and Virginia Blankenship, for example, found that among women, affiliation motivation was associated with physical abuse of an intimate partner.[21]

A spectacular illustration of scorned affiliation seeking revenge through violent power can be found in Wagner's *Götterdammerung*, the concluding opera of his "Ring" tetrology. Believing that her lover, Siegfried, has deceived her, Brünnhilde asks the gods to "teach me revenge as has never been tamed . . . to destroy the man who betrayed her!" (Act 2, scene 4). She then tells the evil Hagen how to kill Siegfried. Later, at his funeral pyre, Brünnhilde rides her horse, Grane, into the flames. Seizing a firebrand, she flings it toward Valhalla, the home of the gods. The whole world catches fire.

Reason and Intellect

As far back as Plato's *Republic*, people have believed that power can be tamed by reason and the intellect.[22] Again, Freud explained how: "The voice of the intellect is a soft one, but it does not rest till it has gained a hearing. Finally, after a countless succession of rebuffs, it succeeds. This is one of the few points on which one may be optimistic about the future of humankind, but it is in itself a point of no small importance."[23] Plato's guardians were to receive specialized training in "harmony" (the study of interrelationships) and "dialectic" (pure intelligence or abstraction), which was supposed to temper their power drives so that they would become ideal rulers of the Republic. In later times, this educational regimen evolved into the modern liberal arts curriculum, designed to produce leaders who can handle power effectively and soberly.[24] Bertrand Russell focused specifically on the effect of the "scientific temper." Psychologists have attempted to specify these broad concepts in terms of more precise variables such as "self-control" or "self-regulation" and "attentional control competencies."[25]

The twentieth century, however, has taught us that reason and the scientific temper are intellectual tools or capacities that can be used in the service of aggressive power as easily as the service of controlled power. Thus, German nationalism, which was to become a scourge of the first half of the twentieth century, was originally the creation of professors and schoolteachers.[26] And shortly after the outbreak of war in 1914, British and German intellectuals and scientists enlisted their talents of reason and intellect in the production of manifestos. On September 18, fifty-two British professors and writers published a letter in the Times, attacking the views of German apologists as "both dangerous and insane." Two weeks later, ninety-three German scientists and intellectuals proclaimed themselves "heralds of truth" and protested the "lies and calumnies with which our enemies are endeavoring to stain the honor of Germany in her hard struggle for existence—in a struggle that has been forced on her."[27] Even Freud wrote to one colleague at the outbreak of the war that "for the first time in 30 years, I feel myself to be an Austrian" and "like everyone else, I live from one German victory to the next"; to another he wrote, "I suddenly mobilized libido for Austria-Hungary."[28] Finally, of course, the optimistic words of Freud and Russell were written before men of reason and the scientific temper created nuclear weapons, that great scourge of the latter half of the twentieth century.

Commenting on this readiness of German and Allied academics to produce learned proofs of the righteousness of their own side's cause so soon after the outbreak of war in 1914, a contemporary *Washington Post* editorial concluded that "the war has given a wide range of evidences of 'reversion to type' on the part of college professors. . . . All of which, doubtless, shows that a polished dome of thought may rear its impassive front above a heart that still thrills with the instincts of patriotism, to the disadvantage of a cool working intellect."[29]

Thus, if Athena was the Greek goddess of wisdom and reason, she was also the goddess of war. To be sure, she usually preferred mediation over battle and relied on skill and strategy rather than blood lust; nevertheless, she alone had access to the weapons of Zeus, and she was always victorious. Like every other human capacity, reason and intellect can be swept up in the hubris of exaggerated self-regard. Qualities of intellect, self-control, and self-regulation can be used to carry out actions that are courageous and moral, but they are also available to facilitate monstrous evils. The memoirs of Rudolf Höss, commandant of the Auschwitz extermination camp during much of World War II, provide a vivid example of the latter corruption of self-control. While watching weeping mothers and screaming children being carried into the gas chambers, Höss wrote, "My pity was so great that I longed to vanish from the scene: yet I might not show the slightest trace of emotion. . . . I was repeatedly asked how I and my men could go on watching these operations, and how we were able to stand it. My invariable answer was that the iron determination with which we must carry out Hitler's orders could only be obtained by a stifling of all human emotions."[30]

The kingdom of intellect easily becomes an arrogant meritocracy in which people who know *some* things come to think that they know everything. Thus in January 2005, Harvard president Lawrence Summers, a respected economist, made a fool of himself and lost the confidence of his faculty when he chose to "think systematically and clinically"—but in blithe ignorance of the extensive social science research on the topic—about the causes of women's underrepresentation in academic science and engineering positions.[31]

In the end, as Nicola Baumann and Julius Kuhl note, qualities of self-regulation, self-control, and intellect have the effect of facilitating people's "behavior according to their emotional preferences."[32] As a result, such qualities are no better or worse than the preferences they serve.

Responsibility

Power is often tamed or tempered by a sense of responsibility. The concept of responsibility involves many components: having concern for others and about the consequences of actions, feeling a sense of obligation, and applying ethical and legal standards to the judgment of one's behavior. David Winter and Nicole Barenbaum have shown that a measure of responsibility based on these themes can channel people's power motivation.[33] When their level of responsibility is high, power-motivated men and women act in socially useful ways and are effective leaders, but if responsibility is low, their power drives assume profligate, impulsive, and aggressive forms.

At the collective level, however, responsibility does not moderate power drives in such a clear-cut Manichaean way. Winter coded government documents, speeches, and other texts from eight crises that escalated to war and eight matched crises that were peacefully resolved. As expected, he found that power motive levels were significantly higher in the "war" crises. Surprisingly, however, levels of responsibility were also significantly higher in these same crises.[34] What is the explanation? When one's own group is believed to be under threat, each component of responsibility may function to release the controls and inhibitions that normally restrain power drives. Thus, in a crisis, it is the other side rather than our own that is judged as violating legal and ethical standards;

"concern for others" becomes concern to protect one's own group; a "concern about consequences" becomes a concern about the consequences of inaction; and feelings of obligation support the belief that we have no other choice. Thus, for example, in his First Inaugural Address in 1861, Abraham Lincoln concluded by addressing the seceding Southern states as follows: "In your hands, my dissatisfied fellow-countrymen, and not in mine, is the momentous issue of civil war."[35]

Religion and Morality

Religious and secular moral codes would seem to be an obvious check on the excesses of power. Many religions advocate the renunciation of power, and almost every major religion teaches rules for the expression of power. Thus, the Gospel of Luke records that before Jesus began his public ministry, he was tempted by Satan: "And the devil said unto him, 'All this power will I give thee, and the glory of them: for that is delivered unto me; and to whomsoever I will I give it. If thou therefore wilt worship me, all shall be thine.' And Jesus answered and said unto him, 'Get thee behind me, Satan'" (Luke 4:6–8).

While we must acknowledge that religion can be an effective restraint on power, we must also recognize that sometimes power appears to hijack religion, turning it to the service of its own goals. As Lincoln ironically noted in his Second Inaugural Address, after four years of bloody civil war, "Both [sides] read the same Bible, and pray to the same God; and each invokes His aid against the other."[36]

Speaking from the balcony of the Imperial Palace in Berlin on July 31, 1914, Kaiser Wilhelm told the crowds in Berlin, "And so I commend you to God. Go forth into the churches, kneel down before God, and implore his help for our brave army." On the other side, a British clergyman would later write: "Not only is this a holy war, it is the holiest war that ever has been waged. The cause is the most sacred that man has been asked to defend. It is the honour of the most High God which is imperiled [sic]. . . . Odin is ranged against Christ, and Berlin is seeking to prove its supremacy over Bethlehem. Every shot that is fired, every bayonet thrust that gets home, every life that is sacrificed, is in very truth 'for His Name's sake.'"[37]

Hijacking the Power-Taming Mechanisms

The preceding sections suggest that every psychological mechanism that might contain or tame power can also be hijacked, that is, subverted by power itself. As a result, the very actions used to tame power can sometimes become subverted to be in the service of power. Freud characterized this phenomenon as a particular form of the "return of the repressed" by "a piece of malicious treachery . . . what has been repressed . . . emerges from the repressing force itself." Freud illustrated the process with an etching by the Belgian artist Félicien Rops: an ascetic monk prays before a cross, on which he sees not Jesus but rather a voluptuous naked woman. (As an analogy, imagine the forces of gluttony disguised as dietary advice, putting forward a "high calorie weight-loss diet.") Thus, it would be worthwhile to understand when, how, and why this hijacking process occurs. Freud suggested that "even trivial similarities suffice for the repressed to emerge behind the repressing force and take effect by means of it."[38]

Social-Structural Candidate Variables

Because psychological mechanisms are not always successful, many theorists and practical politicians have turned to designing social and political structures to accomplish the goal of taming power. In most situations, power is zero sum: that is, increased power for one person entails decreased power for one or more others. Most social-structural controls therefore involve ways of limiting either the desire or the possibility of increasing one's power. In other words, in a world of power, people should "know their place" and keep to it. In the thought of Confucius, power could be tamed if people only knew and confined themselves to their ascribed roles—ruler/ruled, husband/wife, parent/child—and strived to fulfill the responsibilities and obligations of those roles.[39]

"Degree"

William Shakespeare called this arrangement of power *degree*, by which he meant something like the abstract principle behind rank and organization. Power unrestrained by degree causes human society to degenerate into a "wilderness of tigers."[40] In his *Troilus and Cressida*, set in a time when the Trojan War was going badly for the Greeks besieging Troy, Ulysses attributes the breakdown of the Greek cause to a loss of degree:[41]

> *Take but degree away, untune that string,*
> *And, hark, what discord follows! Each thing meets*
> *In mere oppugnancy.*
> *. . .*
> *Then every thing includes itself in power,*
> *Power into will, will into appetite;*
> *And appetite, an universal wolf . . .*
> *Must make perforce an universal prey,*
> *And last eat up himself.*

From the perspective of the hegemon—the person on top, the people with power—degree is an agreeable concept because it reinforces his or her power. However, from the perspective of the subaltern—that is, people without power—the call for degree simply means that, in the words of Thucydides, "the strong do what they can and the weak suffer what they must."[42] In plain language, "degree" means power inequality, and power inequality or "power distance,"[43] especially in societies not used to it, can breed discontent and other negative emotions.[44] In the words of Linda Hill,[45] "powerlessness corrupts."

Institutions

Political philosophers and political scientists study and prescribe ways in which institutions can tame the power of individuals. In the West, the quest for the perfect institutional arrangements is at least as old as Plato's *Republic*. Slogans such as "democracy"[46] and "a government of laws, not of persons," as well as the disciplines of political science and constitutional law, reflect a faith that people can construct certain political arrangements, enshrined in written or unwritten constitutions, as reliable ways to contain power and the people who seek it.

Inevitably, however, institutions reflect the interests of powerful groups and ruling classes that construct them, as Charles Beard demonstrated in his analyses of the U.S. Constitution and the concept of "Jeffersonian democracy."[47] More recently, social scientists have documented the role of class interests in American society in general and key governmental institutions in particular.[48] For example, slavery and sex discrimination were written into the U.S. Constitution. Many American corporations, for example, are controlled by interlocking boards of directors, who determine each others' compensation and select their successors, independent of any formal control from other institutions or market forces. Thus by inscribing Shakespeare's "degree" (that is, existing power differentials), institutions perpetuate corruption of power among power holders and resentment of power among their targets.

Leaders bent on the corrupt or immoral use of power are often able to operate within institutions, directing them to their own purposes. Thus, Adolf Hitler came to power as chancellor of Germany in a perfectly legal, constitutional way; once in power, he seized the opportunity furnished by the Reichstag fire to pass the Enabling Act. From that point on, there were no effective institutional controls to his power.[49]

Separation of Powers

Drawing on the theories of Charles-Louis Montesquieu, the representatives of a small sector of American society (that is, propertied white men) who drafted the U.S. Constitution put their faith in one particular institutional form, the separation of powers. In defense of the new Constitution, John Adams expressed skepticism about any psychological check on power: "Nothing intoxicates the human mind so much as power," so that "it would be preposterous to rely on the discretion of any men." Writing in *The Federalist*, Alexander Hamilton, James Madison, and John Jay argued that "ambition must be made to check ambition."[50]

Sometimes the separation of powers works, and overreaching power is successfully tamed. In 1937, Franklin D. Roosevelt was forced to abandon his plan to "pack" the U.S. Supreme Court, and in 1973–1974, Richard Nixon had to give up the incriminating Watergate scandal evidence that quickly led to his resignation. And in 2005, the attempt of right-wing religious leaders to goad Congress into intervention in the Teresa Schiavo case, thereby overruling a series of consistent state and federal court decisions, collapsed. As one legal filing in the case put it, "Any law that suspends, nullifies, or reverses a final court judgment is an exercise of judicial, not legislative power."[51]

Separation-of-powers arrangements may be inherently unstable over time. Thus the mid-twentieth century saw the rise of the "imperial presidency,"[52] while in the election that marked the end of that century, the U.S. Supreme Court weakened the separation-of-powers doctrine by intervening to overrule the Florida State Supreme Court and assume the power to select the head of the executive branch.

Finally, we must realize that even when they are effective, the separation of powers and federalism doctrines may actually permit monopolies of power—untamed power—at lower levels. Thus in U.S. history, claims of states' rights, ostensibly flowing from the doctrines of federalism and the separation of powers, often simply masked slavery and other forms of discrimination. And "local control" has often meant economic oppression at the local level in company towns.

Taming Power: An Analogy and a Vision

Although the preceding analysis suggests limits to the effectiveness of every personal and structural mechanism for taming power, it need not be a counsel of despair. If power has a dual nature, perhaps we can learn from studying other processes and phenomena that are both useful and destructive.

A Structural Analogy: Power and Fire

Consider fire: it can heat our homes, cook our food, and light our way. Untamed, it can destroy and kill. Like power, fire "shines in heaven" and "burns in hell."[53] Over millennia, humans have learned how to tame fire—to guard and trim it back—so as to secure its beneficent effects and minimize its dangers. For example, fire is confined to certain safe sites, such as furnaces, stoves, and the cylinders of internal combustion engines. These sites, as well as other vulnerable spaces, are protected by fireproofing that uses fire-resistant materials. Finally, firefighters use a variety of fire extinguisher apparatus and techniques to stop unwanted and out-of-control fires. Perhaps the power-fire analogy could be elaborated to suggest ways of "power furnaces," "power-proofing," "power resistance," "power fighting," and "power extinguishers."

Generative Historical Consciousness

When encountered directly, power can impress, fascinate, attract, repel, and terrify. From the perspective of history, however, power often looks very different. Who cares that King James I appointed his favorite George Villiers as Master of the Horse in 1616, the year of Shakespeare's death? Who remembers Christian Ludwig, margrave of

Brandenburg, to whom Johann Sebastian Bach dedicated his match-less *Brandenburg Concertos?* The once-mighty empires of Ashoka, Caesar, Phillip II, and even Benjamin Disraeli have been reduced to monuments and museum pieces. As the Victorian poet Henry Austin Dobson wrote, "The bust outlasts the throne; the coin, Tiberius."[54]

I want to refer to this perspective of history as "historical consciousness"; by that term, I mean the ability to view present actions and alternatives from the distant perspective of history. It is quite different from basing present decisions on the "lessons of history," which often turn out to be wrong.[55] Soviet premier Nikita Khrushchev showed a glimmer of historical consciousness in his reflections on the Cuban missile crisis to the American editor Norman Cousins: "When I asked the military advisers if they could assure me that holding fast would not result in the death of five hundred million human beings, they looked at me as though I was out of my mind or, what was worse, a traitor. . . . It is all such nonsense. What good would it have done me in the last hour of my life to know that though our great nation and the United States were in complete ruins, the national honor of the Soviet Union was intact?"[56]

Building on Khrushchev's comment, some systematic archival and experimental research in psychology suggests the importance of historical consciousness as a way of taming power concerns. In crisis situations, people often distort levels of perceived power drive (hence threat) when they process communications from the "other" side, especially if their power motivation is aroused.[57] In laboratory studies of crises, one of the very few experimental manipulations that counteracts this tendency is the arousal of historical consciousness. Thus, for example, in a study of college students' perceptions of speeches from a 1996 crisis between the United States and Iraq, Markus Kemmelmeier and Winter found that instructing participants to assume an impartial mediator role had no effect on distortion of perceived power and threat. Distortion was removed only by instructing participants to take the perspective of a historian five hundred years in the future, writing a history of the twentieth and twenty-first centuries: "The world has changed greatly. In particular, the political structure of 'nation-states' has undergone tremendous changes. . . . Obviously, the people who made these speeches are long since dead, and you will want to work with wisdom and a sense of long-term perspective when deciding what is worth writing about for your audience of 26th-century readers."[58]

As the *Washington Post* editor wrote at the beginning of World War I, perhaps "the best time for a dispassionate discussion of wars and the causes leading thereto is some centuries after they have been fought to a finish."[59]

Power and Mortality

In "several centuries," of course, we will all be dead. Is it possible to encourage people to view their actions from such a perspective even while they are alive? Perhaps historical consciousness with respect to power has to do with the way in which we handle the undoubted fact of our personal mortality and how we view a future world in which we no longer live. That is, how we view our own mortality determines whether we can tame our power drives. If the prospect of ever shortening time until our own death is experienced as something that diminishes and threatens the self, then our power drives may break through the constraints of love, reason, and morality in a desperate determination to strike sooner rather than later.[60]

Hitler's Anxiety. This sequence can be observed in the words and deeds of Hitler, especially between 1937 and 1939. During 1937, declining health, reinforced by his parents' early deaths and a lifelong fear of cancer, led Hitler to believe he did not have long to live. During the next two years, as his foreign policy became more and more reckless, Hitler's speeches to military leaders were laced with references to "sterility" and the "decline of Germanism," the possibility of his own death, and the consequent certainty that "we could not wait longer." On August 29, 1939, just three days before the German invasion of Poland, Hitler spoke to his entourage over dinner: "I'm now 50 years old, still in full possession of my strength. The problems must be solved by me, and I can wait no longer. In a few years I will be physically and perhaps mentally, too, no longer up to it."[61]

Prospero's Renunciation. There are people who can turn away from the abuse of power or even renounce it completely. Perhaps we can understand how they do this by examining their orientation toward mortality. One of the most clear-cut examples is literary: Shakespeare's character Prospero in *The Tempest.* Having been wrongfully exiled to a lonely island with his daughter, Miranda, Prospero uses magical power to bring about a shipwreck that casts his enemies onto his island. Prospero exults: "At this hour lies at my mercy all mine enemies" (Act IV, Scene 1, lines 258–259). Yet only thirty lines later, Prospero renounces his power: "My charms I'll break," "This rough magic I here abjure," "I'll break my staff," "I'll down my book" (Act V, Scene 1 passim).

Perhaps we can understand the motives for Prospero's sudden transformation by examining what has happened in the scenes immediately preceding his exultation. First, Miranda has been successfully married to Ferdinand (son of the king of Naples, who had driven Prospero into exile). At the wedding celebration, a play within the play is staged, depicting the goddess Ceres and celebrating fecundity. At the end of the play, Prospero dismisses the "actor-spirits" and begins his famous soliloquy about time and death:

> Our revels now are ended. These our actors,
> As I foretold you, were all spirits, and
> Are melted into air, into thin air;
> And like the baseless fabric of this vision,
> The cloud-capped towers, the gorgeous palaces,
> The solemn temples, the great globe itself,
> Yea, all which it inherit, shall dissolve;
> And, like this insubstantial pageant faded,
> Leave not a rack behind. We are such stuff
> As dreams are made on, and our little life
> Is rounded with a sleep [Act IV, Scene 1, lines 148–158].

These earlier events and words suggest that Prospero was able to give up power because of the successful experience of generativity—in Erik Erikson's words, "the ability to lose oneself in the meeting of bodies and minds . . . the interest in establishing and guiding the next generation."[62] The generative theme of the play echoes Shakespeare's own life. Many of his earlier plays portray disasters of untamed power: for example, *Titus Andronicus* (written when Shakespeare was thirty) and *King Lear* (written when he was forty-two). *The Tempest,* with its very different treatment of power, was written in 1611, when Shakespeare was forty-seven—a few years after the marriage of his eldest child, Susanna, and the birth of his first grandchild. It was probably his last full play, and the soliloquy quoted above has been taken to be Shakespeare's personal valedictory to the theater.

Kennedy's Vision. Prospero was a fictional character. Sometimes real-life people—even political leaders—have articulated a generative vision of power, history, and mortality. Thus, in his June 1963 speech at American University, President John F. Kennedy spoke about the kind of peace "that enables men and nations to grow and to hope and to build a better life for their children—not merely peace for Americans but peace for all men and women—not merely peace in our time but peace for all time." Speaking eight months after the Cuban crisis had brought the world close to a thermonuclear holocaust and five months before his own death, Kennedy urged a reexamination of American attitudes toward the Soviet Union in words memorable for their generative vision: "So, let us not be blind to our differences—but let us also direct attention to our common interests and to the means by which those differences can be resolved. And if we cannot end now our differences, at least we can help make the world safe for diversity. For, in the final analysis, our most basic common link is that we all inhabit this small planet. We all breathe the same air. We all cherish our children's future. And we are all mortal."[63]

7

POWER AND MORAL LEADERSHIP

Dacher Keltner, Carrie A. Langner, Maria Logli Allison

Are actions with moral implications disproportionately made by people with power? Resource allocations, punitive acts, the production of knowledge, the dissemination of collective values and morals, and even sexual overtures and advances, many have claimed, are all more typically enacted by people with power. In fact, one prevalent definition of power as the control over the life outcomes and resources of others implicitly intertwines power with one facet of morality: the concern and responsibility for others' welfare.[1] It is perhaps for this reason that social theorists for thousands of years, from Confucius to Plato, have grappled with the question of how leaders are to be guided by ethical and moral concerns.

What is the relationship between power and morality? Are leaders concerned with the moral implications of their decisions? One possible answer to these interrelated questions proceeds as follows. Perhaps people who gain power do so because of their elevated moral and ethical standards. Groups select their leaders and extend power to others, this argument would contend, according to the individual's moral depth, perspective, and stature. Several social forces might give rise to such a state of affairs. People with power have greater access to the institutions and cultural practices that help cultivate the moral and ethical senses. People with power are subject to tremendous social scrutiny. Their actions tend to influence many other people. Both of these processes, which give greater gravity to their actions and deliberations, might make the powerful more reflective of their intentions and actions, and perhaps more morally attuned. Such a state of affairs, where power and elevated morality go hand in hand, might be considered a desirable social condition.

Regrettably, this scenario, where power and the cultivation of moral sensibilities mutually reinforce one another, is hard to reconcile with history's abundant examples of moral abuses by people in power. The same could be said for the most newsworthy, and seemingly systematic, actions of leaders today, for example, the fraud and cover-up perpetrated by Enron executives.[2] In the light of these observations, one might argue that power corrupts moral judgment and unleashes and amplifies the antisocial tendencies of human nature.

In this chapter we argue for a third position regarding the question of the relationship between power and morality. We will contend that power does have a moral direction and that it is oriented toward self-interest. This general claim emerges from a research program on the determinants and effects of social power. We survey a variety of studies on power and related variables such as social status that examine power dynamics—who gains power, how the acquisition of power affects reasoning and action—in spontaneous interactions of individuals in informal social groups and in laboratory's controlled environment.[3] This research, and other findings and their implications, have led to four generalizations that form the heart of this chapter. First, we argue that the acquisition, or distribution, of power is not random. Instead, power tends to be given to people who are more likely to act in an impulsive and self-interested fashion. Second, we argue that the power affects moral judgment through a process of disinhibition leading to impulsiveness and often the pursuit and rationalization of self-interest. Third, we propose that power, through subtle and often unconscious processes, evokes social consensus. The social consensus that power evokes tends to entrench the views and values of those in power. Finally, we consider certain leveling mechanisms that constrain the abuses of power.

Status Endowed: The Rise of the Impulsive

Who attains social power? What kinds of individuals rise in social hierarchies? Answers to these questions are critical to the more general question of the moral direction of power, for if there are certain kinds of individuals who gravitate to positions of power, with certain values or moral orientations, then power is likely to be associated with certain moral views and principles and not others. These questions are all the more important in the light of recent studies by Serena Chen and her colleagues, which demonstrate that power amplifies the preexisting tendencies—whether Machiavellian or altruistic—of the individual.[4] If the individual is prone to self-interested action, power intensifies those self-interested tendencies and behaviors. If the individual is prone to attend to the needs and concerns of others, being in power makes this person all the more communal and prosocial. Who attains positions of power, by implication, will influence what the effects of social power look like.

In addition to dispositional inclinations toward prosocial or self-serving motives, situational factors promoting these different goals are germane. Social and cultural contexts such as competitive corporate environments, the pursuit of political agendas, or cultural values stressing individual achievement can all serve to increase the likelihood of self-interested expressions of power.

Numerous studies suggest that people who are prone to impulsive behavior are likely to attain power. Several studies find that people who are interested in dominating and manipulating others attain social power.[5] Personality traits predict the attainment of power for young adults in informal social groups, such as residence halls, fraternities, and sororities.[6] In particular, the personality traits of interest were Extraversion, which is defined by impulsivity and gregariousness; Conscientiousness, defined by an achievement, goal focus, and clear scruples and standards; and Neuroticism, defined by emotional volatility and anxiety and distress. In these studies, highly extraverted females and males attained higher positions within social hierarchies, typically within the first week of entering into the group. Extraverts, impulsive and excitable by nature, quickly rise in power. Conscientious people, in contrast, tended to attain lower positions in the hierarchy, especially women. And as one might expect, highly neurotic individuals also occupied lower positions within social hierarchies. These findings tell us that the attainment of power is not random with respect to the character of the individual. Nor is the distribution of power merit based. Positions of power are more likely to be inhabited by impulsive, energetic, charismatic individuals who are prone to self-interested actions, precisely the behavior that power permits.

Power and the Pursuit of Self-Interest

In addition to the dispositional factors that characterize those who attain power, we argue that being in a high power role further drives individuals to impulsive action. In a recent theory of the effects of social power, we argued that elevated power increases the likelihood of impulsive action, particularly actions that satisfy the individual's desires, goals, and interests.[7] In more specific terms, we have reasoned that powerful individuals live in environments with abundant rewards, including financial resources, food, physical comforts, beauty, and health, as well as social resources, such as flattery, esteem, attraction, and praise. As Weber observed nearly sixty years ago, people with elevated power tend to enjoy the freedom to act without significant interference from others or serious social consequences.[8] Acting within reward-rich environments and unconstrained by others' evaluations or the consequences of one's actions, people with elevated power should be disposed to act in impulsive fashion that satisfies their current interests and goals.

For complementary reasons, the lack of power should be associated with increased inhibition and constraint. Less powerful individuals tend to have reduced access to material, social, and cultural resources and are more subject to social threats and punishments. Thus, they are more sensitive to the evaluations and potential control of others. For example, less powerful individuals are more likely to be victimized by aggression. This is evident in childhood bullying, which is directed at low-status children,[9] racism and discrimination against minority groups,[10] violence against women,[11] and crime in activities victimizing members of lower classes.[12] Acting in environments with increased punishment, threat, and the lack of resources and aware of the social constraints placed on their behavior, people with reduced power should be disposed to elevated levels of inhibition-related affect, cognition, and behavior.

The preceding arguments suggest that more powerful individuals should show elevated levels of goal-directed, impulsive action. The absence of power, in contrast, should be associated with heightened activity of inhibition-related processes. We have also argued that these effects of power apply at multiple levels of analysis, including the individual, the dyad (for example, within romantic relations), the group (for example, within a work organization or political decision-making body), and the collective (for example, where identity derives from social class, ethnicity, or gender). We make this claim based on the notions that power ultimately involves a subjective process that is similar across these levels of analysis and because the effects of power on action are mediated by similar neurocognitive processes, such as levels of dopamine (which facilitate goal-related action) and serotonin (which is involved in the inhibition of behavior).[13]

The mounting evidence in support of the approach-inhibition theory of power suggests that individuals with power act in impulsive, self-interested fashion, often neglecting social norms, morals, and the concerns of others. Empirical studies have given individuals power within experimental contexts (for example, by allowing one individual to control the resources of another), or they have assessed power as a traitlike disposition within the individual.[14] With these varying methods, studies indicate that people with power are more likely to act in impulsive, and self-interested fashion. Thus, those in power are more likely to consume collective resources.[15] They are more likely to act in sexually forward and often profligate fashion.[16] People who enjoy elevated power have been shown to violate social norms related to gambling and drinking.[17] High-power individuals, both adults and children, have been observed to touch others in ways that are inappropriate to the social context.[18] And still other studies have revealed that people with less power are more likely to be victimized, as exemplified in correlations between power and hate crimes, sexual harassment, and rape.[19] If human nature, as many have reasoned, reflects a tension between self-interest and the interests of others and the greater good, power tips this balance, disposing the individual to act in impulsive, self-interested ways.

Power and the Ideology of Self-Interest

A related issue is how powerful individuals rationalize their impulsive tendencies. We suggest that people in power will espouse moral ethics that justify and facilitate self-interested action. They do so by prioritizing rights and freedoms as moral concerns over other moral values involving duties, obligations, responsibilities to others, need, and caring. Our analysis will necessarily be speculative and extend beyond the current empirical basis; however, it is based on a contemporary psychological study of morality.[20] Its first premise is that morality is broader than previously thought. For decades, empirical psychologists defined morality in arguably narrow terms, in terms of rights, harm, and justice. More recent work has shown in numerous cultures that people make moral judgments according to a broad set of ethical concerns, which include concepts related to duties and obligations, caring, and purity, both bodily and spiritual. Our claim is that power makes people define morality in narrow terms, focusing on rights and self-interest.

Our second guiding assumption, again one that has emerged in recent empirical studies of moral judgment, is that moral views often act as rationalizations for courses of action the individual takes or states of affairs the individual experiences.[21] Moral intuitions have many origins: they emerge out of the individual's experience, they unfold with cognitive development, and they are invoked to explain choices and actions. We argue that power predisposes the individual to act in self-interested fashion, which in turn is rationalized by a certain set of moral constructs.

Power and the Moral Rationalization of Self-Interest

How do individuals in positions of power justify their impulsive actions? Surprisingly few psychological studies have addressed this question. To begin to formulate an answer here, we extrapolate from one germane study that suggests that power may relate to a relatively narrow conception of morality based on individual rights and self-interest.

In this study, Jon Haidt and colleagues asked lower- and upper-class participants in Brazil and Philadelphia to read a number of vivid scenarios that portrayed infractions of varying kinds.[22] For each hypothetical scenario, participants indicated, as a measure of their moral judgment, whether they thought the people in the scenarios should be punished for their actions. Some of these situations involved harm: a boy pushes a girl off a swing that he wants to use. Others involved violations of a social convention: a man eats food with his hands, both in public and private, after washing them. Still others depicted harmless but offensive actions: a family eats the family dog that had been hit by a car; a woman cleans her toilet with cut-up portions of the country's flag.

Participants in both cultures and from both socioeconomic backgrounds were strongly inclined to punish perpetrators of harmful acts (that is, pushing someone off the swings). Intended harm can be thought of as a clear universal moral concern. For every other violation, however, the students of lower socioeconomic status (SES) expressed a greater sense of moral offense. They were more inclined to punish violations of social conventions. They were more likely to punish perpetrators of harmless but offensive and impure symbolic and sexual acts. And in other research, people from lower socioeconomic background are much more likely than those from higher backgrounds to define morality in terms of duties, obligations, and attending to the needs of others.[23]

From this illustrative study, we assume that lower-SES individuals define morality much more broadly than upper-SES counterparts. Lower-SES individuals define morality as including issues of obligation, duty, and purity and attending to the needs of others. Upper-SES individuals, by contrast, define morality in terms of freedoms and individual rights—principles that allow the pursuit of self-interested courses of action by allowing obligations and concern for others to be written off as mere convention in the pursuit of individual goals.

We contend that these class-based differences in the prioritization of moral concerns generalize to social power more generally, for in empirical studies, people from upper-SES backgrounds feel more powerful in their daily lives than do people from lower-SES backgrounds.[24] We also note that similar differences in moral principles emerge in studies of power and the allocation of resources.[25] Whereas low-power individuals prefer the principle of equality or a need-based approach to the allocation of resources, high-power individuals prefer the rule of equity (to each according to his or her contributions), maximizing the likelihood that their self-interest will be satisfied.[26]

Putting these empirical strands together, we contend that power inclines people to pursue self-interested courses of action. This disposition in turn is rationalized by a commitment to an ideology of self-interest, where high-power individuals justify the pursuit of goals and resources in terms of rights and freedoms. These claims echo Jost and colleagues' theory of system justification, the process by which high-power individuals justify societal inequalities with stereotypes of high- and low-status individuals (for example, as innately talented or deserving of their lot in life) and ideologies of meritocracy or individualism.[27]

Power and the Complexity of Moral Judgment

Finally, what about the general complexity of the moral views of those in power? Moral issues, such as the debates over gay marriage, abortion, and interventionist foreign policy, are inherently complex, involving multiple principles and perspectives. Morality involves multiple domains related to rights, freedom, purity, duty, obligation, need, and caring.[28] Moral views therefore can also vary in their complexity and the degree to which they incorporate multiple principles (for example, freedom and duty) and multiple perspectives. Work by Tetlock and colleagues has shown that to the extent that leaders endorse more complex moral-political positions, they are better able to negotiate with adversaries and avoid conflict escalation.[29]

What, then, of the general relationship between power and the complexity of moral views? Numerous empirical studies suggest that the moral views of those in power are simplistic: they lack the hallmark characteristics of more complex positions that incorporate multiple views and interconnect principles within a particular position. Studies of U.S. Supreme Court justices, political leaders, and strangers within social interactions all indicate that high-power individuals reason in less complex fashion and that their moral positions and assertions are defined by more one-sided, simplistic claims.[30] The simplistic moral judgments of those in power are consistent with our overall depiction of those in power as impulsive people who attend to a more limited spectrum of moral concerns.

Is there, then, a moral direction to the nature of power? We would argue that power often disposes individuals to pursue self-interest and endorse moral views that justify the relatively unfettered pursuit of personal goals and desires. Furthermore, research suggests that the moral positions of those in power tend to be fairly extreme, unqualified by alternative views. These claims are hypotheses with partial support that await further empirical study. We now suggest that the social environments of high-power individuals bolster these moral stances.

Power and Solipsistic Social Environments

Thus far we have argued that powerful people are predisposed to pursue courses of action that satisfy self-interest and that they rationalize their actions in part by invoking moral ethics centering on freedoms, rights, and self-interest. How then do these rationalizations of self-interest unfold in social context?

Power by its very nature is a bidirectional process; power, in part, is given by one person to another. This rather remarkable property of human social hierarchies—that high-power individuals gain their positions through the permission of others—was long ago noted by the sociologist Goffman. His analysis of deference and demeanor suggested that it is only through the complicity of others that people enact their social identities.[31] Furthermore, the sociologist Emerson offered the insightful notion that low-power individuals control high-power individuals through affordances of status and respect.[32] Within human social hierarchies, this theorizing implies that low-power individuals constrain the actions of high-power individuals through the social constructive processes involving expressions of respect, admiration, deference, and esteem.

Perhaps low-power individuals, through informal communication processes such as teasing and gossip, and through basic emotional responses, provide checks and balances on those in power. Several empirical studies described below examine whether low-power individuals do indeed constrain high-power individuals in this manner. Overall these studies suggest that high-power individuals are exposed to little, if any, moral critique and tend to evoke consensus from others. This research suggests that high-power individuals live in solipsistic environments that largely support their preexisting views. Several scholars have noted this. For example, Janis, in his analysis of groupthink, noted the problematic tendency for group members to resist contradicting the views of those in power, which adversely affects group decision making.[33] The research examined next suggests that power evokes particularly self-confirming environments for high-power individuals.

Power and the Silencing of Moral Critique

In one line of research, we have investigated the effects of social power on teasing and gossip, two informal communicative processes by which people comment on, and control, the moral tendencies of other group members. Teasing and gossip are particularly interesting from the standpoint of power because they are off-record communicative acts. That is, teasing and gossip offer commentaries, often of a critical nature, on others, but they do so in an indirect or back-channel fashion. In teasing, the commentary is rendered off-record through various linguistic devices, such as hints, exaggerations, metaphors, ironic comments, or alterations in the speed or loudness of the utterance, all of which indicate the statement is in part not literally true and to be taken in the spirit of play. Gossip too is an indirect communicative act, in part through similar linguistic devices that lie at the core of a tease and also due to its hushed, behind-the-scenes character. One might expect that low-power individuals would use teasing and gossip to curb and control the actions of those in power. They might tease and gossip about high-power individuals in ways that highlight their moral shortcomings and foibles and flaws.

Not so. In studies of power and teasing, low-status group members tend to tease others with delicacy and discretion, and in ways in which the provocative content of the tease is greatly diminished.[34] For example, in one study high- and low-status fraternity members were given two initials (for example, A.D.) and asked to make up a nickname and use that nickname to tease high- and low-status peers. The content of the teases was coded for evidence of moral critique and also for evidence of the off-record, linguistic devices that render teases more playful and less critical. This study reveals a telling property of communication by and about high- and low-power individuals. High-power individuals teased both high- and low-status individuals in a direct, morally critical fashion. This is consistent with several other studies showing that high-power individuals in hospitals, in organizations, and on the playground frequently use teasing to critique, bring in line, and inculcate morals in low-power peers.[35]

Perhaps more surprising was the teasing produced by low-power individuals, in particular in relation to the high-power individuals. Low-power individuals were extremely delicate, even laudatory, and certainly hesitant to criticize, the high-status members of their group. We have since replicated this finding in a study of gossip within a female sorority.[36] When sorority members were induced to gossip about a high-status member in a risky situation in which the gossip might get back to the target, a similar pattern emerged: they instilled their critique with ambiguity and off-record markers and gossiped in a more flattering, praiseworthy way. These studies demonstrate the manner in which social feedback is rendered less challenging to high-power individuals. Low-power individuals are not inclined to deliver direct, harsh critique of their high-power counterparts but instead disguise their commentary as more benign by infusing it with praise and linguistic markers of ambiguity.

Studies within political communication have documented a similar pattern of silencing in the communication of low-power individuals.[37] In a laboratory study that prompted participants to discuss affirmative action, students with opposing affirmative action attitudes were paired with a partner of lower or higher trait power. Low-power opponents felt silenced in the political discussion and were judged by independent coders as introducing less disagreement into the conversation. Having power in the political discussion meant less exposure to a partner's disagreement and subsequently a more positive affective experience. In discussions of a political issue, high-power individuals were not restrained by critique or disagreement from their opponents.

Placed within the arguments that we are advancing in this chapter, these studies suggest that high-power individuals are unlikely to hear critiques of their moral views and actions, even in informal social interaction. These studies suggest that the silencing of those with less power critique may be a pervasive phenomenon, ranging from informal communicative acts to direct, structured conversations. As a result, high-power individuals are likely to overestimate the consensus in their moral views and, in turn, attribute greater certainty and universality to those claims.

The Upward Flow of Information to Those in Power

The study of the gossip observed within the sorority points to another process by which informal communication consolidates and entrenches the moral ideologies of those in power.[38] In a first phase of the study of sorority gossip, all members of the sorority indicated who they gossiped about and with whom they gossiped. These sociometric nominations were used to derive a map of the flow of gossip within the sorority to address to whom this morally relevant communication went and whom it targeted.

Given gossip's secretive and back-channel nature, one might have expected gossip to function as a means of critiquing those with power. In this sense, one might think of gossip like other forms of off-the-record communication, the best example being forms of satire, which expose the foibles of the powerful and challenge the legitimacy of hierarchical arrangements. This study suggests instead that gossip lacks this critical, destabilizing function. In fact, it appears to do quite the opposite, at least when risks of reprisal are significant. Gossip transmits valuable social information into the hands of those with power: it consistently flowed to high-status sorority members and targeted group members who were well known but had low status in the group. The recipients of gossip in our study were clearly the agents of social control in the group, managing the discourse that threatened the reputations of those with less power. And this was evident in their actual gossip behavior as well, which we captured in a later phase of the experiment. High-power recipients of gossip tended to gossip in ways that were more critical and damaging to the reputations of others.

Earlier we argued that high-power individuals act in a self-interested fashion and rationalize these acts with certain moral claims. Although one might expect these actions to be subject to critique, our evidence suggests that this is not always the case: communicative processes that typically serve to critique and control—teasing and gossip—are muted and softened when directed at high-power individuals. In addition, communications over explicit disagreements (such as political discussions between opponents) produce little disagreement from low-power discussion partners. These studies suggest that high-power individuals act in social environments that present little critique, skepticism, or challenge and further their control over others.

Power and Mimetic Behavior

In addition to evidence that low-power individuals modify their behavior in deference to high-power individuals, it appears that power also exerts its influence on more deeply rooted and involuntary processes such as emotional experience and attitude shifts. More specifically, recent empirical evidence indicates that low-power individuals shift toward the emotions and attitudes of those individuals in power, often without being aware of these dynamics.

In one study of emotional convergence, friends came to the laboratory at two different times during the year and reported their emotional reactions to different evocative stimuli such as humorous or disturbing film clips.[39] The central question was whether people with less power within a dyadic bond would make more of the change in the emotional convergence process over the course of the year than high-power individuals. That is, did the emotions of low-power individuals, thought by many to be outside volitional control, begin to conform to the emotions of high-power friends over time?

Indeed this proved to be the case: the emotional styles of low-power individuals shifted over the course of the year to resemble the emotional profiles of high-power individuals. Powerful partners' own emotions at a later time point were not predicted by their partner's emotions at Time 1. These findings emerged for both positive and negative emotion. In contrast, the emotions of the less powerful partner at Time 2 were predicted by their partner's prior emotions.

These findings fit one of the well-documented properties of the social interactions of high- and low-power individuals: that low-power individuals attend quite carefully to the actions of high-power individuals, who in turn are relatively unaware of the actions of low-power individuals.[40] This power-related difference in social attention is likely to account for the patterns of emotional convergence. And in fact, in the political discussion study described above, there is further support for this thesis: low-power individuals shifted their attitudes toward affirmative action (reported privately before and after the discussion) in the direction of a higher-power partner's attitude.[41] In contrast, higher-power partners were less likely to shift their attitudes toward their partner's attitudes. More generally, these studies of social interaction suggest that high-power individuals elicit confirmatory patterns of emotions and attitudes. We suggest that the consensus that high-power individuals tend to evoke in those individuals who surround them is likely to enhance the certainty and conviction in their views.

Leveling Mechanisms

We have argued that power can lead to self-interested behavior and disregard for others' well-being through selection pressures for self-interested actors and through situational pressures toward impulsive behavior, moral rationalizations, and solipsistic social environments. But are there processes that check the negative effects of power and encourage moral leadership? Research on situational factors (accountability and reputation) and person factors (responsibility) suggests ways to help curb the tendency of power to produce self-interested behavior.

Accountability

Accountability—the sense that one's actions are personally identifiable and subject to the evaluation of others—often accompanies structural power and acts as a constraint on power. Individuals in power who know they will be held accountable are more likely to consider social consequences and take others' interests into account.[42] This may help explain why U.S. presidents exhibit greater cognitive complexity after they are elected, when they are accountable to a diverse array of constituents, than prior to election.[43] From our perspective, accountability is implicit in the psychology of low-power individuals: they carefully consider how their actions will influence and be judged by others. To the extent that high-power individuals are accountable for specific actions, they should be less likely to show the pattern of impulsive, self-interested action and moral rationalization that we have described thus far. Individuals may behave in a strikingly different fashion as they acquire power and are accountable to others, compared to when their power is firmly entrenched.[44]

Reputation

What, then, is at stake when those in power are accountable to others? What risk does disdain in the eyes of those with less power pose to the powerful? Despite their control over resources, those in power rely on those below them for one of their most important resources: their reputations.[45] The concept of reputation as a leveling mechanism has underscored many theories of how the reckless pursuit of self-interest is constrained in cooperative society. Adam Smith posited that social approbation and disapprobation were critical to sustaining honorable behavior in commerce.[46] In the legal history of defamation law, reputation has been treated as a resource that, when damaged, could impose a measurable economic loss on any person who participates in the marketplace.[47] Even self-interested individuals must maintain honorable behavior to some extent because a damaged reputation results in a loss of trust, which leads to exclusion from the benefits of social exchange. These claims are borne out in the modern online marketplace, where reputation ratings based on customer feedback are created, adjusted, and publicly displayed on a transaction-by-transaction basis. Research based on one popular online marketplace, eBay, has demonstrated that merchants with better reputations are able to attract more customers to their online store and command higher prices for the same merchandise being sold for less by merchants with worse reputations.[48] Compounding the risks associated with losing one's reputation is the negativity bias—the tendency for negative characteristics to exert disproportionate weight in overall impressions of character, suggesting that a good reputation is far easier to damage than a bad reputation is to repair.[49]

Clearly the powerful have much to lose by a damaged reputation. How then are the reputations of high-power individuals jeopardized by their actions and the evaluations of others? Gossip is a primary means of shaping reputations, yet the behavior of those low in power is constrained when gossiping about those in positions of power. In the study of gossip in a sorority, an interesting finding was that despite the more apologetic and off-record nature of their gossip, the lower-status targets of gossip were actually more likely to point out norm violations when gossiping about others. These results suggest that although the risks associated with gossiping about a high-status group member may necessitate more cautious gossip behavior, couched in indirectness and even flattery, the powerful may not completely escape social criticism for their misdeeds. More generally, we might expect the reputational critiques of those in power to be more pronounced and pointed in less structured interactions than those we have studied.

The Responsible Use of Power

Research by Winter and others indicates individual differences in the use of power.[50] One such difference that delineates those who use power impulsively and those who do not is a concern with responsibility. Examining the actions of individuals with high power motivation, those who exhibited a concern for responsibility in addition to a desire for power were successful leaders whose subordinates experienced high morale. In contrast, individuals with high power motivation who had little concern for responsibility demonstrated profligate impulsivity. In another study, responsibility moderated the effect of power on profligate behavior in both men and women.[51] This study indicates that the negative effects of power can be curbed by a concern with responsibility. Why, then, are some individuals more likely to be guided by this concern?

Life span events can increase responsibility. Winter and colleagues have shown that individuals high in the need for power engaged in profligate gambling, drinking, and sexual licentiousness less often when two kinds of life events enhanced their accountability: the presence of younger siblings and the arrival of offspring.[52] In fact, the social responsibilities tied to having a younger sibling or parenthood led high-power individuals to engage in more prosocial, approach-related behaviors, such as involvement in voluntary organizations. In summary, accountability, reputation, and responsibility are all factors that reduce the likelihood of power leading to impulsive, and at times antisocial, self-interested actions.

Conclusions and Future Directions

How are power and morality linked? Will power always corrupt? In this chapter, we have argued that the social processes that give rise to the acquisition of power, and the ways that power affects the individual and the surrounding social environment, have a direction with moral implications: the pursuit, expression, and rationalization of self-interest. Many individuals who rise to power are concerned with self-serving pursuits. Once given power, they are likely to pursue with little constraint their goals, desires, and impulses. And by their very actions, powerful individuals evoke social environments that reinforce these tendencies.

Many of our claims have gone beyond the current data and clearly require empirical examination. The same can be said for our conceptual analysis, which is certain to be subject to boundary conditions we have not elucidated. For example, the very nature of self-interest, whether it prioritizes the concerns of the individual or of kin or community, is certain to vary across context and culture. If so, one might expect our predictions concerning the effects of power on self-interested action and moral rationalization also to vary in their content across individualistic and collectivistic cultures.

For millennia, social theorists have grappled with the question of how power and morality are intertwined. Our analysis is intended to prompt further empirical research and promote a nuanced understanding of the problem of moral leadership.

Part Three

SELF-SACRIFICE AND SELF-INTEREST

8

ORCHESTRATING PROSOCIAL MOTIVES

C. Daniel Batson

The challenge of moral leadership is, I take it, to get people to act more morally. To provide guidance on how one might manage this formidable task, we need to have some sense of what we mean by *moral*.

Much of what we refer to as moral can be subsumed under the notion of giving weight to the interests and desires of others in situations in which our interests and theirs conflict. Although this notion may not cover *propriety morality* (adherence to cultural standards and taboos), it covers *interpersonal morality*. And interpersonal morality encompasses a lot. It includes getting people to recycle, carpool, vote, contribute to public television and community charities, promote justice in society, care for the needy, not harm others, do business honestly, and pay their fair share of taxes. If we can figure out a way to lead toward increased interpersonal morality, I shall be quite content.

Perhaps the most obvious forms of moral leadership are (1) to lead by legislation—whether at the local, state, national, or international level; (2) to lead by example—as did Mahatma Gandhi, Martin Luther King Jr., and Mother Teresa; and (3) to lead by encouraging critical reflection on moral issues and questions—character education. I wish to consider a fourth form of moral leadership: leading by orchestrating the motives that might prompt a person to act morally. The idea behind this less obvious form of moral leadership is that if we can identify the motives that prompt people to act morally, what I shall call *prosocial motives*, then we can play on these motives to get people to act more morally.

Why worry about orchestrating prosocial motives? Why not just play on all the motives available? The reason is that, like different musical instruments in orchestra, different motives can create discord rather than harmony. The challenge is to find a combination that harmonizes to produce positive effects that no one form of prosocial motivation alone can provide.

Motives as Goal-Directed Forces

Following Kurt Lewin, I am thinking of motives as goal-directed forces to obtain or maintain valued states.[1] A valued state is a state one prefers over some other. Mary values State A over State B if she consistently chooses State A over State B, other things being equal. If a negative discrepancy is perceived between a current or anticipated state and a valued state, then obtaining or maintaining the valued state is likely to become a goal.

It is possible—and important—to distinguish among ultimate goals, instrumental goals, and unintended consequences. *Ultimate goals* are the valued states the individual is seeking to reach. "Ultimate" does not here mean "cosmic" or "most important"; it simply refers to the state or states a person is seeking (perhaps unconsciously) at a given time. Each different motive has a unique ultimate goal evoked by a unique value. *Instrumental goals* are sought because they are stepping-stones to ultimate goals. When an ultimate goal can be reached more efficiently by other means, an instrumental goal is likely to be bypassed. Pursuit of a goal, whether instrumental or ultimate, may produce effects—sometimes dramatic—that are not themselves a goal. These are *unintended consequences*.

Four Types of Prosocial Motivation

To identify different prosocial motives, let us consider what values might be pursued by acting morally. There is little doubt that most of us value our own welfare and are motivated to increase it when opportunities arise. *Egoism*, motivation with the ultimate goal of increasing our own welfare, clearly exists. Indeed, virtually every major account of human action in psychology, sociology, economics, and political science assumes that human action is always and inevitably directed toward the ultimate goal of self-benefit.[2] According to this assumption, we act to benefit others or for the good of society only because doing so is an instrumental means to promote our own welfare or is an unintended consequence of promoting our own welfare. Obviously, if this view of human motivation is correct, then anyone wishing to stimulate moral action had best address all appeals to self-interest.

Recent theory and research suggest, however, that this view of human motivation is not correct. Self-interest is a powerful and pervasive motive, but apparently the human capacity for caring is not limited to one's own interest. Three other broad classes of motives have been proposed that involve interests outside ourselves: altruism, motivation with the ultimate goal of increasing the welfare of one or more other individuals as individuals; collectivism, motivation with the ultimate goal of increasing the welfare of a group; and principlism, motivation with the ultimate goal of upholding some moral principle, such as justice.[3]

I suggest that all four of these prosocial motives exist and that each has its own distinct promise and problems as a source of moral action. For a given individual in a given situation, more than one of these motives may be present at once. When this is the case, the motives may either clash or harmonize with one another. Before considering their interplay, however, let me say more about each type of prosocial motivation. Table 8.1 provides an overview of my analysis.

Egoism: Motivation to Benefit Oneself

Egoism is the most obvious motive for acting morally. Action that benefits others or serves the common good can be egoistically motivated if this action is either instrumental to reaching the ultimate

Table 8.1. Four Prosocial Motives

Motive	Ultimate Goal	Strengths	Weaknesses
Egoism	Increase one's own welfare.	Many forms; easily aroused; powerful.	Moral action relates to egoistic motivation only as an instrumental means or as an unintended consequence.
Altruism	Increase the welfare of one or more other individuals.	Powerful; may generalize to group of which other is a member.	May be limited to individuals for whom empathy is felt; moral action relates to altruistic motivation only as an instrumental means or as an unintended consequence.
Collectivism	Increase the welfare of a group or collective.	Powerful; directly focused on common good.	May be limited to in-group.
Principlism	Uphold some moral principle (for example, justice).	Directed toward universal and impartial good.	Often seems weak; vulnerable to rationalization.

goal of self-benefit or is an unintended consequence of reaching this goal. A philanthropist may endow a hospital or university to gain recognition and a form of immortality. A capitalist, nudged by Adam Smith's invisible hand,[4] may create jobs and enhance the standard of living of the community while motivated by relentless pursuit of personal fortune. A student may volunteer at a local nursing home to add community service to her résumé. All three are egoistically motivated. Yet the action of each may be considered beneficial to society and, from a consequentialist perspective, moral.

Reflecting on what motives might induce people to act for the common good, ecologist and social policy analyst Garrett Hardin concluded that egoism is not simply the most obvious. He concluded that it is the only motive sufficiently pervasive and powerful to do the job. Hence, Hardin proposed his Cardinal Rule of Policy: "Never ask a person to act against his own self-interest."[5]

Varieties of Egoistic Motivation.   A number of self-benefits can be the ultimate goal of acting morally. One can act to gain material, social, and self-rewards (for example, pay or prizes, recognition or praise, esteem-enhancement), or to avoid material, social, and self-punishments (for example, fines, avoidance of censure, guilt, shame).

When one looks beyond the immediate situation to consider long-term consequences and intangible benefits for oneself, self-interest becomes enlightened. From an enlightened perspective, one may see that head-long pursuit of self-interest will lead to less long-term personal gain than will acting for the common good. So one may decide to act for the common good today as an instrumental means to reach the ultimate goal of maximizing self-benefit in the long run. Appeals to enlightened self-interest are often used by politicians and social activists trying to encourage action for the public good. They warn us of the eventual consequences for ourselves and our children of pollution or of underfunded schools. They remind us that an unchecked epidemic may reach into our home, or that if the plight of the poor becomes too severe, we may face revolution. The motivation they seek to arouse is egoistic; they threaten our enlightened self-interest.

Nontangible self-benefits of acting morally have sometimes been called *side payments*. One may, for example, act morally as a means to reach the ultimate goal of avoiding social censure or guilt. In his defense of utilitarianism as a moral standard, John Stuart Mill asked, "Why am I bound to promote the general happiness? If my own happiness lies in something else, why may I not give that the preference?"[6] Mill's answer was that we will give our own happiness preference until, through education, we learn the sanctions for doing so. External sanctions stem from social censure (including divine censure); internal sanctions stem from conscience. Sigmund

Freud presented a similar view, as have most social learning and norm theorists since.[7] Side payments are not all negative; there are also nontangible self-rewards of acting morally. People may attend to the interests and desires of others to see themselves—or be seen by others—as caring, concerned, responsible, good people. Pursuit of such side payments may provide great benefit to others. Still, the underlying motivation is egoistic.

Promise and Problems of Egoism as a Source of Moral Action. Egoistic motives offer promise for promoting moral behavior because they are easily aroused and potent. They offer problems because they are fickle. If the egoistically motivated individual finds that self-interest can be served as well or better without giving attention to the interests and desires of others, then others' interests be damned. If he or she can break free from Mill's external and internal sanctions, from the constraint of social and self-censure, from the desire for social and self-esteem, then narrow self-interest reigns supreme.

Altruism: Motivation to Benefit One or More Other Individuals

Altruism is motivation with the ultimate goal of increasing the welfare of one or more individuals other than oneself. Altruism should not be confused with helping behavior, which may or may not be altruistically motivated. Nor should it be confused with self-sacrifice, which concerns cost to self, not benefit to the other.

The most commonly proposed source of altruistic motivation is empathic emotion. By *empathy* I mean other-oriented feelings elicited by and congruent with the perceived welfare of another person. If the other is perceived to be in need, then empathy includes feelings of sympathy, compassion, and tenderness. These feelings appear to be a product not only of perceiving the other as in need but also of valuing the other's welfare. It has been suggested that empathic feelings in turn amplify motivation directed toward the ultimate goal of relieving the empathy-inducing need—altruistic motivation.[8]

Problems.   Although there is now strong evidence that empathy-induced altruistic motivation exists, is it a plausible source of motivation to act morally? Altruism, especially empathy-induced altruism, appears to be directed toward the interest of specific other individuals. It may not be possible to feel empathy for an abstract social category like the community, people with AIDS, the elderly, or the homeless. Furthermore, the likelihood that the needs of different individuals will evoke empathic feelings is not equal because we do not value the welfare of all individuals equally. Empathic feelings are more likely to be felt for those (1) who are close to us such as friends and kin, (2) to whom we are emotionally attached, (3) for whom we feel responsible, or (4) whose perspective we adopt. And like any other emotion, empathic feelings are likely to diminish over time. Underscoring these limits, it has been found that empathy-induced altruism can lead one to act immorally, showing unfair partiality toward a person for whom empathy is felt.[9]

These limits suggest that many of our most pressing moral concerns may evoke little empathy. The people in need are too remote; the problems are too abstract and long term. For this reason, Garrett Hardin dismissed altruism as a potential solution to large-scale social problems such as poverty, homelessness, population control, or pollution: "Is pure altruism possible? Yes, of course it is—on a small scale, over the short term, in certain circumstances, and within small, intimate groups. . . . But only the most naive hope to adhere to a noncalculating policy in a group that numbers in the thousands (or millions!), and in which many preexisting antagonisms are known and many more suspected."[10] Hardin quickly returned to his Cardinal Rule: never ask a person to act against self-interest.

As a source of action for the common good, altruism may be limited in much the same way as egoism. If benefiting the person or persons for whom empathy is felt leads to increased common good, fine. But if it does not, then altruism will not increase the common good; it may even diminish it. Out of concern for the welfare of members of their families, farmers may overwork the land, loggers clear-cut, and fishermen deplete stocks.

Consistent with these observations, it has been found that inducing empathy for one of the other individuals in a group can lead to increased allocation of scarce resources to this individual, to the detriment of the group as a whole, much as increased egoistic motivation might. Indeed, when allocation decisions are under public scrutiny, empathy-induced altruism may pose a more serious threat to the common good than does egoism. There are clear societal sanctions against egoism but not against altruism.[11]

Promise. Still, under certain circumstances, empathy-induced altruism may be a surprisingly powerful motive for promoting the common good. Recent research has shown that inducing empathy for a member of a stigmatized group can lead to more positive attitudes toward the group as a whole. This strategy has been used to improve attitudes toward members of racial and ethnic minorities, gay men, people with AIDS, the homeless, and even convicted murderers. It has also been used to increase not only attitudes toward but also action on behalf of users of hard drugs.[12]

This strategy of prompting moral action by inducing empathy for an individual who is an exemplar of a disadvantaged group is employed in many fundraising ads, whether for children with disabilities, for those needing a Big Brother or Sister, for the homeless, or for starving refugees. Even the needs of the physical environment may not lie beyond the reach of empathy. Think of attempts to personalize these needs by invoking metaphors such as Mother Earth, the rape of the landscape, or dying rivers. Could it be that these personalizing metaphors are used to evoke empathy—and so altruistic motivation—to address environmental needs?

Collectivism: Motivation to Benefit a Group

Collectivism is motivation with the ultimate goal of increasing the welfare of a group or collective. The collective may be small or large, from 2 to over 2 billion. It may be a marriage or a partnership; it may be a sports team, a university, a community, a nation; it may be all humanity. The collective may be one's race, religion, sex, political party, or social class. One need not even be a member of the collective. One may, for example, act to increase the welfare of a racial or ethnic minority, of the homeless, of gays and lesbians, without being a member of these groups. If one values a group's welfare and this welfare is threatened or can be enhanced in some way, then collectivist motivation should be aroused, promoting action to benefit the group.

To illustrate, the person who supports and comforts a spouse, not out of concern for the spouse individually or for the self-benefits imagined but "for the sake of the marriage," is displaying collectivist motivation. So is the person who contributes to the local United Way because it enriches the community. So is the senator who supports building shelters with the ultimate goal of easing the plight of the homeless. So is the rescuer of a Jewish family in Nazi Europe whose ultimate goal is to benefit humanity in whatever way possible. If the person's ultimate goal is to benefit some group, whether large or small, inclusive or exclusive, the motive is collectivism.

Problems. Typically, we care about collectives of which we are members, an *us*. Identifying with a collective or group usually involves recognition of an out-group, a *them* who is not us. Indeed, some have suggested that a them-us comparison is necessary to define a collective.[13] Concern to meet *our* needs may lead to callous indifference to *their* needs. When AIDS was initially labeled as a gay disease, many outside the gay community felt little inclination to help. It was *their* problem.

Promise. In addition to this very real limitation, collectivist motivation has some virtues that egoism and altruism do not. As noted, egoism and altruism are both directed toward the welfare of individuals. Often, however, others' needs are far removed from our self-interest, even enlightened self-interest, and from the interest of those for whom we especially care. Egoism and altruism may be of limited use in encouraging action to meet these needs. Think, for example, of the plight of the homeless in the United States, of poverty and illiteracy in Central America, of pollution, global warming, overpopulation, energy conservation, endangered species—the list goes on and on.

Such group-level needs are particularly difficult to address because they often come in the form of social dilemmas. A social dilemma arises when two conditions are satisfied. First, individuals in a group or collective have a choice about how to allocate personally held scarce resources such as money, time, or energy. Second, allocation to the group provides more benefit for the group as a whole than does allocation to oneself, but allocation to oneself provides more self-benefit than does allocation to the group. Examples include recycling, energy and water conservation, contributing to public television, and supporting charities. In such situations, the action that is best for oneself is to allocate resources to meet one's own needs, ignoring the needs of the group as a whole. But if everyone tries thus to maximize their own welfare, the attempt will backfire. Everyone, including oneself, is worse off. If we appeal to straightforward egoistic—or altruistic—motivation to address the social dilemmas we face, the prognosis looks bleak.

But the situation is rarely this grim. There is considerable evidence that when faced with a social dilemma, whether in a research laboratory or in real life, many people do not seek only to maximize their own welfare. They seek also to enhance the group welfare. The most common explanation for this attention to group welfare is that it stems from collectivist motivation. It is claimed that under conditions of group identity, individuals can and do act with an ultimate goal of increasing the welfare of their group. Whether it is possible to induce such a motive in someone who is not a member of the group is, however, less clear.[14]

Principlism: Motivation to Uphold Moral Principles

Principlism is motivation with the ultimate goal of upholding some moral principle such as justice or the utilitarian principle of the greatest good for the greatest number. It is not surprising that most moral philosophers have argued for the importance of a form of prosocial motivation other than egoism. But most since Immanuel Kant have also argued for a form other than altruism and collectivism. Moral philosophers reject appeals to altruism based on feelings of empathy, sympathy, and compassion because they find these emotions too fickle and circumscribed. They reject appeals to collectivism because it is bounded by the limits of the collective. These philosophers typically call for motivation with a goal of upholding some universal and impartial moral principle.

Kant even argued that the Judeo-Christian commandment to love one's neighbor as oneself should be understood as a moral principle to be upheld rather than as an expression of social identity or personal compassion. Leo Tolstoy echoed Kant's view, calling the law of love "the highest principle of life" and asserting that love should be "free from anything personal, from the smallest drop of personal bias toward its object. And such love can only be felt for one's enemy, for those who hate and offend." Similarly, the utilitarian principle of the greatest good for the greatest number is universal and impartial; it affirms that one should give no more weight to what is good for oneself than to what is good for anyone else.[15]

More recently, philosopher John Rawls has argued for a principle of justice based on the allocation of goods to the members of society from an initial position behind the Veil of Ignorance, where no one knows his or her place in society—prince or pauper, laborer or lawyer, male or female, black or white. Why does Rawls require such a stance? It eliminates partiality and seduction by special interest. A universal, impartial principle of justice is also the basis for Lawrence Kohlberg's Post-Conventional or Principled moral reasoning, the highest level in his stage model of moral development.[16]

Universalist, impartial views of morality have not gone unchallenged. Writers like Lawrence Blum, Carol Gilligan, Thomas Nagel, Nel Noddings, Joan Tronto, and Bernard Williams call for recognition of forms of morality that allow for special interest in the welfare of certain others or certain relationships. In opposition to an ethic based on justice and fairness, these writers propose an ethic of care. Sometimes it seems that they are proposing care as an alternative principle to justice, either as a substitute for justice or in dynamic tension with it. At other times, it seems that they are proposing care as an alternative to principled morality altogether. If care is an alternative principle, then it too might be an expression of principlism; one might act for the public good as a means to uphold the principle of care. If, however, care is a special feeling for another individual, for oneself, or for a relationship that inclines one to act, then care would be a form of altruism, egoism, or collectivism, respectively.[17]

Calls to moral action often appeal to principle. We are told that it is our duty to vote, that it is not fair to leave our litter in the park for someone else to clean up, that we should give our "fair share" to the United Way, that we ought to take care of the community in which we live.

Problems. The major problem with relying on principlism as a source of motivation to act morally is knowing when and how a given principle applies. It may seem that moral principles, at least universal ones, always apply. But it is not that simple.

Most of us are adept at rationalization, at justifying to ourselves— if not to others—why a situation that benefits us or those we care about does not violate our moral principles. Why, for example, the inequalities in the public school systems of rich and poor districts in the United States are not really unjust. Why storing our nuclear waste in someone else's community is fair. Why attacks by our side are regrettable but necessary, whereas attacks by the other side are atrocities. Why watching public television without contributing or forgoing the extra effort to recycle is not wrong. The abstractness of most moral principles, and their multiplicity, makes rationalization easy. Skill in dodging the thrust of moral principles we espouse may explain the weak empirical relation between espousing moral principles and social action.[18] Perhaps moral principles serve more to censure or extol others' actions than to motivate our own. Perhaps adherence to moral principles is only an instrumental goal on the way to the egoistic ultimate goal of benefiting ourselves by avoiding social and self-censure or gaining social and self-esteem.

It is not that we have no moral sensibility. Most of us consider ourselves to be highly moral. Yet when our own interest is best served by violating avowed moral principles, we may find this relatively easy to do. We find ways to see ourselves as fair—or at least not unfair—while avoiding the cost to self of actually being fair. Moral principles are affirmed, but the motivation to uphold these principles seems spotty and weak.

A number of psychological processes may contribute to this weakness of moral motivation. First, people may conveniently forget to think about their moral principles if such an omission serves their own interests. Second, people may convince themselves that their moral principles do not apply either to the specific others whose interests conflict with their own (moral exclusion) or to the specific situation (moral disengagement). Third, people may deceive themselves into believing that they have acted morally even when they have not if there is sufficient ambiguity to allow them to appear moral without having to be moral (moral hypocrisy). Fourth, moral principles may be internalized only to the degree that they are experienced as oughts, not wants.[19]

Promise. More positively, if upholding moral principles can serve as an ultimate goal, defining a form of motivation independent of egoism, then perhaps these principles can provide a rational basis for acting morally that transcends reliance on self-interest or on vested interest in and feeling for the welfare of certain other individuals or groups. This is quite an "if," but it seems a possibility well worth exploring.

Conflict

This analysis of prosocial motivation offers both good news and bad to those aspiring to moral leadership. The good news is the existence of prosocial motives other than self-interest, making available new resources. The bad news is that the multiplicity of motives complicates matters. Different motives for acting morally do not always work in harmony. As long as the welfare of self, others, and various groups is perceived to be distinct, motives to promote the welfare of each can clash with one another—and with motives to uphold moral principles.

Well-intentioned appeals to act morally for egoistic motives can backfire by undermining other forms of prosocial motivation. Indeed, the presence of self-beneficial inducements may lead people to interpret their motivation as egoistic even when it is not. As a result, when the inducements are removed, the behavior may vanish. The common assumption that there is only one motive for acting morally—egoism—can become a self-fulfilling prophecy.[20]

Nor do the other three motives always work in harmony; they also can conflict. For example, altruism can—and often does—conflict with collectivism or principlism. We may ignore the welfare of the group or compromise our principles, not to benefit ourselves but to benefit those individuals about whom we especially care. A father may resist contributing to public television not to buy himself a new shirt but because he feels for his daughter who wants new shoes. An executive may fiddle the books to keep the company afloat not to line his or her own pockets, but out of concern for the workers who would lose their jobs.[21]

Orchestration

Each of the four types of prosocial motivation that I have identified has strengths. Each also has weaknesses. The potential for the greatest good may come from leadership strategies that orchestrate prosocial motives so that the strengths of one can overcome weaknesses of another. Strategies that combine appeals to either altruism or collectivism with appeals to principlism seem especially promising. Motivation to uphold a moral principle like justice may have broad relevance, but it can be weak—vulnerable to oversight and rationalization. Empathy-induced altruism and collectivism are potentially powerful but limited in scope; they produce partiality, special concern for a particular person or persons or for a particular group. Perhaps if we can lead people to feel empathy for the victims of injustice or perceive themselves in a common group with them, then we can get these motives working together rather than at odds. Desire for justice may provide perspective and reason; empathy-induced altruism or collectivism may provide emotional fire and a push toward seeing the victims' suffering end, preventing oversight and rationalization. Consider examples.

At times, history has orchestrated these motives. Something of this sort occurred, I believe, in a number of rescuers of Jews in Nazi Europe. A careful look at data collected by Samuel and Pearl Oliner and their colleagues suggests that involvement in rescue activity frequently began with concern for a specific individual or individuals, or members of a specific group, for whom compassion was felt—often individuals known previously. This initial involvement subsequently led to further contacts and rescue activity and to a concern for justice that extended well beyond the bounds of the initial empathic concern. In several cases, such as in the French village of Le Chambon, the result was dramatic indeed.[22]

Such orchestration also occurred at the time of the bus boycott in Birmingham, Alabama, in the 1950s. The horrific sight on television news of a small black child being literally rolled down the street by water from a fire hose under the direction of Police Chief Bull Connor—and the empathic emotions this sight evoked—seemed to do more to arouse a concern for justice than hours of reasoned argument and appeals to equal rights.

At times there is a human conductor. Such orchestration seemed to lie at the heart of the forms of nonviolent protest in the face of entrenched injustice practiced by Mahatma Gandhi and by Martin Luther King Jr.

Such orchestration can also be found in the writing of Jonathan Kozol. Deeply concerned about the "savage inequalities" in public education between rich and poor communities in the United States, Kozol clearly documents the inequality, but he does far more: he takes us into the lives of individual children. We come to care for them and, as a result, care deeply about the injustice. Kozol's goal is not simply to get us to feel; he wants to get us involved in action to improve funding for schools in poor communities. He pursues this goal by orchestrating the motives of empathy-induced altruism and principlism.[23]

Conclusion

Orchestrating prosocial motives is, I believe, a promising strategy for moral leadership. It appears capable of producing dramatic results. Yet it is a strategy rarely considered. Could this be because the assumption that all human motivation is self-interested has prevented us from even conceiving the possibility of such a strategy? If so, then it may be wise to reexamine this assumption. I think those who do will find the assumption untenable, opening up new possibilities for moral leadership.

9

SELF-SACRIFICE AND SELF-INTEREST

Do Ethical Values Shape Behavior in Organizational Settings?

Tom R. Tyler

The behavioral study of ethics has much to offer those interested in moral leadership. This chapter addresses two central issues. The first is whether people in organizations have ethical values that are related to the characteristics of those organizations. The second is whether those values shape their rule-related behavior. These issues are directly relevant to the question of how to manage ethics in organizations. If people lack sound values or those values do not shape their behavior, then efforts to regulate must focus on curtailing self-interest. This leads to a focus on either sanctions as a way to secure compliance or the use of procedures such as markets to manage allocations in organizations. By contrast, if people have ethical values and those values shape their behavior, it is possible to regulate behavior by appealing to those values. This leads to the possibility of self-regulation, in which people are encouraged to take responsibility for their behavior. They could be encouraged to do so by the leaders of their own organizations or by government authorities, or by both.

Adherence to Rules

Understanding employees' adherence to rules is critical for successful organizational functioning.[1] There has long been extensive evidence that noncompliance with rules is widespread.[2] Such issues of compliance have been dramatically thrust into the public eye through recent highly visible incidents of corporate misconduct. The prevalence and damaging consequences of such noncompliance underscore the importance of identifying effective strategies of employee rule adherence.

Several types of compliance are desirable in workplaces. Organizations first want employees to adhere to organizational policies. Organizational rules and policies stipulate desired employee behavior, and the organization benefits when those policies are followed. For example, organizational rules often specify behaviors about how work should be carried out, when people arrive at work, and so forth. Such rules facilitate coordination among employees and ensure the smooth functioning of the organization.

On the flip side of conformity or deference to organizational policies lies deviant behavior by employees, or behaviors that are damaging and prohibited by organizational rules. For example, employees may use office supplies for personal use or use sick leave when not sick. More seriously, employees may steal or break organizational rules by lying and cheating. This deviant behavior is referred to as rule breaking because it involves the decision to ignore or violate organizational rules. And, of course, legal authorities want to prevent citizens from engaging in rule breaking in their everyday lives.[3]

Naturally companies want to reduce the degree of rule breaking that occurs among employees. For instance, a widely damaging form of inappropriate employee behavior is theft of business supplies and equipment. It is estimated that 30 to 50 percent of all business failures are linked to losses from employee theft, a problem that is ten times more costly than street crime in terms of loss to society and whose costs are often estimated to be in the hundreds of billions of dollars in the United States alone.[4] Again, the extent of these losses, and the suggestion that up to 75 percent of employees engage in some form of theft in their workplace, indicates the magnitude of the challenge posed by trying to manage this problem.

The ability to secure compliance with rules is a key to being successful as a legal or political authority.[5] A litmus test of effective leadership is the ability to secure such compliance, since the decisions of police officers or judges would have little value in resolving disputes or creating social order if people ignored them. Although Americans are generally law abiding, there are widespread instances of noncompliance, in areas ranging from tax nonpayment to the illegal use of software, films, and music.[6] Compliance with law, while frequent, can never be taken for granted.[7] Hence, legal authorities focus on limiting damaging behavior.

The issue of adherence to the law is central to all discussions of effective legal authority. In the specific case of dealing with corporate corruption, the issue of the authoritativeness of law is central to the ability of government to regulate businesses. Without that ability, government regulation lacks the ability to shape the conduct of people in the business arena, either at the level of CEOs or with everyday employees. Despite longstanding debates about the extent to nature of appropriate regulatory strategies, there is dispute that in conflicts, government needs to have the ability to effectively control organizational behavior.

Models of Human Motivation

We live in an era in which the rational or self-interested actor is the dominant image of human motivation shaping policies in management, law, and public policy. This image is central to the perspective taken in dealing with a wide variety of ethical issues in organizations, including efforts to understand how to promote compliance with rules.

Our dominant strategy of regulation has flowed directly from a rational actor perspective on human psychology. That strategy is deterrence, and it motivates rule following by the threat or application of punishment for rule breaking.[8] A similar incentive-based model, which links performance to rewards, is important in work organizations.[9] The most widely practiced model within contemporary America is the command-and-control model, which is based on a rational actor model of a person, as motivated by rewards and costs. In this approach, resources are concentrated at the top of hierarchical authority systems, and those controlling the resources use them to motivate conduct on the part of those below them. One strategy, deterrence, motivates conduct by the threat or use of sanctions when people violate rules. The other strategy, incentives, motivates conduct by rewarding desired behavior.

Evidence suggests that these strategies are effective in many situations. Studies indicate that people's estimates of the likelihood of being caught and punished for wrongdoing influence their behavior in both work and community settings. There are equally clear downsides to the use of incentives and sanctions. One is that they are resource intensive. This is most strikingly true with deterrence, since it is necessary to create and maintain a credible threat of punishment to obtain deterrence effects. Furthermore, organizations are least likely to have the resources to implement these strategies during times of crisis and change, when rule following is more closely linked to organizational viability. Furthermore, these high costs come with modest behavioral effects at best. For example, sanctions explain only a minor aspect of rule following: in one study, around 5 percent[10] and incentives around 10 percent.[11] Finally, the use of command-and-control strategies does not effectively motivate voluntary behavior and may actually undermine it. Hence, it requires the continual expenditure of resources to maintain suitable levels of rule-following adherence.

Is there another approach? More recently there has been a great deal of discussion of markets within organizational settings. Markets are also a mechanism that assumes that people will act in self-interested ways. Market methods focus on creating economic incentives. While these methods have gained new policy prominence, they reflect the same underlying psychology of the person. The advantage of markets is that they rely on incentives rather than sanctions.

Many studies suggest that incentives are a better motivator of behavior; however, neither is a particularly strong force leading to rule following, and neither is a motivator of voluntary behavior.

Another way to describe this distinction between required and voluntary behavior is to separate external and internal forces. The deterrence model reflects a strategy of external regulation because employee behavior is affected by managers through their ability to impose desirable rewards or undesirable sanctions. In communities, the power to sanction similarly rests in the hands of police officers and judges. By contrast, the self-regulatory model relies on internal motivations of individual employees or community residents. This distinction has a long history within social psychology; for example, Kelman distinguishes between compliance based on external contingencies and self-regulation linked to identification and internalization.[12] This distinction is extended to organizational arenas by Kelman and Hamilton[13] and to work settings by O'Reilly and Chatman[14] and Tyler and Blader.[15]

The use of sanctions represents a traditional management strategy to securing employee compliance to organizational rules and policies. My focus here is whether activating employees' ethical values is an effective management strategy for securing their compliance. The use of such a self-regulatory model has been long advocated within discussions of legal regulation of business[16] and has been advanced with particular frequency in recent years.[17] The studies discussed here test whether employees' ethical values can in reality—as hypothesized by self-regulatory models—provide a viable basis for encouraging employee policy adherence.

Alternative Models

The focus of self-regulatory models is on motivating people to defer to laws, rules, and policies. Approaches that rely instead on external sanctions have the limitation that people comply only when there is the risk of being caught and punished for wrongdoing. By contrast, self-regulatory strategies lead people to be personally motivated to follow rules or refrain from breaking them regardless of likelihood of sanctions.

I consider this issue within the context of two types of social settings: work organizations and communities. Within work organizations, my concern is why employees follow workplace rules;[18] in communities I examine why community members defer to the law, the courts, and the police.[19] Within work organizations, managers, ranging from line managers to CEOs, try to create a corporate culture or workplace climate within which employees voluntarily adhere to company policies and rules. Within communities, legal authorities create laws and seek to establish a regulatory climate within which people follow those laws. Of course, work organizations exist within communities, so a further issue is the legal regulation of conduct within the workplace. In all of these settings, the goal is to bring member conduct into alignment with group rules.

I believe that adherence to rules and policies can best be encouraged by drawing on people's values. My approach to addressing this question is empirical and involves interviewing people in both work and community settings. Using questionnaire data and sometimes behavioral observation, I look at the factors that motivate rule-following behavior to demonstrate the influence of values in both work and community settings. My argument is that these empirical findings support the value of a self-regulatory approach based on appeals to employees' ethical values. (The studies are explored at length in publications referenced in the Notes.)

Evidence for the Value-Based Approach

What follows is an overview of the conclusions most relevant to exercise of moral leadership.

Two values are central in motivating compliance. The first is legitimacy—the feeling of responsibility and obligation to follow rules. The second is moral congruence—the judgment that the rules are consistent with one's moral values and therefore should be followed. Legitimacy and moral congruence are similar in that their motivational force comes from within the person and is not directly linked to costs or benefits in the immediate environment. Rather, people are motivated to bring their behavior into line with their own values concerning what is right and proper.

First, we can consider how values shape behavior in the work organization. Here the concern is with whether employees adhere to workplace policies more frequently when they believe that those policies are legitimate or congruent with their moral values. I address this question in a paper jointly authored by Steve Blader of the Stern School of Management.[20] That study involves two samples: a sample of corporate bankers and a sample of American employees.

We compare the impact of two judgments: the likelihood of being caught and punished for rule breaking and the degree to which rule breaking is viewed as illegitimate or morally incongruent. We then explore how well these judgments predict two behaviors: compliance with organizational rules and voluntary deference to those rules. We find that values are more important than sanctions in shaping deference to rules in both a study of corporate bankers and a general sample of employees. The same finding results from an analysis of the antecedents of rule breaking. Successful appeals to values are the most effective way to lessen rule breaking.

A similar analysis can be performed in communities. Tyler and Fagan examine the relationships between the legitimacy of police action and citizens' compliance with the law and cooperation with the police.[21] The sample involves 1,653 New Yorkers and measures three factors affecting law enforcement: (1) citizens' fear of being caught and punished for rule breaking, (2) police effectiveness in fighting crime, and (3) the magnitude of the neighborhood crime problem. The influence of these three factors is then compared to the values index reflecting legitimacy and moral congruence. This index is more influential in shaping both compliance with the law and cooperation with the police than are the instrumental factors. Our finding again underscores the effectiveness of values promoting ethical behavior.

These results are consistent with my earlier findings in a study involving residents of Chicago.[22] This study finds that both legitimacy and moral congruence have a significant influence on compliance with the law. Furthermore, both values, legitimacy and moral congruence, are more important in shaping compliance than the perceived risk of sanctions.

Another example from a study of everyday rule following yields similar conclusions.[23] This study also contrasts the moral congruence of actions with the risk of punishment. It uses three surveys: two on law and one on workplace compliance. The question at issue is: If people consider an action to be wrong, how much does the risk of being caught affect their decision to act? The average beta is 0.10. If there is a low risk of punishment, how much does knowing the morality of an action shape whether you undertake it? The average beta is 0.38. Again, the influence of morality on behavior is greater than is the influence of the risk of punishment. In this case, when people have views about the morality of an action, they are not very strongly influenced by whether it is likely to be sanctioned.[24]

These studies provide guidance on appropriate strategies of management and governance. Values can play an important role in regulation in both work settings and in society more generally. Hence, self-regulation through appeals to values is an alternative approach to deterrence and the use of markets. And these findings suggest that it is an approach that ought to have a relatively significant degree of success.

In addition, a value-based strategy of self-regulation avoids the problems associated with deterrence and market-based approaches in several ways. First, it does not require the continuous use of resources to create and maintain a credible system of surveillance or to reward desired actions. Furthermore, managers and government officials can seek ways to build positive relations with citizens.

The strategic implications of these findings are that we need to structure organizations in ways that encourage people to act on their values. We need to look at the members of organizations and communities and examine what motivates them to view rules as legitimate and consistent with their own moral commitments. This information can then provide the basis for institutional design.[25] It is to the question of institutional design that this discussion now turns.

Procedural Justice

The finding that compliance flows from values leads to the question of what an organization can do to encourage people to view it as legitimate and to view its actions as congruent with their moral values. An extensive literature on procedural justice demonstrates that people's views about legitimacy are linked to their judgments about the fairness of the procedures through which authority is exercised.[26] In fact, widespread evidence from all types of organizations underscores the importance of procedural fairness in work and community settings.[27] Typical of this research is a study by Kim and Mauborgne that finds that procedural evaluations of fairness influence the willingness of subsidiaries to accept corporate strategic policy decisions in multinational organizations.[28] Other studies link the perceived fairness of workplace procedures to employees' willingness to voluntarily help their work groups, to their intention to stay with their company, and to the quality of their job performance.[29] These findings suggest that a key factor in developing supportive values is maintaining procedures that are widely viewed as just.

In employment settings, studies find that workers' perceptions of procedural justice are central to both legitimacy and moral congruence. Examples include two studies of Tyler and Blader, noted previously—one of corporate bankers and the other of a general sample of employees. In both studies, procedural justice is the primary antecedent of both legitimacy and compliance with rules.[30] And as already noted, legitimacy is a key factor promoting compliance. Hence, the challenge in work settings is to manage in ways that employees believe is fair.

Recent corporate scandals in which CEOs and other high-ranking corporate officials have been implicated in unethical behavior make clear that adherence to organizational rules does not always lead to appropriate conduct, since the rules themselves can be inadequate. Hence, these findings speak to situations in which rules can be justified on moral grounds.[31]

Interestingly, the same analysis also suggests that procedural justice is a key antecedent of moral congruence. In other words, the primary cue that employees use to determine whether they feel that their company is pursuing policies consistent with their moral values is the fairness of the way the company makes decisions and treats its employees. This procedural judgment about fairness is more important to assessments of moral congruence than the perceived fairness of the outcome as its benefit to the employee. Such research underscores the importance of having business leaders focus on the procedures by which their organizations exercise authority.

The same is true in other settings. An illustrative example involves the New York City Police Department.[32] In this study, procedural fairness was the primary factor shaping public assessments about whether the New York City Police Department is legitimate and police authority should be respected. Also, the residents of New York indicate that the police department has values congruent with their own when they judge that it exhibits procedural justice. Both of these judgments—legitimacy and moral congruence—have more influence on evaluations and behaviors than do assessments of risk or performance.

The primary implication of the findings outlined is that we can build an effective regulatory system based on appeals to people's values. Both legitimacy and moral congruence shape rule-related behavior. And they do so in work and community settings. These value-based approaches are typically less costly than systems relying on rewards and sanctions.

Implications for Moral Leadership

The literature on leadership generally views the ability to motivate desirable behavior as a key feature of managerial effectiveness.[33] The ability to motivate employees has always been one important component of leadership in work organizations, but this issue has taken on a new importance in recent years in the wake of corporate scandals. To create an ethical workplace, an organization must have appropriate ethical rules and a culture that fosters compliance. A central challenge is how to encourage adherence to rules when individual self-interest pushes in a different direction. Behavior such as stealing office supplies or violating accounting rules can often lead to immediate gains with little risk of detection. In such circumstances, leaders need to be able to motivate their followers to put the interests of the organization above their own.

Leaders need first to care about ethics and create an organization in which ethics matters. They also need the ability to motivate their followers to adhere to ethical policies, even when it is not in their personal self-interest. In recent corporate scandals, leaders were often lacking in both respects. My focus here, however, is on the ability to motivate employees when leaders want to create an ethical workplace. I focus on this issue because that is where my prior research is relevant.

An appeal to values runs counter to the culture of surveillance and sanctions that characterizes most American workplaces. The dominant model of leadership in contemporary management involves command and control. This model concentrates resources at the top of the organizational hierarchy and provides incentives for desirable behavior and sanctions for undesirable behavior. One version of this approach is labeled transactional leadership because it focuses on resource-based transactions between leaders and followers.[34] The underlying assumption is that employee behavior is primarily a reaction to workplace rewards and penalties.

A related outcome-based approach is to motivate workers by ensuring that they receive fair or favorable outcomes. This approach makes the very reasonable assumption that people are motivated by what they receive from organizations. This model suggests that if leaders want to promote adherence to rules, they need to focus on how workers will experience the results.

The procedural justice literature points in a different direction. Although early models linked concerns with procedural justice to outcomes,[35] more recent research suggests that people have more fundamental concerns about the fairness by which authority is exercised, regardless of consequences. Their concerns about procedural justice are, in other words, ethically based.

Research consistently finds that attitudes, values, and behaviors are strongly linked to evaluations of the procedural justice of organizational policies and practices. If leaders are to be effective in motivating those they lead, they must exercise their authority in ways that subordinates experience as fair.[36] I refer to this approach to leadership as process-based leadership.

The root of process-based leadership is the recognition that although leaders are generally interested in motivating followers, they are especially interested in encouraging actions that are internally driven. In other words, leaders would like followers to share their vision and believe that their organizations are intrinsically desirable. If followers internalize the leader's goals, then they need fewer rewards and sanctions and less need for external supervision. For example, employees who want their company to be successful will work extra hours or on weekends without being asked to do so and without being concerned about whether their efforts will be noticed and rewarded. Organizational achievements are valued for their own sake.

Such internal motivation reduces the need for costly surveillance and avoids the limitations of rule-bound frameworks. It is often difficult to specify in advance what is desirable in a given situation, and if employees are given discretion to do what they think is appropriate, it is equally difficult to specify incentives or sanctions. Even when it is clear what is desirable, enforcement may be problematic. Sanctions require a credible surveillance system because employees are motivated to hide noncomplying behavior. Those who are internally motivated require fewer incentives and sanctions.

Defining Procedural Justice

The findings outlined make clear that encouraging moral values is central to the effectiveness of organizations and their leaders. These findings make equally clear that values—legitimacy and moral congruence—turn heavily on procedural justice. To understand how to create institutions that are designed to be responsive to these findings, it is necessary to understand the meaning of procedural justice in greater depth. The model that emerges from prior studies is based on the four components,[37] and each contributes independently to overall procedural justice judgments. Those components are defined by two distinct aspects of organizational processes and two sources of information about procedures.

One aspect of organizational processes considers decision-making procedures. Specifically, the model considers employees' evaluations of the quality of decision making in their organization. These evaluations focus on the neutrality of the decision maker, the objectivity and factual basis of decisions, the consistency of rule application, and the lack of bias.[38]

A second and often equally important issue involves the quality of people's treatment by organizational authorities. Considerations include officials' politeness and dignity and concern for people's rights.

Each of these two aspects of procedures (quality of decision making and quality of interpersonal treatment) can be linked to two sources of information. One involves the rules of the organization. The formal rules and structures of the organization, as well as statements of organizational values, communicate information about organizational procedures. For example, organizations vary in terms of whether they have formal grievance procedures that allow people to voice complaints. They also differ in their vision or mission statements of organizational values. For example, one common provision in such statements is a commitment that individuals will "treat each other with respect, dignity, and common courtesy" and "express disagreements openly and respectfully." This provision specifies the type of procedures that the corporation views as reflecting its values.

The other source of information is an employee's experience with their supervisor or supervisors. Although organizational authorities are constrained by formal institutions and procedures, they also typically exercise considerable discretion—the manner in which they implement decision-making procedures and make decisions in the absence of formal procedures. As a consequence, supervisory personnel have a great deal of flexibility about how they treat colleagues. The same decision-making procedure can be implemented in a way that emphasizes the dignity of those involved, or employees can be treated rudely or dismissively. A similar situation applies in other contexts. Formal laws and rules govern the conduct of law enforcement officers and judges. However, those authorities typically have considerable latitude in how they exercise their authority.

The four-component model argues that each of these aspects of procedural justice plays an important role in perceptions of the fairness of procedures. What bears emphasis is the noninstrumental character of those components. The organizational processes emphasized in this model of procedural justice (quality of decision making, quality of treatment) are not directly linked to evaluations of the favorability or fairness of the outcomes people receive.

Conclusion

The prior analysis makes clear that effective moral leadership needs to pay greater attention to procedural fairness in both public and private sector contexts. A growing body of research demonstrates that perceptions of the quality of organizational decision making and the treatment of individuals strongly influence people's willingness to comply with rules and to act ethically in the best interest of the organization. Rather than focusing largely on rewards and punishments, leaders would do well to appeal to values. To do so, they need to structure workplaces that more effectively draw on employees' own feelings about legitimacy and sense of moral responsibility. Building on individuals' ethical sensibilities is the best way for organizations to bring their practices into line with their principles, as well as with legal regulations and societal interests.

Part Four

SERVING THE PUBLIC THROUGH THE PUBLIC SECTOR

Accountability of Nonprofit Organizations

10

STRATEGIC PHILANTHROPY AND ITS MALCONTENTS

Paul Brest

Accountability lies at the core of the exercise of moral leadership in the nonprofit sector, particularly in philanthropy. Operating nonprofit organizations are accountable to those who fund them and those they have committed to serve. But what about the philanthropists themselves? Of course, they are accountable to adhere to state and federal legal requirements. They also have duties of fair dealing toward the organizations they fund. However, the diversity of goals that philanthropists pursue—goals that are sometimes in direct conflict with each other—makes it difficult to talk about accountability for particular substantive outcomes.

Yet it is not too great a stretch to say that the tremendous tax advantages conferred by the Internal Revenue Code obligate philanthropists to use their funds effectively to achieve their goals, whatever they may be. In this chapter, I address this broader and somewhat metaphoric idea of accountability: the accountability of philanthropists to ensure that their activities, grants, and donations actually make a difference. While I emphasize the obligation of philanthropists and the foundations they establish, their accountability requires that the nonprofit organizations in which they invest be accountable as well.

The absence of such accountability on the part of philanthropists is part of a long tradition that focuses more on the donor's state of mind than on what he or she actually accomplishes. But although it is fine for philanthropy to be motivated by transcendent moral principles—or even by personal satisfaction or community regard and approval—these do not strike me as defensible reasons for spending vast sums of money or claiming the advantageous deductions of section 501(c)(3) of the Internal Revenue Code.

This chapter focuses on the nontranscendent, practical question of how philanthropists—whatever their motivations—can actually make a difference in achieving their goals. This is the core of what has been called *strategic philanthropy*. The first part of the chapter sets out the fundamental tenets of strategic philanthropy and makes the case for it. The second defends strategic philanthropy against its critics.

The Idea of Strategic Philanthropy

Implicit in the term *strategic* is the premise that philanthropists—and the nonprofit organizations they support—have goals that can be achieved more or less effectively and that they ought to deploy their resources to achieve those goals more effectively rather than less. This virtually tautological premise has tremendous implications for how an organization structures and conducts its work.

Let me break the premise down into four parts. I will state them from the philanthropist's point of view, though they have significant implications for the organizations supported by philanthropy:

- Each gift or grant must be designed to achieve articulable goals.

- The philanthropist must believe that an organization to which he or she makes a grant has a sound strategy or plan for achieving those goals and the capacity to implement the plan.

- The philanthropist must have some means of learning of the organization's progress toward their shared goals, especially if the philanthropist is contemplating future investments in the same organization.

- The philanthropist must take account of the benefits, costs, and risks of pursuing the organization's plan in order to assess its effectiveness compared with other ways of achieving the goals.

The philanthropist can perform these activities with extensive diligence or not. He may rely largely on intuition or trust in the organization's leadership, or may engage in independent analysis and fact finding. His approach to these matters will be determined by his time, energy, and financial resources and by the nature of the organizations in the fields of his interest and grant making. But one way or another, these are the essential tenets of strategic grant making. I will discuss them one at a time.

• *Each philanthropic gift or grant must be designed to achieve certain goals.* There is an incredible diversity of objectives that philanthropists may legitimately pursue:

The arts: museums, music, theater, dance—from the High Renaissance to high kitsch, from internationally renowned to tiny neighborhood organizations

Religion: neighborhood churches and megachurches; evangelical missionaries preaching redemption, tolerance, and outright hatred

Social services: housing and feeding the poor, teen pregnancy, and drug prevention programs

Social change: promoting women's choice or prohibiting abortions; advocating for gun control or citizens' right to bear arms

Medicine and health: preventing or curing cancer, Alzheimer's, malaria, and AIDS, as well as the rare disease that afflicted one's beloved family member

This list represents a tiny fraction of the relatively conventional aims of philanthropy. Examples of less conventional ones include the search for extraterrestrial life, identifying asteroids targeting the earth, extrasensory perception, and saving whales and salamanders.

While the choice of goals can be criticized from a moral point of view—Should a philanthropist commission symphonies rather than prevent AIDS? Should he or she support prochoice rather than antiabortion groups?—such questions lie on a different level from the issues considered here, which are relevant to any goals a funder may seek to achieve.[1]

To illustrate the other three points, I will use the example of a philanthropist who has the goal of improving the life opportunities of teenage girls by reducing unplanned pregnancies and who supports an organization that pursues this goal.

• *The philanthropist must believe that an organization has a sound strategy or plan for achieving its goals, and the capacity to implement the plan.* This is where the accountability of the organizations supported by philanthropists comes in, for a philanthropist cannot be accountable for impact in achieving his goals unless he has reason to believe that an organization in which he invests is ready and able to achieve them.

This requires that the organization define its own goals with sufficient clarity that a potential donor can understand them and that the donor can eventually assess the extent to which the organization has achieved them. In addition to describing its goals, the organization must have a plan for accomplishing them. For example, an organization concerned with preventing teen pregnancy may have a plan that provides counseling and access to sexual and reproductive health information. The plan will describe all of the activities the organization must undertake to achieve its goals.

A strategic plan is at least tacitly premised on a theory of how the intended change comes about. For example, providing adolescents with comprehensive, medically accurate sexual and reproductive health information and services increases their ability to make informed decisions, which leads to the delayed onset of sexual activity and increased use of contraception, which in turn leads to a reduction of unplanned pregnancies.

The value of an organization's plan ultimately depends on the validity of the theory underlying it: to the extent the theory is flawed, the plan will not work. At the very least, the theory should be plausible. Ideally, it should be empirically validated. The theory underlying our hypothetical teen pregnancy prevention program is plausible, but so too is a theory that holds that abstinence is the key to teenagers' well-being and that the availability of contraceptives promotes teen sexual activity.

The history of the natural and especially the social sciences suggests that intuitively plausible theories are often wrong.[2] Thus, organizations should aspire to base their work on theories that have previously been evaluated by social scientists and shown to work. Especially because few on-the-ground organizations can afford to undertake such research, philanthropy has a special role to play here. Unfortunately, many philanthropists would rather spend their money "doing something" than learning whether what they are doing actually achieves its intended outcomes.

Finally, one can have a sound, evidence-based strategic plan yet lack the human and financial resources to carry out the proposed work. Thus, the organization also must have a business plan that describes how its resources will be mobilized, and that includes fundraising plans to gain any additional resources necessary for the program's operations.

One way or another, a philanthropist who wants his funds to make a difference must ensure that an organization meets these criteria. But even if an organization were self-sustaining without any philanthropic dollars, it must aspire to meet them if it wishes to be effective in achieving its own ends.

• *The philanthropist must have some means of determining an organization's progress toward their shared goals.* By the same token, even if an organization were economically self-sufficient, it would have to track progress toward its outcomes in order to know whether it is on course and to make corrections where it is not.

Once a strategic plan is drawn up, it is usually easy to identify major indicators of progress to be tracked—for example, the number of counseling appointments kept and missed in the teen pregnancy program. The possible breakdowns in implementation range from individual problems—whether a counselor or youth has missed an appointment—to the wholesale—whether there is a greater demand for reproductive health services than the organization can meet. The items tracked may be of a qualitative as well as a quantitative nature. For example, the success of the teen pregnancy prevention program depends not merely on whether the counselor and youth meet at the appointed time, but on the sessions' success in imparting substantive knowledge or decision-making skills.[3]

I use the term *tracking* rather than *evaluation* to make the point that the collection of data about an organization's progress under the strategic plan does not require social science studies by outside experts. Rather, it calls for the organization's own personnel to obtain systematic feedback from internal systems. Although one should not minimize the cost of designing and implementing those systems,[4] tracking progress is essential to managing any effective organization—whether a business, government agency, or nonprofit.

As one moves from tracking the organization's own activities to assessing outcomes—whether it actually made a difference—the task often becomes more challenging. Consider the organization's challenge in learning how the program has affected its clients' sexual behavior or their number of unplanned pregnancies. This may require gathering and analyzing data that lie beyond an organization's resources. And this is all the more reason for an organization to rely on a strategic plan based on a theory that has been subject to empirical validation by social scientists.[5]

All of this may seem like a daunting task for many nonprofit organizations. Nonetheless, I doubt that any aspect of the planning process—from articulating clear goals and a theory of change through developing a logic model and business plan—can reasonably be abbreviated. After all, these are the plans that will guide the organization's core activities. Realistically, though, an organization may have to make compromises with respect to tracking and focus its efforts toward getting feedback on the processes most critical to its success.

• *The philanthropist must take account of the benefits, costs, and risks of pursuing the organization's plan.* Although the benefits of philanthropic grants are often difficult to quantify, a strategic philanthropist at least implicitly, and sometimes explicitly, takes into account the relationship between the cost of the grant and the benefits it promises to bring. If two programs provide essentially the same service in, say, feeding homeless families, and one costs considerably more than the other, the philanthropist will at least be skeptical about the more expensive one. Indeed, even if it is the only program in town, the cost per meal could be so great as to make a donor consider better uses of his funds.

In these examples, the donor knows pretty much what he is getting for his grant. But a philanthropist addressing many social and environmental issues faces significant uncertainties. Even if the donor to the hypothetical teen pregnancy prevention program knows the cost of counseling sessions, the effects of those sessions on the goal of reducing pregnancies are at least somewhat speculative, and different people may place different values on the benefit of a teen's avoiding a pregnancy. And consider the uncertainties facing a philanthropist who is concerned with developing an AIDS vaccine, changing policies and practices to reduce global warming, protecting large ecosystems, or improving the well-being of the residents of developing countries.

Under these circumstances, one might be tempted to analogize philanthropy that seeks major social change to a day at the races, often with very long odds. However, considering risks in the light of potential social benefits suggests a more apt metaphor: one can think of grants as investments that seek social returns. The metaphor is better not because it is more comforting but because of its core insight that the return on investment is a function of both the expected social impact and the likelihood of achieving it. If philanthropists did not take risks, they would never pursue strategies that seek large-scale changes in education, the environment, or economic development. Nor would they invest in new, relatively untested organizations that have great potential. Although no formulas can substitute for good judgment, an underlying model of investment, risk, and return provides the basis for making big bets, where success is hardly assured but the social payoff is extraordinarily high.

While this metaphor provides a powerful way of conceiving of the work of philanthropy, it does not try to capture the underlying passion that motivates this work. Here there is a significant difference between most for-profit and nonprofit investors. Whereas business investors are (legitimately) motivated by self-interest in seeking a financial return on their investments, philanthropists seek a social return. But a philanthropist who truly cares about making the world a better place would no more want to squander his charitable dollars than a business investor would squander investment funds. A dollar wasted on an organization with a poor strategy or on one that is badly run and thus produces little or no social return could have been spent elsewhere to achieve real impact.

Two Qualifications

While the outcome-oriented model is applicable to the vast majority of nonprofit enterprises, there are at least two situations in which its constraints may need to be relaxed: the fertilization of creativity and the founding of social movements.[6]

Progress in the arts and social and natural sciences depends on the creativity of a diverse array of practitioners, scholars, artists, and thinkers. Jerome Bruner has described creativity in terms of "effective surprise"—a process whereby existing knowledge is converted into something that had not been anticipated.[7] The continual fertilization and development of ideas cannot be accomplished only through the targeted funding of specific projects with determined outcomes, but requires giving creative individuals the space to follow their own lights. To this end, philanthropists support individual artists, universities, and other individuals and institutions that foster and incubate creativity. There are inevitable efficiency losses in the short run. Not all artists and scholars will be industrious, not all of the industrious will be innovative, and not all innovative ideas will be worthwhile. But support for such open-ended creativity has paid off tremendously over time.

None of this lessens the importance of evaluation. While outputs cannot be specified and the process cannot be micromanaged, individual creativity and an institution's capacity to promote its flourishing can be assessed in retrospect. Whether philanthropists invest in institutions with established track records or bet on promising individuals, they will ultimately make wiser choices by regularly obtaining feedback and adjusting their strategy accordingly. At least in this respect, the fertilization of creativity is not radically different from other sorts of philanthropic investments.

The loosening of constraints for founding fields, and particularly social movements, responds to a somewhat different set of dynamics. At its early stages, a social movement is especially subject to "the relative indeterminacy of aim" that the legal philosopher H.L.A. Hart suggests is inevitable in all human affairs.[8] Consider, for example, the goals of civil rights organizations in the early 1960s. Were they concerned with equal treatment or equal outcomes? With integration or self-determination? With only intentional race discrimination or with adventitious discrimination, disparate impact, unconscious discrimination, and affirmative action? While some individuals and organizations had clear views on these matters, for many others the immediate problem of removing traditional forms of discrimination loomed so large as to place these other questions in a hazy distance. Moreover, the civil rights movement consisted of many grassroots organizations with diverse constituencies. Goals were reassessed and clarified over time; strategies were determined by trial and error.

Thus, in the early stages of a social movement, a philanthropist may have little else but the quality of an organization's leadership to guide its grant making. But as a movement matures, so do its organizations, and a philanthropist will rightly expect its leaders to supplement passion and broad vision with clear goals and strategies.

In Defense of Strategic Philanthropy

The general view of philanthropy I have described has a venerable ancestry. Often-cited examples include the Rockefeller and Ford foundations' establishment of the international agricultural research centers that initiated the green revolution, and the efforts by Ford and other foundations after World War II to establish area studies programs with the aim of increasing Americans' knowledge of important regions of the world. More recent examples include George Soros's open society initiatives in Eastern Europe, the Gates Foundation's initiatives to eliminate malaria, and the successful thirty-year campaign by conservative foundations to change the terms of national policy debate in the United States.[9] Strategies are no less important for achieving community-oriented objectives such as feeding and housing the homeless, providing workforce placements for the chronically unemployed, and improving the opportunities for disadvantaged youth.

Despite the obvious advantages of implementing well-thought-out strategies in these and other spheres, this has not been the general approach of the vast majority of America's sixty-five thousand foundations, whose philanthropy tends to be more expressive than outcome oriented. Although there has been increased talk about the value of strategic philanthropy during the past several years, the number of philanthropists—whether individuals or foundations—who have systematically put these ideas into practice remains minuscule. Although the recently publicized financial improprieties of a small minority of foundations present a genuine problem that must be addressed, they pale beside the scandal of the well-intentioned squandering of billions of dollars that have the potential to make one's community, the nation, or the world a better place.[10]

I do not want to minimize the difficulty of doing strategic philanthropy. Developing and implementing strategies is hard work, there are significant risks of failure, and the gratifications of success are often deferred. Most foundations are staffed, if at all, by family members in their spare time. Building their capacity to engage in strategic grant making is a long-term undertaking. But the near-term challenge is to instill the will to acquire that capacity. It is striking how many philanthropists, whose wealth came from pursuing good business strategies, park their strategic instincts outside their foundations' doors.

It is against this background that a handful of writers have suggested that philanthropists might do well to look to the world of business, where the concept of strategic management is well developed and is generally thought to conduce to success.[11] Although funders have hardly rushed headlong to answer the call to strategic philanthropy, the call itself has stirred a small but intense scholarly backlash. Critics of a "strategic," "business," or "investment" approach to philanthropy include two eminent Bay Area philanthropic leaders: Dennis Collins, who retired several years ago as president of the James Irvine Foundation, and Bruce Sievers, who retired as executive director of the Walter and Elise Haas Fund.[12] Of course, there are important differences between the practices of business and philanthropy. But the critics are not concerned with nuance. Rather, they find the very use of business metaphors offensive.

Dennis Collins writes that "'hyperrationalism' and 'managerialism' . . . appear to be crowding out a more values-driven, mission-centered approach to philanthropy and replacing it with a technically based, efficiency-driven, outcome-centered process. In short, supplanting art with a pseudoscience that imagines metrics and matrices are reality rather than a set of useful but limited tools."[13]

Bruce Sievers criticizes what he calls a "business model" of philanthropy:[14]

> Unlike businesses, . . . philanthropic and nonprofit organizations operate in two worlds. One of these is defined by instrumental objectives such as financial stability [or] number of people served. The other world, however, is defined by different end goals of human action: education, artistic expression, freedom of thought and action, concern for future generations, and preservation of cultural and environmental legacies. . . . These ends are the goals and aspirations

of the human experience and are not reducible to the same kinds of categories that define profit margins and make for the most efficient production of widgets.

It is this mission-driven dimension that separates the world of the nonprofit from the world of the for-profit in a fundamental way. "Mission" is even too limited a word to capture all that is entailed in the nature of the nonprofit enterprise; it suggests a single-mindedness of goal that belies the multi-dimensional character of any activity aimed at ameliorating the human condition. "Purpose" or "aspiration" might better describe the goals of organizations that operate in the social sphere. Within their broad purposes, organizations certainly adopt specific tasks, but the point of the overall effort lies beyond these instrumental vehicles. . . . It is poetry rather than metrics that often best captures this dimension of human experience.

Strategic philanthropy . . . suggests that human action can be understood in terms of linear, sequential steps that can be orchestrated in predictable ways to arrive at a goal. . . . But most sophisticated social analysts . . . posit a very different model of social change, one that is stochastic (non-linear, incapable of precise prediction), self-referential, and multi-variant. The . . . business model makes foundations averse to this kind of complexity, leading them to insulate themselves from diversity within the fields in which they operate and to bypass vital areas of social concern that do not fit easily into a linear framework of analysis.

Having made the affirmative case for strategic philanthropy earlier in this chapter, I now defend it against these critics.

The Confusion of Means and Ends

Sievers is absolutely right that philanthropy "operate[s] in two worlds," one defined by instrumental, the other by transcendent objectives. But the two worlds he describes are essentially those of means and ends, and it generally makes good sense not to conflate them.

Philanthropy comes from the heart—from the love of human-kind, as the Greek word connotes. It is love or passion that leads the philanthropist to determine a mission and set ambitious goals. But once he or she has determined these goals, then mind and muscle come in to design and implement a strategy to achieve them. A strategy comprises the unromantic, nitty-gritty working out of the means to accomplish one's goals. It is never an end in itself, only a tool to aid an organization in achieving its mission.

To contrast, as Collins does, a "values-driven, mission-centered approach to philanthropy" with an "efficiency-driven, outcome-centered process" confuses ends and means. In fact, the outcomes sought in an outcome-centered process are precisely the philan-thropist's values and mission. Sievers manifests the same confusion when he says, "Within their broad purposes, organizations . . . adopt specific tasks, but the point of the overall effort lies beyond these instrumental vehicles." The strategically oriented philanthropist would respond, "Absolutely so!"[15]

Grants as Investments Seeking (Larger Rather Than Smaller) Social Returns

There is obviously something deeper that bothers the critics—per-haps two related things: the metaphor of social return on invest-ments and the use of metrics. With respect to the investment metaphor, Sievers observes that there is

a disjunction between [foundations'] central resource—money, which is countable—and social objectives, which generally are not. There is a natural inclination to ask, How much social value can we buy with this money? The proper response, in my view, is that this is the wrong question: rather than seeking to conjure up something that would satisfy the "biggest bang for the buck" requirements of a buyer, those involved in philanthropy ought to pursue the kinds of success appropriate to social organizations.

> . . . SROI [social return on investment] does not and cannot
> adequately account for the complex and intangible human dimen-
> sions of what nonprofit organizations seek to accomplish. The mean-
> ing and import of a ten-year process of policy development, a shift
> in public consciousness, a spark of understanding brought through
> the arts, or the transformation of a single human being in a youth
> development program simply cannot be captured by SROI.[16]

To be sure, the complexities of social forces beyond our control, and even beyond our ken, mean that grant making—especially grant making seeking social change—has far more unknowns than certainties. But program officers must make choices, and the invest- ment metaphor reflects the reality that a grant dollar spent on a poorly designed strategy or a low-performing organization is a lost opportunity to support a more effective one.

Indeed, the investment metaphor serves another critically im- portant function. It gives foundations the space to make "big bets" or, in Dennis Collins's approving phrase, to "swing for the fences."[17] The core insight of the metaphor is that the return on investment is a function of both the anticipated impact and the likelihood of achiev- ing it. If foundations did not take risks, they would never pursue strategies that seek large-scale social change. Nor would they invest in new, relatively untested organizations that have great potential.

Given the large problems that foundations address, their reach will often exceed their grasp—or, to put it bluntly, they will often fail. It is the fact that the social returns they seek, though not quantifiable, are potentially huge by any standard that gives foundation staff and board members the courage to fail. Sievers certainly understands the importance of reaching for the stars, but he does not acknowledge the strategic infrastructure that conduces to grasping success.

Metrics

Perhaps it is less the concept of social return on investment than the idea of subjecting philanthropy to metrics that upsets the crit- ics. Collins talks about a "pseudoscience . . . [of] metrics and matrices." Sievers provides a powerful example of outcomes that are not subject to accounting rules:

> The environmental movement, the rise of the conservative agenda in American political life, and the movement toward equality for the gay and lesbian communities, all aided by significant philanthropic support, have transformed American life in ways that lie beyond any calculations of "return on investment." Of course, we believe that there *have* been calculable returns on investments in these issues, but the point is that these movements have recast the American moral landscape, resulting in enormous change in the way society functions and understands itself, with consequent changes in policy. Commitment of philanthropic resources to these issues was not merely a matter of analyzing increments of inputs and output; it was a moral engagement with wooly, unpredictable issues that called for deeply transformational action.[18]

He writes that "it is poetry rather than metrics that often best captures this dimension of human experience," and that "measurable outcomes . . . may distort an organization's program or actually cause more important, intangible aims to be overlooked."

Well, yes and no. If the point is that philanthropy is more in the nature of a craft than science or economics and that one can seldom quantify the social return on a foundation's investment, there is no disagreement. Likewise, one ought not eschew an important mission because progress cannot be assessed in quantitative units. I have yet to encounter a funder who believes that the goals of massive social change movements are "reducible to the same kinds of categories that define profit margins." Without attempting to quantify social returns, though, the investment metaphor embodies an attitude that presses the staff to use the foundation's resources as effectively as possible.

Most philanthropy, whether practiced by large or small foundations, aims at incremental rather than massive social change. It supports programs to mentor children after school, prevent or treat drug addiction, provide supportive housing for the homeless, help people become productive members of the workforce, and the like. Most such programs have indicators of progress and success that are amenable to quantitative assessment.[19]

Once you have adopted a mission and chosen goals, it is always worth striving to develop quantitative indicators where you can, but with the recognition that many outcomes cannot be assessed this way. A performing arts organization must be concerned with the quality of its productions at least as much as with the size of its audience. And a comprehensive community initiative may have both the objectively evaluable goal of reducing crime rates and the goals of strengthening its residents' subjective sense of trust, community, and well-being.

Anyone who was tempted to look only at metrics in such cases need only consider the distorting effects of teaching to the test on American education. But I think that Collins and Sievers have set up a straw man. In six years in the philanthropic sector, I have not encountered a foundation CEO who did not understand that indicators of success must respond to the program's goals—not vice versa.

Sievers provides only one example of the downside of metrics, and it is a curious one. He suggests that metrics lead to evaluating organizations based on the (small) size of their administrative expenses rather than their accomplishments. But this is precisely what an investment approach guards against. No business views costs in the abstract; rather, it asks whether they are justified in terms of the value they produce. That certainly is the justification for any foundation's having a staff, which is typically its greatest expense. Indeed, it is not evident why a foundation would need much of a staff if it were not strategically oriented.

The Role of Intuition

Related to the critique of metrics, but more radical, one might believe that the demand for anything like a strategic plan is misguided and that a funder should simply trust that an organization leader's or a social entrepreneur's passionate commitment and intuitions will yield results. Along the same lines, a funder might believe in letting a hundred flowers bloom and seeing which turn out to thrive.

One cannot criticize these approaches a priori. Intuition plays an important role in many complex human endeavors and, indeed, is an inescapable part of strategically oriented work. Some people are better at doing than at explaining how they do it—certainly, many are better at talking than doing!—and a good organizational leader or grant maker must have reliable intuitions to parallel the more deliberative aspects of his or her work. But developing reliable intuitions requires getting feedback from the results of one's decisions.[20] A responsible organization and its funders must therefore ultimately determine how well a program succeeded in achieving its mission. My hunch is that most funders whose selection of grantees rely on intuition to the exclusion of a well-thought-out strategic plan do not bother to test their intuitions after the fact.

The Critique of Venture Philanthropy and the Value of General Operating Support

In addition to the general attack on a business model of philanthropy, Sievers criticizes the notion of venture philanthropy—a particular approach that, as the name implies, borrows from the practices of venture capitalists. He focuses on the practices of going to scale, being actively engaged in the management of the grantee's enterprise, using the funder's contacts to secure other investors, and having an exit strategy.[21]

For all of the buzz about venture philanthropy, there are very few funders whose work encompasses most of these practices. In any event, I do not think one can say categorically that they are good or bad. For example, although many organizations are just the right size for their mission, surely it is sometimes valuable to increase an organization's scale or reach.[22] The appropriate level of engagement with a grantee also depends on the circumstances. Although most strategically oriented funders work with an applicant to develop a shared understanding of goals and strategies, and receive and provide feedback during the course of the grant, they are seldom involved in the grantee's management. The rare occasions of higher engagement usually respond to the shared belief that a foundation's staff can add real value to a complex or innovative enterprise. Sievers is surely right that engagement for engagement's sake is not helpful;[23] but once again, I have not encountered funders who have the resources, let alone the desire, to do this. As for using contacts to secure other investors, this strikes me as almost always desirable.

An exit strategy reflects a venture capitalist's expectation that after some period of time, a successful company will go public or be acquired. Though some foundations tend to focus on start-ups, there is no real analog to an exit strategy for the large majority of nonprofit organizations, which will always depend on philanthropic support.[24] That said, philanthropists could learn a couple of valuable lessons from venture capitalists. The first is the importance of supporting an organization as a whole rather than picking and choosing pieces of it. The equivalent in philanthropy is the provision of general operating support—something dear to the heart of every nonprofit organization—rather than funding discrete projects.[25] Second, although they have fairly short time horizons, venture capitalists stay with a company long enough to see it through success at a particular stage—something that contrasts favorably to the modus operandi of many foundations, which impose arbitrary and often counterproductive time limits on their support even for high-performing organizations and often exit because of donor fatigue rather than as a result of any strategy whatever.

In summary, to Bruce Sievers's statement that the business model "has risen to a position of prominence in philanthropic practice," my response is, Would that it were so! I've heard some talk about a business or strategic orientation, but the number of funders who are walking the walk seems small and accounts for an infinitesimal proportion of philanthropic dollars. Indeed, even if foundations were in fact as obsessed with metrics as Collins and Sievers imply, this would be a healthy corrective to a sector that for the most part pays no attention to outcomes whatsoever.

In an excerpt quoted above, Sievers observes that major social change movements arise from a sense of justice that cannot be captured by cost-benefit analysis. Of course, he is right. But since we have recently celebrated the fiftieth anniversary of *Brown v. Board of Education*, it is worth recalling just how outcome-oriented the NAACP Legal Defense Fund was in its support of the most important social change of the twentieth century. Its fundamental strategy was to get the U.S. Supreme Court comfortable with the racial desegregation of professional and graduate schools before pressing the Court to enter the emotionally charged venue of elementary and secondary education. The motivation was the quest for social justice. But the strategy was ruthlessly instrumental and required passing up cries from the heart for immediate action in favor of long-term gains. The foundations that invested in the Legal Defense Fund knew that they were working in partnership with an organization whose leadership not only had its eyes on the prize but had well-thought-out strategies for gaining it.

Sievers and Collins are absolutely right that a sense of mission, commitment, and passion is essential to every aspect of the work of philanthropists and the nonprofit organizations they support. These qualities are what make those committed to social change go to work early and come home late. Strategy is not a substitute for these values but the vehicle for achieving them. Without the capacity to move beyond passion to effective planning and execution, the sector would be left largely with well-meaning efforts that confuse good intentions with real effects.

11

ETHICS AND PHILANTHROPY

Bruce Sievers

The nonprofit sector rests on a foundation of public trust. This trust is based on an assumption that the primary incentives for nonprofit work are neither profit nor power, but rather voluntary action directed toward the public good. For this reason, ethics occupies a central position in the nonprofit sector in a way in which it does neither for the for-profit nor governmental sectors.

This may strike some as a rather idealistic way of describing the complex mixture of motives and purposes that define the nonprofit world, but fundamental justifications for the sector have long been anchored in the concept of trust. For example, legal analysts have emphasized the importance of the nondistribution constraint that imposes an intrinsic limit on self-interested activity on the part of those who operate nonprofits. Economists have pointed to the creation of public goods (in contrast to private goods) as the goal of nonprofit enterprise, and such public goods are always threatened by the problem of unethical free riders. Policy experts have highlighted public trust associated with the tax benefits received by nonprofit organizations. And a long history of charitable support has demonstrated the public's ongoing perception that the work of the sector justifies its trust.

Trust implies ethical behavior. In some respects, this presumption for nonprofits is similar to the presumption of ethical conduct in all professional fields. Because professionals exercise power and authority outside the normal restraints of close governmental regulation, market forces, or political control (and we desire them to remain outside such forces as much as possible), they are assumed to operate according to self-imposed ethical principles. This is why we are so shocked when we learn of the violations of trust by journalists like Stephen Glass and Jayson Blair, the American Medical Association's paid endorsement of medical products, and Enron and WorldCom accountants who were complicit in financial frauds. We defer to professionals' expertise and feel betrayed when then they act dishonestly or deceptively.

The nonprofit sector introduces yet a further elevation of trust expectations because its practitioners not only perform as professionals—in education, health care, environmental protection, or whatever other specific fields in which they may be engaged—they do so with the special benefit of donated funds and volunteer effort directed toward broader public ends. The public benefit yielded by nonprofit professionals and volunteers thus extends beyond performing reliable services for clients; they provide public goods for the benefit of the entire society rather than for themselves or other private recipients. Stated in economic terms, nonprofits provide services to recipients who are not payers and thus commit themselves to avoid exploitation of information asymmetries that, were it not for ethical behavior, might work to the detriment of both donors and clients.

I focus on a particular subset of nonprofit organizations: those that exercise great influence while operating with minimal external control. These are philanthropic foundations, entities endowed by private wealth in pursuit of public purposes. Foundations occupy a particularly crucial place in the universe of the nonprofit sector, and since they have both the resources and the latitude to take the lead in promoting ethical practice, they can reasonably be expected to play a strong role in exercising leadership in the sector.

For the purposes of this chapter, I suggest three levels of ethical issues—from the practical to the broadly theoretical—that apply distinctively to foundations in their role as potential leaders in the nonprofit world.

Funding Ethics

The first is the straightforward issue of ethics as a funding priority. Clearly foundations make funding choices based on a spectrum of reasons, and donors and foundation boards can and should exercise wide discretion in determining which, among the enormous array of potential targets of social concern and interest, they choose as the preferred objects of their support. Freedom of donor discretion is an essential aspect of modern philanthropy, and it has many benefits in stimulating creative, nonbureaucratic, pluralistic solutions to social problems. Social problems and interests are, in effect, limitless, and funds are finite, so it is inevitable that choices be made according to the interests and concerns of the donors and their representatives.

At the same time, systematic thinking is rarely applied to the most important stage of decision making in foundations: the time they are established. Indeed, donor preferences are most often influenced by personal histories, relationships, and experiences that are not typically subject to rigorous critical analysis. The result is that in any given period, foundation funding tends to flow to areas of interest in quite arbitrary ways. There is an irony in this circumstance, in the light of the fact that so much of the field's attention is paid to strategies of grant making after the initial choices have been made.

The idiosyncratic nature of foundation priority setting can create shifting patterns of support often oriented to hot topics of the day, such as elementary education or particular diseases, while fundamentally important but less fashionable arenas of social concern can be easily ignored. I have suggested elsewhere that the subject of ethics—both research and application—is an example of a field with important social consequences that is habitually overlooked by foundations.[1] The entire field of professional ethics—including ethics in medicine, journalism, government, law, and science—receives minimal foundation support. While it is true that financial needs in ethics are less than those in, say, physics research or medical care, for the same reason that electron microscopes and AIDS drugs cost more than fellowships, conferences, and yellow pads, the need for the support of work in ethics is not zero, which is only slightly less than the level of funding actually allocated.

A trend that reinforces this pattern of neglect is an increasingly bottom-line orientation in philanthropy, most recently evident in the contemporary enthusiasm for applying the "business model" to philanthropic practice. The often uncritical importation of this model and its associated conceptual framework—an emphasis on "bang for the buck," measurable outcomes, performance milestones, products, and scaling up—can lead philanthropy to avoid large, philosophically complex, intangible issues such as ethics. Beyond the influences of subjective donor choice, therefore, this reflects an epistemological failing of the field. In his discussion of this phenomenon in other professional fields, Donald Schön called this kind of restricted social perception a form of "selective inattentiveness" to important features of social life.[2]

On a practical level, therefore, there is a need for more serious philanthropic attention to research and application of ethics in professional life. If large health care foundations, for example, were to allocate a small percentage of their grants to medical ethics, and science foundations did the same for scientific ethics, research and education opportunities in ethics would be expanded enormously.

Foundation Accountability

A second level on which ethics and philanthropy have a strong relationship is that of philanthropic accountability. Accountability has in fact been part of the discussion of philanthropy as long as foundations have existed, for example, in the establishment of ancient philanthropic funds that prompted the creation of legal vehicles to ensure their proper and honest administration. The Elizabethan Statute of Charitable Uses of 1601 contained provisions to guarantee the appropriate application of charitable donations to the causes intended by the donors. Congressional oversight of American philanthropy began a century ago concurrent with the creation of the first large general-purpose foundations. The reason for this enduring concern about accountability is simple: the allocation of funds for vital social concerns outside the control of the state or other authority leaves open the clear possibility of abuse.

A contemporary instance of this long-standing concern for philanthropic accountability is to be seen in the current multiple initiatives by both state and national governments that seek to assert greater oversight of the nonprofit sector. An example is the examination by the U.S. Senate Committee on Finance (ongoing in mid-2005) of legislative approaches designed to place more specific financial and operational requirements on foundations and other nonprofits. The stated purpose of such legislation is to ensure greater transparency, public accountability, and socially beneficial application of charitable resources.

The prospect of ever greater regulation raises a fundamental question about the nature of private philanthropy: What is the proper balance between the free exercise of private action in civil society and the obligation to be accountable to the public? Like other professions, philanthropy is accorded wide latitude of operational independence by society to avoid the stifling consequences of bureaucratic or politically motivated influences. But as endowed entities with self-selected boards and self-determined purposes, foundations, and particularly private foundations, have neither market forces nor fundraising requirements to serve as external checks as do most other professional or nonprofit fields. Other than very general scrutiny by state attorneys general, the Internal Revenue Service, and occasional press articles, foundations have little societal oversight.

I am not suggesting that this is necessarily a negative situation. Indeed philanthropic organizations have functioned quite beneficially throughout American history, fostering flexible, proactive, enterprising, sometimes contrarian, and generally helpful social action. Arguably, the combination of freedom and trust accorded these organizations has produced a powerfully productive financial resource for positive social change. Although contributions by individuals consistently exceed those from foundations by a large measure (typically by a factor of eight to one), the ability of foundations to apply their resources in a systematic, focused way over time gives them a unique capacity to contribute to solutions to fundamental social problems.

The problem arises when public trust is violated through carelessness, self-dealing, or outright malfeasance. Absent the mechanisms that ensure popular control over other elites—the market in the for-profit arena and elections in government[3]—foundations, like all other nonprofits, are quite free to set their own rules of behavior. Following several well-publicized missteps and scandals in recent years involving a number of private foundations as well as several large nonprofit organizations, among them the United Way, Red Cross, and Nature Conservancy, there has been greatly increased discussion of the issue of accountability.[4]

When such abuses occur, as they inevitably will in such an unmonitored operating system, the question becomes: What to do? The immediate social reaction is a call for stronger governmental oversight. This is currently evident in increasing state and national legislative efforts to exert more stringent control over the sector. One example is California's Nonprofit Integrity Act of 2004, signed into law by Governor Schwarzenegger, that imposes new requirements on governance and fundraising by California nonprofits. Another is the discussion of legislation under consideration by the U.S. Finance Committee to place stronger regulatory oversight over nonprofits.

These measures are but the latest in an episodic history of governmental regulatory initiatives. Soon after the creation of the modern foundation in the early twentieth century, a suspicious Congress initiated investigations of the Rockefeller, Carnegie, and other foundations. The U.S. Industrial Relations Commission (the Walsh Commission) was the first to conduct such an investigation in 1914, motivated by concern for foundations' "wealth, loosely defined powers, exemption from federal taxation, freedom from public control, subserviency to donors, and benumbing effect on smaller philanthropic agencies and individual giving."[5] The most recent major congressional initiative that created substantial new regulatory provisions over foundations was the 1969 tax act, resulting from hearings conducted by Representative Wright Patman. Throughout the history of these investigations, charges have revolved around a familiar theme: nonprofit organizations, and especially foundations, have the potential to abuse their freedom by operating a closed, self-serving system, and their resistance to calls for greater transparency, accountability, and demonstrable social benefit is counter to the spirit of modern, democratic organizational behavior. Derek Bok, former president of Harvard, put it succinctly: "Of all the institutions in America, philanthropic foundations are surely among the least accountable."[6]

Although the final outcome of the 1969 tax act is now widely regarded as generally positive in its impact on both philanthropy and the nonprofit field as a whole, I suggest that the overall trend toward greater government regulation over the nonprofit sector is actually a negative development, for both the operation of the sector and the public's trust in it. This presents something of a paradox: moves toward greater accountability and oversight are intended to increase ethical behavior and therefore public confidence in the work of the sector. Yet they do not. Why?

The answer is straightforward. Governmental accountability rules arise as mechanisms designed to compensate for a lack of ethical responsibility that has been demonstrated in a field. Thus, the stronger the regulatory mechanisms are, the less is the implicit trust. Onora O'Neill describes this scenario in her 2002 Reith Lecture, *A Question of Trust*:

> The diagnosis of a crisis of trust may be obscure: we are not sure whether there is a crisis of trust. But we are all agreed about the remedy. It lies in prevention and sanctions. Government, institutions, and professionals should be made more accountable. . . . The new accountability takes the form of detailed control. An unending

stream of new legislation and regulation, memoranda and instructions, guidance and advice floods into public sector institutions.[7]

O'Neill warns of the unintended injurious consequences of this barrage of regulatory activity: "The new accountability is widely experienced not just as *changing* but (I think) *distorting the proper aims of professional practice* and indeed as damaging professional pride and integrity."[8] These trends result in an ever expanding "audit culture" that actually undermines public trust. In the United States, for example, there appears to be no evidence that the recent passage of the Sarbanes-Oxley legislation imposing greater accountability on corporate boards has actually increased the public's trust in the corporate sector, despite the fact that the new law has perhaps provided modest reassurance that the violators are more under control. In fact, such efforts to increase government oversight can actually crowd out those to strengthen ethical standards within a field.

The clear implication of this argument is that the foundation community must take the lead in setting standards for its own ethical behavior and in initiating discussions, educational programs, and training sessions to implement them. Past such efforts have been quite timid in their aspirations and weak in their consequences, doing little to establish meaningful standards of behavior for the field. A current Council on Foundations initiative, "Building Strong and Ethical Foundations: Doing It Right," the latest effort aimed at establishing ethically grounded procedures and standards for the operation of foundations, shows promise for taking a next step.

In advocating stronger self-defined standards for the field, however, I want to distinguish between two quite different forms of accountability. While it is necessary and commendable to seek to establish norms of acceptable behavior in the governance and practice of grant making, the attempt to impose rigorous performance standards on the outcomes of foundation or nonprofit activity will not advance their level of ethical responsibility. Here is where Paul Brest and I differ in our interpretations of what is useful and appropriate in monitoring foundations' work. His view is that accountability, in terms of both ethics and public expectations, should include an assessment of foundation productivity; my view is that ethical and public considerations properly have to do with honesty and integrity, not attempts to measure yield. I offer two reasons for this.

First, the sheer number and complexity of variables in the realms of social action make it virtually impossible to arrive at rigorously measurable comparisons of performance among competing nonprofit activities. The vast range of variables involved in social action, the role of the single variable of foundation funding, uncertain time horizons, absence of a uniform feedback mechanism like the market, and lack of conditions for controlled experimentation cumulatively defeat attempts to arrive at precise numerical calculations of results. In purely scientific terms, therefore, the enormous complexity of measuring outcomes all but ensures failure.

Second, beyond the practical problems of measurement, there is a deeper philosophical question about the imposition of interpretive frameworks on social reality. Philosophers from many traditions have addressed this question over time, sharing a common critical stance about distortions that result from imposing a categorical framework grounded in one framework of reference on another.[9] Applied to philanthropic practice, this raises a serious concern about the effect of money and power in defining social reality in conformity with the belief system of the power holder. Those who solicit philanthropic support for their work in the complex arenas of nonprofit activity are particularly vulnerable to such pressures. A current example is the distorting effects of the mandated use of standardized test scores in evaluating educational activity, which, as we frequently hear from teachers, often results in teaching to the test, skewing the educational curriculum in the direction of the tests and translating the end of education into test taking.

Another example is the growing popularity of ratings systems for nonprofits, such as that of Charity Navigator. CN uses financial ratios, such as the ratio of program to administrative expense, to rank charities, including creating "Top Ten" and "Slam Dunk" lists. Despite producing impressive-looking charts and numbers, the ratings are virtually meaningless in terms of assessing the quality and value of the nonprofit organizations. By encouraging a simplistic "bang for the buck" evaluation of nonprofit organizations, such efforts are not only misleading but are positively counterproductive in conveying to the public a distorted message about the nature and purpose of nonprofit work. Even greater distortions occur in cross-cultural contexts.

Philanthropy and Public Goods

A third level on which ethical considerations arise in an important way in philanthropy concerns the role of private wealth in a democratic society. The focus here is on neither questions of philanthropic priority setting nor accountable behavior but on the overall ethical implications of the philanthropic enterprise, that is, the complex responsibility of private sector institutions seeking to address fundamental problems in and potentialities of modern society. This topic is best described under the rubric of concerns about the privatization of the public sphere. While such a complex subject cannot be adequately addressed within the confines of this chapter, I sketch an outline of an argument.

Philanthropy has been an integral part of the evolution of civil society in the West from its earliest origins, both as a moral force for the improvement of humankind and a primary financial resource enabling nonprofit organizations to remain independent of the market and the state. In this role, philanthropy has supplied a base of support for private action, separate from, and often defended against, the state. In the United States, the confrontation between the defense of the prerogatives of private power and the authority of the state occurred early in the nation's history in the struggles between the Federalists and the Jeffersonians. The pivotal *Dartmouth College* case in 1819 provided the definitive initial determination of the rights of private wealth to pursue social purposes through "the [U.S. Supreme] Court's perception of distinct realms of public and private action, and the role of the courts in the protection of private action from public interference."[10]

The subsequent development of the nonprofit sector in the United States reinforced and further refined the interplay between distinct public and private domains of action. At stake have always been two fundamental concerns: the protection of private associational life to operate freely without state intrusion and the ambiguous role of private actors in achieving public ends. The first has been well explored elsewhere and bears on foundations primarily in terms of the regulatory issues raised in the second section above. The second lies at the heart of the role of philanthropy in society.

The core of this second concern has to do with an important distinction between private and public goods and how they are generated. In the commercial sector, private means are used to create private goods. In the governmental sector, public means are used to achieve public goods. In the nonprofit sector, private means are used to create public goods. The consequence for the nonprofit sector is a delicate balancing act between adhering to the dictates of private inspiration and intention, on the one hand, and responsibility to achieve public benefits, on the other.

This balancing act is difficult to maintain because it confronts two fundamental challenges to the creation of public goods in the liberal democratic state: the collective action problem and value pluralism. Each of these two problems, taken separately, creates obstacles to achieving common aims in liberal democracies; together, they create a formidable barrier to channeling private resources in a way that is democratic and has coherence for the benefit of society as a whole.

Todd Sandler has distilled the problem of collective action succinctly in his phrase, "Individual rationality is not sufficient for collective rationality."[11] This conveys the central theme of a large body of work relating to the tragedy of the commons, prisoner's dilemma, free-riding, externalities, the use of common pool resources, and other aspects of the disjuncture between the pursuit of individual interests and the interest of collectivities. The problem is structural. As in the prisoner's dilemma, despite agreement on a common definition of "interest," the forces of individual self-interest can work to defeat the achievement of optimal interests for the group. Garrett Hardin, Mancur Olsen, and many others have demonstrated that the absence of a supervening regulatory power can lead to the diminution and ultimate destruction of the commons.

The problem of value pluralism in a liberal democracy adds a further challenging barrier to the task of achieving common ends. Most notably described by Isaiah Berlin, value pluralism poses a more fundamental problem than that of the practical challenges of reconciling individual interests with a common one because it denies the very existence (or even the possibility, according to Berlin) of a common definition of "good." Values are individually defined and can be ultimately incompatible, so any attempt to forge a common definition of the good society (or a broad sense of the common good within society) is doomed to failure. The general problem of pluralistic values has remained a perpetually unresolved dilemma in liberal democratic theory.

The problems of both collective action and value pluralism converge in the practice of private philanthropy. In a system of free, unfettered private decision making for the allocation of philanthropic resources, there is a presumption of something akin to an invisible hand that rationalizes the entire system for the overall benefit of society.[12] But the incentive of mission achievement works in a foundation much like the incentive of profit in a for-profit enterprise, and the cumulative effect of maximizing individual missions tends to frustrate foundations' potential for collective impact on society. This becomes the philanthropic version of the problem of collective action.

The actions of individual donors and, by extension, foundation boards reflect the effects of value pluralism. Indeed, one of the deepest held principles of private philanthropy is that giving interests should reflect the fundamental convictions of the donors, whether brilliant, inspired, controversial, or wacky. We cherish the ability of

individuals to choose their idiosyncratic paths of inquiry and interest. The question for social policy arises when these involvements
become more than just individual expressions of personal pastimes
or social engagements, but exercises in social power in the form of
particular public agendas advanced by philanthropic actors. In this
situation society is not only accommodating the coexistence of different and potentially conflicting value orientations of its citizens—
an essential characteristic of liberal democracy—but, in addition,
is facilitating the use of major private resources directed by small
groups of people to advance particular causes or value positions
without a broader social response mechanism.

These characteristics of private philanthropy, combined with
an expanding donor base, result in an ever-increasing fragmentation of organized giving.[13] Absent counterforces within or outside
the field that might encourage consideration of the larger collective
consequences of individual funding decisions, philanthropy becomes a magnifier of individually determined interests and goals.
This might be considered unproblematic—the philanthropic equivalent to the marketplace of ideas, in which the best programs, like
the best ideas, float to the top. But the world of private philanthropy, with its financial power and growing social influence, is not
simply a free, transparent, democratic marketplace that expresses
private preferences and beliefs and subjects them to critical feedback. To the contrary, it is a powerful source of social change and
agenda setting operating with minimal external input that steers
major resources to important public purposes.[14]

Several unintended negative consequences can flow from the
pluralism inherent in philanthropy. As Rob Reich has shown in his
study of local philanthropic support flowing into public schools, it
can adversely affect social equity. He documents how private funding can exacerbate the already unequal status of rich and poor school
districts, aggravating an existing lack of fairness in the distribution
of social services.[15] There are many other areas, such as health care,
private education, and particular geographical areas, where similar
questions of equity arise.

Second, philanthropy can distort the public decision-making process through the influence of private wealth in the public arena. The concern voiced early on by the Walsh Commission in its report, charging that "the concentration of wealth in the large foundations, such as the Carnegie and the Rockefeller, was being used by industrial magnates to gain control of the universities and, thereby, the social and educational side of American life,"[16] has remained an ongoing critique by those who object to the "private government" aspect of foundation activity. Michael Walzer has succinctly summarized this position in his observation that "American philanthropy, as currently organized is radically dependent upon . . . 'the princely gift.' Indeed, philanthropy has probably never been organized in any other way. . . . But the price we pay for 'the princely gift' is the power of princes."[17]

Finally, philanthropy can reinforce the deficiencies of the market in the social realm. These deficiencies include both the difficulty of achieving collective goods through market mechanisms[18] and promoting the concept of the market as the preferred vehicle for social decision making. The unfettered pursuit by multiple independent actors of their individually defined social aims results in the collective goods problem described above. Championing a preferred social decision-making model can subtly (or not so subtly) shape public perceptions of the relations between the public and private sectors and options available for social agenda setting.[19]

What might be done about these inherent deficiencies of philanthropy in its pursuit of public purposes? The answer certainly does not lie in the imposition of additional stringent limitations on foundations in the form of stronger governmental regulatory control, which carries with it substantial threats of politicization and bureaucratization. Even Walzer, arguing from a socialist perspective, maintains that a good egalitarian society would include a freely operating philanthropic sector because of the important contribution philanthropy can make to pluralism and civic-mindedness.[20] Philanthropy is an essential contributor to the liberal democratic state, and remedies to its shortcomings should be sought from within rather than outside the field.

I will suggest four possible areas for exploration of ways in which philanthropy might pursue a path toward solving its collective goods problem, in place of its current tendency to reinforce the trends toward fragmentation and privatization. This could be accomplished without inflicting damage on the system of philanthropy itself.

First, the field needs to increase its self-awareness of the problems intrinsic to its own mode of social problem solving: the potential exacerbation of inequality, fragmentation, and the deficiencies of market approaches to the pursuit of collective goods. Second, there should be greater attention in donor education activities to the social implications of fundamental agenda setting, that is, critical analysis of the process by which initial foundation purposes and priorities are established, rather than just attending to issues of effectiveness in grant making. Third, philanthropy could play a much stronger role in championing the importance of the public sphere in contemporary society.[21] Fourth, philanthropy could do more to improve the public decision-making process itself—the means through which the public comprehends and addresses the vast array of decisions on social policy—such as increasing its attention to ways of improving the media and deliberative democracy.

These topics open issues for another discussion. Nevertheless, the ethical implications of the use of important private resources to accomplish vital public purposes are profound, and foundations have the opportunity to take leadership in both examining those implications and addressing them in practice.

Part Five

MORAL LEADERSHIP

Perspectives and Implications

12

EXERCISING MORAL COURAGE

A Developmental Agenda

Linda A. Hill

> Leadership is fundamentally about humanity. It is
> about morality. Your primary job as a leader is to
> see what is good for your organization, and what is
> good for the people who work for you, and to create
> something for the well-being of your fellow citizens.
> —*Franco Bernabé, former CEO of Eni,*
> *Italy's large energy-focused industrial group[1]*

If we expect managers to exercise moral agency and courage, then our first task as their educators is to keep in mind who management students really are and offer them a preview of what managerial life will really be like.[2] Our next responsibility is to provide them with the tools they will need to live consistently with their values while at the same time raising their aspirations for how business can be a positive societal force. If the surveys of M.B.A. graduates are correct, we have some distance to travel to address their developmental needs.[3] Just what are those needs? In this chapter, I elaborate on what management students need to learn based on my experience teaching in an M.B.A. program whose mission is to educate leaders who make a difference in the world.[4]

I thank Joshua Margolis, Maria Farkas, Lisa Pode, Emily Stecker, and Scott Snook for their feedback on drafts of the manuscript for this chapter.

Who Are the Management Students?

The decision to pursue a managerial career is a carefully considered one for most management students. Yet like most inexperienced managers, they are often blinded to the realities of management by their personal motivation and ambitions. They may fail to appreciate that leadership is not only about exercising authority but also about managing interdependencies. Assuming the mantle of leadership confers not only rights and privileges, but also duties and obligations associated with those interdependencies—in short, ethical considerations.

Although ethical dilemmas are the stuff of the everyday lives of leaders, management students often arrive at business school with an underdeveloped moral compass. They are largely unaware of their ethical blind spots. They see themselves as people of character who will not commit the kind of blatant wrongdoing they read about in the newspapers. But they admit they are pragmatists, not idealists.[5] They hope they can dodge ethical minefields, but they fear they will be unable to reconcile financial and ethical imperatives over the course of their careers. For them, the bottom line is just that: the bottom line. They have little idea about how to give voice to their values in the face of countervailing pressures, and even more, they are uncertain of how to change the rules of the game.[6]

Ethical judgment is learned and cultivated over the course of a career. It begins with an understanding of one's personal values. Adversity or crucibles, to use the language of Warren Bennis and Robert Thomas, are especially important to the development of an inner compass or understanding of one's values:

> The crucible experience was a trial and a test, a point of deep self-reflection that forced them to question who they were and what mattered to them. It required them to examine their values, question their assumptions, hone their judgment. And, invariably, they emerged from the crucible stronger and more sure of themselves and their purpose—changed in some fundamental way.

Leadership crucibles can take many forms. Some are violent, life-threatening events. Others are more prosaic episodes of self-doubt.[7]

As it turns out, many management students, especially those who attend leading business schools, have limited experience with adversity. For example, Sharon Parks conducted a three-year study of Harvard M.B.A. students. She found that with some notable exceptions, most in our population had been in the "flow of success," which had required of them little self-reflection about ethical matters, and hence impoverished their development of ethical judgment:

> As a group, they are highly motivated, talented, and bright. Most are graduates of the best secondary and undergraduate schools. Many of the American students, upon graduation from college, were recruited and subsequently trained by some of our most prestigious commercial and financial institutions or by the military. . . . Only a small percentage of them come from elite families, but as a group they do come predominantly from upwardly mobile middle-class backgrounds. Our society seems to work for them.
>
> From some angles of vision, these young adults obviously represent a certain sort of privilege. Yet this particular profile of young adult success seems to have a number of implications that are soberingly significant in terms of the students' potential as future managers and leaders. Specifically, because they have been in the "flow of success," many of them have had less occasion for critical reflection on self and world than others their age. Most are fully capable of critical thought and can work out a strategy within a given set of conditions. But in the absence of significant adversity and/or cross-cultural cognitive dissonance, they have had less experience than have some of their generational peers in recognizing and considering the conditions themselves—the broader social, cultural, political, and economic context within which the conditions themselves rest. Therefore, they remain more vulnerable than might be presumed to the unexamined assumptions of conventional thought and circumstance.[8]

For students like these, John Dean's memoir, a book he so aptly titled *Blind Ambition*, is a cautionary tale of how the flow of success can lead to disaster.[9] Dean served in President Nixon's administration, starting as associate deputy attorney general, moving quickly to become counsel to the president, and ending ignominiously as a convicted criminal for his participation in the Watergate cover-up. Dean's actions were not only morally wrong in themselves, but they also destroyed the career he had so ambitiously constructed. Why and how does this happen? What was it about the situation that led to Dean's demise? What was it about him? These are the questions we ask the management students to ponder.

During the course of the discussion of excerpts from Dean's memoir, the students discover it is too easy to conclude that John Dean was simply a "bad person." Much to their surprise, the vast majority of management students begin to see themselves in John Dean, a "very sobering thought" as one student put it. Like John Dean, they too aspire to climb to positions of considerable power and prestige, preferably as rapidly as possible. Like Dean, they end up recognizing how ill equipped they are to live up to the complexity and responsibility that such positions can entail. They come to see how "fast tracking"—and consequently limited opportunity to develop a moral compass—contributed to his downfall. To close the class, I share Parks's research with the students. The combination of ambition, high need for achievement, and little personal sense of what they consider right and wrong from an ethical standpoint can be a formula for disaster. It is all too easy to slide down the slippery slope of unethical behavior, even when well intentioned.[10]

Leadership—including the ethical dimension—cannot be taught, but it can be learned.[11] It is learned primarily through on-the-job experience and developmental relationships. Our responsibility as educators is to prepare students to be willing and able to take charge of what will be their life-long development. When designing our new required leadership course at Harvard, we took seriously the notion that we could not teach the M.B.A. students to lead. They had to teach themselves. We defined our role with them explicitly as providing them with the critical resources they would need to make the most of on-the-job learning experiences after leaving business school.

While most management students understand that to be effective leaders they must do a great deal of task learning throughout their careers, they often fail to realize that task learning is only half of the equation.[12] Of course, they have to acquire expertise in the technical, conceptual, and human arenas (ethical judgment is based on expertise in all three arenas). But they also have personal learning to do, that is, adopting a psychological perspective, attitudes, and values consistent with their leadership roles and responsibilities. Not only will the management students need to refine their internal gyroscopes for managing the ethical dilemmas they will inevitably encounter, they also will need to learn how to cope with the stresses and negative emotions associated with those encounters.[13] Too often we ignore the emotional challenges of leadership, but as seen in the work of Joshua Margolis and Andrew Molinsky, the capacity to manage their emotions will be critical to their success in treating others with dignity and acting ethically.[14] We should forewarn them that the personal learning can be demanding and at times traumatic.[15] They tend to downplay the self-inquiry, self-reflection, and the consequent personal transformation that personal learning requires.

Unlearning the Myths of the Inexperienced

Management students, like most new and inexperienced managers, have very incomplete and overly simplistic expectations of what it means to manage and lead.[16] In their initial conception of what it means to be a manager, they tend to think of the rights and privileges associated with the managerial role—the formal authority—rather than the duties and obligations. It is usually the power of the position that attracts them to management: "I [had] always wondered what it would be like to be in charge and get people to do things the right way," one new manager explained.

First-time managers are eager to implement their ideas about how to run an effective organization. When they start in their new positions, their primary aim is learning how to exercise their newfound authority and gain control. They erroneously believe that their formal authority will be the primary source of power on which they will rely to influence others. Many adopt a hands-on autocratic approach consistent with their initial notion of the managerial role: the manager as boss. They choose such a style not because they are eager to exercise power over people, but because they want to produce results.

Once they go into their first managerial assignment after school, they soon confront the realities of management. They find themselves enmeshed in a web of relationships with people (subordinates, bosses, peers, groups outside the organization) who make what seem like unending, often ambiguous, or conflicting demands; these demands are the source of most of the ethical dilemmas they will encounter. Consequently their daily routines will often be pressured, hectic, and fragmented and will not fit their expectations of power and control. They will soon learn that formal authority does not guarantee influence. As one manager reported in my research on the transition from individual contributor to manager, being a manager is a daunting task: "The fact is that you really are not in control of anything. The only time I am in control is when I shut my door, and then I feel I am not doing the job I'm supposed to be doing, which is being with the people." Many soon-to-be managers do not realize the profound insight of this statement. In fact, many management students consider "dealing with the people problems" to be a poor use of time and effort. Until they give up the myth of authority for the reality of interdependencies, they will not be able to lead effectively or ethically.

In my own research, it is the ethical dilemmas that arise from these interpersonal relationships that literally keep new managers up at night.[17] Managers are surprised, for example, to discover how stressful and difficult the "burdens of leadership" can be. It is not easy to be "responsible for somebody's life," when it can mean withholding the bonus of a poorly performing employee who hopes to send his child to private school or identifying outsourcing opportunities as part of a dramatic and much-needed turnaround. Thus, management students need to learn that ethical dilemmas are part of the routine practices of leadership. They are characterized less frequently by illegal actions like those of John Dean or the highly visible issues that end up in the *Wall Street Journal* than by concerns about more everyday relationships and responsibilities (making trade-offs among the priorities and concerns of the many constituencies on which managers are interdependent). Joshua Margolis and Andrew Molinsky have reported that "necessary evils," harms done in order to deliver a presumed greater good, are frequent occurrences in organizations.[18]

The importance of being able to manage a complex web of relationships increases as individuals advance in their organizations. The higher up managers move, the more complex their interdependencies with others are going to become and thus the more perplexing their ethical dilemmas. As John Kotter, a prominent leadership researcher noted, ethical judgments include both the interpersonal and the systemic:

> Effective leadership in top posts in modern organizations demands something far more complex than the desire to "do good." It requires sound moral judgment. This means, first of all, a keen sense of all the people or groups who are affected by the firm's operations and decisions. Many will be obvious (e.g., large customers or stockholders), but some won't be (e.g., people living downstream from a plant that uses river water). It requires an appreciation of what their interests are, not just in a narrow economic sense, but in the broadest sense possible. And it requires the capacity to estimate not only the first- or even second-order consequences for all these people of decisions made by the firm, but even third, fourth and beyond.
>
> All the great business and government leaders that I have known have these capacities. And in some sense, this is what most clearly differentiates them from their talented, but more naive or cynical colleagues.[19]

How individuals frame ethical dilemmas affects their capacity to manage them effectively. When they view them as exceptional and apart from business as usual, they are less likely to see their actions as expressions of their values. Instead they are treated as aberrations that are keeping them from their "real work." Mary Gentile wrote:

> One of our observations thus far has been that often folks do not see ethical or moral dilemmas as part of doing business. That is, they think of themselves as just working along, minding their own business, when all of a sudden an ethical challenge inserts itself into the flow of their lives. It threatens to derail them. . . . It was interesting how often folks said "I never expected to encounter this," even when the dilemma they were describing was a classic business ethics situation.
>
> Framing the situation in this way can sometimes have the effect of disabling folks. They feel as if they have stepped out of their competent, action-oriented work identities and somehow a more personal part of themselves is being engaged. This kind of compartmentalization can mean that folks who typically have no problem articulating a contrary position on a problem may silence themselves when it comes to ethical arguments.[20]

Deciding the right thing to do *and* getting it done will be harder than most management students realize.[21] Ethical dilemmas are just that—dilemmas; they usually involve weighing competing factors that make establishing what is right and wrong patently clear. While the tale of John Dean is viewed by the management students as a story about why "ethics pays," they are all too aware that "ethics does not always pay" or pay enough. Economic self-interest and ethical commitment are compatible in some situations but conflicting in others.[22] As Lynn Sharp Paine describes, there is a "zone of acceptability" within which companies operate (Figure 12.1): "In a world that expects companies to create wealth while conducting themselves as moral actors, managers will need to practice what might be termed 'center-driven' decision-making. This term refers

Figure 12.1. Zone of Acceptability

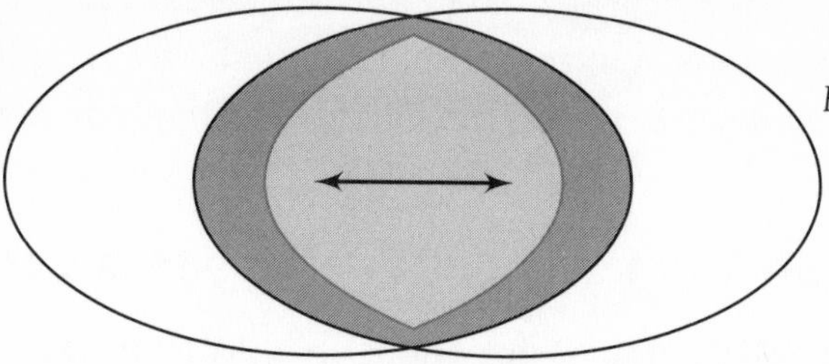

Source: Lynn Sharp Paine, *Value Shift: Why Companies Must Merge Social and Financial Imperatives to Achieve Superior Performance* (New York: McGraw-Hill, 2003), 61. Used by permission of The McGraw-Hill Companies.

to the area of overlap between ethics and economics. . . . Put simply, they will need to marry NPV (net present value) with MPV (moral point of view) analyses."[23]

Management students need help figuring out where the zone of acceptability begins and ends in their given context. They need help figuring out what to do when there is a disconnect between NPV and MPV. Acting consistently with one's values requires moral imagination and courage. If we do not help management students confront the realities of leading, they will not feel a sense of moral agency; rather they will feel like "a puppet in a puppet show," as one individual reported to me.

James Rest identified four categories or levels of moral reasoning: (1) moral awareness or recognition that a situation raises ethical issues, (2) moral decision making or determining what course of action is ethically sound, (3) moral intent or identifying which values should take priority in the decision, and (4) moral behaviors or acting on ethical decisions.[24] Too often we stop short in our education efforts. Attention is focused mostly on moral awareness and decision making at the expense of moral intent and especially moral behavior. I would contend that this is one of the primary reasons many management students feel inadequately prepared to confront ethical dilemmas. Therefore, the moral developmental agenda for management students must include an understanding of how power and influence dynamics work in organizations: the routine flow of ethical dilemmas that arise from interdependencies in organizational life, the limitations of formal authority, and how to acquire power and exercise influence to get things done effectively and ethically.

Doing the Right Thing: Powerlessness Corrupts

Consistent with their misconceptions about what it really means to manage and lead, management students also tend to have a limited understanding of how power and influence dynamics work within organizations.[25] They fail to recognize that political conflict is at the heart of organizational life and that it is not necessarily a negative force. Power and conflict are often the engine for creativity, innovation, and ethical outcomes in organizations.[26] Management students need to learn how to cultivate their own power and exercise influence if they have any hope of being effective and moral leaders.

Too many people become disillusioned and cynical early in their careers about the realities of organizational life. Often it is the most principled among them—those who would never "stoop to playing office politics"—who fall the deepest into apathy and fear. There are, of course, organizations with poisonous political climates filled with plotters and schemers who have little regard for the harm they do. There is, of course, some truth to the popular adage that "nice guys finish last." We all know of unethical or incompetent people who get ahead. And, of course, we all know that "power corrupts."

As individuals progress in their careers and begin to acquire power, they must be vigilant about not abusing it. Indeed, much has been written about how power can corrupt. For instance, David Kipnis studied the "metamorphic effect" power can have on people. He found that the frequent use of power can lead to abuses of power because the power holder increasingly exaggerates his or her own self-worth and devalues the worth of those whom he or she has influenced successfully. Their self-aggrandizement can lead power holders to take liberties that would otherwise be unthinkable. As

David Kipnis pointed out, this psychological phenomenon has been the basis of many famous Greek tragedies:

> The Greek dramatists were particularly sensitive to the fate of persons who were at the high tide of their power and status. . . . The viewer is confronted with the image of great and powerful rulers transformed by their prior successes so that they are filled with a sense of their own worth and importance—with "hubris"—impatient of the advice of others and unwilling to listen to opinions that disagree with their own.[27]

We need only watch the nightly news to find accounts of executives who have engaged in unethical behavior as a result, in part, of their hubris.

In fact, however, powerlessness also corrupts.[28] People with power can shape their environment, whereas the powerless are destined to be molded and constrained by theirs. How often have we heard of people who believed they had no choice but to engage in some unethical act because they did not have the power to change the way things were usually done. Certainly we need to help emerging leaders determine the ethical course of action in a given situation, but also we need to help them figure out how to implement this solution.[29]

Organizations are inherently political entities, and managers who ignore or fail to understand how power and influence work in organizations find it difficult to be effective and ethical on the job. Therefore, it is critical that we help management students develop their diagnostic skills to assess power dynamics in a given situation. They need to learn to think of themselves as anthropologists, eagerly collecting and analyzing data about who really has power and how things really get done in an organization. Power dynamics are a part of the very fabric of an organization, and this is too often taken for granted. Discovering these dynamics requires reading between the lines of the explicit formal structure, policies, and procedures to figure out their informal counterparts. In order to do this, management students need to develop their observation, listening, inquiring, and empathic skills.

These skills will help students anticipate and prepare for the inevitable political conflicts that will arise as they try to behave effectively and ethically. Their analyses of political dynamics will help them understand and predict how people will think and act in response to their decisions and actions. In making sense of situations in which there are perceived conflicts of interests, most people have a tendency to view their own behavior as reflecting honorable motives and rigorous analysis and others' behavior as evidence of self-interested motivation, excessive personal ambition, or irrationality.[30] Careful diagnosis can keep individuals from attributing malicious intentions to those opposing them in an honest conflict, especially when "they win." It encourages them to test their assumptions and adopt a more objective perspective—a critical ingredient for exercising moral judgment. Among other things, management students need to understand: (1) What is power? (2) Why is political conflict inevitable in organizations? (3) Where does power come from, and how can it be acquired? Although it is beyond the scope of this chapter to go into much detail about these specific issues, Table 12.1 provides a broad overview of the perspective presented, summarizing the key concepts shared with students about power and influence.

Many management students erroneously believe that the powerful are those in more senior positions, because they equate power simply with formal authority.[31] Initially, they do not understand that there are many sources of power, and that their responsibilities now include developing their own power and influence in order to manage key interdependencies and relationships.[32] In our required leadership course, the students are provided with a power and influence framework for thinking about how they can learn and contribute to the organization, while acquiring diverse sources of power through experiences (such as stretch assignments) and key relationships (such as sponsors and mentors).[33]

Table 12.1. The Reality of Managing and Leading

	Myth	*Reality*
Basic concept	Authority	Interdependency
Source of power	Formal authority	"Everything but"
Key players	Direct reports	Includes those outside your formal authority
Desired outcomes	Control, compliance	Commitment, judgment
Key competencies	Technical	Technical, human, conceptual

Source: Linda Hill, *Becoming a Manager: How New Managers Master the Challenge of Leadership* (Boston: Harvard Business School Press, 2003), 268.

As managers, they will be responsible for addressing the inevitable trade-offs and for equitably negotiating and integrating their team's interests with those of others, such as superiors or peers in other functional or geographical areas. Rather than engage in political infighting, as much as possible effective managers seek creative win-win solutions and avoid participating in zero-sum negotiation behavior. Once managers begin to understand the political dynamics in their organizations and the degree of interdependence they have with others inside and outside those organizations, they realize that their source of power is not formal authority as they expected but rather, in the words of one manager, "everything but."

This can be a very unsettling revelation. Discovering that formal authority is a limited source of power, new managers must find other ways to get things done. They may tell or ask others to do something, but even their direct reports may not respond. All influential managers have power, but not all powerful managers have influence. What does it take to convert power into influence? The answer is twofold: (1) to be willing and able to empower those on whom they are dependent and (2) to be willing and able to cultivate networks of mutually beneficial relationships with those on whom they are dependent.[34] Initially, the idea of sharing power seems anathema to many of the management students, as it suggests an abrogation of responsibility and control. But a paradox of power that I hope they will discover is that sharing power actually increases a manager's power and hence "control," since it increases commitment. Empowerment promotes trust and thereby increases a manager's ability to exercise influence. By sharing their power, managers can build bridges with others to motivate and inspire them to pursue mutually agreed-on goals. In addition, the excessive use of power often diminishes a person's actual influence, for it can lead to abuses of power. The very powerful may increasingly exaggerate their own self-worth and denigrate others; their self-aggrandizement can cause them to take liberties and exploit others in ways that would otherwise be unthinkable. This in turn causes others to distrust them, which slowly but surely erodes their capacity to influence them. By adopting a policy of empowering others—leveling the "power playing field"—managers can check this insidious process.[35]

The bottom line is that political conflict is at the heart of how organizations function. All managerial decisions involve trade-offs and the need to balance complex and ambiguous issues—those legitimate disagreements about what is best for the organization—that generate political conflict. These conflicts are often ethical dilemmas about both the means and ends of how they do their work. The challenge is not to eliminate conflict but to harness it to the appropriate ends.

The Role of Business as a Societal Force

We need to help management students begin the journey of self-discovery and understand how things really get done in organizations if we expect them to exercise moral agency. Moreover, we need to raise their aspirations if we expect them to enact lives of moral courage. We must urge them to think deeply about the role of business in society and what they hope to accomplish over the course of their business careers. To quote Sharon Parks's research again, an interpersonal orientation to ethics is much more accessible to our M.B.A. students than a systemic one:

Again, their [M.B.A. students] sense of power as individuals (or at least their sense of power as individuals in the role of CEO) seems to be constrained by the limits of an interpersonal imagination; they express little sense of power or imagination in relationship to the socioeconomic fabric of their wider public life. As their generation stands on the threshold of significant new challenges from Asian economies, a unifying Europe, and a reordering of the former Soviet political and economic order, these students await initiations into a more adequate and precise articulation of the dynamics and goals of democratic capitalism. They appear to engage business in an interpersonal mode, as yet unaware of the systemic reach of their personal energy, both actual and potential.[36]

The debate rages on about just what is the appropriate role of business. We should encourage students to familiarize themselves with all sides of the argument.[37] To provide some counterweight to the more prevalent view that "business is simply about making profits," it is important to show them role models of successful executives who hold a broader vision for the corporate world. Among others, we rely on the case of Franco Bernabé, the executive quoted at the beginning of this chapter, to integrate the lessons of moral agency and courage and demonstrate the power of moral leadership.[38] Bernabé is very clear about who he is and what he hopes to accomplish. He understands how power dynamics work and how to exercise influence. He is willing and able to cope with the emotional turmoil and sacrifices of living his values.

In his six-year tenure as CEO of Eni, Italy's energy-focused industrial group, Bernabé led the transformation of the organization from a debt-ridden, government-owned, and politically controlled entity into a competitive and profitable publicly traded corporation focused on energy production. He sold off two hundred companies, dismissed hundreds of managers, installed radically new business structures and systems, and began to create a culture of "clarity, transparency, and rigor." He led this turnaround under the most daunting of circumstances. Several months after his surprise promotion to CEO, much of Eni's senior management team was arrested and jailed on corruption charges. The company's former chairman committed suicide in prison. During the investigation, even Bernabé was accused of taking a substantial bribe. The charge turned out to be based on nothing more than rumor, but as Bernabé recalled, he felt like there was "an atomic bomb exploding on [his] head." Even his mother questioned his innocence.

What explains Bernabé's success? That is the question with which students grapple. They find this case inspirational in part because Bernabé does not fit the mold of the classic charismatic leader. He is unprepossessing and shy to the point of appearing remote. For ten years, he kept a low profile (and was even demoted twice) and then, when opportunity knocked, he seized power more boldly than anyone might have expected.

There are many explanations, but perhaps more than anything else, Bernabé's power to lead comes from within. As he says, "If you are in a very difficult situation . . . what you need is a moral compass to indicate the way. In my case, the compass was my conscience. I decided to do what my conscience considered the right thing to do even if that was very risky." Bernabé's moral compass was pointed toward humanity and justice, and while he did seek consultation from others in difficult times, he ultimately made all important decisions alone so as not to be buffeted by the needs, agendas, or emotions of others.

Students wonder how such a strong moral compass is developed, and according to Bernabé, the answer is *solitudine*, the Italian word for the state of being alone. Although he is reticent about his personal life, Bernabé does share a seminal story from his youth, when he spent his weekends volunteering at an institution for the elderly who had no family or financial support. He saw suffering, loneliness, and injustice there, and he became committed to righting such wrongs. At Eni, he found honest, hard-working employees were having their professional pride stolen by a corrupt minority. And this act of betrayal, he believed, could destroy the whole country. Although all might not agree with his strategic goals for Eni, few ever questioned his motives. Bernabé's idealism and patriotism have earned him widespread respect and are perhaps his greatest sources of power.

As the students learn, Bernabé goes on to face other challenges, and at times he loses the battle, but he never loses what matters most to him: his integrity.[39] How can management students lead a life committed to principles, steadfast in their convictions, and passionate about their endeavors—so much so that they persist despite demotion and despite dangers to their livelihood, their families and perhaps their lives—yet be sufficiently open to learn from others, to be able to acknowledge their own fallibility? Researchers find this to be one of the most difficult competencies to develop. Karl Weick called it "the attitude of wisdom," the ability to commit yourself totally to a plan of action while being open to your own fallibility.[40] All management students must resolve this tension in their own way if they expect to successfully confront the mundane and profound ethical dilemmas of business life.

Moral Leadership: Expanding the Zone of Acceptability

Moral leadership is more than avoiding ethical wrongdoing; it is about making a positive difference in others' lives and in our communities. As Paine points out, the zone of acceptability is context specific and dynamic. In this regard, it is useful to expose management students to leadership challenges and opportunities across the globe, for the practice of capitalism and beliefs about the role of business vary across countries.[41] If we are to meet the mission of my institution, to educate leaders who make a difference in the world, our ultimate challenge is to expand the M.B.A. students' zone of acceptability (Figure 12.2): "An excellent company will be concerned about the consequences of its actions, the rights of its constituencies, and its contributions to the broader community. The challenge is

Figure 12.2. Expanding the Zone of Acceptability

Ethically Sound
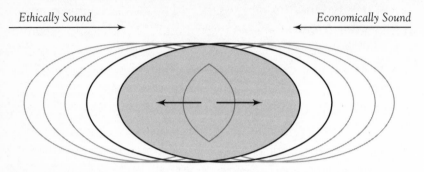
Economically Sound

Source: Paine, *Value Shift* (New York: McGraw-Hill, 2003). Used by permission of The McGraw-Hill Companies.

thus to figure out a practical path of action that will enable the company to remain competitive while respecting the rights of others and minimizing the collateral harms caused by its activities."[42]

Maria Farkas and I are developing a series of teaching materials about the evolution of the new black capitalist class in South Africa.[43] The cases will encourage management students to consider how business can be used as a tool to address societal inequities. For many South African business leaders (of all races and ethnicities), the crucible of apartheid and the ensuing transformation of their country have prepared them to engage some of the most intractable ethical challenges of our times. They define these challenges as being at the very heart of business leadership.

The individuals we are writing about are all revolutionaries in the true sense of the word; they were actively involved, at great personal risk, in the overthrow of apartheid. They were detained, beaten, and had loved ones killed during the struggle. Like their first black president, they see business as a catalyst for social change. Nelson Mandela made the following remarks at the 1997 national conference of the African National Congress, Mafikent, Northwest:

The wider, and critical struggle of our era, [is] to secure an acceptance and actualisation of the proposition that while capital might be owned privately, there must be an institutionalised system of social accountability for the owners of capital. In this context, it may very well be that the success of our strategy for BEE will address not only the objective of the creation of a non-racial South Africa. It might also be relevant to the creation of the system according to which the owners of capital would, willingly, understand and accept the idea that business success can no longer be measured solely by reference to profit. According to this thesis to which we must subscribe, success must also be measured with reference to a system of social accountability for capital, which reflects its impact both on human existence and the quality of that existence.

Their ambition is to become embodiments of Mandela's vision. The cornerstone of their leadership approach is the advancement of marginalized groups through employment, skill transference, and leadership development. For example, Iqbal Survé, a physician by training, was a youth leader in the antiapartheid struggle. He and his wife were very active in the rehabilitation of torture victims, for which he received an award from Amnesty International. In 1995, Survé founded an investment holding company, Sekunjalo (which means "Now Is the Time"). Concerned that black economic empowerment (the term coined to describe, among other things, policies and practices to increase black ownership, leadership, and employment in the economy) was enriching only the few, he and other activist friends founded their company with a clear "manifesto" to improve the lives of the previously disadvantaged. Irene Charnley spent the apartheid years as a tenacious negotiator in the male-dominated National Union of Mineworkers (NUM).[44] The years spent across the negotiating table from the captains of industry, wrestling from them control of black mineworker pension funds, prepared Charnley for her next step as a board member of Johnnic, the NUM's first postapartheid direct investment. Charnley was instrumental in negotiating the complex deals that turned Johnnic from a passive investment holding company into a telecommunications conglomerate. Subsequently she became an executive at MTN, Johnnic's cellular company, where, among other things, she championed international expansion of the company and negotiated a deal for MTN's senior managers to purchase an 18 percent share in MTN. Charnley's story reminds us of the burdens of leadership and what it takes to be a change agent in a hostile environment:

> There were black people in the organization whose confidence had been completely destroyed. People withheld information. People wanted them to fail. They were undermined around every corner. You had to be strong to put up with that stuff. And the black employees knew they could stand up and challenge things because they had the support of the board. They knew that I was there to monitor, police, and make sure that things happened. Because when you are out there, it's like being in the battlefield and you are absolutely alone, and there is nobody protecting your back. But, if you know you are out in the battlefield and there is somebody behind you who is able to spot that person who is going to kill you, then it is better. . . . I said to people, "You have to work extra hard, and if you're a woman you have to work even harder. When people sleep, you work. You have to be the best. People must respect you. And they must be oblivious to your color because of what you deliver. When you don't deliver, they say black people are incompetent. We've had good black people who have quit because they couldn't take the pressure."

For her accomplishments, Charnley was named one of the most powerful women in the world by *Fortune Magazine*. Both Sekunjalo and MTN have won awards for their achievements with regard to their social agendas.

These cases are replete with controversies and lessons. They focus on the key dilemmas these executives have faced in implementing their vision to use business as a catalyst for social change while simultaneously creating value for shareholders (for example, how to gain control with limited capital, how to develop their own business leadership capabilities, how to implement affirmative action policies expeditiously without alienating their white work-force, and how to have the broadest impact on society through choices about the scale and scope of their operations). The South African experience is unique in some respects, but South African executives deal each day with challenges familiar to those operating in emerging markets: limited capital and talent, poor infrastructure, and weak or still-forming state institutions, and large populations of the very poor.[45]

As Survé observed, the competitive pressures of the global econ-omy and the sociopolitical challenges of the African continent demand that businesspeople focus on survival issues such as cash flow and efficiency so that "there [is] limited headspace to spare for broader visions." Our subjects recognize that many of their business colleagues believe their focus on social concerns adds costs to their corporations and compromises their competitive advantage. But during the antiapartheid struggle, these individuals were inspired by what they witnessed firsthand: the power of leaders using ideals to capture the hearts and minds of diverse people, to achieve the mir-acle of the new South Africa. Answering Mandela's charge drives them day and night. As Survé continued:

> Thinking about whether we are able to actually achieve this keeps me awake at night. Because for me, it's not about becoming rich. That's nonsense. That's not me. I can easily walk away from that sort of thing. The thing is, what legacy are we leaving in terms of Black Economic Empowerment in this country? That's what's important.
>
> In my view, it's criminal if you know something is wrong, and you don't correct it. For those who never knew what was wrong, especially whites, I can forgive them because they didn't know what was wrong. We, who have come from our background, we know what's on the other side of this line. We know the issues in the town-ships. We know the poverty that's out there. We know that there are no jobs in this country. We know that there is an enormous skill space possible, that people, if given the opportunities, will grab it. Those of us who know, we have to create that for them, create that

environment of opportunity. No white company's going to do that. Never. We, as a black company, and as a particular type of black company, have to do that. If we don't do that, then we are no different than the others.

I'm not saying don't get rich. I'm saying, you'll get even more wealth here if you do this the right way. We shouldn't be blindly driven in a direction. There are enough models worldwide to show that this can work if we apply our minds to it.

The stories of the emerging black business leaders in South Africa ask the management students to question their assumptions about business and capitalism. As corporations grow in size and influence, public pressure increases for business leaders to consider the impact of their actions on pressing societal concerns. What role could and should business play in communities and nations? At first, we conceived of this case series as being about the move from "activist to capitalist." But as our case protagonists have helped us understand, their challenge is to ensure that their core values and professional identity are not transformed, but rather that they transform others' values and identities instead. Only time will tell if their vision of a "gentler capitalism" is realistic and if these leaders can remain authentic to their principles of humanism and activism.

To date, we have taught only the case about Irene Charnley. The specific action question with which the students must struggle is whether she should link the achievement of affirmative action objectives to compensation. When faced with the question of what to do about increasing the numbers of blacks in business in the post-apartheid context, the students find themselves unable to figure out just what the right thing to do is, nonetheless how to implement it. The majority of students are on principle against affirmative action; it is inconsistent with their belief in meritocracy. But given the history of apartheid, most recognize that without some sort of formal intervention, blacks will remain a "permanent underclass," as many of them put it. The discussions became quite emotional and uncomfortable as faculty and students were confronted with a vexing ethical dilemma. This is not surprising since the subtext of the debates included differing notions about human nature and the limitations and appropriate power of markets, governments, shareholders, and managers. Most found themselves questioning basic and deeply held assumptions. It was reported that many students found the day's discussion to be one of the most important and honest they had had during their time at the School. That said, it was also reported that some professors and students found the class discussion too emotionally charged and the resulting conflict destructive.

We have much to learn about engaging students on the systemic issues of exercising moral leadership, where normative questions about the ends of capitalism are brought into sharp relief. As faculty we must be willing and able to enter into these very murky and complex waters if we want to raise the moral courage and fortitude of our students.[46] Like the reality the management students will encounter when they leave school, ethical concerns must be integrated throughout the curriculum, for the myth of the amoral business leader is just that—a myth. At the very least, I hope the students leave with neither a cynical nor naive but rather a realistic sense of what it means to be a business leader. Along with that realistic perspective should come a number of questions worthy of continual consideration and dialogue over the course of their careers:

- Who do I really work for?
- What are my rights and privileges?
- What are my duties and obligations?
- How do I assess my impact (intended and unintended)?
- What really matters to me?
- Who has benefited from business? Who should?

13

PERSPECTIVES ON GLOBAL MORAL LEADERSHIP

Kirk O. Hanson

As other contributions to this book demonstrate, moral leadership is difficult to define and harder to understand. It is even more difficult to understand moral leadership on the global stage, as it responds to problems that transcend the boundaries of a single nation or culture.

Religious figures, particularly the Roman Catholic popes, leading Muslim imams, and influential rabbis have spoken to the world regarding love and compassion, economic and social justice. Moral leadership by religious leaders, based on a single sect's moral tenets, is perhaps more easily understood. But global moral leadership implies advocacy of values that are universal—truly global—and not the beliefs of a single sect or the values of a single culture.

What Is Global Moral Leadership?

An understanding of the phenomenon of global moral leadership, and how it differs from ethical leadership in general, and even from moral leadership in the context of a single culture, will be an essential part of the study of moral leadership in coming years.

At its essence, moral leadership is about calling others to critical ethical values and the behaviors that emanate from them. In my view, moral leadership is distinct from ethical leadership addressed elsewhere in this book. Ethical leadership is about leading an organization or people to accomplish its core purposes using ethical means. Moral leadership is about leading an organization or people to accomplish an explicitly moral purpose. Moral leadership usually involves transformation, for example, by introducing a people to a new moral value or calling out behavior from the group consistent with a moral value that is not currently practiced.

Fortunately, ethical leaders are common in most societies. Universities, businesses, governments, and nonprofits are led by individuals of conscience who ensure that the operations of their organization are marked by ethical behavior. Ethical leadership in organizations is needed in every society. Corrupt leadership or leadership indifferent to its effects on people is a blight on any society.

Moral leadership may be rarer. We can easily identify Mahatma Gandhi as a moral leader, a man who called his country to religious tolerance and nonviolence and called England to respect for self-determination in India. We also identify Martin Luther King Jr. as a moral leader and reflect on his call for "this nation to rise up and live out the true meaning of its creed: 'We hold these truths to be self evident: that all men are created equal.'"[1] Both Gandhi and King are clearly moral leaders in their own societies. One can also say their influence later transcended their own cultures and societies. But it is harder to identify individuals who transcend individual cultures during their own lifetimes and call people across the globe to the adoption and enactment of universal moral values.

Who Is a Global Moral Leader?

There are some individuals who clearly fit the definition of global moral leader. U.S. President Woodrow Wilson's fourteen points and his creation of the League of Nations mark him, a world political leader, as a global moral leader. That his leadership did not bring his own nation into the League does not diminish his importance and his influence on the creation of the United Nations in 1945. Nobel Peace laureates Oscar Arias and Mikhail Gorbachev were current political leaders who addressed conflicts that transcended their own nations.

Other global moral leaders have never held public office. Mother Teresa, Nobel Peace Prize recipient in 1979, communicated strongly to the entire world that compassion for the poorest and sickest among us is a basic moral duty. She clearly was a global moral leader, though her influence was small at first and grew slowly as her congregation of nuns and her reputation spread.

Some organizations have demonstrated global moral leadership, though one must acknowledge that there is usually an individual leader behind the organizational structure. Among such entities are the International Committee of the Red Cross, which has been honored three times with Nobel Peace Prizes (1917, 1944, 1963), and more recently Médecins Sans Frontières (Doctors Without Borders), which won the Nobel Peace Prize in 1999. In honoring the International Campaign to Ban Landmines in 1997, the Nobel Committee also honored its founder Jody Williams. Each organization championed values of basic human respect and reverence for each human being.

The emerging phenomenon of the individual celebrity as global moral leader is particularly interesting case. Almost fifty years ago, the United Nations Children's Fund (UNICEF) named U.S. entertainer Danny Kaye as its first "Goodwill Ambassador." Kaye and his dozens of successors have traveled the globe drawing attention to the humanitarian and social objectives of UNICEF, UNESCO, UNDP, the United Nations Population Fund, and other United Nations entities that have named Goodwill Ambassadors. In the United States, it has not been uncommon for a Hollywood celebrity to be the spokesperson for a foundation dedicated to eradicating a particular disease or to the compassionate and symbolic "adoption" of foreign children.

In the past six years, the music star Bono has raised the role of celebrity as global moral leader to new prominence. Focusing first on Third World debt relief, Bono traveled the world, meeting with heads of state and promoting forgiveness of the debt of the poorest countries on the globe. From 2004, Bono's attention was focused on

Africa and its many needs. James Traub, writing in the *New York Times Magazine*, reflected:

> Why Africa? Why not, say global warming? Part of the answer is happenstance: Africa is what Bono got swept up into. But Africa, or so Bono feels, needs what only a certain kind of world figure can give—a call to conscience, an appeal to the imagination, a melody or a lyric you won't forget. The cause of ending extreme poverty in Africa speaks to Bono's prophetic impulse. . . . Among his best work is the rallying cry. He often says, "My generation wants to be the generation that ended extreme poverty." There's not much evidence that this is so; but Bono has helped make it so, in part by repeating such resonant phrases.[2]

Wangari Maathai is a Kenyan environmentalist who was awarded the 2004 Nobel Prize for Peace. Breaking with tradition, the Nobel committee awarded Maathai the prize for her advocacy of the concept that "peace on earth depends on our ability to secure our living environment. . . . More than simply protecting the existing environment, her strategy is to secure and strengthen the very basis for ecologically sustainable development."[3] Maathai's Green Belt movement, founded over thirty years earlier, had fought to head off desertification, but through education, family planning, nutrition, and the fight against corruption, she had led the way to peace, according to the committee.

Maathai's grassroots environmental and educational efforts, over a long period of time, had introduced new international understandings of development, human rights, and peace. Her influence could be detected throughout Africa in national policies and the advocacy efforts of others. Is Maathai, not previously a global figure like a Bono, a global moral leader? Her case may remind us that leadership comes in many forms and that global moral values evolve over time.

Characteristics of a Global Moral Leader

One way to understand the phenomenon of global moral leadership is to identify key characteristics that help us identify such leadership and may guide us to further study. Global moral leaders demonstrate several key characteristics:

- A personal commitment to a set of values that transcend a single nation or culture
- The world's (or a region's) need for a key moral value that is not currently widely held or acted on and the leader's insight that this value can be enacted
- The courage to articulate and promote that value, often at significant risk to oneself
- The communication and other skills to promote that value effectively

On Values

Any moral leader needs a personal commitment to values. Global moral leaders need a commitment to values that transcend national boundaries and serve all the world's peoples. But it is often difficult to define which values fit this definition. It is clear that dominant ethical values differ from culture to culture. Where do global moral leaders themselves look to shape their own values and identify the universal values they will promote?

On the World's Needs

The world today faces many critical needs. How does a global moral leader choose the need to address and the moral value to promote? Do moral leaders choose their mission, or is their mission thrust on them by circumstance and encounter with those in need?

On Courage

How does a moral leader marshal the courage to champion a cause or a value? What traits are needed? What disciplines? What support does an individual need to take this path? When a great price is to be paid for being a moral leader, how does that leader react? As Aung San Suu Kyi sits in her home in Burma, what strengths and what support does she need to continue her vigil for democracy and the rule of law there? What courage did she need to resist the temptation to visit her dying husband in England when she knew she would not be allowed to return to Burma?

On the Skills Needed to Be a Moral Leader

What skills are needed to be an effective moral leader, a global moral leader? Presumably most moral leaders need a highly developed communication capability; though Gandhi was not a particularly effective public speaker, he was charismatic in other respects. Moral leaders, one hypothesizes, communicate in several ways. What organizational and strategic skills are needed for success as a global moral leader? To what extent does context determine the skills needed for success?

What Are Global Moral Values?

One of the most difficult challenges is defining the global moral values to be pursued by global moral leaders, values that serve the interests and welfare of all peoples. To many, moral values are culturally bound and relative to one's context. The whole concept of global moral leadership challenges that belief.

Global moral standards have been articulated throughout history by religions, though sometimes with disastrous results. Wars of religion and sectarianism have plagued the world, as rival claims to universality have led only to conflict. Nonetheless, Christianity has made specific attempts to be ecumenical (worldwide), holding councils of all bishops under the rubric of universality. Between 1962 and 1965, the Second Vatican Council of the Roman Catholic church sought to speak of universal values not only to the Roman Catholics of the world, but all peoples. Many give high marks to Pope John Paul II for articulating strongly the values of self-determination and religious freedom and give him credit as the most important force in ending the Soviet Union.

Roman Catholic popes have influenced the development and acceptance of global moral values in another way, through the promulgation of social encyclicals addressing economic and social problems of the modern era. Pope Leo XIII issued the first, "Rerum Novarum," in 1892. His successors through John Paul II have continued this tradition, with John Paul adding "Laborem Exercens" (1981), "Sollicitudo Rei Sociales" (1987), and "Centesimus Annus" (1991).[4] These encyclicals promoted the rights of labor, humane standards for development, ethical capitalism, and the need to make the poor a priority.

In recent years, the fourteenth Dalai Lama, the leader of Tibetan Buddhism, has become a major global moral authority, in part because of his exile after the Chinese takeover of Tibet in 1959, and his stateless identity. While he retained his role as a deposed head of state and advocate for Tibetan independence, the Dalai Lama also began to write and speak to all peoples on basic human values. His published volumes and global appearances made him among the most visible world's moral leaders, and his theology has been widely accepted by Buddhists and non-Buddhists alike.

The modern secular history of universal moral standards dates from 1948 and the adoption by the new United Nations of the Universal Declaration of Human Rights (UDHR).[5] The document, prepared by a commission chaired by American Eleanor Roosevelt, represented a great victory. The commission had convinced Christian and Muslim nations, as well as dictatorships and new democracies in Asia, to accept a common definition of the rights of human beings.

Since 1948, a body of international treaties, conventions, and other forms of agreement have made the rights enumerated in the UDHR more detailed and more binding on nations and peoples. Human rights law has become a global focus. UN councils and directorates have been established to promote various aspects of the UDHR. Similarly, human rights concepts have been embodied in the charters of institutions of international law such as the International Court of Justice.

Perhaps the greatest failing of the UDHR is that it touches only lightly on which government entities, institutions, and individuals have the duties that correspond to rights enumerated in the UNDHR. In the Preamble, the UDHR states that "every individual and every organ of society . . . shall strive by teaching and education to promote respect for these rights and freedoms, and by progressive measures, national and international, to secure their universal and effective recognition and observance." But who really has the responsibility to protect all humans from torture and slavery? Who has the responsibility to ensure freedom of movement, individual consent to marriage, or freedom of religion? Who has the responsibility to fulfill the promise in Article 25 that everyone has a right to "a standard of living adequate for health and well-being"?

Over the past twenty-five years, several attempts have been made to expand our understanding of global moral values by articulating a set of responsibilities to match the rights in the UDHR. In 1997, a group of former presidents and prime ministers known as the InterAction Council[6] drafted, with the help of Roman Catholic theologian Hans Kung, a proposed "Universal Declaration of Human Responsibilities."[7] This proposed document, written to parallel the UDHR, identified the responsibilities of individuals and governments, stating, for example, that "every person . . . has a responsibility to treat all people in a humane way (Article 1)."

While the document attracted modest acclaim, it was opposed and its adoption eventually blocked by advocates of human rights.

These human rights advocates were concerned that more than fifty years of careful legal development to support the UDHR would be weakened by parallel attention to a new document, no matter how well intentioned. Human rights advocates supported the principle that responsibilities were also important, but believed that well-articulated human rights principles were the best protection for the world's peoples.

Since the founding of the InterAction Council in 1985, four other associations, comprising primarily former heads of state and dedicated to the promotion of global moral principles, have been established: the Council of Women World Leaders,[8] the Club of Madrid,[9] the International Ethical, Political and Scientific Collegium,[10] and the Global Leadership Foundation.[11] Each promotes slightly different global moral principles in a slightly different manner, but each seeks to be a global moral actor and to enable the former political leaders who make up their membership to be global moral leaders.

Other contributions to the definition of global moral standards have also emerged. Beginning in 1901, the Nobel Prize Committee of Sweden awarded the Nobel Prize for Peace.[12] The recipients of this prize, which include Woodrow Wilson, Ralph Bunche, and Mikhail Gorbachev, each demonstrated a commitment to peace and to moral values considered universal. Some operated on a global stage, others on a domestic stage to settle conflicts that threatened global peace and security. The Nobel Prize for Peace has often articulated a new global value, as demonstrated in the 2004 award to Wangari Maathai.

A new source of global moral standards in the 1990s was voluntary global codes promulgated by a wide array of institutions, from the United Nations itself to various nongovernmental organizations that serve as advocates for particular causes or peoples. Among the most prominent of these are the UN Global Compact,[13] the Caux Principles,[14] and the to-be-developed ISO 26000,[15] which would address the concerns of many. Each of these codes defines a set of global moral values and key behaviors that embody them. Some of those promulgating these codes have standing in existing organizations like the United Nations, but many others are self-appointed advocates for particular values or moral perspectives.

The debate over which values are truly universal faces yet another hurdle. There is an active debate about whether moral leadership is possible, or even desirable, on the global stage. Articulate voices reason that great nations such as the United States, their leaders and citizens, must pursue the nation's self-interest, not a set of global moral values.

Former U.S. Secretary of State Madeline Albright has suggested that both global moral values and self-interest have a role in foreign policy and that the only question for a foreign policymaker is which comes first. Either self-interest is the basis of foreign policy but at times constrained by morality, or morality is the primary guide and is constrained at times by self-interest.[16]

Conclusion

With globalization will come an increasing discussion of universal moral values and the global moral leadership that would lead us to those values. Global moral leaders who will champion these moral values will include sitting political leaders, former heads of state, nongovernmental organizations, individual activists, and even celebrities. These global moral leaders will have significant impact on the political and social structure of the globe. They will be important political as well as moral actors. Their role, their identity, and their characteristics must be understood.

Notes

Introduction

1. Linda Klebe Treviño and Gary R. Weaver, *Managing Ethics in Business Organizations: Social Scientific Perspective* (Stanford: Stanford University Business Press, 2003), xiii.
2. George Bush, remarks on corporate responsibility, Regent Wall Street Hotel, New York, July 9, 2002, http://www.whitehouse.gov/news/releases/ 2002/07/ 20020709—4.html. For similar views, see Lynnley Browning, "M.B.A. Programs Now Screen for Integrity, Too," *New York Times,* September 15, 2002, B4; Breffni X. Baggot, "Money, Ethics and the M.B.A.," *New York Times,* August 23, 2002, A16; Thomas K. Lindsay, "What Does It Profit a Man to Gain an MBA?" *Los Angeles Times,* November 18, 2002, A13.
3. Tim Carvell, "Endpaper," *New York Times Magazine,* June 6, 2004, sec. 6, 114.
4. Bruce McCall, "Bush, Cheney Blister Shady Business Ethics," *New Yorker,* July 29, 2002, 39.
5. Warren G. Bennis, "Leadership Theory and Administrative Behavior: The Problem of Authority," *Administrative Science Quarterly* 4 (1959): 259. For similar assessments, see Warren G. Bennis and Burt Nanus, *Leaders: The Strategies for Taking Charge* (New York: HarperCollins, 1985): Joseph C. Rost, *Leadership for the Twenty-First Century* (Westport, Conn.: Praeger, 1991), 4–6.
6. Joanne B. Ciulla, "Leadership Ethics: Mapping the Territory," in Joanne Ciulla (ed.), *Ethics: The Heart of Leadership* (Westport, Conn.: Quorum Books, 1998), 3.
7. Ann Colby and William Damon, *Some Do Care: Contemporary Lives of Moral Commitment* (New York: Free Press, 1992), 3, 29; Ciulla, "Leadership Ethics," 3–6; Linda Klebe Treviño and Gary R. Weaver, *Managing Ethics in Business Organizations* (Stanford: Stanford University Business Press, 2003), xiv, 300, 331; Rabindra N. Kanungo and Manuel Mendonca, *Ethical Dimensions of Leadership* (Thousand Oaks, Calif.: Sage, 1996), 10.

8. Rost, *Leadership for the Twenty-First Century*, 7.
9. Lynn Sharp Paine, *Value Shift: Why Companies Must Merge Social and Financial Imperatives to Achieve Superior Performance* (New York: McGraw-Hill, 2003), 4.
10. Rost, *Leadership for the Twenty-First Century*, 38.
11. Rost, *Leadership for the Twenty-First Century*, 18–22.
12. Ciulla, "Leadership Ethics," 9, discussing Bass and Stogdill's *Handbook on Leadership*.
13. Al Gini, "Moral Leadership and Business Ethics," in Ciulla, *Ethics*, 27, 36.
14. Linda Klebe Treviño, Michael Brown, and Laura Pincus Hartman, "A Qualitative Investigation of Perceived Executive Ethical Leadership: Perceptions from Inside and Outside the Executive Suite," *Human Relations* 56, 1 (2003): 23–26.
15. James McGregor Burns, *Leadership* (New York: HarperCollins, 1978), 19.
16. John Gardner, *The Moral Aspect of Leadership* (Washington, D.C.: Independent Sector, 1987), 9, 10, 13.
17. Gardner, *The Moral Aspect of Leadership*, 3. See also Adel Safty, "Moral Leadership: Beyond Management and Governance," *Harvard International Review* 25, 3 (2003): 84, 85.
18. Rost, *Leadership for the Twenty-First Century*, 18, 165.
19. Warren G. Bennis, *Why Leaders Can't Lead: The Unconscious Conspiracy Continues* (San Francisco: Jossey-Bass, 1989), 18.
20. Al Gini, "Moral Leadership: An Overview," *Journal of Business Ethics* 16, 3 (1997): 323, 325. See also Joanne B. Ciulla," What Is Good Leadership?" Kennedy School of Government, Center for Public Leadership, Working Papers, Spring 2004, 1, http://www.ksg.harvard.edu/leadership/workingpapers. html; Barbara Kellerman, *Bad Leadership: What It Is, How It Happens, Why It Matters* (Boston: Harvard Business School Press, 2004), 11–12, 30.
21. Kellerman, *Bad Leadership*, 12.
22. Michael E. Brown and Linda K. Treviño, "Is Values-Based Leadership Ethical Leadership?" in Stephen W. Gilliland, Dirk D. Steiner, and Daniel P. Skarlicki (eds.), *Emerging Perspectives on Values in Organizations* (Greenwich, Conn.: Information Age Publishing, 2003), 151, 153.
23. Philip Selznick, *Leadership in Administration: A Sociological Interpretation* (New York: HarperCollins, 1957), 121–122.
24. J. C. Collins and Jerry I. Porras, *Built to Last: Successful Habits of Visionary Companies* (New York: Business, 1997); Thomas Chappell, *Managing Upside Down: The Seven Intentions of Values-Centered Leadership* (New York: Morrow, 1999); Michael Fullan, *Leading in a Culture of Change* (San Francisco: Jossey-Bass, 2001), 28; Brown and Treviño, "Is Values-Based Leadership Ethical Leadership?" 154.
25. Thomas H. Peters and Robert P. Waterman Jr., *In Search of Excellence: Lessons from America's Best-Run Companies* (New York: HarperCollins, 1982), 245.

26. Peters and Waterman, *In Search of Excellence*, 218, 284, 287.

27. American Management Association, *2002 Corporate Values Survey* (New York: American Management Association, 2002), http://www.amanet.org/research/pdfs/2002_corp_value.pdf; Brown and Treviño, "Is Values-Based Leadership Ethical Leadership?" 155, 165.

28. Rost, *Leadership for the Twenty-First Century*, 92.

29. Noel M. Tichy and Andrew R. McGill (eds.), *The Ethical Challenge: How to Lead with Unyielding Integrity* (San Francisco: Jossey-Bass, 2003), 9 (stood the test of time); Tom Morris, *If Aristotle Ran General Motors: The New Soul of Business* (New York: Holt, 1997), 122 (kindness, concern, respect, honor, strength); Joseph L. Badaracco and Richard R. Ellsworth, *Leadership and the Quest for Integrity* (Boston: Harvard Business School Press, 1999), 100 (honesty and fairness); John Gardner, *On Leadership* (New York: Free Press, 1990), 77 (honor, integrity, tolerance, mutual respect); John Dalla Costa, *The Ethical Imperative: Why Moral Leadership Is Good Business* (Cambridge, Mass.: Perseus Publishing, 1998), 155, 276, 282 (compassion, fairness, honesty).

30. Dalla Costa, *The Ethical Imperative*, 214, 240–248 (moral excellence, moral imagination, moral courage); Bill George, *Authentic Leadership: Rediscovering the Secrets to Creating Lasting Value* (San Francisco: Jossey-Bass, 2003), 17, 20 (moral compass).

31. George, *Authentic Leadership*, 17–18 (lead with heart, be true to core values); Dalla Costa, *The Ethical Imperative*, 89, 155 (not a luxury, value integrity); Morris, *If Aristotle Ran General Motors* (climate of goodness); Sidney Harman, *Mind Your Own Business: A Maverick's Guide to Business, Leadership and Life* (New York: Doubleday, 2003), 62 (evangelist); Tony Manning, *Discover the Essence of Leadership* (Cape Town: Zebra, 2002), 40 (trust yourself); Tichy and McGill, *The Ethical Challenge*, 9 (quoting Jack Welch on doing everything right).

32. Morris, *If Aristotle Ran General Motors*; Wess Roberts, *Leadership Secrets of Attila the Hun* (New York: Time Warner, 1985).

33. Morris's *If Aristotle Ran General Motors* has one of the widest selection of quotations. The fortune cookie is on p. 208.

34. Joseph L. Badaracco, *Leading Quietly: An Unorthodox Guide to Doing the Right Thing* (Boston: Harvard Business School Press, 2002), 34–42, 124.

35. See Tichy and McGill, *The Ethical Challenge*, 117, 282; Badaracco, *Leading Quietly*, 37; George, *Authentic Leadership*, 127; Tom Chappell, *The Soul of a Business: Managing for Profit and the Common Good* (New York: Bantam, 1993).

36. Tichy and McGill, *The Ethical Challenge*, 83.

37. Dalla Costa, *The Ethical Imperative*, 320.

38. Tichy and McGill, *The Ethical Challenge*, 142.

39. Brown and Treviño, "Is Values-Based Leadership Ethical Leadership?" 155–161.

40. In 1913, JC Penney established a code, the first to do so. Treviño and Weaver, *Managing Ethics in Business Organizations*, xviii.

41. Ethics Officer Association, *Business Ethics: Historical Perspective*, http://www.eoa.org/AboutEOA.asp; Paine, *Value Shift*, 5.

42. Dalla Costa, *The Ethical Imperative*, 66.

43. U.S. Sentencing Commission, *Sentencing Guidelines for Organizations* (1991).

44. Paine, *Value Shift*, 2; Treviño and Weaver, *Managing Ethics in Business Organizations*, xviii; Ethics Resource Center, *National Business Ethics Survey 2003* (Washington, D.C.: Ethics Resource Center, 2003), 5–8, http://www.ethics.org/nbes2003/.

45. Paine, *Value Shift*, 2; Ethics Officer Association, *History of the EOA*, http://www.eoa.org/AboutEOA.asp.

46. Harold R. Bowen, *Social Responsibilities of the Businessman* (New York: HarperCollins, 1953). For overviews, see Douglas M. Branson, "Corporate Social Responsibility Redux," *Tulane Law Review* 76 (2002): 1207, 1208–1225; Elisabet Garriga and Domènec Melé, "Corporate Social Responsibility Theories: Mapping the Territory," *Journal of Business Ethics* 53, 1–2 (2004): 51–71, 52–59; Antonio Tencati, Francesco Perrini, and Stefano Pogutz, "New Tools to Foster Corporate Socially Responsible Behavior," *Journal of Business Ethics* 53, 1–2 (2004): 173, 174–176.

47. See Business for Social Responsibility, http://www.basr.org.

48. David Vogel, *The Market for Virtue: The Potential and Limits of Corporate Social Responsibility* (Washington, D.C.: Brookings Institution Press, 2005), 6.

49. Bowen, *Social Responsibilities of the Businessman*.

50. PriceWaterhouse Coopers Management Barometer Survey, May 2003, available in Institute for Global Ethics Newsline, June 9, 2003, http://www.globalethics.org/newsline/members/pastissue2.tmpl?issued=6/9/2003.

51. Gallup Poll, available in Institute for Global Ethics Newsline, August 11, 2003, http://www.globalethics.org/newsline/members/pastissue2.tmpl?issued=8/11/2003.

52. Roper Center for Public Opinion Research, Program on International Policy Attitudes, University of Maryland, June 4, 2004, available in Westlaw Poll database; Claudia H. Deutsch, "New Surveys Show That Big Business Has a P.R. Problem," *New York Times*, December 9, 2005, C1.

53. Roper Center for Public Opinion Research, Peter D. Hart Research Associates, August 29, 2002, available in Westlaw Poll database.

54. 2002 CBS News Poll, available at Institute for Global Ethics Newsline, July 15, 2002, http://www.globalethics.org/newsline/members/pastissue2.tmpl?issued=7/15/2002http://www.globalethics.org/newsline/members/pastissue2.tmpl?issued=7/15/2002.

55. Roper Center for Public Opinion Research, Los Angeles Times Poll, April 1, 2004, available in Westlaw Poll database.

56. Ethics Resource Center, *National Business Ethics Survey*, 16, 51.

57. Career Builder, *Life at Work 2004*, careerbuilder.com, available at Institute for Global Ethics Newsline, May 17, 2004, http://www.globalethics.org/newsline/members/pastissue2.tmpl?issued=5/17/2004.

58. Treviño and Weaver, *Managing Ethics in Business Organizations*, 305.

59. Paine, *Value Shift*, 58.

60. Ethics Resource Center, *National Business Ethics Survey 2003*, iii, 27, 33.

61. Ethics Resource Center, *National Business Ethics Survey 2003*, iii, 43.

62. American Management Association, May 2002 survey, reported in Business Ethics Newsline, available at http://www.globalethics.org/newsline/members/pastissue2.tmpl?issued=5/8/2002.

63. Arthur P. Brief, Janet M. Dukerich, Paul R. Brown, and Joan F. Brett, "What's Wrong with the Treadway Commission Report? Experimental Analysis of the Effects of Personal Values and Codes of Conduct on Fraudulent Financial Reporting," *Journal of Business Ethics* 15 (1996): 183–198.

64. Peter S. Cohan, *Value Leadership: The Seven Principles That Drive Corporate Value in Any Economy* (San Francisco: Jossey-Bass, 2004), 4.

65. Amartya Sen, "Does Business Ethics Make Economic Sense?" *Business Ethics Quarterly* 3 (1993): 46, 48; Kenneth J. Arrow, *Social Choice and Individual Values* (New Haven, Conn.: Yale University Press, 1970).

66. Christopher Stone, *Where the Law Ends: The Social Control of Corporate Behavior* (New York: Waveland, 1991); Kenneth Arrow, "Social Responsibility and Economic Efficiency," *Public Policy* (1973): 313–317. Lawrence E. Mitchell and Theresa A. Gabaldon, "If I Only Had a Heart: Or, How Can We Identify a Corporate Morality," *Tulane Law Review* 76 (2002): 1645, 1655.

67. Vogel, *The Market for Virtue*, 8–9, 166–173.

68. Morris, *If Aristotle Ran General Motors*, 127, 134, 157.

69. The error in judgment is a phrase applied to Salomon Brothers' mishandling of a trader who submitted false bids. For a thoughtful discussion, see Paine, *Value Shift*, 10–12. Other commonly cited examples include fraud by Enron and Tyco and unsafe products by Johns Manville (asbestos) and H. R. Robbins (Dalkon Shields). See Saul W. Gellerman, "Why 'Good' Managers Make Bad Ethical Choices," *Harvard Business Review* (July-August 1986): 85; Dalla Costa, *Ethical Imperative*, 115.

70. Tichy and McGill, *Ethical Challenges*, 84.

71. Peters and Waterman, *In Search of Excellence*, 279. See also Robert C. Solomon, *Ethics and Excellence: Cooperation and Integrity in Business* (New York: Oxford University Press, 1993), 44, 47.

72. Robert Slater, *Jack Welch on Leadership* (New York: McGraw-Hill, 2004), 50, 55. For a discussion of Welch's ethical record, see 133–139; Brown and Treviño, "Is Values-Based Leadership Ethical Leadership?" 166; Gellerman, "Why 'Good' Managers Make Bad Ethical Choices," 90.

73. See Slater, *Jack Welch on Leadership*; Brown and Treviño, "Is Values-Based Leadership Ethical Leadership?"; Gellerman, "Why 'Good' Managers Make Bad Ethical Choices."

74. Stephen J. Garone, *The Link Between Corporate Citizenship and Financial Performance* (New York: Conference Board, 1999), 3; Vogel, *The Market for Virtue*, 4, 29–33; Sandra A. Waddock and Samuel B. Graves, "The Corporate Social Performance-Financial Performance Link," *Strategic Management Journal* 18, 4 (1997): 303–304.

75. Waddock and Graves, "The Corporate Social Performance-Financial Performance Link," 304.

76. Paine, *Value Shift*, 52–53. See also Garone, *The Link Between Corporate Citizenship and Financial Performance*, 6; Garriga and Melé, "Corporate Social Responsibility Theories," 51; Joshua Daniel Margolis and James Patrick Walsh, *People and Profits? The Search for a Link Between a Company's Social and Financial Performance* (Mahwah, N.J.: Erlbaum, 2001); Vogel, *The Market for Virtue*, 23.

77. Waddock and Graves, "The Corporate Social Performance-Financial Performance Link," 304.

78. Margolis and Walsh, *People and Profits?*

79. Elena G. Procario-Foley and David F. Bean, "Institutions of Higher Education: Cornerstones in Building Ethical Organizations," *Teaching Business Ethics* 6, 1 (2002): 101–102.

80. See Treviño and Weaver, *Managing Ethics*, 233, and studies cited in Paine, *Value Shift*, 42–44; see also Kim S. Cameron, David Bright, and Arran Caza, "Exploring the Relationships Between Organizational Virtuousness and Performance," *American Behavioral Scientist* 47, 2 (2004): 766; and Tom R. Tyler and Steven L. Blader, "Social Identity and Fairness Judgments," in Dirk D. Steiner and Daniel P. Starlicki (eds.), *Emerging Perspectives on Values in Organizations* (Greenwich, Conn.: Information Age Publishing, 2003), 67, 69–73.

81. Treviño and Weaver, *Managing Ethics*, 233; Paine, *Value Shift*, 45; Robert B. Cialdini, "Social Influence and the Triple Tumor of Organizational Dishonesty," in David M. Messick and Ann E. Tenbrunsel (eds.), *Codes of Conduct: Behavioral Research into Business Ethics* (New York: Russell Sage Foundation, 1996), 53–56.

82. Garone, *The Link Between Corporate Citizenship and Financial Performance*, 11; Cialdini, "Social Influence and the Triple Tumor of Organizational Dishonesty," 56.

83. Tyler and Blader, "Social Identity and Fairness Judgments," 67–79; Paine, *Value Shift*, 46.

84. Paine, *Value Shift*, 45–46; Cameron, Bright, and Caza, "Organizational Virtuousness and Performance," 773.

85. Garone, *The Link Between Corporate Citizenship and Financial Performance*, 11; Paine, *Value Shift*, 45; Cameron, Bright, and Caza, "Exploring the Relationships Between Organizational Virtuousness and Performance," 770–783.

86. Shari Caudron, "Volunteerism and the Bottom Line," *Industry Week* (February 1994): 13–18; Craig Smith, "The New Corporate Philanthropy," *Harvard Business Review* 74 (May-June 1994): 14; Barbara A. Bartkus, Sara A. Morris, and Bruce Seifert, "Governance and Corporate Philanthropy: Restraining Robin Hood?" *Business and Society* 41, 3 (2002): 319; Cathleen Wild, *Corporate Volunteer Programs: Benefits to Business* (New York: Conference Board, 1993), 20, 21; William J. Holstein, "Office Space: Armchair M.B.A.: The Snowball Effect of Volunteer Work," *New York Times*, November 21, 2004, sec. 13; Garone, "The Link Between Corporate Citizenship and Financial Performance," 11; Jan Larson, "Sweet Charity," *Marketing Tools Magazine* (May 1995): 69; Bill Shaw and Frederick R. Post, "A Moral Basis for Corporate Philanthropy," *Journal of Business Ethics* 12, 10 (1993): 745; Nancy L. Knauer, "The Paradox of Corporate Giving: Tax Expenditures, the Nature of the Corporation, and the Social Construction of Charity," *DePaul Law Review* 44 (1994): 1, 57–60.

87. Charles J. Formbrun, *Reputation: Realizing Value from the Corporate Image* (Boston: Harvard Business School Press, 1996); Grahame Dowling, *Creating Corporate Reputations: Identity, Image, and Performance* (New York: Oxford University Press, 2001); Paine, *Value Shift*, 48–49; Robert B. Cialdini, "Social Influence and the Triple Tumor Structure of Organizational Dishonesty," in David M. Messick, John M. Darley, and Tom R. Tyler (eds.), *Social Influences on Ethical Behavior in Organizations* (Mahwah, N.J.: Erlbaum, 2001). See also Jennifer Reese, "America's Most Admired Corporations," *Fortune*, February 8, 1993, 44; Paine, *Value Shift*, 48–49.

88. Environics International, *The Millennium Poll on Corporate Social Responsibility, 1999*, http://www.environicsinternational.com/news_archives>http://;www.environicsinternational.com/news_archives MPExecBrief.pdf, March 5, 2002. See also Paine, *Value Shift*, 82, 111.

89. Hill and Knowlton, *2001 Corporate Citizen Watch Survey* (New York: Hill and Knowlton, 2001) (one-third to two-thirds consider citizenship); "Caring in the Community," *Management Today* (March 1995): 19–20; Ronald Alsop, "The Best Corporate Reputations in America," *Wall Street Journal*, September 23, 1999, B1, B22 (one-quarter recall boycott).

90. Paine, *Value Shift*, 49; Jonathan M. Karpoff and John R. Lott Jr., "The Reputational Penalty Firms Bear from Committing Criminal Fraud," *Journal of Law and Economics* 36 (1993): 757.

91. Karpoff and Lott, "The Reputational Penalty Firms Bear from Committing Criminal Fraud."

92. Paine, *Value Shift*, 49; Cameron, Bright, and Caza, "Exploring the Relationships Between Organizational Virtuousness and Performance," 773; Holstein, "The Snowball Effect of Volunteer Work."

93. Paine, *Value Shift*, 30; Richard S. Tedlow and Wendy K. Smith, "James Burke: A Career in American Business" (Harvard Business School: Case No. 389–177, 390–030, 1989); Dalla Costa, *The Ethical Imperative*, 217.

94. Paine, *Value Shift*, 49; Michael D. Watkins and Max H. Bazerman, "Predictable Surprises: The Disasters You Should Have Seen Coming," *Harvard Business Review* (March 2003): 72.

95 Paine, *Value Shift*, 30.

96. Paine, *Value Shift*, 76.

97. Vogel, *Market for Virtue*, 4.

98. For examples, see Amar Bhide and Howard H. Stevenson, "Why Be Honest If Honesty Doesn't Pay," *Harvard Business Review* (September-October 1990): 121.

99. Michael Useem, *The Inner Circle of Large Corporations and the Rise of Business Political Activity in the United States and the United Kingdom* (New York: Oxford University Press, 1984), 121–126; Usha C. V. Haley and Stephen A. Stumpf, "Corporate Contributions as Managerial Masques: Reframing Corporate Contributions as Strategies to Influence Society," *Journal Management Studies* 28, 5 (1991): 485–494.

100. Mary Lyn Stoll, "The Ethics of Marketing Good Corporate Conduct," *Journal of Business Ethics* 41, 1–2 (2002): 121, 124.

101. For Aristotle, see *Nichomachean Ethics*, Book 2, Sec. 5–6. For recent work on virtue ethics, see Alaisdair MacIntyre, *After Virtue: A Study of Moral Theory* (South Bend, Ind.: Notre Dame University Press, 1981).

102. Thomas J. Sergiovanni, *Moral Leadership: Getting to the Heart of School Improvement Authentic Leadership* (San Francisco: Jossey-Bass, 1999), 17; Tichy and McGill, *The Ethical Challenge*, 142. See also Gail Sheehy, *Character: America's Search for Leadership* (New York: Morrow, 1988); Robert Coles, *Lives of Moral Leadership* (New York: Random House, 2000); Colby and Damon, *Some Do Care*.

103. John M. Doris, *Lack of Character: Personal and Moral Behavior* (Cambridge: Cambridge University Press, 2002), 93; Philip E. Tetlock, "Accountability: A Social Check on the Fundamental Attribution Error," *Social Psychology Quarterly* 48 (1985): 227–236; Lee Ross, "The Intuitive Psychologist and His Shortcomings: Distortions in the Attribution Process," in Leonard Berkowitz (ed.), *Advances in Experimental Social Psychology* (Orlando, Fla.: Academic Press, 1967), 10.

104. David L. Rosenhan, "Moral Character," *Stanford Law Review* 27 (1975): 925, 926. See also Walter Mischel, *Personality and Assessment* (Hoboken, N.J.: Wiley, 1968), 23–26.

105. Doris, *Lack of Character*, 24–25; Lee Ross and Richard E. Nisbet, *The Person and the Situation* (Philadelphia: Temple University Press, 1991); Deborah L. Rhode, "Moral Character as a Professional Credential," *Yale Law Journal* 94 (1985): 556–562; Walter Mischel and Yuichi Shoda, "A Cognitive-Affective Theory of Personality: Reconceptualizing Situations, Dispositions, Dynamics, and Invariance in Personality Structure," *Psychological Review* 102 (1995): 246–286; M. David Ermann and Richard J. Lundman, *Corporate and Governmental Deviance: Problems of Organizational Behavior in*

Contemporary Society (New York: Oxford University Press, 2001); Ronald R. Sims, "The Challenge of Ethical Behavior in Organizations," *Journal of Business Ethics* 11, 7 (1992): 505; Cialdini, "Organizational Tumor Social Influence and the Triple Tumor of Organizational Dishonesty."

106. James R. Rest (ed.), *Moral Development: Advances in Research and Theory* (New York: Praeger, 1994), 26–39.

107. Treviño and Weaver, *Managing Ethics*, 171; Kenneth D. Butterfield and others, "Moral Awareness in Business Organizations: Influences of Issue-Related and Social Contextual Factors," *Human Relations* 53 (2000): 981, 982; Thomas M. Jones, "Ethical Decision Making by Individuals in Organizations: An Issue-Contingent Model," *Academy of Management Review* 16 (1991): 366, 368, 379. For an overview, see Lynn L. Dallas, "A Preliminary Inquiry into the Responsibility of Corporations and Their Officers and Directors for Corporate Climate: The Psychology of Enron's Demise," *Rutgers Law Journal* 35 (2003): 1, 10–11.

108. Butterfield and others, "Moral Awareness in Business Organizations," 1001.

109. William Damon, *The Moral Advantage: How to Succeed in Business by Doing the Right Thing* (San Francisco: Berrett-Koehler, 2004), 3.

110. Robin Derry, "Moral Reasoning in Work-Related Conflicts," in William C. Federick and Lee E. Preston, *Research in Corporate Social Performance and Policy* 9 (Greenwich, Conn.: 1987), 25, 333 (one-third of managers and professionals); Robert L. Nelson, "Ideology, Practice, and Professional Autonomy: Social Values and Client Relationships in the Large Law Firm," *Stanford Law Review* 37 (1985): 503, n. 32 (finding that only 16 percent of attorneys recalled refusing a case for ethical reasons).

111. Jones, "Ethical Decision-Making by Individuals in Organizations," 376.

112. Nancy Eisenberg, *Altruistic Emotion, Cognition, and Behavior* (Mahwah, N.J.: Erlbaum, 1986), 30–56; Samuel P. Oliner and Pearl Oliner, *Altruistic Personality: Rescuers of Jews in Nazi Europe* (New York: Free Press, 1988), 113, 165–167, 173–175, 228; Martin L. Hoffman, "Empathy and Prosocial Activism," in Nancy Eisenberg, Janusz Reykowski, and Ervin Staub (eds.), *Social and Moral Values: Individual and Societal Perspectives* (Mahwah, N.J.: Erlbaum, 1989); Martin L. Hoffman, "Empathy, Its Limitations, and Its Role in a Comprehensive Moral Theory," in William M. Kurtines and Jacob Gewirtz (eds.), *Morality, Moral Behavior, and Moral Development* (Hoboken, N.J.: Wiley, 1984), 283, 285–287.

113. Albert Bandura, "Moral Disengagement in the Perpetration of Inhumanities," *Personality and Social Psychology Review* 3 (1999): 193.

114. See sources cited in Deborah L. Rhode, *Pro Bono in Principle and in Practice* (Stanford, Calif.: Stanford University Press, 2005), 53–65. For socialization, see Joan E. Grusec, "The Socialization of Altruism," in Nancy Eisenberg (ed.), *The Development of Prosocial Behavior* (Orlando, Fla.: Academic Press, 1982); Virginia A. Hodgkinson and others, *Giving and Volunteering in the United States* (Washington, D.C.: Independent Sector, 1996), 127. For

exposure to injustice, see Richard J. Bentley and Luana G. Nissan, *Roots of Giving and Serving: A Literature Review Studying How School-Age Children Learn the Philanthropic Tradition* (Indianapolis: Indiana University Center on Philanthropy, 1996), 9; Alfie Kohn, *The Brighter Side of Human Nature: Altruism and Empathy in Everyday Life* (New York: Basic Books, 1990), 71. For religious and ideological commitments, see Colby and Damon, *Some Do Care*, 78, 276–279. For political and ethical commitments, see Eva Fogelman, *Conscience and Courage: Rescuers of Jews During the Holocaust* (New York: Random House, 1994), 253–270; Eleanor Brown, "The Scope of Volunteer Activity and Public Service," *Law and Contemporary Problems* 62 (1999): 27, 35; Hodgkinson and others, *Giving and Volunteering in the United States*, 12–13, 87–88.

115. Craig E. Johnson, *Meeting the Ethical Challenges of Leadership: Casting Light or Shadow* (Thousand Oaks, Calif.: Sage, 2004), 70 (quoting Dunlop).

116. John A. Byrne, *Chainsaw: The Notorious Career of Al Dunlop in the Era of Profit-at-Any-Price* (New York: HarperBusiness, 1999), 153. See also Kellerman, *Bad Leadership*, 130–137.

117. Brown and Treviño, "Is Values-Based Leadership Ethical Leadership?" 163.

118. Ronald R. Sims and Johannes Brinkmann, "Enron Ethics (Or: Culture Matters More Than Codes)," *Journal of Business Ethics* 45 (2003): 243, 247. See Bethany McLean and Peter Elkind, *Smartest Guys in the Room: The Amazing Rise and Scandalous Fall of Enron* (New York: Portfolio, 2003).

119. Sims and Brinkmann, "Enron Ethics," 251–253; Dallas, "A Preliminary Inquiry," 53.

120. Donald C. Douglas Langevoort, "The Organizational Psychology of Hyper-Competition: Corporate Irresponsibility and the Lessons of Enron," *George Washington Law Review* 70 (2002): 968, 970.

121. Lawrence Kohlberg, Charles Levine, and Alexandra Hewer, *Moral Stages: A Current Formulation and a Response to Critics* (New York: Karger, 1983); June L. Tapp and Lawrence Kohlberg, "Developing Senses of Law and Legal Justice," *Journal of Social Issues* 27, 2 (1971): 65, 68–69.

122. For different levels, see James Weber, "Managers' Moral Reasoning: Assessing Their Responses to Three Moral Dilemmas," *Human Relations* 43 (1990): 687, 689; Michael Bommer, Clarence Gratto, Jerry Gravander, and Mark Tuttle, "A Behavioral Model of Ethical and Unethical Decision-Making," *Journal of Business Ethics* 6 (1987): 265, 268. For individuals' poor understanding of their own reasoning, see Doris, "Lack of Character," 141.

123. Robert Jackall, *Moral Mazes: The World of Corporate Managers* (New York: Oxford University Press, 1988), 6.

124. Claudia H. Deutsch, "My Big Fat C.E.O. Paycheck," April 3, 2005, sec. 3, 1, 12; John Cassidy, "The Greed Cycle: How the Financial System Encouraged Corporations to Go Crazy," *New Yorker*, September 23, 2002, 68.

125. David Skeel, *Icarus in the Boardroom: The Fundamental Flaws in Corporate America and Where They Came From* (New York: Oxford University Press,

2005), 152–155; Cassidy, "Greed Cycle," 70; Jeff Madrick, "Economic Scene: Where Economists Stand, or Don't Stand, on the Issue of Corporate Scandals," *New York Times,* October 28, 2004, C2; Michael Jensen and Joseph Fuller, "Just Say No to Wall Street: Courageous CEOs Are Putting a Stop to the Earnings Game and We Will All Be Better Off for It," *Journal of Applied Corporate Finance* 14 (2002): 41. For a general critique of executive compensation, see Lucian Bebchuk and Jesse M. Fried, *Pay Without Performance: The Unfulfilled Promise of Executive Compensation* (Cambridge, Mass.: Harvard University Press, 2004). Michael C. Jensen, "How Stock Options Reward Managers for Destroying Value and What to Do About It," Harvard NOM Research Paper No. 04-27; Social Science Research Network eLibrary, http://papers.ssrn.com/abstract+48040, 2001.

126. Cassidy, "Greed Cycle," 76; James Surowiecki, "The Financial Page: Perk Hogs," *New Yorker,* June 14, 2004, 68.

127. Patrick McGeehan, "Listing Perks, But Not as an Endangered Species," *New York Times,* April 3, 2005, sec. 3, 12; Andrew Ross Sorkin, "Tyco Ex-Chief Is Humbled, But Unbowed," *New York Times,* January 16, 2005, A1, A21 (quoting Kozlowski).

128. See Deborah L. Rhode, *In the Interests of Justice* (New York: Oxford University Press, 2000), 171; Lisa G. Lerman, "Blue Chip Bilking: Regulation of Billing and Expense Fraud by Lawyers," *Georgetown Journal of Legal Ethics* 12 (1999): 205, 259–262; Susan Koniak, "When Did Overbilling Become a Habit?" *New York Times,* May 2, 1998, A15.

129. Surowiecki, "The Financial Pages: Perk Hogs," 68. For a general account of the cumulative effects of dishonesty, see Sissela Bok, *Lying: Moral Choice in Public and Private Life* (New York: Pantheon Books, 1978).

130. Treviño and Weaver, *Managing Ethics in Business Organizations,* 275–276, 285–286; James C. Wimbush and Jon M. Shepard, "Toward an Understanding of Ethical Climate: Its Relationship to Ethical Behavior and Supervisory Influence," *Journal of Business Ethics* 13 (1994): 637, 641; Tom R. Tyler and Steven I. Blader, "Social Identity and Fairness Judgments," in Gilliland, Steiner, and Starlicki, *Emerging Perspectives on Values in Organizations,* 67, 69–73.

131. Langevoort, "The Organizational Psychology of Hyper-Competition," 971; Ray F. Baumeister, Todd F. Heatherton, and Dianne M. Tice, "When Ego Threats Lead to Self-Regulatory Failure: Negative Consequences of High Self-Esteem," *Journal of Personality and Social Psychology* 64, 1 (1993): 141.

132. See Martin E. P. Seligman, *Learned Optimism: How to Change Your Mind and Your Life* (New York: Pocket Books, 1998), 100–112; Max H. Bazerman, *Judgment in Managerial Decision Making,* 3rd ed. (Hoboken, N.Y.: Wiley, 2002), 37–39; David M. Messick and Max H. Bazerman, "Ethical Leadership and the Psychology of Decision Making," *Sloan Management Review* 37, 2 (1996): 9; David M. Messick and John M. Darley, "How Organizations Socialize Individuals into Evildoing," in David M. Messick and

Ann E. Tenbrunsel (eds.), *Codes of Conduct: Behavioral Research into Business Ethics* (New York: Russell Sage Foundation, 1996), 13, 16–25; Barry M. Staw, "Knee Deep in the Big Muddy: A Study of Escalating Commitment to a Chosen Course of Action," *Organizational Behavior and Human Performance* 16 (1976): 27; Langevoort, "The Organizational Psychology of Hyper-Competition," 974.

133. See the sources cited in the previous note. Kimberly D. Krawiec, "Accounting for Greed: Unraveling the Rogue Trader Mystery Norms Theory," *Oregon Law Review* 17 (2000): 309, 310.

134. The classic account is Leon Festinger, *A Theory of Cognitive Dissonance* (Stanford, Calif.: Stanford University Press, 1957), 128–134. For more recent accounts, see Eddie Harmon-Jones and Judson Mills (eds.), *Cognitive Dissonance: Progress on a Pivotal Theory in Social Psychology* (Washington, D.C.: American Psychological Association, 1999).

135. Messick and Bazerman, "Ethical Leadership and the Psychology of Decision Making," 76; M. R. Banaji, M. Bazerman, and D. Chugh, "How (Un)Ethical Are You?" *Harvard Business Review* 81, 12 (2003): 56–64.

136. For overviews, see Augusto Blasi, "Bridging Moral Cognition and Moral Action: A Critical Review of the Literature," *Psychological Bulletin* 88, 1 (1980): 1, 37–41; Dallas, "A Preliminary Inquiry," 18.

137. Rest, *Moral Development*, 32–33.

138. See Colby and Damon, *Some Do Care*, 307; Rhode, *Pro Bono in Principle and in Practice*, 61–62, 65.

139. Treviño and Weaver, *Managing Ethics in Organizations*, 181; James R. Rest and Darcia Narvaez, *Moral Development in the Professions* (Mahwah, N.J.: Erlbaum, 1994).

140. John M. Darley and C. Daniel Batson, "From Jerusalem to Jericho: A Study of Situational and Dispositional Variables in Helping Behavior," *Journal of Personality and Social Psychology* 27 (1973): 100.

141. Stanley Milgram, *Obedience to Authority: An Experimental View* (New York: HarperCollins, 1974). For an overview of the Milgram work and its relevance for lawyers, see David Luban, "The Ethics of Wrongful Obedience," in Deborah L. Rhode (ed.), *Ethics in Practice: Lawyers' Roles, Responsibilities, and Regulation* (New York: Oxford University Press, 2000), 95–97, 102–105.

142. Arthur G. Miller, *The Obedience Experiments: A Case Study of Controversy in Social Science* (New York: Praeger, 1986). See Doris, *Lack of Character*, 39–50; Luban, *The Ethics of Wrongful Obedience*, 97.

143. See David Luban, Chapter One, this volume.

144. John Braithwaite, *Crime, Shame and Reintegration* (Cambridge: Cambridge University Press, 1989), 147.

145. John M. Darley and Bibb Latane, "Bystander Intervention in Emergencies: Diffusion of Responsibility," *Journal of Personality and Social Psychology* 8 (1968): 377; Bibb Latane and Steve Nida, "Ten Years of Research on Group Size and Helping," *Psychology Bulletin* 89 (1981): 308.

146. *In re Gutfreund, Securities Exchange Release No. 34-31554* (December 3, 1992).

147. Paine, *Value Shift*, 9–12.

148. See Kellerman, *Bad Leadership*, 146, 155 (discussing the boards overseeing Dunlop and Fastow); Sims and Brinkmann, "Enron Ethics" (discussing the board overseeing Fastow); Skeel, *Icarus in the Boardroom*, 163 (discussing the board overseeing Fastow); Sorkin, "Tyco Ex-Chief Is Humbled, But Unbowed," A1, A21.

149. John R. Kroger, "Enron, Fraud, and Securities Reform: An Enron Prosecutor's Perspective," *University of Colorado Law Review* 76 (2003): 57, 98.

150. J. Scott Armstrong, "Social Irresponsibility in Management," *Journal of Business Research* 5 (September 1977): 185–213.

151. Jackall, *Moral Mazes*; Sims and Brinkmann, "Enron Ethics."

152. Howard Gardner, Mihaly Csikszentmihalyi, and William Damon, *Good Work: When Excellence and Ethics Meet* (New York: Basic Books, 2001); Albert Bandura, Gian Vittorio Caprara, and Laszlo Zsolnai, "Corporate Transgressions Through Moral Disengagement," *Journal of Human Values* 6, 1 (2000): 57–64; Luban, "Making Sense of Moral Meltdowns"; Cialdini, "Social Influence and the Triple Tumor of Organizational Dishonesty"; Luban, "Integrity: Its Causes and Cures," *Fordham Law Review* 72 (2003): 307–310.

153. Kroger, "Enron, Fraud, and Securities Reform," 93.

154. C. S. Lewis, "The Inner Ring," in *They Asked for a Paper: Papers and Addresses* (London: Geoffrey Bless, 1962), 146–147.

155. Luban, "Making Sense of Moral Meltdowns"; Kroger, "Enron, Fraud, and Securities Reform," 97, 98; Messick and Darley, "How Organizations Socialize Individuals into Evildoing," 14–15; Jefferey Sonnenfeld and Paul R. Lawrence, "Why Do Companies Succumb to Price Fixing?" in Kenneth R. Andrews and Donald K. David (eds.), *Ethics in Practice: Managing the Moral Corporation* (Boston: Harvard Business Press, 1989), 184, 191; Diane Vaughn, "Regulating Risk: Implications of the *Challenger* Accident," *Law and Policy* 11 (1989): 330, 333–337; Diane Vaughn, *Controlling Unlawful Organizational Behavior* (Chicago: University of Chicago Press, 1983).

156. Sims and Brinkmann, "Enron Ethics," 252–253.

157. See sources cited in notes 107 to 120. Dallas, *A Preliminary Inquiry*, 28–30; Tim Barnett and Cheryl Vaicys, "The Moderating Effect of Individuals' Perceptions of Ethical Work Climate on Ethical Judgments and Behavioral Intentions," *Journal of Business Ethics* 27 (2000): 351; Randall S. Upchurch and Sheila K. Ruhland, "The Organizational Bases of Ethical Work Climates in Lodging Operations as Perceived by General Managers," *Journal of Business Ethics* 15 (1996): 1083; Wimbush and Shepard, "Toward an Understanding of Ethical Climate," 637.

158. Paine, *Value Shift*, 168–169. See Julia Flynn, Christina Del Ville, and Russell Mitchell, "Did Sears Take Other Customers for a Ride?" *Business Week,*

August 3, 1992, 25; Henry Gilgoff, "Sears Says Trust Us," *Newsday*, June 28, 1992, Business Section, 62.

159. Treviño and Weaver, *Managing Ethics in Organizations*, 225.

160. Nick Bunkley, "Examiner: Greed Sank Enron," *Detroit News*, March 16, 2004, 1C; R. Neal Baxton, the court-appointed examiner for Enron, remarked: "The story of Enron is the story of a perfect storm, of failing in the atmosphere of the overheated markets of the 1990s. . . . All the checks and balances fell short." See also Nancy B. Rapoport, "Enron, Titanic, and the Perfect Storm," in Nancy B. Rapoport and Bala G. Dharan (eds.), *Enron: Corporate Fiascos and Their Implications* (New York: Foundation Press, 2004), 927.

161. Sims and Brinkmann, "Enron Ethics," 252; Skeel, *Icarus in the Boardroom*, 171. See also Langevoort, "The Organizational Psychology of Hyper-Competition."

162. Skeel, *Icarus in the Boardroom*, 164.

163. See Deborah L. Rhode and Paul Paton, "Lawyers, Ethics and Enron," *Stanford Journal of Law, Business and Finance* 8 (2002): 9, reprinted in Rapoport and Dharan (eds.), *Enron*; Barbara Lee Toffler, *Final Accounting: Ambition, Greed, and the Fall of Arthur Andersen* (New York: Broadway Books, 2003), 62; Kroger, "Enron, Fraud, and Securities Reform," 90.

164. Hannah Arendt, *The Life of the Mind* (Orlando, Fla.: Harcourt, 1978), 41; Hannah Arendt, *Eichmann in Jerusalem: A Report on the Banality of Evil* (New York: Penguin Books, 1994), 235–236.

165. See, for example, Tom Chappell, *The Soul of a Business: Managing for Profit and the Common Good* (New York: Bantam, 1996).

166. The same is true of financial performance. For example, of the forty-three exemplary corporations singled out by Peters and Waterman, half were in trouble within five years and all but five within twenty years. Fullan, *Leading in a Culture of Change*, 47. See also John R. O'Neil, *The Paradox of Success: When Winning at Work Means Losing in Life* (New York: Penguin, 2004), 47 (noting how many of Peters's companies had fallen).

167. Cohan, *Value Leadership*, 222–223. For discussion of praise for Enron as one of the most innovative and best companies to work for, see Jean Lipman-Blumen, "Why Do We Tolerate Bad Leaders? Uncertitude, Anxiety, and Meaning," in Warren Bennis, Gretchen M. Spreitzer, and Thomas G. Cummings (eds.), *The Future of Leadership: Today's Top Leadership Thinkers Speak to Tomorrow's Leaders* (San Francisco: Jossey-Bass, 2001), 125–138. For its ethical code, see Cohan, *Value Leadership*, 2; Paine, *Value Shift*, 36; and Vogel, *The Market for Virtue*, 38. For discussion of an award for excellence to Andrew Fastow, see Paul Krugman, "Executives Gone Wild," *New York Times Book Review*, February 8, 2004, 9.

168. Compare Cohan, *Value Leadership*, 238 (quoting Sam Walton) with Eliot Blair Smith, "Wal-Mart Sets New Policy on Ethics," *USA Today*, January

31, 2005, 2B; Deborah L. Rhode, "Up Against the Wal-Mart," *National Law Journal*, July 22, 2002, A25.

169. Johnson, *Meeting the Ethical Challenges of Leadership*, 197; Arrow, *Social Responsibility and Economic Efficiency*; Mark S. Schwartz, "A Code of Ethics for Corporate Code of Ethics," *Journal of Business Ethics* 41, 1–2 (2002): 27–43.

170. Sonnenfeld and Lawrence, "Why Do Companies Succumb to Price Fixing?" 145; Johnson, *Meeting the Ethical Challenges of Leadership*, 197.

171. Schwartz, "A Code of Ethics for Corporate Code of Ethics," 38; Solomon, *Ethics and Excellence*, 98; Johnson, *Meeting the Ethical Challenges of Leadership*, 197.

172. Dalla Costa, *The Ethical Imperative*, 110 (quoting Haas).

173. Melissa S. Baucus and Caryn L. Beck-Dudley, "Designing Ethical Organizations: Avoiding the Long-Term Negative Effects of Rewards and Punishments," *Journal of Business Ethics* 56 (2005): 355; Linda Kelber Treviño, Gary R. Weaver, David G. Gibson, and Barbara Ley Toffler, "Managing Ethics and Legal Compliance: What Works and What Hurts," *California Management Review* 41, 2 (1999): 131, 134–138; Lynn Sharp Paine, "Managing for Organizational Integrity," *Harvard Business Review* (March-April 1994): 113; Treviño and Weaver, *Managing Ethics in Organizations*, 204–205.

174. Treviño, Weaver, Gibson, and Toffler, "Managing Ethics and Legal Compliance," 139; Treviño and Weaver, *Managing Ethics in Organizations*, 216; Schwartz, "A Code of Ethics for Corporate Code of Ethics"; Lisa Girion, "Interest in Corporate Ethics Is Still Weak," *Los Angeles Times*, July 8, 2002, C1, C8 (quoting Ed Petry, executive director of the Ethics Officer Association, concerning the ineffectiveness of many corporate ethics programs).

175. Treviño and Weaver, *Managing Ethics in Organizations*, 155; Johnson, *Meeting the Ethical Challenges of Leadership*, 197; Christine Parker, *The Open Corporation: Effective Self-Regulation and Democracy* (Cambridge: Cambridge University Press, 2002), 26; Dennis K. Berman, "Does Wall Street Finally Need an Ethics Code," *Wall Street Journal*, March 10, 2005, C1.

176. Kimberly D. Krawiec, "Cosmetic Compliance and the Failure of Negotiated Governance," *Washington University Law Quarterly* 81 (2003): 487, 513.

177. Cohan, *Value Leadership*, 2; Jonathan Peterson, "Firms Paying Heed to the Higher Price of Offenses," *Los Angeles Times*, February 13, 2005, C4 (quoting ethics expert Michael Josephson's observation that Enron had one of the nation's best codes of ethics). For the auction, see Paine, *Value Shift*, 36.

178. Treviño and Weaver, *Managing Ethics*, 128.

179. Treviño, Weaver, Gibson, and Toffler, "Managing Ethics and Legal Compliance," 140; Treviño and Weaver, *Managing Ethics*, 217.

180. For studies with different results, see Dallas, *A Preliminary Inquiry*, 32; Schwartz, "A Code of Ethics," 27–28. For research finding no significant relationship between codes and compliance, see Kimberly D. Krawiec,

"Organizational Misconduct: Beyond the Principal-Agent Model," *Florida State University Law Review* 32 (2005): 571, 593; Krawiec, "Cosmetic Compliance," 511; and M. Cash Mathews, "Codes of Ethics: Organizational Behavior and Misbehavior," in William C. Frederick and Lee E. Preston, *Research on Social Performance and Policy* (Greenwich, Conn.: JAI Press, 1987), 125 (finding no significant relationship between adoption of a code and corporation violations).

181. George, *Authentic Leadership,* 127; Treviño and Weaver, *Managing Ethics,* 113; Paine, *Value Shift,* 249; Treviño, Weaver, Gibson, and Toffler, "Managing Ethics and Legal Compliance," 147; Girion, "Interest in Corporate Ethics," C8.

182. U.S. Sentencing Commission Guidelines, Chapter Eight, Sentencing of Organizations, Section 8B2.1, as amended, November 1, 2004.

183. Treviño, Weaver, Gibson, and Toffler, "Managing Ethics and Legal Compliance," 147. See also Girion, "Interest in Corporate Ethics," C8; Parker, *Open Corporation,* 203–204.

184. Berman, "Does Wall Street Finally Need an Ethics Code," C1, C4.

185. Treviño, Weaver, Gibson, and Toffler, "Managing Ethics and Legal Compliance," 143–48; Treviño and Weaver, *Managing Ethics,* 224, 272; Paine, *Managing for Organizational Integrity,* 113.

186. See Dallas, "A Preliminary Inquiry," 43, 57; Chris Moon and Clive Bonny, "Attitudes and Approaches," in Chris Moon and Clive Bonny (eds.), *Business Ethics: Facing Up to the Issues* (London: Economist, 2001), 31–32; W. Michael Hoffman, "Integrating Ethics into Business Cultures," in Moon and Bonny, *Business Ethics,* 43–44, 51.

187. Paine, *Value Shift,* 249; Paine, *Managing Ethics for Organizational Integrity,* 101, 113; Dallas, "A Preliminary Inquiry," 56.

188. Robert C. Camp, *Benchmarking: The Search for Industry Best Practices That Lead to Superior Performance* (Milwaukee, Wis.: Quality Press, 1989); Antonio Tencati, Francesco Perrini, and Stefano Pogutz, "New Tools to Foster Corporate Social Responsibility Behavior," *Journal of Business Ethics* 53, 1–2 (2004): 173, 177.

189. Ethics Resource Center, http:///ethics.org.

190. See Paine, *Value Shift,* 248, 253–256.

191. See the sources cited in notes 79 to 86.

192. Moon and Bonny, "Attitudes and Approaches," 34; Dallas, "A Preliminary Inquiry," 34; Laura L. Nash, *Good Intentions Aside: A Manager's' Guide to Resolving Ethical Problems* (Boston: Harvard Business School Press, 1991), 185.

193. William Verbeke, Cok Ouwerkerk, and Ed Peelen, "Exploring the Contextual and Individual Factors on Ethical Decision Making of Salespersons," *Journal of Business Ethics* 15 (1996): 1175; Dallas, "A Preliminary Inquiry," 34–36; see notes 115 to 120 and 158 to 163.

194. Bebchuk and Fried, *Pay Without Performance*; Gregg Easterbrook, *The Progress Paradox* (New York: Random House, 2003), 268; Deutsch, "My Big Fat CEO Paycheck," sec. 3, 1; Jensen and Fuller, "Just Say No to Wall Street"; Stephen Labaton, "Four Years Later, Enron's Shadow Lingers as Change Comes Slowly," *New York Times*, January 5, 2006, C1; Robert Daines, Vinay B. Nair, and Lewis A. Kornhauser, *Are CEOs Paid for Skill? The Good, the Bad and the Lucky* (Stanford: Stanford University Law School, January 2005); University of Pennsylvania, Institute for Law and Economics Research Paper 05–07; N.Y.U., Law and Economics Research Paper No. 04–035, http://ssrn.com/abstract=622223; Madrick, "Economic Scene," C2.

195. Harris Interactive Polls, September 2, 2003, October 2, 2002, http://www.harrisinteractive.com/harris_poll.

196. Treviño, Weaver, Gibson, and Toffler, "Managing Ethics and Legal Compliance," 142–143; Peter B. Doeringer, "The Socio-Economics of Labor Productivity," in Richard M. Coughlin (ed.), *Morality, Rationality, and Efficiency: New Perspectives on Socio-Economics* (Armonk, N.Y.: M. E. Sharpe, 1991), 108, 112; Moon and Bonny, "Attitudes and Approaches," 29; Dawson, "Toward a Preliminary Inquiry"; Dallas, "A Preliminary Inquiry," 36.

197. Paine, *Value Shift*, 249; Paine, *Managing for Integrity for Organizational Integrity*, 113; Treviño, Weaver, Gibson, and Toffler, "Managing Ethics and Legal Compliance," 142–143; Parker, *Open Corporation*, 50, 94, 203.

198. Dallas, "A Preliminary Inquiry," 40; Hoffman, "Integrating Ethics into Business Cultures," 43–44; Moon and Bonny, "Attitudes and Approaches," 34.

199. Treviño, Weaver, Gibson, and Toffler, "Managing Ethics and Legal Compliance," 142; Heesun Wee, "Corporate Ethics: Right Makes Might," *Business Week OnLine*, April 11, 2002, http://www.businessweek.com/bwdaily/dnflash/apr2002/nf20020411_6350.htm (describing findings of Ethics Research Center 2000 Survey).

200. Vicky Arnold, James C. Lampe, and George G. Sutton, "Understanding the Factors Underlying Ethical Organizations: Enabling Continuous Ethical Improvement," *Journal of Applied Business Research* 15 (Summer 1999): 1, 10; Moon and Bonny, "Attitudes and Approaches," 29–34; Hoffman, "Integrating Ethics into Business Cultures," 50.

201. Lisa Fethertone, "Race to the Bottom," *Nation*, March 28, 2005, 17, 18 (discussing Wal-Mart CEO salary of $23 million); Gary Rivlin and John Markoff, "Tossing Out a Chief Executive," *New York Times*, February 14, 2005, C1 (describing Carly Fiorino's yacht); Treviño and others, *Managing Ethics and Legal Compliance*, 145 (discussing shoe incident).

202. For variations on these questions and the evening news inquiry, see Paine, *Value Shift*, 226; Treviño and Weaver, *Managing Ethics*, 298.

203. John Gibeaut, "Telling Secrets: When In-House Lawyers Sue Their Employers, They Find Themselves in the Middle of the Debate on Client

Confidentiality," *ABA Journal* (November 2004): 39, 73; Roberta Ann Johnson, *Whistleblowing: When It Works—and Why* (Boulder, Colo.: Lynne Rienner Publishers, 2003), 93; C. Fred Alford, *Whistleblowers: Broken Lives and Organizational Power* (Ithaca, N.Y.: Cornell University Press, 2001), 1, 19–20; Robert Pack, "Whistleblowers and the Law," *Washington Lawyer Online* (June 2002): 21, 28; Terance Miethe, *Whistleblowing at Work: Tough Choices in Exposing Fraud, Waste, and Abuse on the Job* (Boulder, Colo.: Westview Press, 1999), 149–208; Myron P. Glazer and Penina M. Glazer, *Whistleblowers: Exposing Corruption in Government and Industry* (New York: Basic Books, 1989), 210.

204. Miethe, *Whistleblowing at Work*, 81, 73–91; Alford, *Whistleblowers*, 20.

205. Glazer and Glazer, *Whistleblower*, 207 (quoting Hugh Kaufman).

206. Johnson, *Whistleblowing*, 50.

207. Alford, *The Whistleblowers*, 31–32; Johnson, *Whistleblowing*, 112 (discussing mixed evidence on hot lines).

208. Alford, *The Whistleblowers*, 21.

209. Dalla Costa, *The Ethical Imperative*, 87.

210. Sarbanes-Oxley Act of 2002, P.L. 107–204, 116 Stat. 745, July 30, 2002.

211. Sarbanes-Oxley Act of 2002, sec. 207, 17 Code of Federal Regulations Part 205 (20043).

212. Parker, *Open Corporation*, 104–106, 204–207; Paine, *Value Shift*, 248; Dalla Costa, *The Ethical Imperative*, 273.

213. Parker, *Open Corporation*, 261–267.

214. Parker, *Open Corporation*, 76–77, 101–103; Tencati, Perrini, and Pogutz, "New Tools to Foster Corporate Social Responsibility Behavior," 175.

215. Parker, *Open Corporation*, 214, 223; Kor Grit, "Corporate Citizenship: How to Strengthen the Social Responsibility of Managers," *Journal of Business Ethics* 53, 1–2 (2004): 97, 105; Risako Morimoto, John Ash, and Chris Hope, "Corporate Social Responsibility Audit: From Theory to Practice," *Journal of Business Ethics* 62 (2005): 315.

216. For proposals to assign auditors from panels, see Skeel, "Icarus in the Boardroom," 188; Jeff Madrick, "Economic Scene: Where Economists Stand, or Don't Stand, on the Issue of Corporate Scandals," *New York Times*, October 28, 2004, C2. For other proposals, see Parker, *Open Corporation*, 278; Alton B. Harris and Andrea S. Kramer, "Corporate Governance: Pre-Enron, Post-Enron," in Christopher L. Culp and William A. Niskanmen (eds.), *Corporate Aftershock: The Public Policy Lessons from the Collapse of Enron and Other Major Corporations* (Hoboken, N.J.: Wiley, 2003), 49, 73–75.

217. Leonard M. Baynes, "Just Pucker and Blow? An Analysis of Corporate Whistleblowing and the Duty of Care, the Duty of Loyalty, and the Sarbanes-Oxley Act," *St. John's Law Review* 76 (2004): 875, 896; David L. Hudson Jr., "No Place to Blow the Whistle," *ABA Journal eReport*, February 1, 2005, http://www.abanet.org/journal/ereprt, 1. For an overview of whistle-

blowing and compilation of legal protections, see National Whistleblower Center, *Labor Day Report: The National Status of Whistleblower Protection on Labor Day, 2002*, and its compilation of legal protections, http://www.whistle blowerlaw.com/protection.htm.

218. U.S. Department of Labor, Occupational Safety and Health Administration, *Protecting Whistleblowers with Job Safety and Health Complaints* (Washington, D.C.: U.S. Government Printing Office, 2000). For a model statute, see the National Whistleblower Protection Act, http://www.whistleblower law.com/protection.htm.

219. Parker, *Open Corporation*, 36, 187–188; Deborah L. Rhode and David Luban, *Legal Ethics* (New York: Foundation Press, 2004), 408.

220. "Caring in the Community," *Management Today* (March 1995): 19–20; Stephen Garone, *The Link Between Corporate Citizenship and Financial Performance* (New York: Conference Board, 1999), 8; Roper Starch Worldwide and Cone/Coughlin Communications, *The 1996 Cone/Roper Study: A Benchmark Survey of Consumer Awareness and Attitudes Toward Cause-Related Marketing* (1996); John A. Yankey, "Corporate Support of Nonprofit Organizations: Partnerships Across the Sectors," in Dwight F. Burlingame and Dennis R. Young (eds.), *Corporate Philanthropy at the Crossroads* (Indianapolis: Indiana University Press, 1996), 13.

221. Vogel, *Market for Virtue*, 46–48; Deutsch, "New Surveys Show That Big Business Has a P.R. Problem," C1.

222. Vogel, *Market for Virtue*, 60; Marc Gunther, *Faith and Fortune: The Quiet Revolution to Reform American Business* (New York: Crown Business, 2004), 35.

223. Vogel, *Market for Virtue*, 60–61; Jeffrey Hollender and Stephen Fenichell, *What Matters Most: How a Small Group of Pioneers Is Teaching Social Responsibility to Big Business* (New York: Basic Books, 2004), 47.

224. Vogel, *Market for Virtue*, 162.

225. Vogel, *Market for Virtue*, 63–64; *2003 Report on Socially Responsible Investing Trends in the United States (Social Investment Forum, 2003)*, 16, available at http://www.socialinvest.org.

226. Deutsch, "My Big Fat C.E.O. Paycheck." For other proposals, see Bebchuk and Fried, "Pay Without Performance," 189–200; Kevin J. Murphy, "Explaining Executive Compensation: Managerial Power Versus the Perceived Cost of Stock Options," *University of Chicago Law Review* 69 (2002): 847, 867–868.

227. Deutsch, "New Surveys Show That Big Business Has a P.R. Problem," C1.

228. For increased activity, see Peterson, "Firms Paying Heed to the Higher Price of Offenses," C4. For resource needs, see, for example, the Corporate Crime Report, http://www.corporatecrimereporter.com/, and the Web site of the Association of Certified Fraud Examiners, http://www.cfenet.com/.

229. See the sources cited in David A. Skeel Jr., "Shaming in Corporate Law," *University of Pennsylvania Law Review* 149 (2001): 1811; John Braithwaite, *Crime, Shame, and Reintegration* (Cambridge: Cambridge University Press,

1989); Dan M. Kahan and Eric A. Posner, "Shaming White Collar Criminals: A Proposal for Reform of the Federal Sentencing Guidelines," *Journal of Law and Economics* 42 (1999): 365; Theresa A. Gabaldon, "Corporate Conscience and the White Man's Burden," *George Washington Law Review* 70 (2002): 944, 949.

230. Parker, *Open Corporation*, 239–240, 283–289.

231. For example, Wharton has hired an outside firm to do background checks on a randomly selected group of applicants. Lynnley Browning, "M.B.A. Programs Now Screen for Integrity, Too," *New York Times*, September 15, 2002, B4. The Tuck School at Dartmouth is asking applicants to self-report grades and test scores and will then corroborate them against official transcripts.

232. For example, Harvard asks recommenders to "comment on the applicant's behavior (e.g. respect of others, honesty, integrity, accountability for personal behavior) within your organization and in the community." Harvard Business School, M.B.A. Application Form, Class of 2003. For the five-point scale, see Rick Gladstone, "Weeding Out the Bad Apples (Before They Get to Harvard)," *New York Times*, September 8, 2002, B3; Browning, "M.B.A. Programs Now Screen for Integrity, Too," B4.

233. Gladstone, "Weeding Out the Bad Apples," B3; Harvard Business School, M.B.A. Application Form.

234. Browning, "M.B.A. Programs Now Screen for Integrity," B4 (quoting Ann L. McGill).

235. William J. Holstein, "Screening for Ethics: How One School Does It," *New York Times*, November 20, 2005, H1 (quoting Gabriel Hawawini).

236. Ronald R. Sims, "The Challenge of Ethical Behavior in Organizations," *Journal of Business Ethics* (1992): 513; Cialdini, "Social Influence and the Triple Tumor Structure of Organizational Dishonesty"; Messick, Darley, and Tyler, *Social Influences on Ethical Behavior in Organizations*.

237. Walter Mischel and Yuichi Shoda, "A Cognitive-Affective Theory of Personality: Reconceptualizing Situations, Dispositions, Dynamics, and Invariance in Personality Structure," *Psychological Review* 10 (1995): 246.

238. James Flanigan, "Slipshod Business Ethics a Poor Example for Youth," *Los Angeles Times*, October 30, 2002, C1, 13.

239. Bush, remarks on corporate responsibility, http://www.whitehouse.gov/news/releases/2002/07/ 20020709-4.html. For similar views, see Browning, "M.B.A. Programs Now Screen for Integrity, Too," B4; "Money, Ethics and the M.B.A.," *New York Times*, August 25, 2002, A16; Thomas K. Lindsay, "What Does It Profit a Man to Gain an MBA?" *Los Angeles Times*, November 18, 2002, A13; Penelope Patsuris, "Can Integrity be Taught?" *Forbes on Line*, October 4, 2002, http://www.forbes.com/2002/10/04/1004_virtue.htm/; Rebecca Spence, "Letter to the Editor," *New York Times*, August 23, 2002, A16; Robert Prentice, "An Ethics Lesson for Business Schools," *New York Times*, August 20, 2002, A2.

240. "MBA Candidates Demand Ethics over Earnings," *Business Ethics Newsline*, September 3, 2002, http://www.globalethics.org/newsline/members/current issue2.tmpl. See also Frederic E. Greenman and John F. Sherman III, "Business School Ethics–An Overlooked Topic," *Business and Society Review* 104, 2 (Summer 1999): 171, 173–174.

241. Geoffrey Keynes (ed.), *Selected Essays of William Hazlitt: 1778–1830* (New York: Random House, 1948), 222.

242. See Rhode, *In the Interests of Justice,* 200; William H. Simon, "The Trouble with Legal Ethics," *Journal of Legal Education* 41 (1991): 65, 66; Robert Granfield and Thomas Koenig, "'It's Hard to Be a Human Being and a Lawyer': Young Attorneys and the Confrontation with Ethical Ambiguity in Legal Practice," *West Virginia Law Review* 105 (2002–2003): 495.

243. Deborah L. Rhode, "The Professional Responsibilities of Professors," *Journal of Legal Education* 51 (2001): 158, 164.

244. Robert S. Shiller, "How Wall Street Learns to Look the Other Way," *New York Times,* February 8, 2005, A1, 33; Jeff Gottlieb, "Enron Ethics—The Business Course, UC Irvine Business Ethics Class: In a Word, Enron," *Los Angeles Times,* July 9, 2002, B1, B4; John R. Farnsworth and Brian H. Kleiner, "Trends in Ethics Education at US Colleges and Universities," *Management Research News* 26 (2003): 130–140; Brian Hindo, "Where Can Execs Learn Ethics?" *Business Week Online,* June 13, 2002, http://www.businessweek.com/bwdaily/dnflash/june2002/nf20020613_6153.htm; Daniel G. Arce, "Conspicuous by Its Absence: Ethics and Managerial Economics," *Journal of Business Ethics* 54, 3 (2004): 261; Andrea L. Stake, "Area Business Schools Are Not Rushing to Add Courses on Ethical Behavior as a Result of the Enron Scandal," *Providence Journal-Bulletin,* April 7, 2002, F-1.

245. Christopher S. Stewart, "A Question of Ethics: How to Teach Them?" *New York Times,* March 21, 2004, E11; Harsh K. Luthar and Ranjan Karri, "Exposure to Ethics Education and the Perception of Linkage Between Organizational Ethical Behavior and Business Outcomes," *Journal of Business Ethics* 61 (2005): 353.

246. Stewart, "A Question of Ethics." See also Greenman and Sherman, "Business School Ethics," 172.

247. Robert A. Giacalone, "A Transcendent Business Education for the 21st Century," *Academy of Management Learning and Education* 3 (2004): 415, 416. For student attitudes, see Stewart, "A Question of Ethics," E11.

248. Rhode, "In the Interests of Justice," 201; Granfield and Koenig, "'It's Hard to be a Human Being and a Lawyer,'" 519, 521–522; Thomas W. Dunfee and Diane C. Robertson, "Integrating Ethics in the Business School Curriculum," in Thomas Donaldson and Thomas W. Dunfee (eds.), *Ethics in Business and Economics* (Brookfield, Vt., and Aldershot, England: Ashgate/Dartmouth, 1997), 513.

249. Irving Kristol, "Ethics Anyone? Or Morals?" *Wall Street Journal*, September 15, 1987, sec. 1, 32. See also Michael Levin, "Ethics Course: Useless," *New York Times*, November 25, 1989, A23; Barbara Kellerman, "Bad Leadership" (address before the Commonwealth Club of San Francisco, January 10, 2005).

250. Paul R. Tremblay, "Shared Norms, Bad Lawyers, and the Values of Casuistry," *University of San Francisco Law Review* 36 (2002): 659, 673. See Thane Bellomo, "Letter to the Editor," *New York Times*, February 14, 2005, A4: "We had classes on ethical behavior. But if you are a rotten person going into B-school, you will probably still be a rotten person when you come out."

251. Levin, "Ethics Courses: Useless," A23.

252. Solomon, *Ethics and Excellence*, 6.

253. See the research summarized in Rhode, "The Professional Responsibility of Professors," 165; John M. Doris, "Lack of Character," *Personality and Moral Behavior* (2002): 123; Jim Heskett, "What Can Business Schools Do to Avoid Bad Apples?" *Harvard Business School Online*, September 2, 2002, http://hbswk.hbs.edu/pubitem.jhtml?id=3084&t=heskett; James R. Rest, "Can Ethics Be Taught in Professional Schools? The Psychological Research," *Easier Said Than Done* (Winter 1988): 22; James S. Leming, "Curricular Effectiveness in Moral Values Education: A Review of Research," *Journal of Moral Education* 10 (1981): 147; Ann Colby and Thomas Ehrlich, "Higher Education and the Development of Civic Responsibility," in Thomas Ehrlich (ed.), *Civic Responsibility and Higher Education* (Phoenix, Ariz.: Oryx Press, 2000), xxi.

254. Penelope Patsuris, "Can Ethics Be Taught?" *Forbes.com*, October 4, 2002 http://www.forbes.com/2002/10/04/1004_virtue.htm/ (quoting Tom Donaldson).

255. Patsuris, "Can Integrity Be Taught?" (quoting Alexei Marcoux).

256. Lipman-Blumen, "Why Do We Tolerate Bad Leaders?" 163.

257. Jenny B. Davis, "Corporate Crime Fighter: Ex-Prosecutor Teams with Prisoners to Teach Ethics to Executives," *ABA Journal* (February 2003): 26; "Convicted Business Executives to Teach Students About Ethics," Institute for Global Ethics," *Ethics Newsline*, http://www.globalethics.org/newsline/members/issue.tmpl?articleid=07220215562058; Giacalone, "A Transcendent Business Education for the 21st Century," 418.

258. Treviño and Weaver, *Managing Ethics*, 339.

259. For similar calls for research, see Treviño and Weaver, *Managing Ethics*, 328–341; Parker, *Open Corporation*, 245.

260. Jim Collins, *Good to Great: Why Some Companies Make the Leap . . . and Others Don't* (New York: HarperCollins, 2001), 21, 38.

261. Collins, *Good to Great*, 215.

262. Collins, *Good to Great*, 215.

263. Mukul Pandya and others, *Lasting Leadership: What You Can Learn from the Top 25 Business People of Our Times* (Upper Saddle River, N.J.: Wharton

School Publishing, 2005), xv. Among those singled out for ethical qualities were James Burke, of Johnson & Johnson, for his handling of the Tylenol recall; Muhammad Yunus, Grameen Bank, for creating microeconomic opportunities in impoverished communities; and George Soros, of the Open Society Institute, for using his fortune built on high-risk currency speculation to fund progressive social change, for his cleanup of the Solomon Brothers trading scandal, and for his concern about executive compensation.

264. The discussions of Lee Iacocca are silent on his devaluation of safety concerns. Jack Welch's profile reveals nothing about his celebrated affair and conflict of interest with a *Harvard Business Review* editor. The account of Sam Walton's transformation of Wal-Mart omits discussion of the company's appalling labor record. Pandya and others, *Lasting Leadership*.

Chapter One

1. See David Luban, "Contrived Ignorance," *Georgetown Law Journal* 87 (1999): 957–980.

2. Here I am adopting the analysis of my colleague Don Langevoort. See Donald C. Langevoort, "Managing the 'Expectations Gap' in Investor Protection: The SEC and the Post-Enron Reform Agenda," *Villanova Law Review* 48 (2003): 1139–1163.

3. See generally Arthur Isak Applbaum, *Ethics for Adversaries: The Morality of Roles in Public and Professional Life* (Princeton, N.J.: Princeton University Press, 1999).

4. See Deborah L. Rhode and David Luban, *Legal Ethics*, 4th ed. (New York: Foundation Press, 2004), 215–218, and sources cited there.

5. The case is *Washington State Physicians Insurance Exchange & Association v. Fisons Corporation*, 858 P.2d 1054 (Wash. 1993).

6. *United States v. Regent Office Supply*, 421 F.2d 1174 (2nd Cir. 1970).

7. William Bratton, "Enron and the Dark Side of Shareholder Value," *Tulane Law Review* 76 (2002): 1275–1361.

8. Melvin J. Lerner, *The Belief in a Just World: A Fundamental Delusion* (New York: Plenum, 1980).

9. Lerner, *The Belief in a Just World*, 20–21.

10. Robert Swaine, *The Cravath Firm and Its Predecessors, 1819–1947* (privately printed, 1946), 1:667.

11. Ronald H. Coase, "The Nature of the Firm," *Economica* 4 (1937): 386.

12. Robert Jackall, *Moral Mazes: The World of Corporate Managers* (New York: Oxford University Press, 1988), 17–25.

13. Jackall, *Moral Mazes*, 17.

14. Marc Bloch, *Feudal Society*, trans. L. A. Manyon (Chicago: University of Chicago Press, 1961), 145.

15. Bratton, "Enron and the Dark Side of Shareholder Value," 1293.

16. Jackall, *Moral Mazes*, 91–100.

17. Michael Lewis, *Liar's Poker* (New York: W.W. Norton, 1989), 64–70.

18. Donald C. Langevoort, "The Organizational Psychology of Hyper-Competition: Corporate Irresponsibility and the Lessons of Enron," *George Washington Law Review* 70 (2002): 968–975.

19. Former dot-commer Michael Wolff portrayed this world vividly in his 1998 best seller, *Burn Rate: How I Survived the Gold-Rush Years on the Internet* (New York: Simon & Schuster, 1998).

20. Leon L. Festinger and J. M. Carlsmith, "Cognitive Consequences of Forced Compliance," *Journal of Abnormal and Social Psychology* 58 (1959): 203; see also the discussion in Lee Ross and Richard E. Nisbett, *The Person and the Situation: Perspectives of Social Psychology* (Philadelphia: Temple University Press, 1991), 66.

21. I discuss this paradox at greater length, including extensive references to the social psychology literature, in David Luban, "Integrity: Its Causes and Cures," *Fordham Law Review* 72 (2003): 279–310. Part of my discussion in this section draws on this article.

22. See Ross and Nisbett, *The Person and the Situation*, 30–35.

23. Bibb Latané and John Darley, *The Unresponsive Bystander: Why Doesn't He Help?* (Upper Saddle River, N.J.: Prentice Hall, 1968); for a literature review, see Bibb Latané and Steve Nida, "Ten Years of Research on Group Size and Helping," *Psychological Bulletin* 89 (1981): 308.

24. C. S. Lewis, "The Inner Ring," in *They Asked for a Paper: Papers and Addresses* (London: Geoffrey Bles, 1962), 146.

25. Lewis, "The Inner Ring," 147.

26. Craig Haney, William Banks, and Philip Zimbardo, "Interpersonal Dynamics of a Simulated Prison," *International Journal of Criminology and Penology* 1 (1973): 81; Philip G. Zimbardo, W. Curtis Banks, Craig Haney, and David Jaffe, "A Pirandellian Prison," *New York Times Magazine*, April 8, 1973. There is a terrifically interesting slide show and analysis of the Stanford Prison Experiment, put together by lead experimenter Philip Zimbardo, available on the Internet: Philip B. Zimbardo, *Stanford Prison Experiment: A Simulation Study of the Psychology of Imprisonment Conducted at Stanford University*, http://www.prisonexp.org.

27. Craig Haney and Philip Zimbardo, "The Socialization into Criminality: On Becoming a Prisoner and a Guard," in June Louin Tapp and Felice J. Levine (eds.), *Law, Justice, and the Individual in Society: Psychological and Legal Issues* (New York: Harcourt School, 1977), 207.

28. Haney and Zimbardo, "The Socialization into Criminality," 207–209.

29. These famous experiments are described in Stanley Milgram, *Obedience to Authority: An Experimental Approach* (New York: HarperCollins, 1974).

30. I take these suggestions from Luban, "Integrity," 307–310.

31. Milgram, *Obedience to Authority*, 203–204.

Chapter Two

1. David Messick and Max Bazerman, "Ethical Leadership and the Psychology of Decision Making," *Sloan Management Review* (Winter 1996): 9–22; Mahzarin Banaji, Max Bazerman, and Dolly Chugh, "How (Un)Ethical Are You?" *Harvard Business Review* 81 (December 2003): 56–64.

2. U.S. Senate, Permanent Subcommittee on Investigations of the Committee on Governmental Affairs, "The Role of the Board of Directors in Enron's Collapse," July 8, 2002, 26–27.

3. John M. Darley and C. Daniel Batson, "'From Jerusalem to Jericho': A Study of Situational and Dispositional Variables in Helping Behavior," *Journal of Personality and Social Psychology* 27 (1973): 100–108.

4. See Chapter Five in this volume.

5. Deborah G. Ancona, Gerardo A. Okhuysen, and Leslie A. Perlow, "Taking Time to Integrate Temporal Research," *Academy of Management Review* 26 (2001): 512–529; Leslie Perlow, "The Time Famine: Toward a Sociology of Work Time," *Administrative Science Quarterly* 44 (1999): 57–81.

6. Derek Parfit, *Reasons and Persons* (Oxford: Clarendon Press, 1984).

7. Our data suggest that novice professionals are more sensitive to ethical considerations, yet veteran professionals are more adept at managing the multiple considerations that arise. Research across many professional fields, ranging from medicine to engineering, suggests that novices and veterans bring different strengths and sensibilities to a task. Therefore, structural mechanisms designed to integrate professionals with different levels of experience can prove highly beneficial. See Niteesh K. Choudhry, Robert H. Fletcher, and Stephen B. Soumerai, "The Relationship Between Clinical Experience and Quality of Health Care," *Annals of Internal Medicine*, February 15, 2005, 260–273; Marco Iansiti, *Technology Integration: Making Critical Choices in a Turbulent World* (Boston: Harvard Business School Press, 1997).

8. Research on learning and proficiency suggests this approach toward managing time. Ironically, that research indicates that construing a challenge as a learning opportunity can produce better performance than focusing on performing well. Researchers thus encourage people to frame anxiety-provoking situations less as performance tasks and more as learning opportunities. See Carol S. Dweck, *Self-Theories: Their Role in Motivation, Personality and Development* (Philadelphia: Psychology Press, 1999); Amy C. Edmondson, "Framing for Learning: Lessons in Successful Technology Implementation," *California Management Review* 45, 2 (2003): 34–54.

9. For an extensive account of Betty Vinson's misgivings in committing accounting fraud, see Susan Pulliam, "How Following Orders Can Harm Your Career," *CFO.com*, October 3, 2003, http://www.cfo.com/article.cfm/ 3010537/2/c_3036075?f=insidecfo, accessed July 12, 2005.

10. Psychologists have documented the discrepancy between decisions made under the cool shade of reason and actions taken under the hot impulse of emotions and drives. See Max Bazerman, Ann Tenbrunsel, and Kimberly Wade-Benzoni, "Negotiating with Yourself and Losing: Making Decisions with Competing Internal Preferences," *Academy of Management Review* 23 (1998): 225–241; George Loewenstein, "Out of Control: Visceral Influences on Behavior," *Organizational Behavior and Human Decision Processes* 65 (1996): 272–292; Janet Metcalfe and Walter Mischel, "A Hot/Cool-System Analysis of Delay of Gratification: Dynamics of Willpower," *Psychological Review* 106 (1999): 3–19.

11. Stanley Milgram, *Obedience to Authority* (New York: Harper Torchbooks, 1975), 27–31.

12. Ruth Barcan Marcus, "Moral Dilemmas and Consistency," in C. W. Gowans (ed.), *Moral Dilemmas* (New York: Oxford University Press, 1987), 188–204.

13. T. M. Scanlon, *What We Owe to Each Other* (Cambridge, Mass.: Belknap Press of Harvard University Press, 1998).

14. James G. March, *A Primer on Decision Making* (New York: Free Press, 1994). Joel Podolny has proposed another illuminating distinction, contrasting the "logic of person" and the "logic of position," which he uses to explain how people relate to the actions they take in ethical situations. See Joel Podolny, *The Logic of Position, the Meaning of Leadership* (New York: Oxford University Press, forthcoming).

15. Joshua Margolis, Andrew Molinsky, and Katherine Decelles, *Ethical Orientation and the Moral Content of Managerial Work* (Boston: Harvard Business School, 2005).

16. Adam Grant and others, *Identity and Procedural Injustice in Delivering Unfavorable Outcomes: When Prosocial Identity Undermines Prosocial Behavior* (Ann Arbor, Mich.: University of Michigan, 2005).

17. John Darley, "How Organizations Socialize Individuals into Evildoing," in David M. Messick and Ann E. Tenbrunsel (eds.), *Codes of Conduct: Behavioral Research into Business Ethics* (New York: Russell Sage Foundation, 1996), 13–43.

18. Solomon Asch, "Effects of Group Pressure upon the Modification and Distortion of Judgments," in H. Guetzkow (ed.), *Groups, Leadership, and Men* (Pittsburgh, Pa.: Carnegie Press, 1951), 177–190.

19. Banaji, Bazerman, and Chugh, "How (Un)Ethical Are You?" 56–64; Jonathan Haidt, "The Emotional Dog and Its Rational Tail: A Social Intuitionist Approach to Moral Judgment," *Psychological Review* 108 (2001): 814–834; Messick and Bazerman, "Ethical Leadership and the Psychology of Decision Making," 9–22.

20. John Rawls, *A Theory of Justice* (Cambridge, Mass.: Harvard University Press, 1971).

Chapter Three

1. Ann E. Tenbrunsel and David M. Messick, "Ethical Fading: The Role of Self-Deception in Unethical Behavior," *Social Justice Research* 17 (2004): 223–236.
2. David M. Messick and Keith P. Sentis, "Fairness and Preference," *Journal of Experimental Social Psychology* 15 (1979): 418–434.
3. Rushworth M. Kidder, *How Good People Make Tough Choices* (New York: Fireside, 1995).
4. Marcia P. Miceli and Janet P. Near, *Blowing the Whistle* (Lanham, Md.: Lexington Books, 1992).
5. Tenbrunsel and Messick, *Ethical Fading*, 223–236.
6. David M. Messick, Suzanne Bloom, Janet P. Boldizar, and Charles D. Samuelson, "Why We Are Fairer Than Others," *Journal of Experimental Social Psychology* 21(1985): 480–500.
7. Karen L. Cates and David M. Messick, "Frequentistic Adverbs as Measures of Egocentric Biases," *European Journal of Social Psychology*, 26 (1996): 155–161.
8. Susan E. Squires, Cynthia J. Smith, Lorna McDougall, and William R. Yeack, *Inside Arthur Andersen* (Upper Saddle River, N.J.: Prentice Hall, 2003); Barbara L. Toffler, *Final Accounting* (New York: Broadway Books, 2003).
9. Hazel Markus and Robert B. Zajonc, "The Cognitive Perspective in Social Psychology," in Gardner Lindzey and Elliot Aronson (eds.), *Handbook of Social Psychology* (New York: Random House, 1985), 1:137–230.
10. Roland Huntford, *The Last Place on Earth* (New York: Random House, 1999).
11. Robert Falcon Scott, *Scott's Last Expedition: The Journals* (New York: Carrol and Graf, 1996), 441.
12. Kurt Eichenwald, *Conspiracy of Fools* (New York: Broadway Books, 2005).
13. Eichenwald, *Conspiracy of Fools*, 590.
14. Eichenwald, *Conspiracy of Fools*, 590.
15. Kidder, *How Good People Make Tough Choices*.
16. Joseph L. Badaracco, *Leading Quietly* (Boston: Harvard Business School Press, 2002; Stanley Milgram, "Behavioral Study of Obedience," *Journal of Abnormal Psychology* 67 (1963): 371–378; Herbert C. Kelman and V. Lee Hamilton, *Crimes of Obedience* (New Haven, Conn.: Yale University Press, 1989).
17. Miceli and Near, *Blowing the Whistle*.

Chapter Four

1. Russell Hardin, "Representing Ignorance," *Social Philosophy and Policy* 21 (2004): 76–99.

2. See Deborah Rhode, "Why the ABA Bothers: A Functional Perspective on Legal Codes," *Texas Law Review* 59 (1981): 689–721.

3. David Hume, *A Treatise of Human Nature*, ed. David Fate Norton and Mary J. Norton (1739–1740; New York: Oxford University Press, 2000), book 3.

4. Russell Hardin, "The Artificial Duties of Contemporary Professionals," *Social Service Review* 64 (1991): 528–541; Rena A. Gorlin (ed.), *Codes of Professional Responsibility: Ethics Standards in Business, Health, and Law* (Washington, D.C.: Bureau of National Affairs, 1999); Judith Andre, "Role Morality as a Complex Instance of Ordinary Morality," *American Philosophical Quarterly* 28 (1991): 73–80.

5. It has perhaps more often been religious, but I will not address religious ethics here.

6. H. A. Prichard, "Does Moral Philosophy Rest on a Mistake?" in H. A. Prichard, *Moral Obligation and Duty and Interest* (New York: Oxford University Press, 1968), 48.

7. Immanuel Kant, *Prolegomena to Any Future Metaphysics*, trans. Paul Carus (La Salle, Ill.: Open Court, 1902), 6. In Kant's own time, such philosophers as Thomas Reid initiated this "modern" line of inquiry.

8. God evidently botched the process in many cases.

9. This is a big issue that cannot be settled here. See Russell Hardin, *Morality Within the Limits of Reason* (Chicago: University of Chicago Press, 1988), 178–191.

10. Thomas Nagel, "Ruthlessness in Public Life," in Thomas Nagel, *Mortal Questions* (Cambridge: Cambridge University Press, 1979), 75–90.

11. Russell Hardin, "Institutional Morality," in Robert E. Goodin (ed.), *The Theory of Institutional Design* (Cambridge: Cambridge University Press, 1996), 126–153.

12. Lon L. Fuller, "Human Interaction and the Law," in Lon L. Fuller, *The Principles of Social Order*, ed. Kenneth Winston (Durham, N.C.: Duke University Press, 1981), 212–246. Fuller holds that law is a facility enabling men to live a satisfactory life in common. The purpose is something like Thomas Hobbes's mutual advantage.

13. Kenneth E. Scott, "Two Models of the Civil Process," *Stanford Law Review* 27 (1975): 937–950.

14. My account here is based on service on this board during 1998–2001.

15. Ronald Dworkin, *Freedom's Law* (Cambridge, Mass.: Harvard University Press, 1996); Richard A. Posner, *The Problematics of Moral and Legal Theory* (Cambridge, Mass.: Harvard University Press, 1999).

16. Richard A. Posner, "Reply to Critics," *Harvard Law Review* 111 (May 1998): 1796–1823.

17. Neil R. Luebke, "Conflict of Interest as a Moral Category," *Business and Professional Ethics Journal* 6 (Summer 1987): 66–81; Michael Davis, "Conflict of Interest," *Business and Professional Ethics Journal* 6 (Summer 1982): 17–27. The phrase "conflicting interests" appeared in a U.S. court case in 1941.

18. Conflicts of interest seem now to be rampant. For a few indicative cases across many arenas of professional life, see Karen S. Cook, Russell Hardin, and Margaret Levi, *Cooperation Without Trust?* (New York: Russell Sage Foundation, 2005), 5–6, 46–47, 104–110, 117–120, 124–129.
19. Nagel, "Ruthlessness in Public Life," 80.
20. Reinhold Niebuhr, *Moral Man and Immoral Society: A Study in Ethics and Politics* (New York: Scribner, 1932).
21. Hume, *A Treatise of Human Nature*, 3.2.11.2.
22. Hardin, "The Artificial Duties of Contemporary Professionals," 529.
23. G. E. Moore, *Principia Ethica* (Cambridge: Cambridge University Press, 1903).
24. Hardin, "Institutional Morality."

Chapter Five

1. Iris Chang, *The Rape of Nanking: The Forgotten Holocaust of World War II* (New York: Basic Books, 1997).
2. Anne Barstow, *Witchcraze: A New History of the European Witch Hunts* (New York: HarperCollins, 1994).
3. Theodore W. Adorno, Else Frenkel-Brunswick, Daniel J. Levinson, and R. Nevitt Sanford, *The Authoritarian Personality* (New York: HarperCollins, 1950).
4. Lee Ross, "The Intuitive Psychologist and His Shortcomings," in Leonard Berkowitz (ed.), *Advances in Experimental Social Psychology* (Orlando, Fla.: Academic Press, 1977), 173–220.
5. Harry C. Triandis, *Culture and Social Behavior* (New York: McGraw-Hill, 1994).
6. Stanley Milgram, *Obedience to Authority* (New York: HarperCollins, 1974).
7. Thomas Blass, *The Man Who Shocked the World: The Life and Legacy of Stanley Milgram* (New York: Basic Books, 2004).
8. Robert C. Cialdini, *Influence: Science and Practice* (Needham Heights, Mass.: Allyn and Bacon, 2001).
9. Susan T. Fiske, Lasana T. Harris, and Amy J. C. Cuddy, "Why Ordinary People Torture Enemy Prisoners," *Science* 306 (2004): 1482–1483.
10. William Golding, *Lord of the Flies* (New York: Perigee, 1954).
11. Philip Zimbardo, "The Human Choice: Individuation, Reason, and Order Versus Deindividuation, Impulse and Chaos," in W. J. Arnold and D. Levine (eds.), *Nebraska Symposium on Motivation* (Lincoln: University of Nebraska Press, 1969), 237–307.
12. John Watson, "Investigation into Deindividuation Using a Cross-Cultural Survey Technique," *Journal of Personality and Social Psychology* 25 (1973): 342–345.
13. Al Bandura, "Mechanisms of Moral Disengagement," in Walter Reich, (ed.), *Origins of Terrorism: Psychologies, Ideologies, Theologies, States of Mind* (Cambridge: Cambridge University, 1990), 161–191.

14. Al Bandura, Bill Underwood, and Michael E. Fromson, "Disinhibition of Aggression Through Diffusion of Responsibility and Dehumanization of Victims," *Journal of Personality and Social Psychology* 9 (1975): 253–269.

15. Sam Keen, *Faces of the Enemy: Reflections on the Hostile Imagination* (New York: HarperCollins, 2004).

16. Christopher Browning, *Ordinary Men: Reserve Police Battalion 101 and the Final Solution in Poland* (New York: Aaron Asher Books, 1992).

17. Browning, *Ordinary Men*, xvi.

18. Adolph Hitler, *The New Order* (*The Third Reich*), T. L. Brooks (ed.) (Alexandria, Va.: Time-Life Books, 1989), 101–102.

19. Philip Zimbardo, "Mind Control in Orwell's *1984*: Fictional Concepts Become Operational Realities," in M. Nussbaum, J. Goldmsith, and A. Gleason (eds.), *Jim Jones' Jungle Experiment in 1984: Orwell and Our Future* (Princeton, N.J.: Princeton University Press, 2005).

20. Philip Zimbardo, "On Transforming Experimental Research into Advocacy for Social Change," in M. Deutsch and H. Hornstein (eds.), *Applying Social Psychology: Implications for Research, Practice, and Training* (Mahwah, N.J.: Erlbaum, 1975), 33–66.

21. For a detailed chronology and fuller account of the behavioral reactions that followed, readers are referred to the above references, and P. G. Zimbardo, C. Maslach, and C. Haney, "Reflections on the Stanford Prison Experiment: Genesis, Transformation, Consequences," in T. Blass (ed.), *Obedience to Authority: Current Perspectives on the Milgram Paradigm* (Mahwah, N.J.: Erlbaum, 1999), 193–237, and to our Web site: www.prisonexp. org.

22. Bibb Latane and John Darley, *The Unresponsive Bystander: Why Doesn't He Help?* (New York: Appleton-Century-Crofts, 1970).

23. John Darley and Dan Batson, "From Jerusalem to Jericho: A Study of Situational and Dispositional Variables in Helping Behavior," *Journal of Personality and Social Psychology* 27 (1973): 100–108.

24. Philip Zimbardo, "Abu Ghraib: The Evil of Inaction, and the Heroes Who Acted," *Western Psychologist Newsletter* (August 2004): 4–5.

25. Martha K. Huggins, Mika Haritos-Fatouros, and Philip G. Zimbardo, *Violence Workers: Police Torturers and Murderers Reconstruct Brazilian Atrocities* (Berkeley: University of California Press, 2002).

26. Mika Haritos-Fatouros, *The Psychological Origins of Institutionalized Torture* (London: Routledge, 2003).

27. Christina Maslach, *Burnout: The Costs of Caring* (Upper Saddle River, N.J.: Prentice-Hall, 1982).

28. Ellen J. Langer, *Mindfulness* (Reading, Mass.: Addison-Wesley, 1989).

29. Erich Fromm, *Escape from Freedom* (New York: Holt, 1941).

Chapter Six

1. Bertrand Russell, *Power: A New Social Analysis* (London: Allen & Unwin, 1938), Chap. 18.
2. Roger Brown, *Social Psychology* (New York: Free Press, 1965), Chap. 2.
3. Robert J. House, William D. Spangler, and James Woycke, "Personality and Charisma in the U.S. Presidency: A Psychological Theory of Leader Effectiveness," *Administrative Science Quarterly* 36 (1991): 364–396.
4. Lord Acton (John E. E. Dalberg Acton), "Letter to Mandell Creighton, April 5, 1887," in Gertrude Himmelfarb (ed.), *Essays on Freedom and Power* (New York: Free Press, 1948), 364.
5. David Kipnis, *The Powerholders* (Chicago: University of Chicago Press, 1976); David Kipnis, *Technology and Power* (New York: Springer Verlag, 1990); Annette Y. Lee-Chai and John A. Bargh (eds.), *The Use and Abuse of Power: Multiple Perspectives on the Causes of Corruption* (Philadelphia: Psychology Press, 2001).
6. Michael Adams, *Fire and Ice: The United States, Canada, and the Myth of Converging Values* (Toronto: Penguin Canada, 2003), 39.
7. Lee-Chai and Bargh, *Use and Abuse*.
8. The Tao, section 48, http://www.kbnet.co.uk/artemis/tao/tao.htm (accessed April 14, 2005).
9. Abigail Stewart and Andrea Dottolo, "Socialization to the Academy: Coping with Competing Social Identities," in Geraldine Downey and others (eds.), *Navigating the Future: Social Identity, Coping and Life Tasks* (New York: Russell Sage, 2005). See also Ella Edmondson Bell and Stella Nkomo, "Armoring: Learning to Withstand Racial Oppression," *Journal of Comparative Family Studies* 29 (1998): 285–295.
10. Marcus Tulius Cicero, *Letters to His Friends* (Cambridge, Mass.: Harvard University Press, 1953), 2:527.
11. David G. Winter, *The Power Motive* (New York: Free Press, 1973); David G. Winter, "Power Motivation," in Alan E. Kazdin (ed.), *Encyclopedia of Psychology* (New York: Oxford University Press and American Psychological Association, 2000), 6:264–266.
12. Hans J. Morgenthau, "Love and Power," *Commentary* 33 (1962): 248.
13. Sigmund Freud, "Why War?" (1933), in James Strachey (ed.), *The Standard Edition of the Complete Psychological Works of Sigmund Freud* (London: Hogarth, 1964), 22:212.
14. David C. McClelland, *Power: The Inner Experience* (New York: Irvington, 1975), 280, 296, Chap. 9.
15. David G. Winter, "Power, Affiliation and War: Three Tests of a Motivational Model," *Journal of Personality and Social Psychology* 65 (1993): 532–545.

16. Carrie A. Langner and David G. Winter, "The Motivational Basis of Compromise and Concessions: Archival and Experimental Studies," *Journal of Personality and Social Psychology* 81 (2001): 711–727.

17. David C. McClelland and David H. Burnham, "Power Is the Great Motivator," *Harvard Business Review* (March-April 1976): 100–110, 159–166; House, "Personality and Charisma"; David G. Winter, "Leader Appeal, Leader Performance, and the Motive Profiles of Leaders and Followers: A Study of American Presidents and Elections," *Journal of Personality and Social Psychology* 52 (1987): 196–202.

18. Samuel A. Stouffer, Arthur A. Lumsdaine, Marion Harper Lumsdaine, and Robin M. Williams Jr., *The American Soldier*, Vol. 2, *Combat and Its Aftermath* (Princeton, N.J.: Princeton University Press, 1949); Robin M. Williams, "The American Soldier: An Assessment, Several Wars Later," *Public Opinion Quarterly* 53 (1989): 160–166.

19. http://warisreal.blogspot.com/ (accessed May 23, 2005).

20. David G. Winter, *Personality: Analysis and Interpretation of Lives* (New York: McGraw-Hill, 1996), Chap. 5.

21. Avonne Mason and Virginia Blankenship, "Power and Affiliation Motivation, Stress, and Abuse in Intimate Relationships," *Journal of Personality and Social Psychology* 52 (1987): 203–210.

22. As Robert F. Kennedy, speaking in 1968 immediately after the assassination of Martin Luther King Jr., put it, "Let us dedicate ourselves to what the Greeks wrote so many years ago: to tame the savageness of man and make gentle the life of this world." http://www.americanrhetoric.com/speeches/robertkennedyonmartinlutherking.html (accessed May 10, 2005).

23. Sigmund Freud, *The Future of an Illusion* (1927), in *Standard Edition*, 21:53.

24. David G. Winter, David C. McClelland, and Abigail J. Stewart, *A New Case for the Liberal Arts* (San Francisco: Jossey-Bass, 1981), 72–76, 138–139, 167–168. In later centuries, study of Greek and Roman classics was presumed to prepare young men to rule the far-flung British Empire; see Philip Woodruff, *The Men Who Ruled India* (London: Jonathan Cape, 1953).

25. Julius Kuhl, "A Functional-Design Approach to Motivation and Self-Regulation: The Dynamics of Personality Systems and Interactions," in Monique Boekaerts, Paul R. Pintrich, and Moshe Zeidner (eds.), *Handbook of Self-Regulation* (Orlando, Fla.: Academic Press, 2000), 111–169. See also Roy F. Baumeister, Todd F. Heatherton, and Diane Tice, D. M., *Losing Control: How and Why People Fail at Self-Regulation* (Orlando, Fla.: Academic Press, 1994); Walter Mischel and Ozlem Ayduk, "Self-Regulation in a Cognitive-Affective Personality System: Attentional Control in the Service of the Self," *Self and Identity* 1 (2002): 115ff.

26. Hans Kohn, *The Mind of Germany: The Education of a Nation* (New York: Scribner, 1960).

27. The British letter was published as "Britain's Destiny and Duty," *Times*, September 18, 1914, 3. Signers included G. K. Chesterton, Arthur Conan

Doyle, Thomas Hardy, the moral philosopher A. C. Bradley, and the historian George Macaulay Trevelyan. (George Bernard Shaw refused to sign.) An English translation of the German manifesto was reprinted in *Current History: A Monthly Magazine: The European War,* Vol. 1: *From the Beginning to March, 1915* (New York: New York Times Company, 1915), 185–187. Signers included ten Nobel laureates and nine professors of theology, as well as physicist Max Planck and psychologist Wilhelm Wundt. Einstein refused to sign, and Planck later withdrew his signature.

28. Freud letters to Karl Abraham on July 26 and August 25, 1914, in Hilda C. Abraham and Ernst L. Freud (eds.), *A Psycho-Analytic Dialogue: The Letters of Sigmund Freud and Karl Abraham 1907–1926* (London: Hogarth), 186, 193; letter to Sándor Ferenczi on August 23, 1914, in Ernst Falzeder and Eva Brabant, eds., *The Correspondence of Sigmund Freud and Sándor Ferenczi,* Vol. 2, *1914–1919* (Cambridge, Mass.: Harvard University Press), 13. After enlisting in July 1914, the Austrian writer Hugo von Hofmannsthal wrote to a friend, "Believe me, all of us here, down to the last man, are entering into this business and all its possible consequences, with a resolution, even a joy, which I have never before experienced and would never have thought possible." See R.J.W. Evans, "The Habsburg Monarchy and the Coming of War," in R.J.W. Evans and Hartmut Pogge von Strandmann, *The Coming of the First World War* (Oxford: Clarendon Press, 1988), 50. (Evans assembled quotations along the same lines from other "creative modernist" intellectuals, 46–54.)

29. "Professors and War," *Washington Post,* September 24, 1914, 6.

30. Rudolf Höss, "Autobiography of Rudolf Höss," in Jadwiga Bezwińska and Danuta Czech, eds., *KL Auschwitz Seen by the SS* (Óswiecim, Poland: Państwowe Muzeum, 1972), 78–79.

31. Michael D. Young, *The Rise of the Meritocracy, 1870–2033: An Essay on Education and Equality* (Harmondsworth, Mddx.: Penguin, 1963); Lawrence Summers, "Remarks at National Bureau of Economic Research Conference on Diversifying the Science and Engineering Workforce," January 14, 2005, http://www.president.harvard.edu/speeches/2005/nber.html (accessed April 16, 2005).

32. Nicola Baumann and Julius Kuhl, "How to Resist Temptation: The Effects of External Control Versus Autonomy Support on Self-Regulatory Dynamics," *Journal of Personality* 73 (2005): 467.

33. David G. Winter and Nicole B. Barenbaum, "Responsibility and the Power Motive in Women and Men," *Journal of Personality* 53 (June 1985): 335–355.

34. David G. Winter, "Comparing 'War' and 'Peace' Crises: The Role of Motivation, Responsibility, and Integrative Complexity" (paper delivered at the Twentieth Annual Scientific Meeting of the International Society of Political Psychology, Kraków, Poland, July 1997).

35. Abraham Lincoln, "First Inaugural Address," http://www.bartleby.com/124/pres31.html (accessed May 12, 2005).

36. Abraham Lincoln, "Second Inaugural Address," http://www.bartleby.com/124/pres32.html (accessed May 22, 2005).

37. Kaiser Wilhelm II, "Speech from the Balcony of the Royal Palace, Berlin," July 31, 1914, http://www.lib.byu.edu/~rdh/wwi/1914/willytalk.html (accessed May 22, 2005); Basil G. Bouchier, "For All We Have and Are" (London: Skeffington, 1916).

38. Sigmund Freud, "Delusion and Dream in Jensen's Gradiva" (1907), in *Standard Edition* 9:35–36; see also Sigmund Freud, *Moses and Monotheism* (1939), in *Standard Edition*, 23:1–137.

39. Confucius, *The Analects of Confucius*, trans. and ed. Simon Leys (New York: Norton, 1997).

40. Phrase from William Shakespeare's *Titus Andronicus*, Act III, Scene 1, line 53.

41. William Shakespeare, *Troilus and Cressida*, Act I, Scene 3, lines 109–1111, 119–124.

42. Thucydides, *History of the Peloponnesian War*, Book 5, section 89.

43. Geert Hofstede, *Culture's Consequences: Comparing Values, Behaviors, Institutions, and Organizations Across Nations*, 2nd ed. (Thousand Oaks, Calif.: Sage, 2001), Chap. 3.

44. Dacher Keltner, Deborah H. Gruenfeld, and Cameron Anderson, "Power, Approach, and Inhibition," *Psychological Review* 110 (2003): 265–284; see also Chapter Seven, this volume.

45. Presentation at the conference on "Moral Leadership" at the Stanford University Center on Ethics, February 24–25, 2005; see Chapter Twelve, this volume.

46. Russell, *Power*, Chap. 18.

47. Charles A. Beard, *An Economic Interpretation of the Constitution of the United States* (New York: Macmillan, 1913); Beard, *Economic Origins of Jeffersonian Democracy* (New York: Macmillan, 1915).

48. G. William Domhoff, *The Powers That Be: Processes of Ruling Class Domination in America* (New York: Random House, 1978); Domhoff, *State Autonomy or Class Dominance? Case Studies on Policy Making in America* (New York: Aldine de Gruyter, 1996); Domhoff, *Who Rules America? Power and Politics in the Year 2000* (Mountain View, Calif.: Mayfield, 1998); C. Wright Mills, *The Power Elite* (New York: Oxford University Press, 1956); Domhoff, *The Power Elite and the State: How Policy Is Made in America* (New York: Aldine de Gruyter, 1990).

49. Ian Kershaw, *Hitler, 1889–1936: Hubris* (New York: Norton, 1999), Chaps. 10–11.

50. Charles-Louis de Secondat, baron de La Brède et de Montesquieu, *The Spirit of the Laws* (1748), Book 11, http://www.constitution.org/cm/sol_11.htm #001 (accessed May 12, 2005); John Adams, "Letter 26" [to Dr. Price], in *A Defence of the Constitutions of Government of the United States of America* (1787), http://www.constitution.org/jadams/ja1_26.htm (accessed May 12, 2005); Alexander Hamilton, James Madison, and John Jay, "The Structure

of the Government Must Furnish the Proper Checks and Balances Between the Different Departments," in *The Federalist: A Commentary on the Constitution of the United States* (1788), Federalist Paper no. 51, http://www.constitution.org/fed/federa51.htm (accessed May 22, 2005).

51. Brief filed March 22, 2005, with the U.S. Court of Appeals, Eleventh Circuit, on behalf of appellees in *Schiavo et al.* v. *Schiavo et al.*, http://reports.tbo.com/reports/schiavo/petition1.doc (accessed May 1, 2005).

52. Arthur M. Schlesinger Jr., *The Imperial Presidency* (Boston: Houghton Mifflin, 1973); Stephen Graubard, *Command of Office: How War, Secrecy, and Deception Transformed the Presidency from Theodore Roosevelt to George W. Bush* (New York: Basic Books, 2004).

53. Gaston Bachelard, *The Psychoanalysis of Fire*, trans. Alan C. M. Ross (London: Routledge & Kegan Paul, 1964), 7. The metaphorical linkages of power and fire may run deeper: charismatic leaders are often described with images of fire and light. For example, after Gandhi's death, India's prime minister, Nehru, said, "The light has gone out of our lives and there is darkness everywhere." Jawaharlal Nehru, *Nehru on Gandhi* (New York: John Day, 1948), 127. And the colors red and black, preferred by power-motivated people (Winter, *Power Motive*, 188–190), are associated with fire and its ashes. On the connections between fire, sexuality, and the control of power, see also Sigmund Freud, "The Acquisition and Control of Fire" (1932), in *Standard Edition* 22:183–193.

54. In his poem "Ars Victrix" (1876), http://www.poemhunter.com/p/m/poem.asp?poet=33330&poem=394107 (accessed May 22, 2005).

55. Yuen Foong Khong, *Analogies at War: Korea, Munich, Dien Bien Phu, and the Vietnam Decisions of 1965* (Princeton, N.J.: Princeton University Press, 1992); Ernest R. May, *"Lessons" of the Past: The Use and Misuse of History in American Foreign Policy* (New York: Oxford University Press, 1973); Richard E. Neustadt and Ernest R. May, *Thinking in Time: The Uses of History for Decision-Makers* (New York: Free Press, 1986).

56. Norman Cousins, "The Cuban Missile Crisis: An Anniversary," *Saturday Review*, October 15, 1977, 4.

57. David G. Winter, "Asymmetrical Perceptions of Power in Crises: A Comparison of 1914 and the Cuban Missile Crisis," *Journal of Peace Research* 40 (2003): 251–270; Bill E. Peterson, Richard M. Doty, and David G. Winter, "Laboratory Tests of a Motivational-Perceptual Model of Conflict Escalation," *Journal of Conflict Resolution* 38 (1994): 719–748.

58. Markus Kemmelmeier and David G. Winter, "Putting Threat into Perspective: Experimental Studies on Perceptual Distortion in International Conflict," *Personality and Social Psychology Bulletin* 26 (2000): 800.

59. "Professors at War," *Washington Post*, September 24, 1914, 6.

60. Psychological research on terror management theory is relevant to this point; see Holly A. McGregor, Joel D. Lieberman, and Jeff Greenberg, "Terror Management and Aggression: Evidence That Mortality Salience Motivates

Aggression Against Worldview—Threatening Others," *Journal of Personality and Social Psychology* 74 (1998): 212–220; Sheldon Solomon, Jeff Greenberg, and Tom Pyszczynski, "Fear of Death and Social Behavior: The Anatomy of Human Destructiveness," in Richard W. Bloom and Nancy Dess (eds.), *Evolutionary Psychology and Violence: A Primer for Policymakers and Public Policy Advocates* (Westport, Conn.: Praeger), 129–136.

61. On Hitler's physical and mental state in 1937, see Ian Kershaw, *Hitler, 1937–1945: Nemesis* (New York: Norton, 2000), 36–37. The phrases are from an adjutant's notes taken at a briefing for military chiefs of staff in November 1937; see Max Domarus (ed.), *Hitler: Speeches and Proclamations, 1932–1945* (Wauconda, Ill.: Bolchazy-Carducci, 1992), 963–972 passim. The August 1939 quotation is from Kershaw, *Nemesis*, 228, 907 note 324. Other vivid examples include (1) a speech to Nazi propaganda leaders in mid-October 1937: "He, Hitler, would not live much longer. . . . In his family, men did not grow old. Also both his parents had died young. It was hence necessary to face the problems which absolutely had to be resolved (Lebensraum) as quickly as possible—so that this would occur while he was still alive" (Domarus, *Hitler*, 959); (2) a conversation with the British ambassador on August 24, 1939: "He was, he said, 50 years old: he preferred war now to when he would be 55 or 60" (Neville Henderson, in Ernest L. Woodward and others, eds., *Documents on British Foreign Policy 1919–1939*. Third Series, Vol. 7—*1939*, London: Her Majesty's Stationery Office, 1954, 201); and (3) a speech to his military commanders in chief on November 23, 1939, twelve weeks after the invasion of Poland: "Everything is determined by the fact that the moment is favorable now; in six months it might not be so any more. As the last factor I must in all honesty describe my own person: Irreplaceable. Neither a military man nor a civilian could replace me. . . . I am convinced of my powers of intellect and of decision. . . . The fate of the Reich depends only on me" (Domarus, *Hitler*, 1887).

62. Erik H. Erikson, *Childhood and Society* (New York: Norton, 1950), 231.

63. John F. Kennedy, "Commencement Address at American University" (June 10, 1963), in *Public Papers of the President of the United States: John F. Kennedy, 1963* (Washington, D.C.: Government Printing Office, 1964), 460, 462.

Chapter Seven

1. Richard M. Emerson, "Power-Dependence Relations," *American Sociological Review* 27 (1962): 31–41; Susan T. Fiske, "Controlling Other People: The Impact of Power on Stereotyping," *American Psychologist* 48 (1993): 621–628.

2. Kurt Eichenwald, *Conspiracy of Fools: A True Story* (New York: Broadway Books, 2005).

3. Dacher Keltner, Deborah Gruenfeld, and Cameron P. Anderson, "Power, Approach, and Inhibition," *Psychological Review* 110 (2003): 265–284.

4. Serena Chen, Annette Y. Lee-Chai, and John A. Bargh, "Relationship Orientation as a Moderator of the Effects of Social Power," *Journal of Personality and Social Psychology* 80 (2001): 173–187; see also Adam Galinsky, Deborah H. Gruenfeld, and Joseph C. Magee, "From Power to Action," *Journal of Personality and Social Psychology* 85 (2003): 453–466.

5. David M. Buss and Kenneth H. Craik, "The Act Frequency Approach to Personality," *Psychological Review* 90 (1983): 105–126; Harrison G. Gough and Pamela Bradley, *CPI Manual* (Palo Alto, Calif.: Consulting Psychologists Press, 1996); Edwin I. Megargee, "Influence of Sex Roles on the Manifestation of Leadership," *Journal of Applied Psychology* 53 (1969): 377–382; David S. Wilson, David Near, and Ralph R. Miller, "Machiavellianism: A Synthesis of the Evolutionary and Psychological Literatures," *Psychological Bulletin* 119 (1996): 285–299.

6. Cameron P. Anderson, Oliver P. John, Dacher Keltner, and Ann M. Kring, "Who Attains Social Status? Effects of Personality and Physical Attractiveness in Social Groups," *Journal of Personality and Social Psychology* 81 (2001): 116–132.

7. Keltner, Gruenfeld, and Anderson, "Power, Approach, and Inhibition."

8. Max Weber, *The Theory of Social and Economic Organization* (New York: Oxford University Press, 1947).

9. Dacher Keltner, L. Capps, A. M. Kring, R. C. Young, and E. A. Heerey, "Just Teasing: A Conceptual Analysis and Empirical Review," *Psychological Bulletin* 127 (2001): 229–248.

10. James Sidanius, "The Psychology of Group Conflict and the Dynamics of Oppression: A Social Dominance Perspective," in S. Iyengar (ed.), *Explorations in Political Psychology* (Durham, N.C.: Duke University Press, 1993).

11. Peggy Reeves-Sanday, "The Socio-Cultural Context of Rape: A Cross-Cultural Study," in L. L. O'Toole (ed.), *Gender Violence: Interdisciplinary Perspectives* (New York: New York University Press, 1997).

12. Michael R. Gottfredson and Michael J. Hindelang, "Sociological Aspects of Criminal Victimization," *Annual Review of Sociology* 7 (1981): 107–128.

13. F. Gregory Ashby, Alice M. Isen, and U. Turken, "A Neuropsychological Theory of Positive Affect and Its Influence on Cognition," *Psychological Review* 106 (1999): 529–550.

14. Cameron P. Anderson, Oliver P. John, and Dacher Keltner, "Self-Perceived Power: An Individual Difference Measure," manuscript in preparation; Jennifer Berdahl and Paul Martorana, "Effects of Power on Influence, Expression, and Emotion During a Controversial Discussion," *Experimental Journal of Social Psychology* (under review); Daphne B. Bugental and Jeffrey C. Lewis, "The Paradoxical Misuse of Power by Those Who See Themselves as Powerless: How Does It Happen?" *Journal of Social Issues* 55 (1999):

51–64; Elizabeth Cashdan, "Smiles, Speech, and Body Posture: How Women and Men Display Sociometric Status and Power," *Journal of Nonverbal Behavior* 22 (1998): 209–228.

15. Daniel Ward and Dacher Keltner, "Power and the Consumption of Resources," unpublished manuscript, University of California, Berkeley, 2000.

16. David G. Winter, *The Power Motive* (New York: Free Press, 1973); D. G. Winter, "The Power Motive in Women—and Men," *Journal of Personality and Social Psychology* 54 (1988): 510–519.

17. David G. Winter and Nicole Barenbaum, "Responsibility and the Power Motive in Women and Men," *Journal of Personality* 53 (1985): 335–355.

18. Brenda Major and Richard Heslin, "Perceptions of Cross-Sex and Same-Sex Nonreciprocal Touch: It Is Better to Give Than Receive," *Journal of Nonverbal Behavior* 6 (1982): 148–162.

19. Michael V. Studd, "Sexual Harassment," in D. M. Buss and N. M. Malamuth (eds.), *Sex, Power, and Conflict* (New York: Oxford University Press, 1996); Reeves-Sanday, "The Socio-Cultural Context of Rape"; Donald P. Green, Janelle S. Wong, and Dara Z. Strolovitch, "The Effects of Demographic Change on Hate Crime," working paper no. 96–06, Institution for Social and Policy Studies, Yale University, 1996.

20. Jon Haidt, "The Emotional Dog and Its Rational Tail: A Social Intuitionist Approach to Moral Judgment," *Psychological Review* 108 (2001): 814–834.

21. Haidt, "The Emotional Dog and Its Rational Tail."

22. J. Haidt, S. Koller, and M. Dias, "Affect, Culture, and Morality, or Is It Wrong to Eat Your Dog?" *Journal of Personality and Social Psychology* 65 (1993): 613–628.

23. James R. Rest, "Morality," in J. Flavell and E. Markman (eds.), *Handbook of Child Psychology* (Hoboken, N.J.: Wiley, 1983), 3:556–629; Kristin Vasquez, Dacher Keltner, David H. Ebenbach, and Tracy L. Banaszynski, "Cultural Variation and Similarity in Moral Rhetorics: Voices from the Philippines and the United States," *Journal of Cross-Cultural Psychology* 32 (2001): 93–120.

24. Cameron P. Anderson, Oliver P. John, and Dacher Keltner, "Self-Perceived Power: An Individual Difference Measure," manuscript in preparation.

25. Kenneth Rasinski, "What's Fair Is Fair . . . or Is It? Value Differences Underlying Public Views of Social Justice," *Journal of Personality and Social Psychology* 53 (1987): 201–211.

26. Rasinski, "What's Fair Is Fair . . . or Is It?"

27. John T. Jost and Mahzarin R. Banaji, "The Role of Stereotyping in System-Justification and the Production of False Consciousness," *British Journal of Social Psychology* 33 (1994): 1–27; James R. Kluegel and Eliot R. Smith, *Beliefs About Inequality* (New York: Aldine de Grader, 1986).

28. Vasquez, Keltner, Ebenbach, and Banaszynski, "Cultural Variation and Similarity in Moral Rhetorics."

29. Philip E. Tetlock, "Cognitive Style and Political Belief Systems in the British House of Commons," *Journal of Personality and Social Psychology* 41 (1984): 365–375.

30. Deborah H. Gruenfeld and Jared Preston, "Upending the Status Quo: Cognitive Complexity in US Supreme Court Justices Who Overturn Legal Precedent," *Personality and Social Psychology Bulletin* 26 (2000): 1013–1022; D. Keltner and R. J. Robinson, "Defending the Status Quo: Power and Bias in Social Conflict," *Personality and Social Psychology Bulletin* 23 (1997): 1066–1077.

31. Erving Goffman, *Interaction Ritual* (New York: Anchor Books, 1967).

32. Emerson, "Power-Dependence Relations."

33. Irving L. Janis, *Groupthink* (Boston: Houghton Mifflin, 1982).

34. Dacher Keltner, R. C. Young, E. Heerey, C. Oering, and N. D. Monarch, "Teasing in Hierarchical and Intimate Relations," *Journal of Personality and Social Psychology* 75, 5 (1998): 1231–1247.

35. Keltner and others, "Just Teasing."

36. Maria Logli Allison, Randall C. Young, Dacher Keltner, and Kenneth H. Craik, "Gossip as Reputational Control in Social Hierarchies," manuscript in preparation.

37. Carrie A. Langner, Dacher Keltner, and Serena Chen, "Power and Attitude Expression," manuscript in preparation.

38. Maria Logli Allison, Randall C. Young, Dacher Keltner, and Kenneth H. Craik, "Gossip as Reputational Control in Social Hierarchies," manuscript under review.

39. Cameron P. Anderson, Dacher Keltner, and Oliver P. John, "Emotional Convergence Between People over Time," *Journal of Personality and Social Psychology* 84 (2003): 1054–1068.

40. Fiske, "Controlling Other People."

41. Langner, Keltner, and Chen, "Power and Attitude Expression."

42. Philip E. Tetlock, "The Impact of Accountability on Judgment and Choice," in M. Zanna (ed.), *Advances in Experimental Social Psychology Vol. 25* (Orlando, Fla.: Academic Press, 1992), 331–376; Jennifer S. Lerner and Philip E. Tetlock, "Accounting for the Effects of Accountability," *Psychological Bulletin* 125 (2000): 255–275.

43. Philip E. Tetlock, "Pre- to Post-Election Shifts in Presidential Rhetoric: Impression Management or Cognitive Adjustment," *Journal of Personality and Social Psychology* 41 (1981): 207–212.

44. Gruenfeld and Preston, "Upending the Status Quo."

45. Maria Logli Allison, "A Functional Approach to Reputation," manuscript in preparation.

46. Adam Smith, "Report Dated 1766," in R. L. Meek, D. D. Raphael, and P. G. Stein (eds.), *Lectures on Jurisprudence* (New York: Oxford University Press, 1978), 538–541.

47. Robert C. Post, "The Social Foundations of Defamation Law: Reputation and the Constitution," *California Law Review* 74 (1986): 691–742.

48. Stephen S. Standifird, "Reputation and e-Commerce: eBay Auctions and the Asymmetrical Impact of Positive and Negative Ratings," *Journal of Management* 27 (2001): 279–295.

49. John J. Skowronski and Donal E. Carlston, "Negativity and Extremity Biases in Impression Formation: A Review of Explanations," *Psychological Bulletin* 105 (1989): 131–142.

50. David G. Winter and Nicole Barenbaum, "Responsibility and the Power Motive in Women and Men," *Journal of Personality* 53 (1985): 335–355; David G. Winter, "Comparing 'War' and 'Peace' Crises: The Role of Motivation, Responsibility, and Integrative Complexity" (paper presented at the annual meeting of the International Society of Political Psychology, Kraków, Poland, 1997).

51. Winter and Barenbaum, "Responsibility and the Power Motive in Women and Men."

52. Winter and Barenbaum, "Responsibility and the Power Motive in Women and Men."

Chapter Eight

1. Kurt Lewin, *Field Theory in Social Science* (New York: HarperCollins, 1951).

2. See Donald T. Campbell, "On the Conflicts Between Biological and Social Evolution and Between Psychology and Moral Tradition," *American Psychologist* 30 (1975): 1103–1126; Jane J. Mansbridge (ed.), *Beyond Self-Interest* (Chicago: University of Chicago Press, 1990).

3. See C. D. Batson, *The Altruism Question: Toward a Social-Psychological Answer* (Mahwah, N.J.: Erlbaum, 1991); C. D. Batson, "Why Act for the Public Good? Four Answers," *Personality and Social Psychology Bulletin* 20 (1994): 603–610; Christopher Jenks, "Varieties of Altruism," in Jane J. Mansbridge (ed.), *Beyond Self-Interest* (Chicago: University of Chicago Press, 1990), 53–67.

4. Adam Smith, *An Inquiry into the Nature and Causes of the Wealth of Nations* (1776; Chicago: University of Chicago Press, 1976).

5. Garrett Hardin, *The Limits of Altruism: An Ecologist's View of Survival* (Bloomington: Indiana University Press, 1977), 27.

6. John Stuart Mill, "Utilitarianism," in John Stuart Mill and Jeremy Bentham, *Utilitarianism and Other Essays* (1861; London: Penguin Books, 1987), 299.

7. Sigmund Freud, *Civilization and Its Discontents*, trans. J. Strachey (1930; New York: Norton, 1961).

8. C. D. Batson, "Prosocial Motivation: Is It Ever Truly Altruistic?" in L. Berkowitz (ed.), *Advances in Experimental Social Psychology* (Orlando, Fla.: Academic Press, 1987), 20:65–122; C. Daniel Batson, Cynthia L. Turk,

Laura L. Shaw, and Tricia R. Klein, "Information Function of Empathic Emotion: Learning That We Value the Other's Welfare," *Journal of Personality and Social Psychology* 68 (1995): 300–313; Martin L. Hoffman, "Empathy, Role-Taking, Guilt, and Development of Altruistic Motives," in T. Lickona (ed.), *Moral Development and Behavior: Theory, Research, and Social Issues* (New York: Holt, 1976), 124–143.

9. C. D. Batson, Tricia R. Klein, L. Highberger, and L. L. Shaw, "Immorality from Empathy-Induced Altruism: When Compassion and Justice Conflict," *Journal of Personality and Social Psychology* 68 (1995): 1042–1054; Ezra Stotland, "Exploratory Studies of Empathy," in L. Berkowitz (ed.), *Advances in Experimental Social Psychology* 4 (Orlando, Fla.: Academic Press, 1969), 4:271–313.

10. Hardin, *Limits of Altruism*, 26.

11. C. D. Batson et al., "Two Threats to the Common Good: Self-Interested Egoism and Empathy-Induced Altruism," *Personality and Social Psychology Bulletin* 25 (1999): 3–16; C. D. Batson, Judy G. Batson et al., "Empathy and the Collective Good: Caring for One of the Others in a Social Dilemma," *Journal of Personality and Social Psychology* 68 (1995): 619–631.

12. C. D. Batson, J. Chang, R. Orr, and J. Rowland, "Empathy, Attitudes, and Action: Can Feeling for a Member of a Stigmatized Group Motivate One to Help the Group?" *Personality and Social Psychology Bulletin* 28 (2002): 1656–1666; C. D. Batson, Marina P. Polycarpou, and E. Harmon-Jones, "Empathy and Attitudes: Can Feeling for a Member of a Stigmatized Group Improve Feelings Toward the Group?" *Journal of Personality and Social Psychology* 72 (1997): 105–118; John F. Dovidio, Samuel L. Gaertner, and J. D. Johnson, "New Directions in Prejudice and Prejudice Reduction: The Role of Cognitive Representations and Affect" (paper presented at the Annual Meeting of the Society of Experimental Social Psychology, St. Louis, Mo., October 1999); Terri K. Vescio and Miles Hewstone, "Empathy Arousal as a Means of Improving Intergroup Attitudes: An Examination of the Affective Supercedent Hypothesis," unpublished manuscript, Pennsylvania State University, 2001; Terri K. Vescio, G. B. Sechrist, and M. P. Paolucci, "Perspective Taking and Prejudice Reduction: The Mediational Role of Empathy Arousal and Situational Attributions," *European Journal of Social Psychology* 33 (2003): 455–472.

13. For example, Henri Tajfel and John C. Turner, "The Social Identity Theory of Intergroup Behavior," in S. Worschel and W. Austin (eds.), *Psychology of Intergroup Relations* (Chicago: Nelson-Hall, 1986), 7–24.

14. G. Alfano and Gerald Marwell, "Experiments on the Provision of Common Goods by Groups III: Non-Divisibility and Free Riding in 'Real' Groups," *Social Psychology Quarterly* 43 (1981): 300–309; Marilynn B. Brewer and Roderick M. Kramer, "Choice Behavior in Social Dilemmas: Effects of Social Identity, Group Size, and Decision Framing," *Journal of Personality and Social Psychology* 50 (1986): 543–549; Robyn M. Dawes, J. McTavish,

and H. Shaklee, "Behavior, Communication, and Assumptions About Other People's Behavior in a Commons Dilemma Situation," *Journal of Personality and Social Psychology* 35 (1977): 1–11; Robyn M. Dawes, Alphons J. C. van de Kragt, and John M. Orbell, "Cooperation for the Benefit of Us—Not Me, or My Conscience," in J. J. Mansbridge (ed.), *Beyond Self-Interest* (Chicago: University of Chicago Press, 1990), 97–110; Roderick M. Kramer and Marilynn B. Brewer, "Effects of Group Identity on Resource Use in a Simulated Commons Dilemma," *Journal of Personality and Social Psychology* 46 (1984): 1044–1057; John M. Orbell, Alphons J. C. van de Kragt, and Robyn M. Dawes, "Explaining Discussion-Induced Cooperation," *Journal of Personality and Social Psychology* 54 (1988): 811–819; T. Yamagishi and K. Sato, "Motivational Bases of the Common Goods Problem," *Journal of Personality and Social Psychology* 50 (1986): 67–73.

15. Immanuel Kant, *Critique of Practical Reason and Other Works on the Theory of Ethics*, 4th ed., trans, T. K. Abbott (1785; White Plains, N.Y.: Longman, 1898), sec. 1, para. 13; Tolstoy, "The Law of Love and the Law of Violence," in *A Confession and Other Religious Writings*, trans. J. Kentish (1908; London: Penguin Books, 1987), 230; Mill, "Utilitarianism."

16. John Rawls, *A Theory of Justice* (Cambridge, Mass.: Harvard University Press, 1971); Lawrence Kohlberg, "Moral Stages and Moralization: The Cognitive-Developmental Approach," in T. Lickona (ed.), *Moral Development and Behavior: Theory, Research, and Social Issues* (New York: Holt, 1976), 31–53.

17. Lawrence Blum, *Friendship, Altruism, and Morality* (London: Routledge, 1980); Carol Gilligan, *In a Different Voice: Psychological Theory and Women's Development* (Cambridge, Mass.: Harvard University Press, 1982); Thomas Nagel, *Equality and Partiality* (New York: Oxford University Press), 1991; Nel Noddings, *Caring: A Feminine Approach to Ethics and Moral Education* (Berkeley: University of California Press, 1984); Joan Tronto, "Beyond Gender Differences to a Theory of Care," *Signs* 12 (1987): 644–663; Bernard Williams, "Persons, Character, and Morality," in Bernard Williams (ed.), *Moral Luck: Philosophical Papers 1973–1980* (Cambridge: Cambridge University Press, 1981), 1–19.

18. Antonio Blasi, "Bridging Moral Cognition and Moral Action: A Critical Review of the Literature," *Psychological Bulletin* 88 (1980): 1–45.

19. See Albert Bandura, "Social Cognitive Theory of Moral Thought and Action," in W. M. Kurtines and J. L. Gewirtz (eds.), *Handbook of Moral Behavior and Development*, Vol. 1, *Theory* (Mahwah, N.J.: Erlbaum, 1991), 45–103; C. D. Batson, "Justice Motivation and Moral Motivation," in M. Ross and D. T. Miller (eds.), *The Justice Motive in Everyday Life* (Cambridge: Cambridge University Press. 2002), 91–106; C. D. Batson, Diane Kobrynowicz et al., "In a Very Different Voice: Unmasking Moral Hypocrisy," *Journal of Personality and Social Psychology* 72 (1997): 1335–1348; David M. Bersoff, "Why Good People Sometimes Do Bad Things:

Motivated Reasoning and Unethical Behavior," *Personality and Social Psychology Bulletin* 25 (1999): 28–39; Ervin Staub, "Moral Exclusion, Personal Goal Theory, and Extreme Destructiveness," *Journal of Social Issues* 46 (1990): 47–64.

20. See C. D. Batson, Nadia Ahmad, and Jo Ann Tsang, "Buying Kindness: Effect of an Extrinsic Incentive for Helping on Perceived Altruism," *Personality and Social Psychology Bulletin* 4 (1978): 86–91; C. D. Batson, J. Fultz, P. A. Schoenrade, and A. Paduano, "Critical Self-Reflection and Self-Perceived Altruism: When Self-Reward Fails," *Journal of Personality and Social Psychology* 53 (1987): 594–602; Dale T. Miller and Rebecca K. Ratner, "The Disparity Between the Actual and Assumed Power of Self-Interest," *Journal of Personality and Social Psychology* 74 (1998): 53–62; Arthur A. Stukas, Mark Snyder, and E. Gil Clary, "The Effects of 'Mandatory Volunteerism' on Intentions to Volunteer," *Psychological Science* 10 (1999): 59–64.

21. See Batson et al., "Two Threats to the Common Good"; Batson, Batson et al., "Empathy and the Collective Good"; Batson, Klein et al., "Immorality from Empathy-Induced Altruism."

22. Samuel Oliner and Pearl Oliner, *The Altruistic Personality: Rescuers of Jews in Nazi Europe* (New York: Free Press, 1988).

23. Jonathan Kozol, *Savage Inequalities: Children in America's Schools* (New York: Crown, 1991).

Chapter Nine

1. For a review of this evidence, see Tom R. Tyler and Steve L. Blader, *Cooperation in Groups* (Philadelphia: Psychology Press, 2000).

2. William C. Frederick, *Values, Nature, and Culture in the American Corporation* (New York: Oxford University Press, 1995); M. Healy and J. Iles, "The Establishment and Enforcement of Codes," *Journal of Business Ethics* 39 (2002): 117–124; Joel Mintz, "Scrutinizing Environmental Enforcement," *Journal of Land Use and Environmental Law* 17 (2001): 127–148; E. M. Rice, "The Corporate Tax Gap: Evidence on Tax Compliance by Small Corporations," in Joel Slemrod (ed.), *Why People Pay Taxes* (Ann Arbor: University of Michigan Press, 1992); David R. Simon and D. Stanley Eitzen, *Elite Deviance*, 3rd ed. (Needham Heights, Mass.: Allyn and Bacon, 1990); D. B. Spence, "The Shadow of the Rational Polluter: Rethinking the Role of Rational Actor Models in Environmental Law," *California Law Review* 89 (2001): 917–998.

3. It might initially seem that rule following and rule breaking would be two sides of the same coin. Empirically they are found to be related but not the same. One reason is that employees may break rules by stealing or cheating for reasons of personal gain that are unrelated to their views about and willingness to pursue company policies while working. An employee might, for

example, willingly pursue company policies when working but consistently falsify expense reports or hours worked.

4. Jerald Greenberg, "The STEAL Motive: Managing the Social Determinants of Employee Theft," in Robert Giacalone and Jerald Greenberg (eds.), *Antisocial Behavior in Organizations* (Thousand Oaks, Calif.: Sage, 1997).

5 Tom R. Tyler, *Why People Obey the Law* (New Haven, Conn.: Yale University Press, 1990).

6. Tom R. Tyler, "Compliance with Intellectual Property Laws: A Psychological Perspective," *International Journal of Law and Politics*, 29 (1997): 219–235; Tom R. Tyler, "Citizen Discontent with Legal Procedures," *American Journal of Comparative Law* 45 (1997): 871–904.

7. See Tom R. Tyler and Yuen J. Huo, *Trust in the Law* (New York: Russell Sage Foundation, 2002).

8. Tyler, *Why People Obey the Law*.

9. Tyler and Blader, *Cooperation in Groups*.

10. Robert MacCoun, "Drugs and the Law: A Psychological Analysis of Drug Prohibition," *Psychological Bulletin* 113 (1993): 497–512.

11. Tyler and Blader, *Cooperation in Groups*.

12. Herbert C. Kelman, "Compliance, Identification, and Internalization," *Journal of Conflict Resolution* 2 (1958): 51–60.

13. Herbert C. Kelman and V. Lee Hamilton, *Crimes of Obedience* (New Haven, Conn.: Yale University Press, 1989).

14. Charles O'Reilly and Jennifer Chatman, "Organizational Commitment and Psychological Attachment," *Journal of Applied Psychology* 71 (1986): 492–499.

15. Tyler and Blader, *Cooperation in Groups*.

16. Philip Selznick, *Law, Society, and Industrial Justice* (New York: Russell Sage Foundation, 1969).

17. M. Aalders and T. Wilthagen, "Moving Beyond Command and Control: Reflexivity in the Regulation of Occupational Safety and Health and the Environment," *Law and Policy* 19 (1997): 415–443; John Darley, Tom Tyler, and Kenworthy Bilz, "Enacting Justice: The Interplay of Individual and Institutional Perspectives," in M. A. Hogg and J. Cooper (eds.), *The Sage Handbook of Social Psychology* (Thousand Oaks, Calif.: Sage, 2003); N. Gunningham and J. Rees, "Industry Self-Regulation," *Law and Policy* 19 (1997): 363–414; C. Rechtschaffen, "Deterrence vs. Cooperation and the Evolving Theory of Environmental Enforcement," *Southern California Law Review* 71 (1998): 1181–1272; M. Suchman, "Managing Legitimacy: Strategic and Institutional Approaches," *Academy of Management Review* 20 (1995): 571–610; Tom R. Tyler, "Trust and Law-Abidingness: A Proactive Model of Social Regulation," *Boston University Law Review* 81 (2001): 361–406; Tom R. Tyler and John M. Darley, "Building a Law-Abiding Society: Taking Public Views About Morality and the Legitimacy of Legal Authorities into

Account When Formulating Substantive Law," *Hofstra Law Review* 28 (2000): 707–739.

18. Tom R. Tyler, "Promoting Employee Policy Adherence and Rule Following in Work Settings: The Value of Self-Regulatory Approaches," *Brooklyn Law Review* 70 (2005): 1202; Tom R. Tyler, "Managing Conflicts of Interest Within Organizations: Does Activating Social Values Change the Impact of Self-Interest on Behavior?" in Don Moore, Daylian Cain, George Loewenstein, and Max Bazerman (eds.), *Conflicts of Interest* (Cambridge: Cambridge University Press, 2005); T. R. Tyler and S. L. Blader, "Can Businesses Effectively Regulate Employee Conduct? The Antecedents of Rule Following in Work Settings," *Academy of Management Journal* 48, 6 (2005): 1143–1158.

19. Tom R. Tyler and Jeff Fagan, "Legitimacy and Cooperation: Why Do People Help the Police Fight Crime in Their Communities?" unpublished manuscript, Psychology Department, New York University, 2005.

20. Tyler and Blader, "Can Businesses Effectively Regulate Employee Conduct?"

21. Tyler and Fagan, "Legitimacy and Cooperation."

22. Tyler, *Why People Obey the Law*.

23. Tom R. Tyler, "Managing Conflicts of Interest Within Organizations: Does Activating Social Values Change the Impact of Self-Interest on Behavior?" in Moore, Cain, Loewenstein, and Bazerman (eds.), *Conflicts of Interest*.

24. However, as in prior findings, they are influenced by risk assessments. The influence occurs but is small in magnitude. It would therefore be inaccurate to depict people as uninterested in instrumental issues. They are interested in risk and shape their behavior in response to risks. However, this is not the primary factor shaping their behavior. See Tyler, "Managing Conflicts of Interest Within Organizations."

25. Robert E. Goodin, *The Theory of Institutional Design* (Cambridge: Cambridge University Press, 1996); D. Jaffee, *Organization Theory: Tension and Change* (New York: McGraw-Hill, 1996).

26. Jason Sunshine and Tom R. Tyler, "The Role of Procedural Justice and Legitimacy in Shaping Public Support for Policing," *Law and Society Review* 37 (2003): 513–547; Tyler and Huo, *Trust in the Law*.

27. J. A. Colquitt and others, "Justice at the Millennium: A Meta-Analytic Review of 25 Years of Organizational Justice," *Journal of Applied Psychology* 86 (2001): 425–445; J. Greenberg and R. Cropanzano (eds.), *Advances in Organizational Justice* (Stanford: Stanford University Press, 2001); Tyler and Blader, *Cooperation in Groups*; Tom R. Tyler and others, *Social Justice in a Diverse Society* (Boulder, Colo.: Westview Press, 1997).

28. W. C. Kim and R. A. Mauborgne, "Procedural Justice, Attitudes, and Subsidiary Top Management Compliance with Multinationals' Corporate Strategic Decisions," *Academy of Management Journal* 36 (1993): 502–526.

29. Tyler and Blader, *Cooperation in Groups*.

30. Steve L. Blader and Tom R. Tyler, "What Constitutes Fairness in Work Settings?" *Human Resource Management Review* 12 (2003): 107–126; Steve L. Blader and Tom R. Tyler, "A Four Component Model of Procedural Justice," *Personality and Social Psychology Bulletin* 29 (2003): 747–758.

31. Obviously it is also important to recognize that authorities can be immoral. Herbert Kelman and V. Lee Hamilton's book, *Crimes of Obedience* (New Haven, Conn.: Yale University Press, 1988), speaks to the situation in which people are being encouraged to engage in immoral actions by legitimate authorities.

32. Tyler and Fagan, "Legitimacy and Cooperation."

33. Tom R. Tyler, "Justice, Identity and Leadership," in Daan van Knippenberg and Michael A. Hogg (eds.), *Leadership and Power: Identity Processes in Groups and Organizations* (Thousand Oaks, Calif.: Sage, 2003); Tom R. Tyler, "Process-Based Leadership: How Do Leaders Lead?" in David M. Messick and Roderick M. Kramer (eds.), *The Psychology of Leadership: New Perspectives and Research* (Mahwah, N.J.: Erlbaum, 2005).

34. For a discussion of models of leadership, see Tom R. Tyler and David DeCremer, "Process-Based Leadership: Fair Procedures and Reactions to Organizational Change," *Leadership Quarterly,* 16 (2005): 529–545.

35. John Thibaut and Laurens Walker, *Procedural Justice: A Psychological Analysis* (Mahwah, N.J.: Erlbaum, 1975).

36. E. Allan Lind and Tom R. Tyler, *The Social Psychology of Procedural Justice* (New York: Plenum, 1988); Tom R. Tyler and E. Allan Lind, "A Relational Model of Authority in Groups," in M. Zanna (ed.), *Advances in Experimental Social Psychology* 25 (New York: Academic Press, 1992), 115–192.

37. Blader and Tyler, "What Constitutes Fairness in Work Settings?"; Blader and Tyler, "A Four Component Model of Procedural Justice."

38. Lind and Tyler, "The Social Psychology of Procedural Justice"; Tyler and Lind, "A Relational Model of Authority in Groups."

Chapter Ten

1. I also do not address another set of important pragmatic questions about how broadly a philanthropist should define her or his goals and how many different goals she should address.

2. Douglas Martin, "Joan McCord, Who Evaluated Anticrime Efforts, Dies at 73," *New York Times,* March 1, 2004.

3. Much of the qualitative data needed to track the teen pregnancy program can be gained through interviews, tests, and questionnaires. The quality of performing arts presentations is assessable—and assessed—by critics and, in the case of grantees, by their funders' program staff. And community members' sense of well-being can be ascertained by surveys. Often data of these sorts, though essentially subjective, can be put in quantitative form, just as

essay exams are graded. As in the case of intrinsically quantitative data, this lends itself to comparisons—across time, across programs, and across participants. Whether the relevant data are ultimately quantifiable, however, tracking progress and success must respond to the program's goals—not vice versa—and a system that ignored relevant indicators and goals would not only be worthless, but harmful.

4. Indeed, funders should be ready to support their grantees' development of such systems. For example, the Hewlett Foundation made a grant to REDF, a regranter and technical assistance provider for workforce development, to enable the organizations it supports to track the services delivered to individuals and the impact of those services on their lives over time.

5. Even when the desired outcome occurs, one cannot always be sure that it resulted from the intervention. For example, after New York adopted a "broken windows" strategy for reducing crime, crime rates declined significantly—but they also declined throughout the nation, including in cities that had done business as usual. See, for example, Steven D. Levitt, "Understanding Why Crime Fell in the 1990s: Four Factors That Explain the Decline and Six That Do Not," *Journal of Economic Perspectives* 18, 1 (Winter 2004): 163–190. Conversely, it is possible for a good strategy to fail to achieve the desired outcome because of some unforeseeable circumstance that can be guarded against in the future.

6. I am indebted to Jane Mansbridge for the observation about social movements.

7. Jerome S. Bruner, *On Knowing: Essays for the Left Hand* (Cambridge, Mass.: Harvard University Press, 1962), 18.

8. H.L.A. Hart, *The Concept of Law*, 2nd ed. (New York: Oxford University Press, 1994), 128.

9. See Kenneth Prewitt, "The Foundation and the Liberal Society" (speech to the Hudson Institute, Washington, D.C., May 5, 2004); and Jeff Krehely, Meaghan House, and Emily Kernan, *Axis of Ideology: Conservative Foundations and Public Policy* (Washington, D.C.: National Committee for Responsive Philanthropy, 2004).

10. Even on the generous assumption that the largest forty foundations are highly strategic, they account for less than 30 percent of foundation giving. See Foundation Center, *Foundation Yearbook* (New York: Foundation Center, 2003), 53.

11. See Jed Emerson, *The Funder's Perspective: Grantmaking as an Investment Strategy* (San Francisco: The Roberts Foundation, 1996); Michael E. Porter and Mark R. Kramer, "Philanthropy's New Agenda: Creating Value," *Harvard Business Review* (November-December 1999): 126–127; Christine W. Letts, William Ryan, and Allen Grossman, "Virtuous Capital: What Foundations Can Learn from Venture Capitalists," *Harvard Business Review* (March-April 1997): 37.

12. See also Stanley Katz, "What Does It Mean to Say That Philanthropy Is 'Effective'? The Philanthropists' New Clothes" (speech to the American Philosophical Society, Philadelphia, April 23, 2004).

13. Peter Karoff, "The Art of Philanthropy," in H. Peter Karoff (ed.), *Just Money: A Critique of Contemporary American Philanthropy* (Boston: Philanthropic Initiative, 2004), 64.

14. Bruce Sievers, "Philanthropy's Blindspots," in H. Peter Karoff (ed.), *Just Money*, 131–133.

15. Of course, especially when seeking large-scale social change, one's understanding of the ends being sought may change in the course of implementing a strategy. Indeed, as the classic case of Alexander Fleming's discovery of penicillin suggests, unanticipated events may lead to the pursuit of entirely new ends. But openness to the unanticipated presupposes that something was originally anticipated—indeed, usually planned for.

16. Sievers, "Philanthropy's Blindspots," 131–133.

17. Dennis Collins, "The Art of Philanthropy," in H. Peter Karoff (ed.), *Just Money*, 67.

18. Sievers, "Philanthropy's Blindspots," 38.

19. For example, REDF, a regranter and technical assistance provider for workforce development, has developed a management information system to enable the organizations it supports to track the services delivered to individuals and the impact of those services on their lives over time. See http://www.redf.org/about_oasis.htm.

20. See Robin Hogarth, *Education Intuition* (Chicago: University of Chicago Press, 2001).

21. Bruce Sievers, "If Pigs Had Wings: The Appeals and Limits of Venture Philanthropy" (address to the Waldemar A. Nielsen Issues in Philanthropy Seminar, Georgetown University, Washington, D.C., November 16, 2001), http://www.philanthropyuk.org/documents/BruceSievers.pdf.

22. Bridgespan Group, "Growth of Youth-Serving Organizations" (March 2005), http://www.thebridgespangroup.org/PDF/Clarkpdfs/Growth%20of%20Youth-Serving%20Orgs%20-%20White%20Paper.pdf.

23. It reminds me of the verse in Marlo Thomas's children's song, "Helping": "Some kind of help is the kind of help that helping's all about,/And some kind of help is the kind of help/we all can do without," in Marlo Thomas, *Free to Be You and Me*, Arista Records, CDU Part #1109804, rpm.

24. Sometimes governments may step in to fund an organization. Exit is also justified when the organization has achieved its mission or is chronically underperforming because of poor management, because it is committed to a flawed strategy, or simply because it is not doing as good a job as other organizations in the same sector.

25. Though Collins and Sievers do not address the point, it is worth emphasizing that general operating support can be every bit as strategic as any other

approach to funding. See Paul Brest, "Smart Money: Strategic General Operating Support," *Stanford Social Innovation Review* (Winter 2003).

Chapter Eleven

1. Bruce Sievers, "Philanthropy's Blindspots," in H Peter Karoff (ed.), *Just Money: A Contemporary Critique of American Philanthropy* (Boston: TPI Editions, 2004).
2. See Donald Schön's general discussion of epistemological issues in professional life in his *The Reflective Practitioner: How Professionals Think in Action* (New York: Basic Books, 1983).
3. Charles Lindblom provides an insightful analysis of this process of social control in *The Market System: What It Is, How It Works, and What to Make of It* (New Haven, Conn.: Yale University Press, 2001).
4. A recent Brookings Institution report noted, "The number of Americans who express little or no confidence in charitable organizations increased significantly between July 2001 and May 2002, and remains virtually unchanged to this day." The study attributes this recent decline to "controversies surrounding disbursement of the September 11 relief funds and subsequent nationally-visible scandals surrounding the Nature Conservancy and several private foundations" (Paul Light, "Fact Sheet on the Continued Crisis in Charitable Confidence," Brookings Institution, September 13, 2004, 1). Beyond such violations of legal and ethical precepts, other aspects of foundation behavior can undermine public confidence as well, such as a lack of speed and courtesy in responding to inquiries and the allocation of excessive compensation and benefits. Because these practices lie outside the reasonable realm of regulation by government, they revert to the personal judgments of foundation board and staff members. A 1991 report produced by Independent Sector, "Obedience to the Unenforceable," captured the essential character of adjudicating these behaviors. Here, the most effective way to promote ethical practices is for the field to take the lead, in this case through individual foundations' modeling best practices. An example is the growing agreement among foundations that the traditional practice of accepting free tickets to arts and other events should be discouraged. Over a decade ago, a few foundations on the West Coast decided not to accept such "freebies" on the grounds that it could be seen as clouding the grantor-grantee relationship and that it in fact deprived the ticket-donating organizations needed income (reasoning that if foundation staff wished to go to the events, they should pay for their tickets). Although this was not an ethical issue of large significance, the traditional practice added to the image of foundations as comfortably ensconced centers of power. Beginning from this small base, the practice of paying for tickets has spread widely through the field.

5. Robert H. Bremner, *American Philanthropy*, 2nd ed. (Chicago: University of Chicago Press, 1988), 113.

6. Derek Bok, "Mute Inglorious Wizards: A Plea for Foundations to Devote Their Money to Funding Talent," *New York Times Book Review*, November 17, 1996, 43.

7. Onora O'Neill, *A Question of Trust* (Cambridge: Cambridge University Press, 2002), 45–46.

8. O'Neill, *A Question of Trust*, 50.

9. For example, Gilbert Ryle's concept of "category mistake" and distinction between "thin" and "thick" descriptions (Gilbert Ryles, *The Concept of Mind*, Chicago: University of Chicago Press, 1949); A. N. Whitehead's "fallacy of misplaced concreteness" (Alfred North Whitehead, "An Enquiry Concerning the Principles of Natural Knowledge," in *Science and the Modern World: Lowell Lectures*, New York: Macmillan, 1925, 64, 72); and Donald Schön's "selective inattentiveness" (Donald Schön, *The Reflective Practitioner*, London: Avebury, 1983).

10. Mark D. McGarvie, "The Dartmouth College Case and the Legal Design of Civil Society," in Lawrence Friedman and Mark McGarvie (eds.), *Charity, Philanthropy, and Civility in American History* (Cambridge: Cambridge University Press, 2003), 100.

11. Todd Sandler, *Collective Action* (Ann Arbor: University of Michigan Press, 1992).

12. This of course presumes that one views the goal of private philanthropy as benefiting society (in accordance with the public benefit provisions written into federal tax law and state regulatory legislation) and not just as an extension of the prerogatives of personal wealth.

13. The number of foundations in the United States has now grown to approximately seventy thousand (a threefold expansion since the early 1990s), and the nonprofit sector has grown significantly faster in the past decade than have the for-profit sector or governmental sectors.

14. An early example of philanthropic influence was the transformation of American medical education initiated by the Rockefeller Foundation. A more recent one is the much discussed impact of conservative foundations on the American political agenda over the past two decades.

15. Rob Reich, "Philanthropy and Its Uneasy Relationship to Equality," forthcoming.

16. Marion R. Fremont-Smith, *Foundations and Government: State and Federal Law and Supervision* (New York: Russell Sage Foundation, 1965), 561.

17. Michael Walzer, "Socialism and the Gift Relationship," *Dissent* (Fall 1982): 436.

18. This poses a kind of ironic second-order problem of collective goods, since, as Todd Sandler has pointed out, charities are themselves entities that generally pursue public goods and consequently face their own challenges in

overcoming obstacles to the provision of public goods. See Sandler, *Collective Action*, 107–111.

19. Especially over the past two decades, there has been an increasing emphasis on (along with corresponding criticism of) the transfer of social services previously seen as public sector responsibilities to the market arena. See, for example, Peter W. Singer, *Corporate Warriors: The Rise of the Privatized Military Industry* (Ithaca, N.Y.: Cornell University Press, 2003); Ed Skloot, "Evolution or Extinction: A Strategy for Nonprofits in the Marketplace," (2005) www.surdna.org/speeches/eoe.html; Derek Bok, *Universities in the Marketplace: The Commercialization of Higher Education* (Princeton, N.J.: Princeton University Press, 2003); Lester Salamon, *Holding the Center: America's Nonprofit Sector at a Crossroads* (New York: Nathan Cummings Foundation, 1997).

20. Walzer, "Socialism and the Gift Relationship," 435–441.

21. For a clear statement of this need, see Mark Rosenman's commentary, "Grant Makers Must Focus on Government's Role," *Chronicle of Philanthropy*, February 17, 2005, 35.

Chapter Twelve

1. Linda Hill and Suzy Wetlaufer, "Leadership When There Is No One to Ask: An Interview with Eni's Franco Bernabe," *Harvard Business Review* 76, 7 (2003): 93.

2. For the purposes of this discussion I equate moral leadership with making a positive difference in the world. Needless to say, this is not a theoretically precise definition, but it is the working definition that I have relied on in my role as an educator of M.B.A. students.

3. The Aspen Institute Business and Society Program periodically surveys M.B.A. students at leading business schools on how well their business school education has prepared them to address ethical challenges. In 2002, one in five students reported that they were receiving no preparation, and the majority said they were only being prepared "somewhat." See Aspen Institute, "Where Will They Lead? M.B.A. Student Attitudes About Business and Society," Aspen Institute's Business and Society Program, May 2003.

4. I am not an expert about moral leadership. The observations offered in this chapter are based primarily on two experiences: serving as faculty chair of the creation of the first required M.B.A. course, Leadership and Organizational Behavior, and serving as faculty chair of the schoolwide Leadership Initiative whose mandate is to ensure that we stay on the cutting edge of leadership research and leadership development. My thinking on moral leadership has been greatly influenced by my colleagues who teach in our required course on Leadership and Corporate Accountability. This chapter focuses on what we should be teaching, not on how we should be teaching it, an equally vexing topic. For instance, there are special challenges in

teaching individuals like M.B.A. students about the human side of business leadership. See, for example, Chris Arygris, "Teaching Smart People How to Learn," *Harvard Business Review* 69, 5 (1991): 99–109.

5. Greg J. Dees and Peter Cramton, "Shrewd Bargaining on the Moral Frontier: Toward a Theory of Morality in Practice," *Business Ethics Quarterly* 1 (1991): 135–167.

6. For an excellent literature review of the relevant research and a description of an ambitious project to develop moral leadership in M.B.A. programs, see Mary Gentile, "Giving Voice to Values" (paper presented at the Aspen Institute Business and Society Program, June 2005). Gentile describes most eloquently our challenge as educators, that is, to help M.B.A. students "give voice to their values with both genuineness and skill and share that capacity with others" in the face of countervailing pressures. Admittedly, some M.B.A. students may have values that will lead to the exploitation of others, but like Gentile, I assume most are well intentioned. I too am inspired by the research on "positive deviance" such as that of Kim S. Cameron, Jane E. Dutton, and Robert E. Quinn, (eds.), *Positive Organizational Scholarship: Foundations of a New Discipline* (San Francisco: Berrett-Koehler, 2003); Robert H. Frank, *What Price the Moral High Ground? Ethical Dilemmas in Competitive Environments* (Princeton, N.J.: Princeton University Press, 2004); and Mary Seligman, *Learned Optimism: How to Change Your Mind and Your Life* (New York: Pocket Books, 1990).

7. Warren G. Bennis and Robert J. Thomas, "Crucibles of Leadership," *Harvard Business Review* 80 (2002): 41.

8. Sharon D. Parks, "Is it Too Late? Young Adults and the Formation of Professional Ethics," in Thomas R. Piper, Mary C. Gentile, and Sharon D. Parks (eds.), *Can Ethics Be Taught? Perspectives, Challenges and Approaches* (Boston: Harvard Business School Press, 1993), 25.

9. John Dean, *Blind Ambition: The White House Years* (New York: Simon & Schuster, 1976).

10. When I first taught the case of John Dean (based on excerpts from his memoirs), I was shocked to discover how many M.B.A. students identified with him. I do not intend to claim that John Dean was indeed well intentioned, but I have come to understand how circumstances can subvert ethical intention or judgment, especially when an individual has not developed a clear sense of his or her values. For a discussion of how to use Dean's memoirs as a teaching vehicle for M.B.A. students, see Linda Hill and Joshua Margolis, "Blind Ambition: Teaching Note," Harvard Business School, No. 494-1994. For a related discussion of how even experienced managers can allow their ambition to interfere with their capacity to lead a meaningful life, see Howard Stevenson and Laura Nash, *Just Enough: Tools for Creating Success in Your Work and Life* (Hoboken, N.J.: Wiley, 2004).

11. For a discussion of how individuals learn to manage and lead (which includes the human and ethical dimension), see, for example, Bruce Avolio

and Fred Luthans, *The High Impact Leader: Moments Matter in Accelerating Authentic Leadership Development* (New York: McGraw-Hill, 2005); Warren G. Bennis and Robert J. Thomas, *Geeks and Geezers: How Era, Values and Defining Moments Shape Leaders* (Boston: Harvard Business School Press, 2002); Linda Hill, *Becoming a Manager: How New Managers Master the Challenge of Leadership* (Boston: Harvard Business School Press, 2003); Morgan McCall Jr., *High Flyers: Developing the Next Generation of Leaders* (Boston: Harvard Business School Press, 1998); and Henry Mintzberg and Jonathan Gosling, "Educating Managers Beyond Borders," *Academy of Management Learning and Education* 1, 1 (2002): 64–75. For a specific discussion of ethical development, see Piper, Gentile, and Parks (eds.), *Can Ethics Be Taught?*

12. For a discussion of task and personal learning, see, for example, Douglas T. Hall, "Dilemmas in Linking Succession Planning to Individual Executive Learning," *Human Resource Management* 25 (1986): 235–265. Too often educators neglect personal learning. For a critique of M.B.A. education, see Henry Mintzberg, *Managers Not M.B.A.s: A Hard Look at the Soft Practice of Managing and Management Development* (San Francisco: Berrett-Koehler, 2003).

13. See, for example, Hill, *Becoming a Manager*, 175–193.

14. Joshua Margolis and Andrew Molinsky are conducting one of the few studies of the "lived experiences" of individuals facing ethical dilemmas. Their preliminary results suggest that the ability of an individual to manage his or her emotions is an important determinant of the person's capacity to treat others with "dignity" and cope effectively with necessary evils. See, for example, Joshua D. Margolis and Andrew Molinsky, "Necessary Evils and Interpersonal Sensitivity in Organizations," *Academy of Management Review* 30 (2005): 245–268.

15. Personal learning frequently involves making oneself vulnerable, admitting what one does not know, taking risks, and experimenting with new ways of being and doing. See, for example, Linda Hill, "New Manager Development for the 21st Century," *Academy of Management Executive* 18 (2004): 121–126. As Scott Snook, a retired professor from West Point, pointed out, there are certain things a leader must be, certain things he must know, and certain things that he must be able to do. Scott Snook, "Be, Know, Do: Forming Character the West Point Way," *Compass: A Journal of Leadership* 1, 2 (2004): 16–19. We have figured out how to change knowledge and skill, but it is the transformation of being—the identity, character, worldviews, and values—about which we still know the least as educators.

16. One of my primary areas of research concerns the transition from individual contributor to manager and the myths new managers hold about their new positions. Unless otherwise indicated, all quotations from unspecified managers in this chapter are based on data collected for that research. See, for example, Hill, *Becoming a Manager*.

17. See Hill, *Becoming a Manager,* especially 197–193.

18. See Margolis and Molinsky, "Necessary Evils and Interpersonal Sensitivity in Organizations."

19. John P. Kotter, *Power and Influence* (New York: Free Press, 1985), 153.

20. Gentile, "Giving Voice to Values," 12–13.

21. For research based on interviews of managers facing ethical dilemmas at work, see, for example, Barbara L. Toffler, *Managers Talk Ethics: Making Tough Choices in a Competitive Business World* (Hoboken, N.J.: Wiley, 1986); Joseph L. Badaracco Jr., *Defining Moments: When Managers Must Choose Between Right and Right* (Boston: Harvard Business School Press, 1997). Also see Laura Nash and Scotty McLennan, *Church on Sunday, Work on Monday: The Challenge of Fusing Christian Values with Business Life* (San Francisco: Jossey-Bass, 2001).

22. See, for example, Joshua D. Margolis and James P. Walsh, "Misery Loves Companies: Rethinking Social Initiatives by Business," *Administrative Science Quarterly* 48 (2003): 268–305; and Joshua D. Margolis and James P. Walsh, *People and Profits? The Search for a Link Between a Company's Social and Financial Performance* (Mahwah, N.J.: Erlbaum, 2001).

23. See, for example, Lynn Sharp Paine, *Value Shift: Why Companies Must Merge Social and Financial Imperatives to Achieve Superior Performance* (New York: McGraw-Hill, 2003), 223.

24. James Rest (ed.), *Moral Development: Advances in Research and Theory* (New York: Praeger, 1994).

25. While there are many different definitions of power, I define power as the potential of an individual (or group) to influence another individual or group. Influence, in turn, is the ability to change the behavior, attitudes, or values of that individual or group. It is easier to change behavior than attitudes and, in turn, attitudes than values.

26. Some express hope that with the new models of flat and lean corporations (of hierarchy, function, and geography), politics has largely been eradicated. This notion is not only unrealistic but also undesirable. Conflict among the different constituencies in an organization can be healthy and productive. To eliminate political conflict, managers would have to eliminate diversity, including the division of labor and specialization. Specialization is often necessary for organizational efficiency and productivity. Diversity and conflict are also essential ingredients for creativity and innovation. See, for example, Dorothy Leonard and Walter C. Swap, *When Sparks Fly: Igniting Group Creativity* (Boston: Harvard Business School Press, 1999).

27. David Kipnis, *The Powerholders* (Chicago: University of Chicago Press, 1976), 169.

28. For example, as Elizabeth Ross Kanter observed, it is powerlessness that often leads to ineffective, petty, and dictatorial managerial styles. Elizabeth Ross Kanter, "Power Failure in Management Circuits," *Harvard Business Review* 57, 7 (1979): 65–75.

29. For examples of how individuals can exercise moral imagination and courage, see Joseph L. Badaracco, *Leading Quietly: An Unorthodox Guide to Doing the Right Thing* (Boston: Harvard Business School Press, 2002); and Deborah Meyerson, *Tempered Radicals: How Everyday Leaders Inspire Change at Work* (Boston: Harvard Business School Press, 2003).

30. See, for example, Hill, *Becoming a Manager*.

31. The distribution of power and influence in organizations is generally aligned with the contextual realities they face. The leaders and dominant coalitions are those who have access to resources of control contingencies critical to the organization's performance. Power will generally shift as the organization's critical contingencies change (for example, when a company changes strategic direction in response to competitive pressures). Nevertheless, it is important that students understand that this process can be subverted and power abused. An individual's power and influence can extend far beyond the original or legitimate bases that created it. Dominant coalitions have been known to act primarily to maintain their power position rather than the best interests of the organization. The distribution of power and influence can become institutionalized and thereby endure well beyond its usefulness. People with power do not give it up easily. They create structures, policies, and procedures to guarantee their power. The organizational culture that develops further helps to support and consolidate their power. It is no wonder that it often takes a revolution to overthrow an entrenched elite. Organizations have begun to create more checks and balances to prevent these corruptions of power, such as the increased number of outside directors on organizational boards or the development of codes of conduct. I hope students will come to see that having checks and balances is often a good thing; it protects even "good people" from temptation. For discussions of power dynamics in organizations, see, for example, Kotter, *Power and Influence*; Jeffrey Pfeffer, *Managing with Power: Politics and Influence in Organizations* (Boston: Harvard Business School Press, 1992); and Gerald R. Salancik and Jeffrey Pfeffer, "Who Gets Power and How They Hold On to It: A Strategic Contingency Model of Power," *Organizational Dynamics* 5, 3 (1977): 2–6.

32. See, for example, Mahzarin R. Banaji, Max Bazerman, and Dolly Chugh, "How Un(Ethical are You)?" *Harvard Business Review* 81, 12 (2003): 56–64; Max Bazerman, *Judgment in Managerial Decision Making* (Hoboken, N.J.: Wiley, 2005); and Deborah Messick and Max Bazerman, "Ethical Leadership and the Psychology of Decision Making," *Sloan Management Review* (Winter 1996): 9–22.

33. How much power and influence an individual accrues is context specific and, hence, dynamic. If the context changes, other things being equal, the individual's power and influence will change. Much of an individual's power stems from the activities they perform and their location in the organization. But to capitalize on the full potential for power inherent in a position,

individuals need to have the necessary personal attributes. Indeed, a person's power is determined by two sets of factors: positional and personal characteristics. In a module of career management, students are given a power and influence framework for thinking about their development. They are offered insights on how to acquire power and influence over the course in their careers in a manner that will allow them to establish credibility and contribute to the success of the organization. When I first presented this framework to the students, I entitled it "Developmental Strategies." I soon changed the title to "Developing Power and Influence" a much more compelling title for ambitious M.B.A.s eager to have impact. See Linda Hill, "Managing Your Career," Harvard Business School, No. 494–082, 1998, for the reading on career development assigned in the required M.B.A. leadership course.

34. For discussions about the strategies and tactics managers can rely on to exercise influence given the limits of formal authority, see, for example, Wayne Baker, *Networking Smart: How to Build Relationships for Personal and Organizational Success* (New York: McGraw-Hill, 1994); Michael Watkins, *The First Ninety Days: Critical Success Strategies for New Leaders at All Levels* (Boston: Harvard Business School Press, 2003); Allan R. Cohen and David L. Bradford, *Influence Without Authority* (Hoboken, N.J.: Wiley, 1990); and David Krackhardt and Jeffrey R. Hanson, "Informal Networks: The Company Behind the Chart," *Harvard Business Review* 71, 7 (1993): 104–111.

35. See Linda Hill, "Power Dynamics in Organizations," Harvard Business School, No. 494–08, 1995, and Linda Hill, "Exercising Influence," Harvard Business School, No. 494–080, 1994, for readings assigned to M.B.A.s on how to think about acquiring power and exercising influence in ways that are effective for the individual, effective for the organization and ethical.

36. Sharon D. Parks, "Is it Too Late? Young Adults and the Formation of Professional Ethics," in Thomas R. Piper (ed.), *Can Ethics Be Taught? Perspectives, Challenges and Approaches* (Boston: Harvard Business School Press, 1993), 40.

37. Milton Friedman's argument that the sole concern of business should be shareholder maximization is alive and well. See, for example, Clive Crook, "The Good Company," *Economist* 374, 8410 (2005): sp. sec., 3–4; Milton Friedman, *Capitalism and Freedom* (Chicago: University of Chicago Press, 1982); and Milton Friedman, "The Social Responsibility of Business Is to Increase Its Profits," *New York Times Magazine*, September 13, 1970, 17–21. For readings that make the counterargument, see, for example, Adrian Cadbury, "Ethical Managers Make Their Own Rules," *Harvard Business Review* 65, 9 (1987): 69–73; Mihaly Csikszentmihalyi, *Good Business* (New York: Penguin Group, 2003); Mihaly Csikszentmihalyi, William Damon, and Howard Gardner, *Good Work: When Excellence and Ethics Meet* (New York: Basic Books, 2001); William Damon, *The Moral Advantage: How to Succeed in Business by Doing the Right Thing* (San Francisco: Berrett-Koehler, 2004);

William George, *Authentic Leadership: Rediscovering the Secrets to Creating Lasting Value* (San Francisco: Jossey-Bass, 2003); William Greider, *The Soul of Capitalism: Opening Paths to a Moral Economy* (New York: Simon & Schuster, 2003); Charles Handy, "What's a Business For?" *Harvard Business Review* 80, 12 (2002): 49–55; Amartya Sen, "Does Business Ethics Make Economic Sense?" *Business Ethics Quarterly* 3 (1993): 46–48; and Noel M. Tichy and Andrew R. McGill, *The Ethical Challenge: How to Lead with Unyielding Integrity* (San Francisco: Jossey-Bass, 2003).

38. Linda Hill, Jennifer Suesse, and Mara Willard, "Franco Bernabé at Eni (A)," Harvard Business School, No. 498–034, 2002; "Franco Bernabé at Eni (B)," Harvard Business School, No. 498–035, 1997; "Franco Bernabé at Eni (C)," Harvard Business School, No. 498–040, 1997; and "Franco Bernabé at Eni (D)," Harvard Business School, No. 498–041, 1997.

39. Linda Hill and Kristin Doughty, "Franco Bernabé: Reflections on Telecom Italia," Harvard Business School, No. 400–060, 2000.

40. Karl Weick, "The Collapse of Sense-Making in Organizations: The Mann Gulch Disaster," *Administrative Science Quarterly* 38 (1993): 628–653. Donald Schön has a similar notion of "double vision," in Donald Schön, *Educating the Reflective Practitioner* (San Francisco: Jossey-Boss, 1990).

41. For examples of the illustrative power of comparative work, see, for example, Handy, "What's a Business For?" 49–55. Handy contrasts the Anglo-American notion of companies as profit-maximizing agents for their shareholders with the European notion of companies as communities and how that impacts how executives in each region think about outsourcing and layoffs, for instance. Much of the comparative work on the role of business has been done in emerging markets. See, for example, V. Kasturi Rangan, "Lofty Missions, Down-to-Earth Plans," *Harvard Business Review* 82, 3 (2004): 112–119; V. Kasturi Rangan, Karim Sohel, and Sheryl K. Sandberg, "Do Better at Doing Good," *Harvard Business Review* 74, 3 (1996): 42–51; and V. Kasturi Rangan and John Quelch, "Profit Globally, Give Globally," *Harvard Business Review* 81, 12 (2003): 16–17.

42. Paine, *Value Shift*, 243.

43. My coauthor on this work is Maria Farkas, formerly my research associate and currently a sociology doctoral student at the University of Michigan. We have made a number of presentations about the research but have completed only one published document about the research, a teaching case about Irene Charnley described below. The other quotations are based on interviews with the subjects of our research.

44. See Linda Hill and Maria Farkas, "Irene Charnley at Johnnic Group (A)," Harvard Business School, No. 405–059, 2005; "Irene Charnley at Johnnic Group (B)," Harvard Business School. No. 403–171, 2003; and "Irene Charnley at Johnnic Group (C)," Harvard Business School, No. 405–061, 2005.

45. For more examples of business leaders committed to achieving both financial and social imperatives, see, for example, C. K. Prahalad, *The Fortune at the Bottom of the Pyramid: Eradicating Poverty Through Profits* (Philadelphia: Wharton School Publishing, 2005).

46. In their insightful book on ethics education, Thomas Piper and his coauthors identified faculty development as a critical barrier to the development of M.B.A. students' capacity for moral leadership. Many faculty still do not understand what, if any, role they should play in the development of M.B.A. students' ethical judgment; despite growing evidence to the contrary, they still believe that there is nothing to be taught. Others recognize there are lessons to be imparted, but also realize how ill prepared they are to lead student discussions of ethical dilemmas. See Piper, Gentile, and Parks (eds.), *Can Ethics Be Taught?*

Chapter Thirteen

1. Martin Luther King Jr., "I Have a Dream" (speech delivered on the steps of the Lincoln Memorial, Washington, D.C., August 28, 1963).

2. James Traub, "The Statesman," *New York Times Magazine,* September 18, 2005, 80ff.

3. Norwegian Nobel Committee, "The Nobel Peace Prize 2004," press release, October 8, 2004.

4. See www.vatican.va/holy_father/john_paul_ii/encyclicals/.

5. See www.un.org/Overview/rights.html.

6. See www.interactioncouncil.org.

7. See www.interactioncouncil.org/udhr/declaration/udhr.pdf.

8. See www.womenworldleaders.org.

9. See www.clubmadrid.org.

10. See www.collegium-international.org.

11. See www.fwdklerk.org.za.

12. For a list of Nobel Peace Prize winners, see www.nobelprize.org/peace/.

13. See www.unglobalcompact.org/portal/.

14. See www.cauxroundtable.org/principles.html/.

15. For information on the planned development of ISO 26000, see http://www.iso.org/iso/en/commcentre/pressreleases/2005/Ref953.html.

16. Madeline Albright (speech at the Commonwealth Club, Santa Clara, Calif., February 12, 2004).

Acknowledgments

One distinguishing characteristic of ethical leadership is full recognition of collaborators in a common venture. This book grows out a collective effort that owes many debts. It began with the Conference on Moral Leadership, which launched a new university-wide Center on Ethics at Stanford in February 2005, and a companion conference at Harvard University on Moral Leadership and the Right to Rule. The conferences were cosponsored by the Center for Leadership, Development and Research (CLDR) at the Stanford Graduate School of Business and the Edmond J. Safra Foundation Center for Ethics, the Center for Public Leadership, the Center for Business and Government, and the Hauser Center for Nonprofit Organizations at Harvard. That collaboration was made possible by the directors of those centers: Beth Benjamin (director, CLDR) at the Stanford Graduate School of Business, Barbara Kellerman (research director) at the Center for Public Leadership, and Dennis F. Thompson (director) and Arthur Applbaum (acting director 2004–2005) at the Safra Center for Ethics.

At Stanford, the conference was organized by a planning committee of faculty: Deborah Gruenfeld, Roderick Kramer, and Dale Miller; and also by the center's superb program coordinator, Bisera Rakicevic-More. In this, as in all other center efforts, its greatest debt is to the associate director, Lawrence Quill, to whom this book is dedicated. For his vision, values, and moral leadership, the Stanford community and I will always be grateful.

About the Authors

Maria Logli Allison is a doctoral candidate in the social and personality psychology program at the University of California, Berkeley. Her research addresses the nature of social reputation and gossip, emotion, and prosocial behavior in social hierarchies.

C. Daniel Batson is professor of psychology at the University of Kansas. He has conducted a number of experiments on various forms of prosocial motivation and is the author of *The Altruism Question: Toward a Social-Psychological Answer* (1991) and a chapter in *The Handbook of Social Psychology* (4th ed., 1998). He received his Ph.D. in psychology from Princeton University.

Paul Brest is the president of the William and Flora Hewlett Foundation in Menlo Park, California. He received an A.B. from Swarthmore College and an LL.B from Harvard Law School. He joined the Stanford Law School faculty in 1969, where his research and teaching focused on constitutional law and problem solving/decision making. From 1987 to 1999, he served as the dean of Stanford Law School. Brest is coauthor of *Processes of Constitutional Decisionmaking* (4th ed. 2000) and currently teaches a law school course on Problem Solving, Decision Making, and Professional Judgment. He holds honorary degrees from Northeastern Law School and Swarthmore College and is a member of the American Academy of Arts and Sciences.

Kirk O. Hanson is executive director of the Markkula Center for Applied Ethics at Santa Clara University and University Professor of Organizations and Society. In 2001, he retired from Stanford University, where he taught business ethics in the Graduate School of Business for twenty-three years. Hanson specializes in organizational ethics in business, government, and public benefit institutions. He has consulted with over sixty leading corporations and organizations, speaks widely on corporate ethics, and has served as an ethics expert witness in many legal cases. Hanson was the founding president of the Business Enterprise Trust, an organization created in 1988 by national leaders in business, labor, media, and academia to promote exemplary behavior in business. He has held graduate fellowships and research appointments at the Yale Divinity School and the Harvard Business School.

Russell Hardin is professor in the Department of Politics at New York University. His current research interests are in rational choice, collective action, morality behind the law, and moral and political philosophy. He received a Ph.D. in political science from the Massachusetts Institute of Technology in 1971.

Linda A. Hill is the Wallace Brett Donham Professor of Business Administration in the Organizational Behavior Area at the Harvard Business School. She is unit chair of Organizational Behavior, faculty chair of the Leadership Initiative, and faculty chair of the Young Presidents' Organization Presidents' Seminar. She is the author of *Becoming a Manager: Mastery of a New Identity, Power and Influence Customized Course Module*, and *Becoming a Manager: How New Managers Master the Challenges of Leadership* (2nd Edition). Hill's consulting and executive education activities have been in the areas of managing change, managing interfunctional relationships, globalization, career management, and leadership development.

Dacher Keltner is professor of psychology at the University of California (UC) at Berkeley and director of the Berkeley Center for the

Development of Peace and Well-being. He received his B.A. from UC Santa Barbara in 1984, his Ph.D. from Stanford University in 1989, and then completed a three-year postdoctoral fellowship in affective science with Paul Ekman at UC San Francisco. He has conducted empirical studies in three areas of inquiry. A first look is at the determinants and effects of power, hierarchy, and social class. A second is concerned with the morality of everyday life, and how we negotiate moral truths in teasing, gossip, and other reputational matters. A third and primary focus is on the biological and evolutionary basis of the benevolent affects, including compassion, awe, love, gratitude, and laughter and modesty. He is the author of over sixty-five articles on these topics. He has received several awards, including the 2001 Positive Psychology prize for research excellence, the 2002 Western Psychological Association prize for outstanding research for an investigator under forty, and the UC Berkeley Letters and Science Distinguished Teaching award. His research has been supported by several private foundations and the National Institutes of Health.

Carrie A. Langner is a postdoctoral fellow in the Health Psychology Program at the University of California, San Francisco. She received her doctoral degree in psychology from the University of California, Berkeley. Her research focuses on social power and status, politicized collective identity, political attributions, and political attitudes.

David Luban is the Frederick Haas Professor of Law and Philosophy at Georgetown University. He has been a visiting faculty member at the Yale Law School, Harvard Law School, University of Melbourne, Dartmouth College, the Max Planck Institute for Foreign and International Private Law (Hamburg), and the Max Planck Institute for European Legal History (Frankfurt). His recent publications include *The Ethics of Lawyers*, which he edited, and *Legal Modernism and Legal Ethics*, coauthored with Deborah L. Rhode. His extensive published work has focused on a range of topics in legal ethics, the social responsibility of lawyers, law and philosophy, jurisprudence, and social justice.

Joshua Margolis is an assistant professor of business administration in the Organizational Behavior unit at Harvard Business School. He teaches Leadership and Organizational Behavior in the M.B.A. program and previously taught the introductory ethics course, Leadership, Values, and Decision Making. Margolis received his B.A. from Yale University and his A.M. (in sociology), and Ph.D. in organizational behavior from Harvard University, where he has also been a Fellow in the Program in Ethics and the Professions. He joined the HBS faculty in 2000 after spending three years on the faculty at the University of Michigan Business School as a Fellow in the Society of Scholars. His research focuses on the distinctive ethical challenges that arise in organizations and how managers can navigate these challenges with practical effectiveness and moral integrity, especially in perform-or-else settings. Margolis has published his work in *Administrative Science Quarterly, Business Ethics Quarterly,* and *Journal of Management,* and along with James P. Walsh, he authored the book, *People and Profits: The Search for a Link Between a Company's Social and Financial Performance.*

David Messick is the Morris and Alice Kaplan Professor of Ethics and Decision in Management at the Kellogg School of Management of Northwestern University. He has held this position since 1991 and is part of Kellogg's Management and Organization Department. Previously he was a professor of psychology at the University of California, Santa Barbara, where he had been a faculty member since 1964. Messick's teaching and research interests are in the ethical and social aspects of decision making and information processing, and the psychology of leadership. He is the author of more than 150 articles, chapters, and edited books, and his scholarly work has been published in prominent academic journals. Recently he has been named the codirector of the newly endowed Ford Motor Company Center for Global Citizenship at Kellogg.

Andrew Molinsky is an assistant professor of organizational behavior at Brandeis University's International Business School, with a joint appointment in the Department of Psychology. He received his Ph.D. in organizational behavior and M.A. in psychology from Harvard University. He also holds a master's degree in international affairs from Columbia University and a B.A. in international affairs from Brown University. After completing his Ph.D., he spent two years on the faculty at the Marshall School of Business at the University of Southern California. Molinsky's research examines the challenges people face in performing emotionally demanding aspects of their jobs. Specifically, his work focuses on the difficulties entailed in adapting behavior in foreign cultural environments and on the moral and psychological challenges involved in performing "necessary evils" (causing harm for a perceived greater good) in professional work. He has developed courses in Managing Across Cultures and in Managing Difficult Conversations to help train students to handle these challenges. He also teaches a core course in organizational behavior.

Deborah L. Rhode is the Ernest W. McFarland Professor of Law and Director of the Stanford Center on Ethics. She is the former chair of the American Bar Association's Commission on Women in the Profession, and the former president of the Association of American Law Schools. Rhode graduated summa cum laude from Yale College and Yale Law School. After clerking for Supreme Court Justice Thurgood Marshall, she joined the Stanford faculty. She is the author or coauthor of seventeen books and over one hundred and fifty articles on professional ethics; and gender, law, and policy.

Bruce Sievers is in his third year as the Haas Center Visiting Scholar at Stanford University. After completing graduate work as a Fulbright Scholar at the Freie Universität Berlin, he became the founding chief executive officer of the California Council for the Humanities between 1974 and 1983 and served as executive director of the Walter and Elise Haas Fund from 1983 to 2002. He was a member of the Council on Foundations board of directors and chair of Northern California Grantmakers. Currently, he holds a Senior Fellow position with Rockefeller Philanthropy Advisors. Sievers teaches an undergraduate course on civil society and philanthropy at Stanford and consults with faculty, students, and Haas Center staff on philanthropy and work in the independent sector. He is currently working on a project titled, Between Public and Private: Philanthropy, Civil Society and the Fate of the Commons. He received his B.A., M.A., and Ph.D. from Stanford University.

Tom R. Tyler is professor at New York University. He teaches in the Psychology Department and the law school. His research explores the dynamics of authority in groups, organizations, and societies. In particular, he examines the role of judgments about the justice or injustice of group procedures in shaping legitimacy, compliance, and cooperation. He is the author of several books, including *The Social Psychology of Procedural Justice* (1988), *Why People Obey the Law* (1990), *Trust in Organizations* (1996), *Social Justice in a Diverse Society* (1997), *Cooperation in Groups* (2000), and *Trust in the Law* (2002).

David G. Winter is professor of psychology at the University of Michigan. He was educated at Harvard University and the Oxford University. He previously taught at Wesleyan University and has been a visiting faculty member at the Massachusetts Institute of Technology, Harvard, College of the Holy Cross, University of Amsterdam, and Peking University. Winter is a personality and social psychologist with a special interest in political psychology. His research has focused on power and power motivation, the motivational bases of leadership, and the psychological aspects of conflict escalation, war, and peace. He is the author of *The Power Motive: Motivating Economic Achievement* (with D. C. McClelland), *A New Case for the Liberal Arts* (with D. C. McClelland and A. J. Stewart), and recently *Personality: Analysis and Interpretation of Lives*, as well as numerous papers in psychological journals. He also translated and edited Otto Rank's *The Don-Juan Legend*. He is a past president of the International Society of Political Psychology.

Philip G. Zimbardo is an internationally recognized scholar, educator, researcher, and media personality, winning numerous awards and honors in each of these domains. He has been a Stanford University professor since 1968, having taught previously at Yale, New York University, and Columbia. Zimbardo's career is noted for raising public awareness about psychology through his popular PBS-TV series, *Discovering Psychology*, along with many text and trade books, among his three hundred publications. He was recently president of the American Psychological Association.

Index

A

Abu Ghraib Prison, 82, 134, 142, 147, 152–155, 159

Accountability: as constraint on power, 191–192; encouraging, 156, 157; in philanthropy, 229–230, 249–250, 252–258; for public officials, 112–113; reducing cues for, 140

Accounting firms: public trust and, 250; reasons for complicity of, 32, 63

Acknowledgment of error, 156

Acton, Lord, 159, 207

Adams, J., 170

Adams, M., 159–160

Adelphia, 57

Adversarial settings, 58–61. *See also* Competition

Adversity, moral development through, 268–270, 282

Affiliation, 161–162

Affirmative action, 120, 190–191, 285–289

Africa, 108, 109, 284–289, 293–294

African National Congress, 284–285

Agents, 77, 78, 92–93

Agnew, S., 121, 123–124

Agricultural research centers, 238

AIDS, 205

Albright, M., 300

Allison, M. L., 177

Altruism: collectivism and, 210–212; conflicts with, 210; empathy-enduced, 202–204, 210–212; motivation of, 199, 200, 202–204; nearness and, 22, 203–204; power attainment and, 179; principlism and, 210–212; self-interest and, 203, 210–212

Altruism scale, 155–156

Ambition, in management students, 268–270

Ambivalence, 84–90, 93

American culture: capitalism in, 63–67; competitiveness of, 57–61; success worship in, 61–63

American Management Association, 13

American Medical Association, 250

American University, 175

Amin, I., 129

Amnesty International, 285

Anglo-Saxon common law, 119

Anonymity: aggressive behavior and, 135–137, 140, 143–145; reducing, 157; in Stanford Prison Experiment, 143–145

Anonymous hot lines, 109, 110

Antitrust violations, 10

Anxiety: of mortality, 173; power attainment and, 179–180

Apartheid, 284, 287–288

Approach-inhibition theory of power, 181–182

Appropriateness, logic of, 91

Area studies programs, 238

Arendt, H., 32

Arias, O., 292

Aristotle, 15, 21

Armstrong, J. S., 28–29

Arrogance: intellectual meritocracy and, 164–165; moral reasoning and, 25; power and, 276–277, 280

Arrow, K. J., 14

Arthur Andersen (AA): client-business priority of, 32; obstruction of justice case of, 58, 99–100

Arts philanthropy, 231, 236–237

Ashoka, 172

Aspen Institute, 48
Athena, 164
Attitudinal convergence, 190–191
Attributional charity, 152
Audit culture, 256
Augustine, Saint, 68
Aung San Suu Kyi, 296
Authentic leadership, character and, 21
Authoritarian personality, 131
Authority: management students' beliefs about, 271–272, 278, 279; obedience to, 106–107, 132–135, 151; resisting immoral, 106–107, 151–152, 155–157

B

Bach, J. S., 172
Bad Leadership (Kellerman), 7
Badaracco, J. L., 107
Bandura, A., 138
Barenbaum, N. B., 165
Bargh, J. A., 159, 160
Barstow, A., 130
Bass, B. M., 5
Batson, C. D., 82, 146, 197
Batson, N., 72
Baumann, N., 165
Bausch & Lomb, 47
Beard, C., 169
Behavior modification, 131
Belgian army, 137
Beliefs: cognitive dissonance and, 67–69; intuitionism and, 115, 125; of management students, 271–272, 278, 279, 288
Bennis, W. G., 3, 7, 268–269
Berlin, I., 260
Bernabé, F., 267, 281–283
Bible, 166
Birmingham bus boycott, 211
Blader, S. L., 217, 219, 221
Blair, J., 250
Blaming others, 29, 66; causal selection and, 101; for evil, 130–132; self-awareness of, 75; self-serving bias and, 100
Blankenship, V., 162
Blind Ambition (Dean), 270
Bloch, M., 65
Blum, L., 207
Board of Education, Brown *vs.*, 247
Boards: diffusion of responsibility in, 28–29; oversized agendas of, 81–82; power and, 169
Boesky, I., 59

Boiled frog syndrome, 29, 74. *See also* Incremental wrongdoing
Bok, D., 255
Bono, 293–294
Bottom-line mentality: at Enron, 23, 31–32, 65–66; in management students, 268–270; moral awareness and, 22, 23; moral conduct and, 31–32, 38; postapartheid development and, 287; reforming compensation systems and, 44; social role of business *versus*, 281–283. *See also* Culture; Financial performance
Bowdlerization, 100
Bowen, H. R., 11
Brandenburg Concertos, 172
Brazil policemen, 147–149
Brest, P., 229, 256–258
Bribery: ethical fading in, 98; of public officials, 121, 123–124
Brown *vs.* Board of Education, 247
Browning, C., 141
Bruner, J. S., 236
Buddhism, 297
Bunche, R., 299
Bureaucracies, 30, 65, 70–71
Burke, E., 146
Burma, 296
Burnout, 154
Burns, J. M., 6
Bush, G. W., 47, 49, 159
Business, social role of, 280–289
Business for Social Responsibility, 11
Business plan, nonprofit, 233–234
Business schools: candidate screening for, 45–47, 50; curricula in, 47–51; developing moral leaders in, 267–289; developmental needs in, 267–280; ethics-promoting strategies for, 45–51; teaching power dynamics in, 276–280; teaching social change in, 280–289. *See also* Management students; Research
Bystander intervention: diffusion of responsibility and, 27; in group *versus* individual contexts, 27, 69–70; time constraints and, 26–27, 82, 146–147

C

Caesar, 172
California's Nonprofit Integrity Act of 2004, 254

Cambodia, U.S. bombing of, 123–124
Capitalism: business school education and, 283–289; feudal and socialist character of, 63–67; moral effects of, 200; Protestant ethic and, 61; in South Africa, 284–289; venture, 245, 246
Care, ethic of, 207–208
Carnegie Foundation, 254, 262
Cates, K. L., 99
Causal selection or cleansing, 100–101
Caux Roundtable Principles for Business, 38, 299
Celebrities, as global leaders, 293–294
Center-driven decision-making, 274–275
"Centesimus Annus," 297
Centralization, 64–65
Ceres, 174
Character: evil and, 130–132, 153–154; lens of, 77, 78, 92; overvaluing of, 21, 46–47, 58–59, 131, 134; power attainment and, 179–180; role of, 21–22; screening for, 45–47, 50
Charismatic leaders, 159, 161, 180
Charity Navigator (CN), 257–258
Charnley, I., 285–286, 288–289
Chatman, J., 217
Chemical manufacturers, 65–66
Chen, S., 179
Chicago, Board of Ethics of, 115, 118
China, ethical judgment in, 105
Christianity, 297
Cicero, 160
Cigarette manufacturers, 129
Civic virtue, eleven-step plan for, 156–157
Civil proceedings: discovery abuse in, 60; limitations of, 44
Civil rights movement, 107, 108, 237, 247, 292
Civil War, 166
Climate, 30–31. See also Culture
Clinton, B., 112
Club of Madrid, 299
Coase, R. H., 64
Cognitive biases: in moral conduct, 21, 25–26, 29–30; in moral judgment, 95–102, 182–183; teaching, in business schools, 49–50; unawareness of, 95, 101. See also Cognitive dissonance; Fundamental attribution error
Cognitive controls, suspension of, 139–140

Cognitive dissonance, 25–26, 29; awareness of, 74–75; moral meltdowns and, 67–74
Collective action problem, 259–263
Collectivist cultures, 131, 194
Collectivist motivation, 199, 200, 204–206, 210
Collins, D., 239–247
Collins, J. C., 52
Command-and-control approach, 216, 223
Common law, 117–118, 119
Commonwealth of Oceana (Harrington), 118–119
Communication, of low-power people, 186–189
Communication skills, 296
Communities, rule adherence in, 218, 219
Compassion, in right-*versus*-right conflicts, 91, 103, 105. See also Empathy
Compensation: moral conduct and, 31, 32, 38–39; moral judgments and, 24–25; reform of, 44. See also Executive compensation; Reward systems
Competition: American capitalism and, 63–67; environment of, 57–61, 67; success worship and, 61–63, 67
Complexity: as deterrent to whistleblowing, 109; failure to address, in leadership ethics literature, 9; of moral motives, 209–210; of moral views, by power status, 184–185; of real-world ethical situations, 78–80; of right-*versus*-right decisions, 102–105
Compliance officers, 37
Compliance programs, value of, 34–37. See also Ethics initiatives and programs
Concentration camps, 130, 141–142, 164
Conflicts of interest: appearance of, 121–122; of public officials, 121–122
Conformity: conflicting desires in, 96–97; nonprofit performance evaluation and, 257; resisting, 157. See also Social or peer pressure
Confucius, 168, 177
Congruence, 218–220, 221–222, 224–226
Connor, B., 211
Conscience: internal sanctions of, 201–202; plasticity of, 73–74
Conscientiousness, 179–180
Consensus, social, 22, 178
Conservative foundations, 238

Consumer power, 43

Contractual obligation, 134

Conventional stage, 24

Corporate philanthropy, 20

Corporate social responsibility: assessment of, 38; emergence of, 11; ethical climate and, 33; extent of, 11; financial impact of, 16–20; rankings on, 42, 43; social role of business and, 280–290; strategies for promoting, 42–44; teaching management students about, 280–289

Corporations, economic paradox of, 64–65

Cost-benefit analysis, in strategic philanthropy, 235–236, 247

Cost-effectiveness, of moral leadership, 15–20

Council of Women World Leaders, 299

Council on Foundations, 256

Counterattitudinal advocacy, 68

Courage: developing moral, 267–289; in ethical judgment, 96–97, 106–110; of global moral leaders, 296; to resist immoral authority, 106–107, 151–152; to risk unpopularity, 107–108; in whistleblowing, 108–110

Cousins, N., 172

Creativity, philanthropic support of, 236–237

Criminal prosecution and liability: ignorance defense in, 57–58; limitations of, 44; of public officials, 124

Crisis situations, power distortion in, 172–173

Critical thinking, 156

Critique. See Dissent

Cuban missile crisis, 172

Cults, 143

Culture, organizational: assessment of, 37–38; integration of ethics in, 37–39; moral awareness and, 22–23; moral conduct and, 30–33, 37–39; moral reasoning and, 24–25. See also Bottom-line mentality; Situational context

Curricula, ethics, 47–51

Customers, passing loss onto, 66

Cynicism, 276

D

Dalai Lama, 297

Darley, J. M., 26–27, 82, 97, 146

Dartmouth College case, 258–259

Davidow, C., 72

Dean, J., 270, 273, 274

Decision making: barriers to ethical, 95–110; center-driven, 274–275; components of ethical, 22–30, 275–276; philanthropy and, 262; procedural fairness in, 225, 226. See also Ethical dilemmas; Moral judgment; Moral reasoning

Defense contracting scandals, 1, 10

Defense Industry Initiative, 10

Dehumanization: at Abu Ghraib, 154; moral disengagement and, 138–139; nearness and, 22–23; in Stanford Prison Experiment, 143–145

Deindividuation, 135–137, 154

Democracy, 169, 170–171; philanthropy and, 253–255, 256–263

Deterrence strategy, 215–217, 219–220

Diffusion of responsibility, 27–30, 135, 156

Dignity, 225, 226

Discovery abuse, 60

Discrimination, 181

Disengagement strategies, 29. See also Moral disengagement

Disinhibition, 178

Disraeli, B., 172

Dissent: encouragement of, 40–41; manipulation of, 135; power status and, 186–188; suppression of, 25–26, 30, 41, 186–188

Dissonance. See Cognitive dissonance

Diversity, respecting, 157

Dobson, H. A., 172

Doctors: ambivalence in, 84–85, 86, 89; resistance of, to immoral authority, 106; right-versus-right conflicts of, 102–103; self-construal of, 90; time pressures of, 80–81, 83–84

Doctors Without Borders, 293

Donaldson, T., 50

Donor preferences, 251, 260–261, 263

Dopamine, 181

Dot-com era, 67

Drug dealers, 129

Duncan, D., 58, 99–100

Dunlop, "C." A., 23, 28

Dworkin, R., 119–120

E

eBay, 35

Ebbers, B., 57

Economics: American capitalist, 63–69; command *versus* market, 64–65; lens of, 78, 92. *See also* Capitalism
Economies, new *versus* old, 65–66
Ecumenicalism, 297
Educational inequalities, 211–212, 261
Educational strategies: for developing moral leadership, 45–47, 267–289; for recruitment into evil, 142–143
Ego strength, 26
Egoism, 199–202, 210. *See also* Self-interest
Eichenwald, K., 101
Eichmann, A., 32
Einstein, A., 161
Elizabethan Statute of Charitable Uses of 1601, 252–263
Emerson, R. M., 186
Emotions: convergence of, 190–191; experience of ambivalence and, 84–90; learning to manage, 271; power status and, 179–180, 190–191
Empathy: altruistic motivation and, 202–204, 210–212; justice and, 210–212; nearness and, 22–23, 203–204
Employee(s): motivation and, 215–220, 222–224; passing loss onto, 66; rule adherence of, 213–226; values and, 218–226
Employee evaluation systems, competitive, 32, 65–66
Employee involvement, in development of codes, 36
Employee perceptions: of corporate ethics, 12–13, 38–39; of fairness in reward systems, 25, 38–39; of leaders' lack of ethics, 25; of procedural justice, 221–226
Employee performance, impact of moral leadership on, 17–18
Employee satisfaction, impact of moral leadership on, 17
Employee theft, 105, 214, 223
Empowerment, 279–280
Enabling Act, 169
Encyclicals, 297
Enemy label, 140, 142
Enforcement: limited impact of, 15, 35; of public service ethics, 115–116, 120–121, 122–124; strategies for, 44–45. *See also* Regulation; Sanctions

Eni, 267, 281–283
Enron, 50, 57, 178, 250; accountant's complicity in, 32, 63; board meeting agenda at, 81–82; corporate social responsibility of, 33; document shredding of, 58; employee evaluation system of, 32, 65–66; ethics code of, 35; executive and board compensation at, 28, 32; jokes about, 2; lawyers' complicity in, 72; misleading language of, 99–100; profits-at-any-costs culture of, 23, 31–32, 65–66; shooting the messenger at, 30; whistle-blowing at, 108–109
Environmental issues: enducing empathy for, 204; global moral leadership for, 294
Erikson, E. H., 175
Ethic of care, 207–208
Ethical codes: on conflict of interest, 121–122; as control of power, 166–167; extent of, 10, 34; global, 299–300; limitations of, 34–37; prepackaged, 36; for public officials, 111, 115, 118–122, 125; standards for, 42
Ethical dilemmas and conflicts: ambivalence in, 84–90, 93; cognitive dissonance and, 25–26, 29, 67–74; in competitive settings, 57–61; conflicting principles in, 96, 102–105; effects of power on, 184–185; firsthand experience of, 78–79; incremental wrongdoing and, 29, 70–72, 74; interpersonal relationships and, 272–281; power status and simplification of, 184–185; practical challenges of, 79–93; right-*versus*-right, 96, 97, 102–105; teaching, in business schools, 49–50, 272–276, 283–289
Ethical fading, 95, 97–102
Ethical leadership. *See* Moral leadership
Ethics: a priori *versus* conventional, 113, 114–116, 277; defined, 4–5; integration of, 37–39, 50–51; and leadership effectiveness, 5–7; philanthropy and, 249–263. *See also* Moral conduct; Moral leadership; Morality
Ethics field: historical background on, 1; moral leadership in, 1–4; philanthropic funding of, 251–252. *See also* Research

Ethics initiatives and programs: educational, 45–51; evaluation of, 37; historical background on, 10–15; skepticism about, 1–2, 12–13; societal, 41–45; strategies for, 33–53; value of, 34–37

Ethics officers, 10–11

Ethics Resource Center, 12, 13, 38

Ethics training, extent of, 10. *See also* Business schools; Management students

Ethnocentric bias, 102

Eton, 114

Euphemisms, 29, 95, 98–100

Evictions, conducting, 79, 86

Evil: banality of, 32; conditions for, 131–155; definition of, 129; dispositional explanations of, 130–132, 153–154; dynamics of, 129–157; of inaction, 146–147; manifestations of, 129–130; necessary (evils), 79–93, 273; promoting resistance to, 155–157

Executioners, 147–149

Executive attitudes, 13–14

Executive compensation: disparity between employee compensation and, 38–39; downsizing, 39, 44; excessive, 24–25, 32, 38–39; government regulation of, 44

Exit strategy, 246

Experience, firsthand: importance of, 78–79; for management students, 270–271, 278; practical challenges and, 79–93

Extraversion, 179–180

F

Fagan, J., 219

Failure: fear of, 62–63; responses to, 66–67

Fairness/unfairness: ethical climate and, 31, 38; in-group bias and, 26; procedural justice and, 221–226; in reward systems, 25, 38–39; in right-*versus*-right conflicts, 91, 103, 105; self-serving judgments of, 95–96. *See also* Justice

Farkas, M., 284

Fascism, 157

Fastow, A., 23, 28, 57, 61, 71, 72, 81

Fastow, L., 57

Federal sentencing guidelines, 35, 36

Federalism, 170–171, 258–259

Federalist, The, 170

Ferdinand, 174

Financial performance: corporate social responsibility and, 16–20; reputation for ethics and, 18–19. *See also* Bottom-line mentality

Fiske, S., 134

Florida State Supreme Court, 170

Ford Foundation, 238

Foreign policy, 300

Fortune, 286

Foundations. *See* Philanthropy; Strategic philanthropy

Frederick, I., 152–155

Free-riding, 259

Freedom: of philanthropic foundations, 253–255, 258–263; refusing to sacrifice, 157; surrender of, 134

Freud, S., 161, 162–164, 167, 201–202

Fuller, L. L., 117

Fundamental attribution error: character screening and, 46–47; in explaining evil, 131, 134; moral character and, 21

Fundraising ads, 204

G

Gallup Poll, 12

Gandhi, M., 107–108, 197, 211, 292, 296

Gardner, J., 6

Gates Foundation, 238

General Motors (GM), 15

Generativity, 171–175

Genocide, 141–142

Genovese, K., 69–70, 146, 147

Gentile, M., 274

German nationalism, 163–164, 166–167. *See also* Nazi Germany

Gilligan, C., 207

Glass, S., 250

Global Crossing, 58

Global Leadership Foundation, 299

Global moral leadership: defined, 291–292; examples of, 292–294; perspectives on, 291–300; problems of, 15; skills for, 296; teaching, in business school, 283–289; values of, 295, 296–300

Goals: of global moral leaders, 295; instrumental, 198, 240–241; philanthropic, types of, 231–232; strategic philanthropy and, 230–236, 239–240; ultimate, 198; unintended, 198

God, 115, 130
Goffman, E., 186
Golding, W., 135–136
Good Samaritan experiment, 26–27, 146–147
Good to Great (Collins), 52
Goodwill Ambassadors, 293
Gorbachev, M., 292, 299
Gossip, 186–189, 193
Government regulation. *See* Regulation
Graft, honest *versus* dishonest, 119, 121
Grantmaking. *See* Philanthropy; Strategic philanthropy
Greek philosophers, 1, 169
Greek society and politics, 168, 169, 277
Greek tragedies, 277
Green Belt movement, 294
Green revolution, 238
Group identity, 206
Group pressure. *See* Social and peer pressure
Groupthink, 186
Gun control, 112–113

H

Haas, R., 34
Haas Fund, 239
Haidt, J., 183–184
Hamilton, A., 170
Hamilton, V. L., 107, 217
Hand, L., 117–118
Hand rule, 117–118
Handbook on Leadership (Bass and Stogdill), 5
Hanson, K. O., 291
Hardin, G., 200–201, 203, 260
Hardin, R., 111
Haritos-Fatouros, M., 148–149
Harrington, J., 118–119
Hart, H.L.A., 237
Harvard Business School, 45–46, 269–271
Hatred, education for, 142–143
Hayek, F., 64
Hazlett, W., 48
Health care philanthropy, 231, 261
Helping behavior, 202. *See also* Altruism; Bystander intervention
Heroes and heroism, 77, 78, 151–152
Hierarchies, 65–69, 186
Hill, L. A., 169, 267
Historical consciousness, 171–173
Hitler, A., 6, 7, 129, 131, 141, 142, 143, 169, 173

Hitler's Final Solution (Endlösung), 141–142, 143
Hobbes, T., 117
Hollywood heroes, 62, 293–294
Holocaust: power dynamics and, 32, 130, 131, 133, 141–143, 159, 164; rescuers in, 205, 211
Höss, R., 164
Hubris, 164
Huggins, M., 148–149
Human Area Files, 137
Human rights, 297–300
Hume, D., 113, 123, 125
Humility, 152
Hussein, S., 7, 129, 159
Hypocrisy, 209

I

Icarus, 75
Ideology, 134, 182–183
If Aristotle Ran General Motors, 9, 15–16
Imprisonment, 143–145. *See also* Abu Ghraib; Stanford Prison Experiment
Impulsiveness: constraints on, 191–194; power and, 178, 179–184
In-group biases, 26, 29–30; collectivist motivation and, 205; reducing, 157; sense of responsibility and, 165–166
Inaction: evil of, 146–147; instrumental, 160
Incentives. *See* Pay-for-performance; Reward systems
Incremental wrongdoing: awareness of, 156; as influence tactic, 135; moral disengagement and, 139; as slippery slope, 29, 70–72, 74
India, self-determination movement in, 107–108, 197, 211, 292, 296
Individual rights, belief in, 183–184, 185–186
Individual-*versus*-institutional arrangements, 113, 116–117, 118–121, 124–125
Individualist cultures, 131, 194
Individuation, 136–137
Influence professionals, 134
Influence tactics, 134–135, 276–280. *See also* Power
Information: fragmentation of, 30, 70–72; upward flow focus of, 188–189
Inhibition, powerlessness and, 180–182
"Inner Ring, The" (Lewis), 29–30

Inquisition, 130–131, 148
Insider-trading scandals, 10, 58–59, 74
Institutional design. *See* Organization structure and design
Integrity: development of, 283; self-deception and, 68–69
Intellect, 162–165
Intensity, 22
InterAction Council, 298–299
Interdependencies, 272–276, 278–280
Internal Revenue Service, 229, 230, 253
International bribery, 10
International Campaign to Ban Landmines, 293
International Committee of the Red Cross, 293
International companies, assessment of, for corporate social responsibility, 38
International Court of Justice, 298
International Ethical, Political and Scientific Collegium, 299
International treaties and conventions, 298
Interpersonal relationships: perceptions of procedural justice and, 225–226; power through, educating management students in, 271–276, 278–281
Intuition: ethics based on, 114–115, 125, 182–183; philanthropy based on, 244–245
Investment banking, 36
Investors: corporate social responsibility and, 44; grantmakers as, 235–236, 241–242
Iraq, 162, 172–173. *See also* Abu Ghraib Prison
ISO 26000, 299
Italian Job, The, 62

J

Jackall, R., 24, 65–66
James I, King, 171
Janis, I. L., 186
Jay, J., 170
Jeffersonian democracy, 169, 258–259
Jesus, 159, 166, 167
John Paul II, Pope, 297
Johnnic, 285–286
Johnson, A., 112
Johnson & Johnson, 19
Jones, J., 143
Jost, J. T., 184
Judgment. *See* Moral judgment

Justice: assessment of organizational, 38; employee satisfaction/performance and, 18; ethic of care *versus,* 207–208; *versus* mercy, 105; as moral principle, 199, 206, 207–208, 210–212; procedural, 221–226; retributive, 25. *See also* Fairness/unfairness

K

Kant, I., 114, 207
Kaye, D., 293
Keen, S., 140
Kellerman, B., 7
Kelman, H. C., 107, 217
Keltner, D., 177
Kemmelmeier, M., 172–173
Kennedy, J. F., 175
Kenya, 294
Kidder, R. M., 96, 103–105
Kim, W. C., 221
King, M. L., Jr., 107–108, 197, 211, 292
King Lear (Shakespeare), 175
Kipnis, D., 159, 276–277
Kissinger, H., 123–124
Kohlberg, L., 24
Kotter, J. P., 273
Kozlowski, L. D., 24–25, 28, 57
Kozol, J., 211–212
Kristol, I., 49
Krushchev, N., 172
Kuhl, J., 165
Kung, H., 298

L

"Laborem Exercens," 297
Langner, C. A., 177
Language: dehumanizing, 138–139, 151; euphemistic, 29, 95, 98–100; rhetorical, 135
Lasting Leadership, 52–53
Latane, B., 97, 146
Law: adherence to, 215, 219; international, 298
Law school curricula, 48
Lawyers, complicity of, 63, 71–72
Lay, K., 23, 57, 81, 101
Layoff decisions, 79, 85–86, 88–89, 90, 104
Le Chambon, 211
Leaders: ethical commitment of, 39–41; evil and, 129–130; global moral,

292–300; power and, 177–194. *See also* Moral leadership
Leadership (Burns), 6
Leadership effectiveness: ethics and, 5–7; models of, 5–7; values-based motivation and, 222–224
Leadership Secrets from Attila the Hun, 9
League of Nations, 292
Learning, through experience, 270–271. *See also* Experience, firsthand
Lee-Chai, A. Y., 159, 160
Legal control, of public officials, 117–118, 118–121. *See also* Regulation
Legitimacy, 218–220, 221, 224–226
Leo XIII, Pope, 297
Lerner, M. J., 62
Letter, D., 31
Levi Strauss, 34
Lewin, K., 198
Lewis, C. S., 29–30, 70–71, 74
Lewis, M., 66
Libertarians, 112–113
Life span events, 193–194
Lincoln, A., 162, 166
Lipman-Blumen, J., 50
LJM1, 81
Lord of the Flies (Golding), 136, 137
Losers: capitalism and, 63–69; disparagement of rule-abiding, 62–63, 67
Love, 161–162, 207
Loyalty: conflict between truth and, 104; corporate social responsibility and, 18; feudalism and, 65; in-group bias and, 26; peer pressure and, 29; professional deformation and, 124
Luban, D., 57
Ludwig, C., 171–172
Luke, Gospel of, 159, 166

M

Maathai, W., 294, 299
Machiavelli, 5, 179
Madison, J., 170
Malaria, 238
Malleus Maleficarum, 130
Man Who Shot Liberty Valance, The, 62
Management students: developing moral leadership in, 267–289; developmental deficiencies of, 267–280; interpersonal competency for, 271–276, 278–281; myths of, 271–276, 279; power and, 276–280; screening candidate, 45–47,

50; values of, 268–270; zone of acceptability for, 283–289. *See also* Business schools
Mandela, N., 107–108, 284–285, 287
Manifestos, 163–164
Mao Tse-tung, 129
March, J. G., 91
Marcus, R. B., 88
Margolis, J., 77, 271, 273
Market approach: to moral behavior in organizations, 216–217, 220; philanthropy and, 262
Market for Virtue, The (Vogel), 44
Mason, A., 162
Mauborgne, R. A., 221
M.B.A. graduates, 267. *See also* Business schools; Management students
McClelland, D. C., 161
Means *versus* ends: ideological justification of, 134; morality in, 6–7; strategic philanthropy and, 240–241
Médecins San Frontières, 293
Media, blaming the, 101
Meese, E., 121
Meltdowns. *See* Scandals
Merari, A., 149–150
Merrill Lynch, 58
"Message to the Public" (Scott), 100–101
Messick, D. M., 95, 97, 98, 99
Metrics, in philanthropy, 233–234, 241–244, 246–247, 256–258
Micelli, M. P., 96, 109
Milgram, S., 27, 73, 75, 86–87, 97, 106–107, 132–134, 135, 136, 142, 155, 156
Milgram's shock experiments, 142; blaming and, 75; obedience and, 106–107, 132–134, 135; observer reactions in, 86–87; peer pressure and, 27, 73, 74; reverse of, 155–156
Milken, M., 59
Mill, J. S., 125, 201, 202
Mimetic behavior, 190–191
Mind control, 143
Mindfulness, 156
Misconduct. *See* Moral conduct; Scandals
Mission: of moral leaders, 295; philanthropy and, 240–241, 260
Modeling: of ethical misconduct, 39; of evil, 151, 154; of morality, 197
Molinsky, A., 77, 271, 273
Montesquieu, C.-L., 170

Moore, G. E., 125

Moral Aspect of Leadership, The (Gardner), 6

Moral awareness: defined, 22; influences on, 22–23; strategies for maintaining, 74–75

Moral conduct and behavior: defined, 22; dimensions of, 20–33, 77–80; lenses on, 77–79, 92; power status and, 177–194; values-based self-regulation for, 215–226

Moral congruence, 218–220, 221–222, 224–226

Moral courage. *See* Courage

Moral disengagement, 138–139, 154, 209

Moral intent or motivation: conflicts among, 209–210; defined, 22; factors in, 26–27; orchestrating, 210–212; types of, 198–209. *See also* Motivation; Prosocial values; Self-interest

Moral judgment: barriers to, 95–110; complexity of, by power status, 184–185; by detached observers, 86–88; developing, 267–289; dimensions of, 95–110; philosophical approaches to, 78; power and, 178, 182–185; reward systems and, 24–25; self-interest and, 182–183

Moral leadership: character traits and, 21–22; characteristics of, 295–296; commitment to, 39–41; cost-effectiveness of, 15–20; defining, 4–9, 20, 197; developing, in business school, 267–289; dimensions of, 20–33, 77–80; effectiveness and, 5–7; employee motivation and, 222–224; ethical leadership and, 291–292; examples of, 292; extent of research on, 2–3, 9; forms of, 197–198; global, 291–300; historical background on, 10–15; parodies of, 1–2; perceptions of, 12–13; power and, 177–194; practical challenges of, 77–93; prosocial motives and, 197–212; of public officials, 111–125; strategies for, 33–53

Moral Mazes (Jackall), 24

Moral philosophy: business ethics and, 1; intuitionism and, 114–115, 125, 182–183; lens of, 78, 92; on politics, 125

Moral point of view (MPV), 275

Moral reasoning: among judges, 120; defined, 22; factors in, 23–26; principlism and, 207; stages of, 24, 275–276

Morality: defined, 4–5, 197; interpersonal, 197, 271–276, 278–281; power status and, 177–194; a priori *versus* conventional, 113, 114–116; propriety, 197. *See also* Ethics

Morgenthau, H. J., 161, 162

Mortality, 173–175

Mother Teresa, 197, 293

Motivation: goal-directed forces and, 198; internal, 224; models of, 215–217; procedural justice and, 221–226; prosocial, types of, 198–212; self-regulation and, 217–226; values and, 218–226. *See also* Moral intent or motivation; Prosocial values and motives

MTM, 286

Mutual funds, 11

My Cousin Vinnie, 62

My Lai, 160

N

NAACP, 247

Nagel, T., 116, 207

Nanking, rape of, 130

Napoleonic Code, 119

National security fears, 134, 149, 152, 157

National Union of Mineworkers (NUM), 285–286

Native Americans, extermination of, 160

Nature Conservancy, 254

Nazi Germany: cooption of power in, 169; Hitler's anxiety and, 173; Holocaust and, 32, 130, 131, 133, 141–142, 159, 164, 205, 211; youth reeducation in, 142–143

Near, J. P., 96, 109

Nearness: altruism and, 203–204; moral awareness and, 22–23

Necessary evils, 273; ambivalence in, 84–90; approaches to, 91; examples of, 79; practical challenges of, 79–93

Negotiation, 107, 185, 279

Net present value (NPV), 275

Neurocognitive processes, 181

Neuroticism, 179–180

New York Police Department, 108, 109, 219, 222

New York Times Magazine, 2, 294

New York University, 47

New Yorker, 2

Niebuhr, R., 123

Nightly Business Report, 52

9/11, 130, 132, 159
1984, 143
Nixon, R., 112, 123, 170, 270
Nobel Peace Prize, 292, 293, 294, 299
Noddings, N., 207
Nonprofit organizations: accountability
    in, 229–230, 252–258; corporate
    social responsibility rankings by, 42;
    ethics and, 249–263; general operat-
    ing support for, 245–247; nondis-
    tribution constraint of, 249; ratings
    systems for, 257–258; scandals in,
    254. See also Philanthropy; Strategic
    philanthropy
Nonviolent protest, 211

O

Obedience: influence tactics for, 134–
    135; Milgram's shock experiments
    on, 106–107, 132–134; resistance to
    authority versus, 106–107, 151–152,
    155–157
Objectivity, illusion of, 95
Observer reactions, to ambivalence,
    86–88
Ocean's 11, 62
Office supply theft, 105, 214, 223
Oliner, P., 211
Oliner, S., 211
Olsen, M., 260
O'Neill, O., 255–256
Online marketplace, 192
Open society initiatives, 238
O'Reilly, C., 217
Organization structure and design:
    building pauses and second-looks
    into, 83–84; covering, in academic
    research, 51–52; covering, in business
    school, 50; employee rule adherence
    and, 213–215; moral conduct and, 30,
    78; power constraint through, 167–
    171; for procedural justice, 221–226;
    to promote ethical values, 220–226;
    public service ethics and, 116–117,
    125
Organizations: employee rule adherence
    in, 215–226; political realities in,
    276–280; values in, 219–226
Orwell, G., 143
Out-groups, 205
Outcomes assessment, in philanthropy,
    233–234, 242–247, 256–258

Oversight: of philanthropic foundations,
    252–258; of public officials, 25, 111,
    120–121

P

Paine, L. S., 19, 274–275, 283
Palestinian suicide bombers, 149–151
Paley, W., 125
Palmer, M., 101
Palo Alto Police Department, 144–145
Parenthood, 193–194
Parks, S. D., 269, 270, 280–281
Parodies, 1–2
Patman, W., 255
Pauses, 83–84
Pay-for-performance: to motivate con-
    duct, 215–216; organizational culture
    of, 24–25
Peer pressure. See Social or peer pressure
Peoples Temple, 143
Performance assessment, organization,
    37–38; shortfalls, 66–67
Perp Walk, 57
Personal bias, 95–96, 101–102
Peters, T. H., 7, 16
Pharmaceutical board experiment, 28–29
Philanthropy: accountability in, 229–230,
    249–250, 252–258; business model
    in, 239–240, 246–247, 252, 256–258;
    corporate, 20; ethics and, 249–263;
    fragmentation in, 261, 263; for general
    operating support, 245–247; historical
    background on, 238, 256–257; metrics
    in, 233–234, 241–244, 246–247,
    256–258; mission and, 240–241, 260;
    priority-setting in, 251–252, 260–261,
    262–263; and public goods, 249, 256–
    263; self-regulation by, 256–258; stra-
    tegic, 229–247; types of objectives of,
    231–232; venture, 245–247. See also
    Strategic philanthropy
Philip Morris, 52
Phillip II, 172
Physical appearance, 135–138
Plato, 162, 163, 169, 177
Plunkett, G. W., 119, 121
Pluralism, 259–263
Pol Pot, 129
Politeness, 225–226
Politics: de facto party realignment
    and, 112–113; enforcement and,
    116, 120–121, 122–124; ethics and,

111–112; institutional standards and, 118–120, 124–125; moral philosophy and, 125; power constraint through, 167–171; regulation and, 113, 117–118; teaching management students about, 276–280. *See also* Power; Public service leadership

Popes, 297

Popular literature, on ethics and leadership, 2–4, 9, 33, 51, 52–53. *See also* Research

Popularity: desire for, 96–97; risking, 96–97, 106, 107–108

Posner, R. A., 120

Postconventional stage, 24, 207

Power: acquisition and distribution of, 168–169, 178, 179–185; approach-inhibition theory of, 181–182; corrupted, 159–160, 169, 276–280; degree of, 168–169; differential, 143–145, 154, 168–169; historical perspective on, 171–173, 178; interpersonal *versus* authoritarian, 271–276, 278–281; low-power people and constraint of, 186–191; mechanisms for leveling, 178, 191–194; mechanisms for taming, 159–175; and mimetic behavior, 190–191; moral judgment and, 178, 182–185; moral leadership and, 177–194; mortality and, 173–175; philanthropy and, 256–263; positive side of, 159; psychology of, 129–157, 159–167, 177–194, 276–280; responsible use of, 193–194; separation of (powers), 170–171; sharing, 279–280; social-structural controls of, 167–171; and solipsistic social environments, 185–191; subversion of repressed, 167; teaching management students about, 272–280; zero sum, 167–168, 279. *See also* Evil

Power (Russell), 159

Powerlessness and low-power people: and constraints on high-power people, 186–194; corruption of, 276–280; evil and, 144–145, 168–169; informal communication of, 186–187; moral leadership and, 182–191

Powers Committee, 72

Preconventional stage, 24

Preferential treatment, 102

Presidency, U.S., 170, 191

Presidential impeachments, 112, 117, 123

Price-fixing scandals, 1

Prichard, H. A., 114, 125

Princeton seminarians, 26–27

Principles: conflicting, 96, 102–105, 209–210; for public leadership, 111; rationalization with, 208–209; values and limitations of, 206–209

Principles of Moral and Political Philosophy, The (Paley), 125

Principles of the United Nations Global Compact, 38

Principlism, 199, 206–209, 210–212

Prisoner's dilemma, 259, 260

Privatization, 258–263

Procedural justice. *See* Justice

Process-based leadership, 224

Professional deformation, 124

Profit myopia. *See* Bottom-line mentality

Propaganda, 140

Propriety, 197

Prosocial values and motives: conflicts among, 209–210; orchestrating, 210–212; power attainment and, 179; rule adherence and, 213–226; types of, 198–209

Prospero, 174–175

Protestant ethic, 61

Psychological dimension: lens of, 77–78, 92; in management education, 270–271; of moral meltdowns, 67–74; of power, 129–157, 159–167, 177–194, 276–280; suggestions for dealing with, 74–75

Public goods, philanthropy and, 249, 256–263

Public perceptions: of corporate ethics, 12; of corporate social responsibility, 18; of executive compensation, 38

Public policy strategies, 41–45. *See also* Regulation

Public service ethics: conflicts of interest and, 121–122; division of labor in, 118–121; enforcement of, 115–116, 120–121, 122–124; immoral policies and, 123–124; individual-level morality *versus* institutional arrangements in, 113, 116–117, 118–121, 124–125; morals for, 111–125; a priori *versus* conventional ethics in, 113, 114–116; trusteeship and, 112

Public trust: in philanthropy, 249–250, 253–258; public officials and, 112. *See also* Accountability

Punishment: power *versus* powerlessness and, 180–181, 183–184; values-based self-regulation *versus*, 215–226

Purchasing behavior, 43

Q

Question of Trust, A (O'Neill), 255–256

Quiet leadership, 107

R

Rabin, I., 108

Racism, 181

Rambo, 62

Rankings, 42, 43

Rationalization, 25, 178; principlism and, 208–209; of self-interest, 182–186

Rawls, J., 207

Reason, as power-taming mechanism, 162–165. *See also* Moral reasoning

Recognition, for moral behavior, 156

Red Cross, 254, 293

Regent Office Supply, United States *vs.*, 60–61

Regulation: limitations of, 14–15; of philanthropic foundations, 252–256, 262–263; of public officials, 113, 117–118; rule adherence and, 215; strategies for, 41–45. *See also* Enforcement; Sanctions

Reich, R., 261

Religion, 166–167, 231, 296–297

Reporting requirements, strategies for, 42

Republic (Plato), 162, 163, 169

Republican party, 112–113

Reputation: as constraint on power, 192–193; financial value of ethical, 18–19; impact of ethical behaviors on, 17; value of, 192; whistle-blowing and, 109

"Rerum Novarum," 297

Rescue activity motives, 211

Research: limitations of existing, 2–3, 9, 33, 51, 52–53; needs for, 33–34, 51–53; philanthropic funding of, 251–252

Resource allocation: collectivist motivation and, 206; empathy-induced altruism and, 204; justice principle and, 207

Respect, 157, 225–226

Response biases, 13

Responsibility: conditions for, 193–194; as power-taming mechanism, 165–166; promoting, 156

Rest, J. R., 22, 23, 30, 275–276

Résumé fraud, 47

Retaliation for whistle-blowing: fear of, 40, 109; government protection from, 43; revenge, 162

Retributive justice, 25

Return on investment, in grants, 235–236, 241–244, 247, 256–258

Reward systems: employee conduct and, 38–39; moral conduct and, 31; moral judgment and, 24–25; to reward moral behavior, 156; rule adherence and, 215–217, 223; strategies for altering, 44. *See also* Compensation; Executive compensation

Rhode, D. L., 1, 113

Rigas, J., 57

Rigas, T., 57

Right-*versus*-right conflicts, 96, 97, 102–105; educating students for, 272–276

Right-*versus*-wrong approach: to ethical conflicts, 103; in public service ethics, 114–116

Risk and risk taking: against all odds, 66–67; moral courage and, 106–110, 296

Rockefeller Foundation, 238, 254, 262

Role holders, failure of public institutions *versus*, 116–117

Roles: assigning, as influence tactic, 134, 144–145; conflicts of interest and, 121–122; ethics of, 124–125; power and, 167–169, 178; self-construal and, 90–93; that encourage ethical misconduct, 123–124

Roman Catholic Church, 130, 297

Roosevelt, E., 297–298

Roosevelt, F. D., 170

Root, E., 63

Rops, F., 166

Ross, L., 130

Royal Dutch Shell, 19

Rule adherence: employee, 213–226; legal authority and, 215; motivation and, 215–226; values and, 218–220

Rule breaking, employee, 213–215
Rules: communication of organizational, 225; vague and coercive, 135, 144
Russell, B., 159, 163

S

Sadat, A., 108
Salomon Brothers, 27–28
Sanctions: from conscience, 201–202; costs of, 216; internal and external, 201–202; for public officials, 122–124; from social censure, 201, 202; strategies of, 44–45, 215–217; values-based self-regulation *versus*, 215–226. *See also* Enforcement; Punishment
Sandler, T., 259–260
Sarbanes-Oxley Act, 41–42, 256
Savings-and-loan scandals, 1, 59
Scandals: bottom-line mentality and, 31–32, 38, 58–67; cognitive dissonance and, 67–74; dimensions of, 57–75; epidemic of, 57–59; ethics field and, 1; ethics initiatives in response to, 1–2, 10–11, 223; ethics programs present in, 35, 221–222; examining, in business school, 50; history of, 58–59; information fragmentation and, 30; in nonprofit organizations, 254; peer pressure and, 69–74; public trust and, 250, 255; reward systems and, 38
Schiavo, T., 170
Schön, D. A., 252
Schwarzenegger, A., 254
Scientific temper, 163
Scott, R. F., 100–101
Scrushy, R., 57
Sears Roebuck, 31
Second Circuit Court of Appeals, 60–61
Second looks, 83–84
Second Vatican Council, 297
Securities and Exchange Commission (SEC) cases, 13–14, 27–28, 99
Securities fraud, 1, 10
Sekunjalo, 285, 286
Self-awareness: individual, 74–75; in philanthropy, 263
Self-construal, 79, 90–93
Self-doubt, 75
Self-evaluation: legal requirements for corporate, 45; reducing concerns for, 140
Self-fulfilling prophecy, 210

Self-interest: altruism and, 203, 210–212; assumption of, 210, 212; collectivism and, 205–206, 210–212; conflicts of interest and, 121; constraints on, 191–194; corporate social responsibility and, 20; egoism and, 199–202, 210; enlightened, 201; foreign policy and, 300; ideology of, 182–183; moral reasoning and, 24–26; as motive for moral conduct, 199–202, 210–212; philanthropy and, 260; power status and, 178, 179, 180–184, 185–186; rationalization of, 182–184, 185–186; side payments and, 201–202; zone of acceptability and, 274–275, 283–289
Self-reflection: encouraging, 156; lack of, in management students, 269–270; teaching, in business schools, 49–51
Self-regulation: employee values and, 213, 217–226; of philanthropic foundations, 256–258; reason and, 163–164
Self-sacrifice, 202
Self-serving bias, 100
Selznick, P., 7
Sen, A., 14
Sentis, K. P., 95
Separation of powers, 170–171
Serotonin, 181
Serpico, F., 108, 109
Sexual harassment, 120
Shakespeare, W., 168, 169, 171, 174–175
Shaming, 44–45
Shareholder interests, 14, 18, 23
Shiesinger, J., 153
Siblings, 193–194
Side payments, 201–202
Sievers, B., 239–247, 249
Situational context: built-in conflicts in, 102–105; evil behavior and, 131–155; firsthand experience in, 78–79; of moral behavior, 26–30; of moral meltdowns, 57–67; of power attainment, 179; practical challenges related to, 79–93; undervaluing of, 21, 46–47, 131, 134. *See also* Culture
Situational incentives, 24–25
Skilling, J., 23, 57, 61, 62, 66
Slippery-slope phenomenon, 97–98. *See also* Incremental wrongdoing
Smith, A., 192, 200
Social change: business as catalyst for, 280–289; global moral leadership for,

291–300; philanthropy for, 231, 243–244, 247, 253–254, 256–263
Social movements: global moral leadership and, 291–300; moral leaders and, 292; philanthropy and, 231, 243–244, 247, 253–254, 256–263
Social or peer pressure: conformity and, 96–97, 133; evil behavior and, 133, 151, 154; impact of, on moral behavior, 27, 29–30, 69–74; resisting, 74–75, 157
Social proximity of consequences, 22
Social Responsibilities of the Businessman (Bowen), 11
Social return on investment, 235–236, 241–244, 247, 256–258
Social role of business, 280–289
Social services philanthropy, 231, 261
Social-structural controls, 167–171
Socialism, 262
Socialization, 29
Socioeconomic status (SES): belief in punishment and, 183–184; power and, 180–181, 183–184
Socrates, 75
Soldiers, 137–138, 140, 162
Solipsistic social environments, 185–191
"Sollicitudo Rei Sociales," 297
Solzhenitsyn, A., 132
Sorority gossip, 187–189, 193
Soros, G., 238
South Africa, 108, 109, 284–289
South Pole expedition, 100–101
Soviet Union, 172, 175, 297
Stalin, J., 6, 7, 98, 129
Stallone, S., 62
Standard and Poor 500 companies, social and financial performance of, 17
Standardized test scores, 257
Stanford Prison Experiment, 142, 147; Abu Ghraib and, 154; described, 73–74, 143–145
States' rights, 170–171
Stigmatized groups, empathy-induced altruism for, 204
Sting, The, 62
Stock options, 24, 66
Stogdill, R. M., 5
Stouffer, S., 162
Strategic philanthropy: ancestry of, 238; challenges of, 238–239; concepts and processes of, 230–236; for creativ-

ity, 236–237; critique of, 238–245, 252, 256–258; defense of, 238–245; for social movements, 236–237, 243–244, 247; venture philanthropy and, 245–247
Strategic plan, philanthropic, 232–233, 244–245
Stress, 154–155, 271
Stretch assignments, 278
Success: credit-taking for, 100; worship of, 61–63, 67
Suicide bombers, 149–151, 152
Sullivan, S., 86
Summer, L., 164–165
Sunbeam, 23, 28
Sunday school morality, 58, 59–60. *See also* Right-*versus*-wrong approach
Supervisors, quality of treatment by, 225–226
Survé, I., 285, 287–288
Surveillance, employee, 223, 224
Sustainable development, 294
Swartz, M., 57

T

Tammany political machine, 119
Taoism, 160
Tax Act of 1969, 255
Tax-exempt status, 229, 230, 249
Team players, 29
Teasing, 186–188
Teenage pregnancy prevention, strategic philanthropy approach to, 232–236
Tempest, The (Shakespeare), 174–175
Temple, N., 58, 99–100
Tenbrunsel, A. E., 95, 97, 98
Terrorism, 130, 132, 134, 149–152
Tetlock, P. E., 185
Texaco, 41
Textile manufacturers, 65–66
Third World debt relief, 293–294
Thomas, R. J., 268–269
Thucydides, 168
Tiberius, 172
Tibetan Buddhism, 297
Time management, 82–84
Time pressure: bystander intervention and, 26–27, 146–147; managing, 93; in organizational settings, 80–84
Times, 163
Titus Andronicus (Shakespeare), 175

Tolstoy, L., 207
Torture, 130, 134, 147–149, 152–155, 298
Tracking progress, in strategic philanthropy, 233–234, 241–244
Trade-offs: attending to ambivalence and, 88–89; interdependencies and, 273, 278–280; short-term *versus* long-term, 104
Trade press publications, on values-laden leadership, 9
Tragedy of the commons, 259, 260
Transactional leadership, 6, 223
Transformational leadership, 6
Traub, J., 294
Treblinka, 141–142
Troilus and Cressida (Shakespeare), 168
Trojan War, 168
Tronto, J., 207
Trudeau, G., 1
Trust No Fox, 142–143
Trustees, public, 112. *See also* Public service leadership
Tyco, 24–25, 28, 57
Tylenol recall, 19
Tyler, T. R., 213, 217, 219, 221
Tyrants, 129, 169

U

Ulysses, 168
UNDP, 293
UNESCO, 293
Uniforms, 137–138, 144–145
Unintended consequences, 198; of self-interest, 200
United Nations, 38, 292, 297–300
United Nations Children's Fund (UNICEF), 293
United Nations Population Fund, 293
UN Global Compact, 299–300
United States, global moral leadership and, 300
United States *vs.* Regent Office Supply, 60–61
U.S. Congress, 170, 252–254
U.S. Constitution, 169, 170–171
U.S. Department of Justice (DOJ), 99, 123
U.S. Industrial Relations Commission, 254–255, 262
U.S. Senate: Enron investigation by, 81–82; nonprofit oversight by, 252–253, 254–255, 262
U.S. Sentencing Commission, 10

U.S. Supreme Court: Andersen case and, 58; on private action, 259; school desegregation and, 247; separation of powers and, 170
U.S. Treasury Department, 27
United Way, 205, 254
Universal Declaration of Human Responsibilities, 298–299
Universal Declaration of Human Rights (UDHR), 297–298, 299
University of Chicago, 46
Unpopularity, risking, 96–97, 106, 107–108
Utilitarianism: greatest good for the greatest number principle of, 206, 207; political ethics and, 125; self-interest and, 201
Utopia, 118–119

V

Value added, for corporate donations, 20
Value pluralism, 259–263
Value statements, 8
Valued states, 198
Values: global moral, 295, 296–300; in management students, 268–270; organizational characteristics and, 213, 219–226; rule adherence and, 218–226; self-regulation through, 213, 217–226; universal, 296–300. *See also* Prosocial values
Values-based leadership, 7–10
Ventura, J., 62
Venture philanthropy, 245–247
Victims: dehumanization of, 138–139; denigration of, 29, 62; powerlessness and, 181, 182
Vietnam War, 123–124, 160
Villiers, G., 171
Vinson, B., 86
Vogel, D., 20, 44
Von Mises, L., 64

W

Wagner, R., 160, 162
Wal-Mart, corporate social responsibility of, 33
Wall Street Ethics, 1
Wall Street Journal, 49, 71, 101, 273
Walsh Commission, 254–255, 262
Walter and Elise Haas Fund, 239

Walton, S., 33
Walzer, M., 262
War: historical consciousness and, 172–173; power-taming mechanisms and, 161, 162, 163–164, 165–166; psychology of evil and, 137–138, 140; of religion and sectarianism, 296–297
Washington Post, 164, 173
Watergate, 1, 170, 270, 273, 274
Waterman, R. P., Jr., 7, 16
Watkins, S., 108–109
Watson, J., 137
Wayne, J., 62
Weber, M., 61, 180
Weick, K., 283
Welch, J., 16
Wharton School, 28–29, 52
Whistle-blowing: belief in futility of, 96, 109, 110; deterrents and barriers to, 40, 70, 109–110; moral courage and, 108–110; positive recognition for, 156; protections for, 40, 42, 43, 109, 110. *See also* Retaliation for whistle-blowing

Wilhelm II, Kaiser, 166
Williams, B., 207
Williams, J., 293
Wilson, W., 160, 292, 299
Win-win approach, 279–280
Winners, worship of rogue, 61–63
Winter, D. G., 159, 165, 172–173, 193
Witch hunts, 130
World War I, 172–173
World War II, 173
WorldCom, 58, 86, 250

Y

Yale College, 133
Youth: Nazi reeducation of, 142–143; suicide bombers, 149–151

Z

Zero sum, 167–168, 279
Zeus, 164
Zimbardo, P. G., 82, 129, 148–149
Zone of acceptability, 274–275, 283–289